Doubt, Atheism, and
the Nineteenth-Century
Russian Intelligentsia

Doubt, Atheism, and the Nineteenth-Century Russian Intelligentsia

Victoria Frede

THE UNIVERSITY OF WISCONSIN PRESS

Publication of this volume has been made possible,
in part, through support from the
ANDREW W. MELLON FOUNDATION.

The University of Wisconsin Press
1930 Monroe Street, 3rd Floor
Madison, Wisconsin 53711–2059
uwpress.wisc.edu

3 Henrietta Street
London WC2E 8LU, England
eurospanbookstore.com

Printed in the United States of America

Library of Congress Cataloging-in-Publication Data
    Frede, Victoria.
    Doubt, atheism, and the nineteenth-century Russian intelligentsia /
    Victoria Frede.
    p.   cm.
  Includes bibliographical references and index.
  ISBN 978-0-299-28444-2 (pbk.: alk. paper)
  ISBN 978-0-299-28443-5 (e-book)
    1. Atheism—Russia—History—19th century.   2. Russia—Religion—
History—19th century.   3. Anti-clericalism—Russia—History—19th
century.   4. Intellectuals—Russia—History—19th century.   I. Title.
BL2765.R8F74   2011
211´.808631094709034—dc22
2011011567

This book is dedicated to my brother,
EDWARD FREDE

Contents

Illustrations

Acknowledgments

Members of the imperial Russian intelligentsia lived their lives in conversation, arguing or just exchanging their thoughts in drawing rooms, stairways, streets, and taverns, as well as in letters and poems. This book seeks to show how these conversations shaped the outlook of particular individuals—and of the intelligentsia as a whole—with regard to the question of the existence of God. It is fitting that I should begin by acknowledging some of the people whose conversations shaped the ideas that went into this book. Many played a formative role in defining its contours and helping me resolve my doubts about the claims I wished to advance. Reginald E. Zelnik, who supervised the project when I began it as a graduate student, did not live to see the fruits of his labor. Neither did Nicholas V. Riasanovsky, who served on my dissertation committee. Others at Berkeley—former teachers, colleagues, and friends—helped see it through to fruition: Yuri Slezkine and Irina Paperno suffered most. Andrew Barshay, Elizabeth Berry, John Connelly, John Efron, Robin Einhorn, David Hollinger, Martin Jay, Thomas Laqueur, Rebecca McLennan, Maureen Miller, Michael Nylan, Ethan Shagan, Jonathan Sheehan, Wen-Hsin Yeh, and Viktor Zhivov all read the manuscript and discussed it with me. Carla Hesse deserves special thanks. Conversations with friends and colleagues at other universities were no less important: Claudia Verhoeven, John Randolph, Konstantine Klioutchkine, Michael Kunichika, Alexander Martin, James Sheehan, Richard Wortman, Daniel Orlovsky, Susan Morrissey, and Elise Kimerling Wirtschafter. Three reviewers for the University of Wisconsin Press offered incisive advice for the improvement of the manuscript, most notably David McDonald and Gary Hamburg.

As I worked on the manuscript, I presented individual chapters to Russian history *kruzhki* at Stanford, Swarthmore, and Columbia University, to my fellows at the Harriman Institute, as well as to a reading group in religious studies sponsored by the Townsend Center at Berkeley. I discussed my work with colleagues at East Carolina University and benefited from their support. Alissa Leigh offered valuable comments on an earlier draft of this book. I owe an exceptional debt to three friends who shared their knowledge—and living quarters—with me in Russia: Iuliia Fedorova, Maria Mayofis, and Ilya Kukulin.

Research toward this book was made possible by the following grants and institutions: IREX, ACTR, the Harriman Institute at Columbia University, East Carolina University, the University of California at Berkeley, and the Hellman Family Faculty Fund. Great thanks are also due to the librarians and archivists at the Russian State Library and Russian National Library, the Library of the Russian Academy of Sciences, Russian Historical Library, Ulianovsk Regional Library, the State Archive of the Russian Federation, Russian State Historical Archive, and the Russian State Historical-Military Archive.

I am grateful to Gwen Walker at the University of Wisconsin Press for her patience and critical judgment. Beth Gianfagna and Mary Rorty made my writing more elegant and accessible. Tatiana Linkhoeva helped smooth out rough edges. Eric Johnson assisted me in creating the index. Finally, I would like to thank Edward Frede and Dorothea Frede, veterans of all my campaigns.

Note on Transliteration and Translation

The transliterations in this book follow both the Library of Congress system and conventions used in nonspecialist publications. A few first names have been anglicized (Aleksandr has become Alexander). Last names have been rendered in the form most familiar to western readers (Butashevich-Petrashevskii has become Petrashevsky). Spellings in the endnotes and bibliography all cohere with the Library of Congress system. Translations are mine unless otherwise indicated.

In quotations throughout the book, brackets around ellipses indicate places where I have left out part of the text. Ellipses without brackets denote suspension points that are found in the original text.

Doubt, Atheism, and the Nineteenth-Century Russian Intelligentsia

Introduction

Youngsters like us," Ivan Karamazov tells his brother Alesha, "must first and foremost resolve the eternal questions; that is our concern. The youth of Russia speaks of nothing but those timeless questions right now." Alesha, the hero of Dostoevsky's *The Brothers Karamazov*, agrees that the two most important are the existence of God and the immortality of the soul.[1] In nineteenth-century Russia, educated people came to view these questions as central to defining their identity and believed it was the moral obligation of every thinking person to attempt to answer them. This book is about why that mode of inquiry became laden with such meaning and how atheism—disbelief in the existence of God—came to be regarded by one segment of Russia's youth as the only viable answer.

The question of the existence of God, though a problem central to modern Western philosophy, took on a peculiarly intensive, existential quality in Russia. Whereas in France, Great Britain, and Germany, metaphysical doubt could and did resolve itself into polite agnosticism by the end of the nineteenth century, in Russia, by contrast, it deepened into a struggle for the salvation of both the individual and the country as a whole. What were the circumstances that leant these questions such intensity? The explanation lies in the unique relationship of Russian writers and thinkers to an autocratic state that founded its ideology on Orthodox faith, the way that relationship intersected with and became infused by new thinking from beyond imperial borders, and the changing social composition of Russian educated society over the course of the century. Finally, there was the small size of the Russian intelligentsia, with its tightly defined codes of comportment, in which actions and reactions could take on their own motive force.

3

At one level, this investigation offers a linear account of how a negative stance, centering on doubt, unfolded in the first half of the nineteenth century, changed under the influence of new intellectual traditions, and was replaced by the positive assertion of an atheistic worldview. At another, deeper level it is about why the question of the existence of God became the crucible in which the identities of educated Russians were formed and allegiances defined.

The question was all the more contentious because many members of educated Russian society continued to believe that there could be no morality and no reason for living without faith in a transcendent God. *The Brothers Karamazov* (1880) neatly illustrates this dilemma in its analysis of the proposition that, without faith in the immortality of the soul, "everything is permissible." Ivan Karamazov is the one to pose it, provoking uproar in the provincial town where the novel is set by telling a group of ladies that a person who does not believe is not only free but obliged, to commit the most heinous acts conceivable.[2] In exploring this idea, Dostoevsky drew on views that prelates of the Russian Orthodox Church had been pressing ever since the mid-eighteenth century. Senior clergymen responded to the rising importation of Western philosophical and theological tracts by warning that many of these were dangerous texts, which could all too easily lead the reader astray—into unbelief. It was in their sermons that the terms *ateizm, deizm,* and *naturalizm* first entered Russian-language print.[3] Loss of faith, they claimed, could not but devastate the individual and must be accompanied by debauchery, insanity, despair, and suicide. Their message—that there could be no middle course between Orthodox faith and depraved godlessness— quickly found its way into the secularized sphere of high culture in the second half of the eighteenth century. Every leading writer, from Sumarokov and Derzhavin to Kheraskov, Emin, and Fonvizin, joined the choir, decrying atheism or godlessness to demonstrate that they had not been corrupted by contact with Western ideas but maintained their piety (however vaguely defined). By the time Dostoevsky wrote his best-known novels, atheism had become a very real phenomenon. Yet the view that atheism could only led to despair and self-annihilation remained influential. In Dostoevsky's *The Possessed* (1872), the would-be atheist, Aleksei Kirillov, found that suicide was the formula by which he must overcome God: "God is the pain of the fear of death. Whoever triumphs over pain and fear, shall become God. [. . .] Whoever dares to kill himself is [a] god. Now anyone can ensure that there shall be no God and nothing shall be."[4]

Intellectual historians have often commented that "ruthless" logic was a trademark of the so-called intelligentsia. To Michael Confino, the "sense of obligation to seek ultimate logical conclusions—in thought as well as in life—at whatever cost" was one of the Russian intelligentsia's defining characteristics.[5] The primary function of debates about religion was to lead the individual toward the discovery of truth; such debates were not meant to supply one a forum in which to express one's personal opinions. Debates of this kind were recorded in diaries, carried on in letters, commemorated in memoirs, and replicated in the best-known fiction of the day. That sense of obligation to engage in these conversations went hand in hand with an assumption that one should have firm beliefs and convictions and live one's life in accordance with those beliefs and convictions. This was the task that educated youths set themselves not only in their writings and conversations but in their own lives and in their interactions with others.

Russian intellectuals sensed an obligation to seek ultimate logical conclusions, but the conclusions they reached were neither internally consistent nor lasting. The country's writers and thinkers lived harder and died younger than their average Western counterparts, and they could change viewpoints with dizzying speed. The need to capture the intensity of a moment of intellectual discovery while balancing it against the vagaries of contemplation and the passage of time has posed a problem for historians of Russian thought ever since they began their work in the early twentieth century.[6] A *profession de foi* (or *manque de foi*) is necessarily delivered with a gusto that suggests some final conclusion has been reached, but in nineteenth-century Russia, such a testament might accurately reflect its writer's opinions for only days, sometimes for weeks and months, rarely for years, and almost never for a lifetime.

In Russia, the "eternal questions" were addressed in youth, as individuals ventured to define their place in society, to confront the compromises that public life entailed, and to determine for themselves what their contribution to the life of the nation ought to be. Their explorations began in the early nineteenth century, under the banner of romanticism, a movement that accorded unprecedented powers to the young. It was in the early nineteenth century that the notion of "youth" as culturally and philosophically distinct from "old age" established itself in Russian social consciousness.[7] Russia came to think of generations as forever inventing themselves anew. Petr Chaadaev complained that his contemporaries appeared to live without memory: "With each step we take forward out past experience disappears without recall."[8] Most romantics

viewed this as an advantage, likening adolescents to Adam in the
Garden of Eden prior to the fall: as yet uncorrupted, they possessed
unique faculties of perception and insight. They had not yet been—but
were about to be—exposed to evil. Nor had they yet learned to bow to
social convention, permitting them to carry their beliefs over into life.[9]
If there was a time in which life and thought could be brought into
harmony in romantic Russia, it was in youth.

The private lives of Russian intellectuals in the nineteenth century, as
Isaiah Berlin once observed, were almost as important to their fellows
as their artistic and intellectual achievements. Indeed, the assessment
of a literary work always depended in some measure on the reader's
judgment of the author's moral integrity.[10] Knowledge about a writer's
intimate affairs was essential if his or her work was to be evaluated
correctly. The capacity of educated Russians to carry out their answers
to the "eternal questions" in their daily lives was also seen as a test of
integrity. This demand for integrity was partly a response to romantic
conceptions, according to which behavior and thought must blend into
one, indistinguishable whole. It was also a response to the pressures
posed by the imperial state, which insisted on its right to regulate the
private morality and religious beliefs of its subjects.

To escape from their elders and superiors and test their answers to
the eternal questions in freedom, youths gathered in "circles" (*kruzhki*).
Drawing rooms, bedrooms, taverns, and stairwells were the sites of their
ruminations and debates, which could last to the break of dawn. Circles
are at the center of attention in this book. Long recognized as a key
institution in the life of the intelligentsia, circles have largely been treated
as associations through which charismatic intellectual figures conveyed
their ideas to lesser lights.[11] Those charismatic figures remained the
focus for historians of Russian thought, who sought to show how each
one was "transformed by an encounter with some idea, most commonly
of European origin."[12] While recognizing that encounters with ideas,
including Western philosophical ideas, were important, this study
departs from the tradition of writing about the intelligentsia by demon-
strating that meetings of minds were communal affairs, shaped by
friendship and infatuation as well as betrayal.

Subjecting Russian circles to careful study helps to uncover why,
between the 1820s and 1840s, doubt became a core part of the nascent
intelligentsia and to show how exchanges over the eternal questions took
shape in and shaped the lives of specific people. It further elucidates how,
at the end of the 1840s and 1850s, some educated Russians repudiated

doubt to embrace the most radical possible answer to the eternal questions by rejecting the existence of God and demonstrates why this rejection became so compelling. In the 1860s, atheistic Russian youths were forced to resolve a new problem, namely how life ought to be lived in the absence of God. The argument is not that the intelligentsia was atheistic by definition but that atheism was one particularly provocative answer to the eternal questions that lent meaning to the lives of educated Russians.

The Russian intelligentsia was the product of Europe's last, great ancien régime, in which every person's life was woven into an elaborate system of hierarchies—from serfs, soldiers, merchants, priests, and that catch-all social category, the *raznochintsy*, to the nobility and the tsar. All of them were expected to contribute, in one way or another, to the life of the Russian state, and this was especially true of Westernized, educated society, which until the mid-nineteenth century was composed largely of the nobility. The ideological and social pressures that members of educated society were subjected to helped bring about the crisis of faith described in this book.[13]

Peter the Great created the first secular schools in Russia in the early eighteenth century to furnish the state with military officers and officials. He devised the Table of Ranks that attached state service to social status, making education a requirement for service, and service the only means by which men could accumulate prestige and wealth. At the highest rungs, however, success depended entirely on the good disposition of the tsar. Whether at court, in St. Petersburg and Moscow, or on their estates, noblemen in the era of the Enlightenment lived to satisfy the tsar's expectations. The "emancipation of the nobility" in 1762 did little to change their sense of obligation to monarch and state.[14]

Russia's press was itself the creation of the absolutist state and was regulated with great care to serve its purposes: the propagation of news about the court, the law, and good morals. The handful of newspapers and journals published in the second half of the eighteenth century served an exceedingly small literate population. Writers and readers consisted largely of the nobility in St. Petersburg and Moscow. The leading literary journals of the later eighteenth century were almost never printed in runs larger than eight hundred copies per issue. Up to the middle of the nineteenth century, most writers combined literary activities with positions in the bureaucracy and military; indeed, many regarded writing as a form of state service.[15]

The home, too, was a "private theater of civic distinction" in which, as John Randolph has argued, noblemen were expected to display their loyalty to "St. Petersburg's culture of power." In the late eighteenth century, the nobility acquired new "desires for independence, self-invention, and societies and intimacies of their own making." They wished to model their own lives, spiritually and intellectually; they sought to attain self-perfection and hoped that these labors would inspire their contemporaries to do the same. Even so, the state expected full concordance between the nobility's "private reason" and officially sponsored civic ideals. Individual priorities were never meant to clash with the cultural and political priorities of the monarch.[16] No Western monarch could rival the power that the Romanovs exercised over educated society in the eighteenth and nineteenth centuries.

In the early nineteenth century, however, tensions between state ideals and the "private reason" of some noblemen became increasingly difficult to overlook. Doubt—about the meaning and purpose of life and Providence, as well as about the extent to which the individual had access to the divine—was one of the expressions of this conflict and first became a theme in Russian literary journals and almanacs in the mid-1820s. The articulation of such doubt was a reaction by intellectuals to an increasingly conservative state, which sought ever more aggressively to shape the outlook of the nobility. This shift in policy, which began under Alexander I, was formulated in response both to the French Revolution and Napoleonic Wars and to the perception that the nobility had become morally corrupt under Catherine II. Doubt was the quintessential assertion by some members of the nobility of their determination to develop an alternative set of ideals about what a meaningful life might look like and on what basis such a life might be justified. It was a private, religious stance with profound political implications: not all doubters were interested in overthrowing autocracy, but they certainly did oppose the imperial state's growing ambition to shape the minds and lives of its subjects.

The Romanovs made extensive use of the Orthodox Church in justifying their hold on power. Peter the Great had done much to secularize the Russian state, subordinating the church to the monarchy and relaxing the hold of Orthodox morality over elite life.[17] Yet he continually emphasized his status as a Christian monarch, chosen by God to preserve the faith of his subjects.[18] He made annual confession and communion a legal requirement for all Orthodox Christians in 1716 and passed stringent laws mandating the investigation of all blasphemers and heretics. They were to be punished by flogging and by having their tongue pierced with a hot poker.[19] From the mid-eighteenth century onward, however, monarchs seldom relied on such violent spectacles to assert their status as protectors of the Orthodox faith.[20] Instead, they used public ceremonies such as the coronation to demonstrate the tsar's faith and his status as God's anointed representative charged to use his autocratic powers to defend Orthodoxy and preserve the morals of the Russian people.[21]

What constituted Orthodoxy as a set of theological propositions remained vague in the eighteenth century. The church's sacred texts had been brought to the Russian principalities from the Byzantine Empire prior to its collapse in the fifteenth century. In both Russia and Byzantium, enormous authority was accorded to the writings of the church fathers, whose wisdom was deemed unsurpassable. Unlike in Byzantium and (more notably) the Catholic West, however, Russians did not supplement these readings with the study of classical philosophy. This omission, as Francis J. Thompson suggests, made "the development of serious original intellectual thought in the sphere of theology, let alone philosophy" very difficult. The corpus of theological writings produced in Medieval and early modern Russia remained exceedingly small; Russia did not even possess a theological academy until the seventeenth century.[22] The weakness of the native theological tradition had profound effects on religious life in the eighteenth century, as clergymen hungry for reading matter turned to Catholic and Protestant theological writings. In the eighteenth and early nineteenth century, as Russian Orthodox hierarchs sought to compose a native theological corpus for the benefit of the clergy, they often found themselves drawing on Western tracts. George Florovsky, who studied their sermons and catechisms closely, commented that the church seemed to have lost its bearings as to what constituted Orthodox theology.[23]

Among the laity, reading habits were even more diffuse. In the eighteenth century, the division between clergy and laity became increasingly marked as the state transformed the Russian Orthodox clergy into a separate estate, or hereditary caste. Efforts were made to introduce a rigorous system of schooling for sons of priests and deacons; owing to funding shortages, however, few graduates of Russia's seminaries could rival Russia's Westernized nobility in erudition. Moreover, as politesse became increasingly important to the eighteenth-century nobility, priests came to be regarded as ill mannered and unsophisticated.[24] As Marc Raeff notes, the eighteenth century saw a rapid decline in the "social and

intellectual authority" of the Orthodox Church among the nobility.[25] In
the nineteenth century, according to Gregory Freeze, educated Russians
remained convinced that the church had "become a mere instrument of
the secular state," even as it attempted to assert its independence.[26]

Clergymen, for their part, tended to look askance at their worldly
countrymen.[27] Prelates of the Russian Orthodox Church believed that
scripture had to be read with extreme caution and preferably be kept
out of the hands of laymen; even catechisms were not made widely
available in the eighteenth century. The sacred word came to literate
Orthodox believers in the form of prayer books, church calendars,
saints' lives, and sermons.[28] These might be supplemented by pietist
and mystical tracts, which were eagerly read by members of the wealthy,
Westernized nobility in the late eighteenth and early nineteenth centuries,
though they continued to identify themselves as Orthodox Christians.[29]
This hybrid religious culture could emerge precisely because the nobility's grasp of the differences between Orthodox and other kinds of
theology was tenuous.

Familiarity with Western philosophical traditions in eighteenth-
century Russia was not altogether great either. Gary Marker has observed
that there was almost no demand in eighteenth-century Russia for translations of works by Descartes, Hobbes, Locke, or Berkeley. "Monte-
squieu's *Spirit of the Laws*, for example, came out in a single Russian-
language edition of 600 copies in 1775. By the mid-1780s most of these
copies were still unsold, and even at a discounted price they drew only
scant attention from booksellers."[30] Russians enjoyed reading works by
Voltaire, but they showed almost no interest in his most radical tracts,
such as "The Catechism of an Honest Man" (1763). His most popular
works in Russia were the ones that were philosophically and theologi-
cally least demanding, such as *Candide* (1759).[31] This can scarcely be
surprising: very few noblemen possessed the kind of education that
would have made his more challenging works attractive. Russia did
not have a university until 1755, when one was opened in Moscow. The
nobility tended to view university education as an unnecessary distraction from state service, and this did not begin to change until the early
nineteenth century.[32]

The relative weakness of theological and philosophical training
among the nobility helps explain why the many deist and atheist tracts
produced in Western Europe during the eighteenth century found little
resonance in Russia.[33] The philosophical and theological apparatus of
eighteenth-century British and French deists was weighty: Voltaire

could not have ridiculed Catholic theology as he did without the benefit of a Jesuit education.[34] As Alan Charles Kors observes, published atheist tracts by D'Holbach and Naigeon, which "burst upon the French reading public" beginning in 1770, were deeply informed not only by the work of Locke, Hobbes, and Berkeley but also by Catholic apologetic writings. These, in turn, were grounded in seventeenth-century debates between Aristotelian and Cartesian theologians.[35]

The intellectual context was essential to the reception of new ideas. In his foundational study *The Problem of Unbelief in the Sixteenth Century: The Religion of Rabelais* (1942), Lucien Febvre argued that atheism, the contention that God does not exist, could become "thinkable" only in the seventeenth and eighteenth centuries, when a modern philosophical vocabulary and new expectations as to the certainty of scientific, philosophical, and theological propositions had taken root in western Europe.[36] When new manuscripts from the early modern period were discovered, historians challenged Febvre's chronological frame. They also questioned his definition of unbelief: he had been willing only to recognize a form of unbelief that bore the features of modern atheism.[37] Even so, Febvre's work compelled historians to situate ideas in their cultural context and to question which ideas were indeed thinkable. Some scholars went further by asking what ideas could be spoken of, inquiring into the limits of self-expression.[38] In this book, the process by which doubt and atheism became "speakable" will be as central as the one by which they became thinkable.

Historians of nineteenth-century atheism have continued to ask how philosophical, theological, and scientific developments transformed the conditions of faith in the modern world, showing how intellectuals were forced to reconsider not only religious certainties but the very nature of religious certainty.[39] Religious certainty was a core concern for Russian intellectuals, too. Yet, unlike in the West, debates over doubt and the existence of God in nineteenth-century Russia did not center on philosophical challenges to the status of the Bible or the truth of theological doctrine. One of the core contentions of this book is that educated Russians, while influenced by Western philosophers, did not view the establishment of a philosophically compelling critique of faith in God as their principal concern. Nor did the availability of a philosophical vocabulary and scientific concepts automatically generate disbelief in God. Life experience, as well as political and social status, also played a role in defining refusals of faith. Challenges to the existence of God were further shaped by existing cultural assumptions about what it meant to lose faith, and by the particular content of the faith held by individuals. Proponents of

Russian atheism did not develop a frame of thought from which every vestige of Orthodox Christian culture had been eradicated; rather they continually drew on the vocabulary of faith and salvation in articulating the meaning that the life of the unbeliever must hold. From a philosophical perspective, their comments on doubt and the atheism they espoused lacked rigor, but this did not deprive them of force.

Deism made almost no inroads among educated Russians until the late eighteenth century; atheism found even fewer adherents until the middle of the nineteenth century. Even so, church and state grew increasingly anxious about the religious allegiances of the secular elite. The French Revolution only heightened such concerns. It confirmed the belief, widely held among educated Russians, that challenges to Orthodox Christianity would inevitably lead to social unrest and anarchy. Revolutionary excesses were blamed squarely on the French philosophes, whose atheist tracts were said to have destroyed the conscience of the French people and enflamed their passions. Voltaire's library, which Catherine II had so proudly transported to St. Petersburg, was now locked away in the basement of the Hermitage and remained there for half a century.[40]

The state had to preserve the Orthodox faith, because only faith could preserve the state. In the nineteenth century, state officials regarded the observance of Orthodox Christian practices as an indicator of the political reliability of the nobility, of personal fidelity to tsar and fatherland. Fear of God was the only guarantee that noblemen would fulfill their obligations to the state and exercise their power as landholders and serf owners conscientiously.[41] A nobleman who consistently failed to attend confession and communion would not be prosecuted, but, if he was an official or a military officer, he might find his chances for promotion diminished and social standing undermined. The political police that Nicholas I created, the Third Section of His Majesty's Own Chancellery, began every interrogation by asking whether the subject had attended church and taken communion. A person who neglected this duty would likely be labeled *neblagonadezhnyi*—unreliable, untrustworthy, a person to be removed from the fabric of Russian society lest it be corrupted by his presence.

Books were considered no less dangerous than people. During the eighteenth century, the Holy Synod sought to regulate the publication of all writings pertaining to the Orthodox faith.[42] Toward the end of the century, the state solidified and institutionalized a second apparatus to control secular literature, and the number of censors and volume of material they handled rapidly grew in the early nineteenth century, as the readership of Russia's periodical press expanded.[43] By 1840, that readership numbered around twenty thousand. Censors, recruited from the literary world, came to play a key role in Russian intellectual life. These "men of good will somehow saddled with the unhappy burden" of excising what might be objectionable required the cooperation of editors and writers to ensure that the system functioned smoothly.[44] To guarantee that they performed their duties diligently, Nicholas I ordered officials of the Third Section to monitor censors' work. Publishing in imperial Russia did not resemble a game of cat and mouse: authors cooperated with the system by censoring their own works in advance, which was essential if they wished to see their works in print. This remained true even in the early reign of Alexander II, who relaxed laws on censorship and permitted the emergence of a vibrant journalistic culture. By the 1860s, journalists had become professionals who did not need to supplement their incomes by working in the bureaucracy or military, and growing numbers came from outside the nobility. Still, their ability to publish and therefore to earn an income depended on their willingness to play by the state's rules.

The strictures of censorship never meant that authors were utterly unable to express their views in print, however. Journalists continually pushed against the boundaries of what the state deemed acceptable. In the early nineteenth century, Russian writers discovered fiction, poetry, and literary criticism as key genres in which they could indirectly voice their opinions about society, politics, and religion. Even so, printed media could offer only a partial view of the author's outlook, and this had major consequences for literary life. It brought the question of personal integrity into sharper focus: writing for print was political, and it involved constant compromise on the part of the author. All readers of Russian journals from the late eighteenth century onward were aware of this problem, and this, in turn, drew their attention to the private lives of Russian intellectuals. Authors' personal choices and actions helped supplement a picture of a mind that could be rendered only partially in print. On a more intimate level, they offered readers further food for thought on the painful subject of the compromises individuals made on a daily basis. The question that most intensely tested personal pliability was the question of faith in the existence of God. An individual's stance on this issue defined his or her place in the regime and willingness to tear the fabric of a deeply hierarchical society.

The word "intelligentsia" did not come into widespread use until the 1860s, but the roots of the concept can be traced to the early nineteenth century. Its meaning has long been controversial. A few decades ago, many historians agreed that intelligentsia referred to a social category, a view that has recently been challenged.[45] In this study, intelligentsia is identified with a set of expectations, articulated in ever more pressing terms during the nineteenth century, that to be an educated person brought with it certain obligations toward the nation and toward humanity. Being a member of the intelligentsia meant holding oneself and others to this standard: Russia's educated minority believed it was called on—morally obligated—to point Russia and the world at large toward a better future. The enormity of this task heightened the importance assigned to addressing and resolving the eternal questions, for the future had, until then, been understood as the domain of Providence. When they invoked the word "intelligentsia," Russians referred to a distinctive set of norms about what it meant—or ought to mean—to be an educated person in imperial Russia. Educated people were to be the "consciousness of the nation."[46]

These expectations were never more vocally honored than when they were breached. More often than not, writings produced about the intelligentsia by its members were accusatory in tone, informing Russia's educated society that it had failed to live up to its calling.[47] This remained true in the twentieth century, when *Signposts* (*Vekhi*), a collection of essays about the intelligentsia, was published in 1909 under the editorship of the literary historian Mikhail Gershenzon. *Signposts* came to define the intelligentsia in historical memory. Written in the wake of the 1905 revolution, it was intended to alert educated society that it had forgotten its true calling amid all the political upheaval. Over the past half century, Gershenzon claimed, "a handful of revolutionaries has been going from house to house and knocking on every door: 'Everyone into the street! It's shameful to stay at home!' [. . .] No one lived; everyone engaged in civic affairs (or pretended to do so). [. . .] A day passes, and who knows why; today things are one way, and tomorrow a sudden fancy will turn everything upside down." Instead of "taking the risk" of formulating an independent worldview, young people allowed themselves to be guided by established doctrines and intellectual fads.[48] Other contributors to *Signposts*, too, excoriated the intelligentsia for having allowed itself to become doctrinaire, intolerant, and fanatical. Atheism was one of the doctrines that bothered them most. The revolutionary intelligentsia had constructed a religion out of atheism, demanding the worship of humankind and anathematizing the worship of God.[49] After the 1917 revolution, *Signposts* seemed prophetic. Nikolai Berdiaev, one of its contributors, was later to argue that the revolution had been a historical inevitability. Soviet communism was not just a misguided attempt to construct a utopia on the basis of Western ideas but the product of the innate millenarianism of the Russian mind, a quest to create a heaven on earth—an atheist heaven. Members of the intelligentsia had become missionaries of this cause well before they discovered Marx.[50]

Beginning in 1921, Soviet historians devoted dozens of studies to projecting a certain form of atheism—a Bolshevik type—backward into history. Atheism, they asserted, was a product of Western scientific materialism: all true scientists were materialists and therefore atheists. Atheism was also an attendant feature of political rebellion and class struggle, manifesting itself among déclassé intellectuals, laborers, and peasants.[51] Western historians tended to dismiss Soviet studies as tendentious, yet they, too, approached the Russian intelligentsia as a handmaiden of the revolution. They agreed that atheism had been a core feature of the revolutionary intelligentsia beginning in the 1860s, but their comments on the topic were usually cursory.[52] In the west, no alternative account of why the question of the existence of God had been accorded such importance by Russian intellectuals emerged.

To treat atheism as a doctrine is, in some way, to miss its most salient feature. In Russia, it was less a statement about the status of God than it was a commentary on the status of educated people in an authoritarian state that sought ever more forcefully to regulate the opinions and beliefs of its subjects. The state's promotion of Russian Orthodox piety and insistence on intellectual conformity made adherence to the faith of the church appear hypocritical, an abdication of the individual's duty to pursue knowledge and truth. Young people needed new answers to the questions of how to live and what to live for. In his article for *Signposts*, Mikhail Gershenzon upbraided his contemporaries for failing to address precisely these issues.[53] Looking into the intelligentsia's past, however, he noted that there had been a time, in the 1830s, when members of the educated elites had organized their lives around finding the answers, when they allowed themselves to be consumed by doubts.[54] Doubt itself provided the answer to the question of how to live. Even as doubt became an intellectual stance that was de rigueur among aspiring noble intellectuals, however, overt atheism remained impermissible.

As young people from outside the nobility sought entrance into literary society in the mid-nineteenth century, they found that they were largely unwelcome. Some of them, sons of merchants and clergymen, would respond by rejecting the nobility and its high culture, and some would also reject doubt in favor of a more radical position: atheism. Social identity helped shape the way in which individuals formulated disbelief. Social circumstances did not produce atheism, but social resentments facilitated its expression. Those young *raznochintsy* most troubled by the limitations of their upbringing and present circumstances came to think that their break with the past entailed the rejection of faith in God. To them, God came to symbolize both a system of hierarchy, which they repudiated, and a connection to their own history, which they wished to overcome. Though they described their abandonment of faith in God as an act of liberation, this abandonment was always accompanied by a sense of crisis, by a feeling that one was launching oneself into a void. The consequences were unforeseeable. Whatever their answer to the question of the existence of God, few educated Russians were prepared to announce themselves satisfied: questioning had become the intelligentsia's reason for being.

Readers accustomed to the long-established narrative of the intelligentsia's formation will notice the relative absence in this study of some familiar figures, such as Chaadaev, the Slavophiles, and Dostoevsky. A broad and diverse scholarship has served admirably to place their religiously informed perspective in its historical and cultural context.[55] The goal of my book is to return our attention to the equally important story of doubt and atheism, to show how each took root in the thought and practice of five generations of imperial-era intellectuals and became a core feature, to be celebrated or reviled, by the Russian intelligentsia. Here, the choice has been for depth over breadth. The individuals and groups who figure in this study were selected largely for pragmatic reasons: these are the people who produced the most extensive records of their loss of faith, doubt, and disbelief, in a society where such records were rarely left behind.[56]

This book is divided into three parts, corresponding to three phases of thought about the eternal questions. Part 1 shows how the quest to answer them began and manifested itself in the articulation of doubt among two intellectual groups, or "circles," in Moscow: the Wisdom Lovers, a group of aristocratic poets in the 1820s (chapter 1), and the Westernizers of the 1830s and 1840s (chapter 2). Moscow was sufficiently far from the courtly world of St. Petersburg to afford the noble elites more leeway for intellectual experimentation. Both groups drew on German idealism—a philosophy that senior state officials condemned—to argue that the calling of every educated person was to identify the deeper meaning that underlies nature and history, the divine essence or purpose behind the world's infinite diversity. Doubt about one's relationship to the divine must form a key part of that quest. Indeed, during the 1840s, the content of doubt expanded to include the very existence of God. Doubt came to be viewed as the mode of thought that made the life of the educated person meaningful.

Part 2 shifts attention from Moscow to St. Petersburg, where the growth of the educated population led to the emergence of a vibrant cultural atmosphere in the 1840s. A circle of young townsmen, who have so far been left out of historical studies, aspired to join the literary elites but found themselves excluded (chapter 3). Nikolai Chernyshevsky and Nikolai Dobroliubov, too, encountered obstacles as sons of priests but were more successful in placing themselves at the center of St. Petersburg's journalistic world in the late 1850s. They became the core of the historiography on the intelligentsia (chapter 4). Doubt could not satisfy this generation: coming from outside the nobility, some would dismiss doubt as an aristocratic weakness and affectation. Many had been radicalized by their authoritarian upbringing in the exceedingly conservative state of Nicholas I. They did not merely wish to affirm that they belonged to the ranks of educated people in Russia (petty bureaucrats, teachers, students, and doctors), but wished to guide them. To assert their authority, they began by challenging Russia's highest authority—God. In articulating their views, they, too drew on Western philosophy, especially the writings of Ludwig Feuerbach, though they also responded to native traditions: those of the earlier intelligentsia.

Part 3 investigates how educated Russians who accepted the proposition that God does not exist attempted to reorient themselves in the 1860s. Students who rejected the state's efforts at liberal reform joined the revolutionary movement (chapter 5). Many were sons of priests and deacons, and they conceived of the popular rebellion they anticipated in apocalyptic terms. They also believed, however, that the "new people" could not create a "new world" unless they cast off the "old Adam": faith in God. Not every atheist was a member of the revolutionary movement, however. During his short but brilliant career as a literary journalist, Dmitrii Pisarev, the son of an impoverished nobleman, struggled with the question of how an individual could find principles to live by in the absence of faith (chapter 6). Individuals, he claimed, must reject faith in God along with other established beliefs and instead orient themselves around a purely inner sense of truth. Pisarev was thus the first intellectual to fully explore the implications of what it meant to be a modern, secular individual. As he discovered, however, a purely inner sense of truth offered people neither intellectual nor emotional stability. Both approaches to living without God—one communitarian and revolutionary, the other individualistic and introspective— remained highly influential in the early twentieth century, when the revolution that everyone expected finally occurred.

The developments described in this book are multifaceted and influenced Russian intellectual life in the late nineteenth and early twentieth century in varied ways. Doubt continued to find expression along side of a millenarian faith in the salvation of the Russian people; friendship remained the object of worship for some, while others attempted to live without a faith of any kind. Some chapters in this book help explain where the Bolsheviks' state religion—militant atheism—came from. Drawing on Marxism, many revolutionaries remained convinced of the necessity of atheism as a predicate of revolution. Yet that atheism was not the only product of the developments outlined here, nor should the atheism that was first elaborated in the mid-nineteenth century be understood solely in these terms. It was the outcome of a long quest to find answers to the question of how to live after the answers offered by the state and the church had been rejected. The book's primary purpose is to show how and why "the youth of Russia spoke of nothing but those timeless questions."

Part 1

Doubt

1

Forbidden Fruit

The Wisdom Lovers

Alexander Koshelev could not remember a more joyful time in his life than the night he spent in the late 1820s in St. Petersburg with Aleksei Khomiakov and Vladimir Odoevsky debating the "finitude and infinity" of the world. The matter could not easily be resolved, and that was part of its appeal. When Koshelev and Khomiakov finally left Odoevsky's home at about three in the morning, they continued their argument on the stairs, in the coach, and in front of Khomiakov's house. Only at dawn would they part ways, after a perplexed neighbor opened her window and exclaimed (in German): "My God and Lord, what is this?"[1]

Though several Wisdom Lovers moved to St. Petersburg in the late 1820s, it was in Moscow that they first came together. In 1823, Prince Odoevsky founded a secret society, the Society for the Love of Wisdom (Obshchestvo liubomudriia), in his rooms in Gazetnyi pereulok, not far from the Kremlin. There, the crowning object was a skull posted with a sign that read "Dare to Know!" ("Sapere Aude!").[2] Though the society's immediate purpose was modest—to study and discuss the philosophy of Friedrich Wilhelm Joseph Schelling—its mission was titanic. In conversation with one another, its members aimed to resolve the mysteries of the universe and to investigate the world in its infinite diversity so as to uncover the higher principle that organized it. In doing so, they would reconcile the divine and the material. They were pantheists, who believed that God, spirit (or the Absolute), is inseparable from nature. The Wisdom Lovers were interested in the status of not only the divine but also the individuals who sought truth—the ways their quest might influence their moral and spiritual condition and their relationship with the society surrounding them. Drawing on German idealist philosophy and romantic literary theory, they grew convinced that no one could grasp the Absolute or divine principle without suffering doubt about his capacity for such knowledge.[3]

Never before in Russian letters had doubt been valued as part of the process by which an individual could grasp divine truth. Within a decade, the concept of doubt, developed by the Wisdom Lovers, was firmly established as essential to the way of thinking and mode of life of young Russian romantics. It was central to the poetics and fiction of Mikhail Lermontov, the premier romantic writer of the 1830s, and was frequently invoked in the correspondence, poetry, literary criticism, and philosophical writings of the young idealists of the 1830s generation, in the circles of Vissarion Belinsky and Alexander Herzen. One Wisdom Lover whom Belinsky and Herzen particularly admired was Dmitrii Venevitinov, both as an exceptional poet and as a critic of the state.[4] Yet the debt they owed Venevitinov and other Wisdom Lovers as proponents of doubt was immediately forgotten. This lapse of memory may be attributed to the depth with which doubt ingrained itself in Russian high culture: doubt quickly became so central to the lives of young romantics that it was difficult to conceive of it as the product of any particular cultural or philosophical movement. In addition, it seems that in the 1830s and 1840s, former Wisdom Lovers welcomed this erasure of the historical record. Several of them came to be known as romantic conservatives, as Orthodox "Slavophiles." Their later Orthodoxy caused historians to gloss over their advocacy of doubt at this early stage.[5] Indeed, doubt itself was rarely mentioned in studies of the history of early nineteenth-century Russian thought.

Doubt was, according to the Wisdom Lovers, a state of uncertainty about one's ability to grasp the higher unity amid the chaos of the surrounding world. They were acutely aware, however, that the truth seeker might come to doubt the very existence of the higher, unifying principle, a state that spelled damnation for anyone who was unable to overcome it. Searching for the antidote to despair, they saw friendship itself as the key to the restoration of hope and faith.

The Wisdom Lovers' inspiration to thoroughly comprehend the world's fundamental truths came from German idealist philosophy and romantic pantheism, though their emphasis on doubt appears to have been Russian in origin. Alexander Pushkin had introduced the word in the mid-1820s into two works that the Wisdom Lovers especially admired: chapter two of *Eugene Onegin* and the poem "My Demon." Pushkin, in turn, was stimulated by the politics of Alexander I (reigned 1801–25).

In the wake of the Napoleonic wars, Alexander I set out to reform the court and the Russian nobility, which he believed had grown prone to immorality and selfishness in the later eighteenth century. Together with senior officials whom he promoted to top ministerial positions, he sought to encourage religious morality, drive out corruption in the bureaucracy, and foster a sense of responsibility toward the Russian people. Nicholas I (reigned 1825–55), in so many ways different from his older brother, shared this sense of purpose. While their efforts succeeded in garnering the support of a large portion of the nobility, their policies of reform spelled an unprecedented intrusiveness into the nobility's private lives, creating opposition in some circles.

The Wisdom Lovers were among those who found the new state-sponsored piety repellant. They found efforts to combat freethinking among the educated elites particularly distasteful. The hostility that state officials and prelates of the Orthodox Church expressed toward doubt and idealist philosophy seems to have increased their appeal. The Wisdom Lovers were not antistate: like all young noblemen, they assumed that they would eventually join the civil administration. Nor were they antichurch: in embracing German idealism, they did not consider themselves apostates of the Orthodox Christian faith, because they had not been trained to think of Orthodoxy as a rigid system of theological doctrines. Rather, they resented the new confidence with which state officials attempted to intervene in the intellectual and ethical formation of members of the nobility and reacted by putting forward an alternative worldview, to which doubt was central.

The Wisdom Lovers were young at the time they established the Society for the Love of Wisdom in 1823. Among the founders, Prince Vladimir Odoevsky, president, was the oldest. At nineteen or twenty, he could already boast several published short stories, which had appeared in the Moscow journal the *Messenger of Europe* (*Vestnik Evropy*) in the early 1820s. Dmitrii Venevitinov, secretary, was eighteen and of delicate health. He was born into a noble family that was not only of ancient lineage but also highly cultured: Venevitinov's mother, Anna Nikolaevna Venevitinova, was a Moscow *salonnière* and a distant relative of Alexander Pushkin. Venevitinov's friends treasured him for his poetic talent. Ivan Kireevsky, seventeen, held the most prestigious literary connections:

his mother, Avdotia Elagina, was hostess of Moscow's most important literary salon. She was the niece of the great poet Vasilii Zhukovsky, who was much favored at court in St. Petersburg. Alexander Koshelev, also seventeen, was talented neither as a philosopher nor as a poet, but he was an enthusiastic participant in the group's debates. He was the nephew of a highly prominent St. Petersburg freemason and courtier. Of the official members of the society, Nikolai Rozhalin, seventeen, was the only one who did not come from a family of noble stock: his father, the grandson of a priest, had worked his way up to hereditary nobility through the Table of Ranks. What Rozhalin lacked in family prestige, he made up through intellectual sophistication.

Other young and well-connected friends also played an integral role in the life of the group, though they were not official members of the society. Vladimir Titov came from an ancient noble family, widely known for the musicality of its leading representatives. Aleksei Khomiakov was the precocious son of a wealthy Muscovite dandy; he was at once a source of consolation and despair to his pious mother, who upbraided her son for his German mannerisms and begged him to cut his shoulder-length hair: he insisted on wearing it in the pageboy style like the rest of his friends. The pug-nosed Stepan Shevyrev could trace his lineage back several centuries, and he was responsible for including Mikhail Pogodin, the son of a freed peasant, in the activities of the group. Aged twenty-three, Pogodin was the eldest person associated with the Wisdom Lovers, but they tended to treat this commoner with disregard.

Born into noble families with close connections to the literary giants of the day, the Wisdom Lovers did not need to break into the literary world; on the contrary, they were marked by a comfortable sense of superiority within it. These nine young men came forward at a time when older members of the cultured elites still clung to the aesthetic codes of the Enlightenment, which maintained its dominance over Russian high culture much longer than in western Europe.[6] By promoting idealism, romanticism, and doubt, they were asserting a right to cultural leadership within the elite, which they regarded as intellectually backward. Simultaneously, they attempted to defend the intellectual autonomy of the nobility against encroachments by the imperial state and Russian Orthodox Church.

The Wisdom Lovers signaled their allegiance to romanticism by favoring such genres as the aphorism and the fragment, alongside metaphysical poetry. They printed these works in their own almanac,

Aleksei Khomiakov. Portrait by unknown artist, undated. In Dmitrii Venevitinov, *Stikhotvoreniia, Proza* (Moscow: Nauka, 1980). (Fyodor I. Tiutchev Museum, Muranovo.)

Stepan Shevyrev. Pencil sketch, undated. In Dmitrii Venevitinov, Stepan Shevyrev, Aleksei Khomiakov, *Stikhotvoreniia*, edited by Mark Aronson and Ivan Sergievskii (Leningrad: Sovetskii pisatel', 1937), between 98 and 99.

which they named *Mnemosyne* (*Mnemozina*) (1824–25), after the mother
of the muses. A short while later, they created a journal, the *Moscow
Messenger* (*Moskovskii vestnik*) (1827–30). Their readership was then still
very small and dominated by the nobility in Moscow and St. Petersburg.
Mnemosyne had only 157 subscribers, and the readership of the *Moscow
Messenger* was only marginally greater.[7] Yet the Wisdom Lovers did not
envision a mass audience for their writings. The cultural world they
inhabited was self-consciously elitist.

Their youth gave them a distinct advantage in their intellectual
mission. Unmarried and unencumbered by positions of responsibility
in state service, they could dedicate their time to discussing poetry and
philosophy. Indeed, they viewed youth as a time when individuals
ought to experiment with art, science, and philosophy, to question the
meaning of life and the established order so as to find their place in the
world. The Wisdom Lovers enjoyed the best education that money and
family connections could provide. Fluent in French, Russian, and
German, they also learned Latin and, in some cases, Greek. Their tutors
included professors at Moscow University. Men of lowly status, sons
and grandsons of priests, these professors were welcomed into their
homes as valued servants.

When custom dictated that Wisdom Lovers should begin to work,
their families arranged their assignments to the Archives of the Ministry
of Foreign Affairs in Moscow, where the few hours they spent in the
offices were often dedicated to the composition of short stories.[8] Publishing their writings was not a problem either: the Wisdom Lovers
could call on their former teachers to support them. Thus, Ivan Snegirev,
once their tutor, now a professor of logic at Moscow University and
state censor, was cajoled into signing off on volumes of *Mnemosyne*.[9]
Finally, their fine education and high birth made the Wisdom Lovers
welcome guests at Moscow's literary societies and salons, including the
most prestigious one, hosted by Ivan Kireevsky's mother. As the St.
Petersburg journalist and novelist Faddei Bulgarin put it with poisonous
disdain, they were "momma's boys, that is: the rear column of the
phalanx patronized by blind fortune. [. . .] They are our dandies,
fashionables, grooms of all brides, in love with any woman whose nose
does not grow out of the back of her head and who can pronounce *oui*
and *non*. They are the ones who set the tone among the Muscovite
youth at promenades, at the theater, and in the drawing rooms. This
rank even provides Moscow with its philosophers of the latest style,
among whom everything is full beyond the brim apart from common

sense; [they are] weavers of rhythm and desperate judges of letters and sciences."[10]

The Wisdom Lovers' reputation for frivolity endured beyond their lifetimes. In historical scholarship, they have often been contrasted with the Decembrists, to whom they were connected by birth and friendship. The Decembrists were remembered for cultivating austere mores and a "serious" manner.[11] They risked (and in some cases, sacrificed) their lives by opposing the ascension of Nicholas I to the throne and occupying Senate Square in St. Petersburg in December 1825, demanding social and political freedom, while the Wisdom Lovers sat comfortably in Moscow discussing Schelling. The poets were frightened when conspirators in the uprising were arrested and investigated; they quickly disbanded their society, even though they continued to meet and cooperate in literary ventures.

The differences between the two groups should not be exaggerated. Both sought to defend noble autonomy against the state. Some Decembrists viewed the study of German philosophy with suspicion, but not all did.[12] As Iurii Lotman has shown, one of the Decembrists' primary objectives was to bring "philosophical speech" and thought into the norms of everyday interaction, lending even their carousing a philosophical seriousness.[13] This was a project that the Wisdom Lovers evidently shared. And while some Wisdom Lovers, notably Odoevsky and Khomiakov, expressed disapproval of the Decembrists' politics, others were sympathetic. In his memoirs, Koshelev recalled attending a soirée in February or March 1825 at which Kondratii Ryleev and other Decembrists were present and made their views known. Dazzled, Koshelev spent the next day telling what he had heard to Venevitinov, Kireevsky, and Rozhalin, who apparently shared his enthusiasm.[14] Their excitement carried over into their philosophical and literary endeavors, which reached a high point in the months leading up to the Decembrist uprising and continued as the Decembrists were arrested, tried, and either pardoned, executed, or exiled. It was between 1825 and 1827 that the Wisdom Lovers published their most explicitly romantic and pantheist poems, along with the writings in which they defended doubt. Only after Venevitinov died in March 1827 did the group lose coherence, backing away from the more daring implications of its thought.

To appreciate what was daring about the Wisdom Lovers' stance, one must consider the delicate status of philosophy in Russia in the 1820s.

In the years following the Napoleonic wars, conservatism took hold of the state as well as Russian high society. Alexander I grew fearful that the peace and stability he strove to create through his Holy Alliance was being undermined everywhere by a spirit of freethinking. "Free-thinking" (*vol'nodumstvo*) was a vague term that could apply to any expression of personal opinion: an individual who spoke his mind necessarily engaged in an act of self-assertion that challenged social and political hierarchies. Small wonder that Alexander I banned all secret societies, including Masonic lodges, in 1822.[15] The government, Alexander believed, needed to go still further to protect the Russian people from the forces of darkness by attacking one core cause of the problem: philosophy.

By the late eighteenth century, Russia's conservative, Westernized elites had already begun to use the word "philosophy" interchangeably with "Freemasonry," "freethinking," "skepticism," and "irreligion." In the gloomy atmosphere of the mid-1810s, senior officials in the Ministry of Enlightenment were inclined to agree, viewing philosophy as a source of religious, political, and social rebellion. Mikhail Magnitskii, one of the leaders of the campaign against intellectual independence, warned that the prince of darkness was approaching and had made philosophy his insidious weapon. Operating through professors at "godless universities," the dark prince was said to be using philosophical considerations to administer "the subtle poison of unbelief and hatred for legitimate powers [*zakonnye vlasti*]." The philosophy of the French Enlightenment was easily identifiable as dangerous for its promotion of atheism and natural law. The philosophy of German idealism, especially that of Schelling, however, was more nefarious, for it promoted atheism under the cloak of piety and preached freedom as the ultimate goal of human development.[16]

German idealism is best understood as a philosophical system that takes the observation of the process of cognition in the individual to be central to a correct understanding of the world. Immanuel Kant argued that we can know the world only as it is represented in our minds. Later idealists would claim that the world itself exists only as we perceive it, that we in fact construct or create the world in the process of representing it to ourselves. Under the influence of romanticism, Friedrich Wilhelm Joseph Schelling imbued the process of cognition with religious meaning. By themselves, our impressions of the world around us are fragmentary and chaotic. Only through intuition do we become aware of the higher unity, which is nothing less than the Absolute, spirit, or God. As the

Absolute reveals itself through human consciousness, it undergoes development; the Absolute cannot become complete without realizing itself in this way. It is not difficult to see why, even in Germany, Schelling's views provoked controversy: God was no longer an independent agent acting on the world from outside but had become spirit, acting in and through nature and humanity. Moreover, Schelling had collapsed faith into knowledge rather than preserving it as a separate, active faculty.[17]

In the 1810s, Schelling's philosophy had only just arrived in Russian universities. It was being taught most notably by Professors Vellanskii and Galich in St. Petersburg and by Professors Davydov and Pavlov in Moscow. Within years of their appointments, Galich and Davydov, together with teachers at other universities, were being investigated by officials at the Ministry of Spiritual Affairs and Public Enlightenment, who attempted to dismiss them. In most cases, the inferior social status of these men made them easy prey.[18] It is unlikely that many of these officials read Schelling's works or even the works of the professors they attacked. Prince Alexander Golitsyn, who headed the Ministry of Spiritual Affairs and Public Enlightenment, appears to have trusted Magnitskii; in an 1822 report to the Committee of Ministers, he called idealism a "perverse system of doubting the authenticity of divine revelation" that sought to replace "it with the false reasoning and insolent conjectures [*lzheumstvovaniiami i derznovennymi dogadkami*] of alleged scholars and philosophers." The "system," he claimed, had already undermined Christian faith, transforming believers into "pagan wise men [*mudrovateli*]." It threatened not only to destroy the church but also to dissolve social hierarchies and undermine all obedience to the state authorities, which would lead to revolution and "tempestuous chaos."[19]

The philosophy professors in question were unable to head off such criticisms and dire predictions. Galich, for example, attempted to allay suspicions about the status of doubt in philosophy. "Doubt" and "skepticism" are a central part of philosophical reasoning, he admitted, but they are valuable only because they reinforce faith in revealed truths. Indeed, there is no better way to "extol the grace" of revelation "than by the deep abasement of the natural powers of understanding and will." He claimed that a "detailed representation of the endless errors of self-confident reason," that is, skepticism, was the best way to prove "the necessity of faith." Though these words were intended to reassure his readers, "doubt" and "skepticism" were red flags to officials, who used them against Galich as evidence of his freethinking.[20] There could, apparently, be no justification for doubt: invoking it for any purpose was dangerous. Galich was stripped of the right to lecture at St. Petersburg University and forced to earn his living as a private tutor.[21]

While the Ministry of Enlightenment faced few challenges as it ferreted out idealist professors in St. Petersburg, Kharkov, and Kazan, it encountered some resistance in Moscow. The city was shielded by its status as the empire's secondary capital, and its high-ranking officials resented interference from St. Petersburg. For a brief moment, Moscow became the envy of the empire.[22] Ivan Davydov was able to hang on to his position for a few years despite repeated and heavy attacks by Magnitskii. He taught Schelling's philosophy at Moscow University and at the elite school attached to it, the Moscow Boarding School for the Nobility (Moskovskii blagorodnyi pansion), until 1826, when he was fired because of intervention from St. Petersburg. That year, a ban that lasted for twenty years was placed on all lectures in philosophy at the university.[23] Davydov was one of the Wisdom Lovers' favorite teachers at the boarding school, where Odoevsky, Shevyrev, and Titov studied in the late 1810s and early 1820s.

The invasiveness of the new spirit of conservatism can be observed in a collection of essays produced by students of the Moscow Boarding School and printed in 1824. One of the first articles in the collection warned readers against "false enlightenment," the "wisdom of the serpent," and "brazen dreaming," which could only lead to rampant violence, including murder and robbery. The virtuous and righteous wise man, by contrast, was one who staked his happiness on "religion and the Gospels" and on "filial submission to the Heavenly Father." "Only the brazen dreamer doubts!"[24] The same rhetoric would be invoked, two years later, by Nicholas I in the wake of the Decembrist uprising. The manifesto of July 13, 1826, announcing the execution of five Decembrists, offered the state's only systematic explanation of the revolt. It characterized the Decembrists as immoral youths carried away by "willfulness of thought" (*svoevol'stvo myslei*) and "brazen dreaming." The blame lay in bad habits of mind, which society had tolerated; Russia would never be safe until they had been eradicated.[25]

The Wisdom Lovers, by choosing German idealism as their source of intellectual sustenance, were clearly defying the official culture of St. Petersburg. They founded their society a year after Alexander I had banned all secret societies, and they dedicated it to the discussion of the philosophy that Magnitskii and Golitsyn condemned as a source of freethinking, atheism, and political chaos. Though they nominally disbanded the society after the Decembrist uprising, they persisted in defending one of the aristocracy's prerogatives, the exploration and assimilation of Western culture. The fact that the fruits they found were forbidden was clearly an important source of the attraction.[26]

If the Wisdom Lovers defied the state's efforts to ban German idealist philosophy, they ignored efforts by Russian Orthodox prelates to assert the status of the church as the only source of divine wisdom. The Westernized nobility had grown wayward over the preceding half century: while its members continued to practice the rites of the Orthodox Church, many were drawn to pietistic, Catholic, and mystical thought. Until the early 1820s, the church had seldom been able to intervene. Now, Orthodox prelates saw an opportunity and joined the state campaign against freethinking, attempting to rein in the proliferation of "false wisdom" among the nobility. Their efforts did not impress the Wisdom Lovers, however, who steadfastly asserted that divinity could be found and expressed anywhere: in nature, music, sculpture, and mathematics but especially in philosophy and poetry.

Scholarly literature has been divided in its representations of the Wisdom Lovers' attitudes toward Christianity and religion more generally; naturally, assessments have also differed for each member of the group. The outlook of its central figures, Venevitinov and Odoevsky, along with Koshelev, has variously been referred to as "materialism" or "skepticism" or as simply "indifference" to Christianity.[27] Some scholars note that Khomiakov was always a firm believer, while others confidently refer to his poetry in the 1820s as "pantheist."[28] "Pantheist" is also the label that is used here, with the caveat that the Wisdom Lovers never applied it to themselves, preferring to leave their status as Orthodox Christians open.

The decision to embrace pantheism was not occasioned by a grave crisis of faith in Orthodox Christianity: the Wisdom Lovers are unlikely to have worried about the incompatibility of these two systems of thought, because most (with the possible exception of Khomiakov) were not raised to think of Orthodoxy as a system of rigorous theological doctrines. Their religious upbringing was in no way untypical of noble children in the first two decades of the nineteenth century. Generally, parents concentrated on teaching their children prayers and liturgical hymns, but the reading habits of noble boys depended very much on the family in which they were raised. Saints' lives, which emphasized the practical application of church doctrine to the everyday behavior of virtuous Christians, formed the core of the devotional reading of most children. Some parents also instructed their children in scripture by telling them what they knew of the Bible. Reading the Bible was more complicated: Bibles were not widely available in print at the beginning of the nineteenth century. Many families would have owned handwritten copies in Old Church Slavonic, which some fathers read with their children.[29] Yet it is unclear how well most noblemen understood Old Church Slavonic in the early nineteenth century. Georges Florovsky wryly observed that Alexander I preferred reading the New Testament in De Sacy's French translation.[30]

Not only were Slavonic Bibles relatively scarce in Russia in the early nineteenth century but so were catechisms and other Orthodox theological tracts. In the eighteenth century, the most highly literate noblemen had already grown used to compensating for this deficit by importing books, including Catholic and Protestant theological tracts, though mystical and pietist literature appears to have held special appeal.[31] Soon, Russians were translating mystical literature and even producing tracts of their own: one particularly influential example was Ivan Lopukhin's *Some Characteristics of the Interior Church* (1798). According to Alexander Martin, pietist and mystical tracts gained appeal as the sentimental codes of the late Enlightenment prompted the educated elite to look for delicate and tender feeling in religion. The Orthodox Church came to appear "coldly ritualistic and intellectually ossified" to members of the Westernized nobility.[32]

The piety practiced in the homes of Wisdom Lovers would tend to suggest that, at the dawn of the nineteenth century, most members of Russia's high nobility did not see a need to choose between Orthodox religiosity and mysticism or pietism, both of which were influential at court in the early reign of Alexander I. All the Wisdom Lovers were raised as Orthodox Christians, and this was especially true of Aleksei Khomiakov, whose mother was famed for the close attention she paid to the performance of the liturgy in the family chapel and for her punctilious observation of all fasts.[33] Other Wisdom Lovers, however, appear to have been exposed at an early age to non-Orthodox forms of piety as well. Ivan Kireevsky, for example, was the son of Vasilii Kireevsky, famed in Moscow as a man of austere piety. Yet Ivan was named after his godfather, the famous mystic Ivan Lopukhin, who bestowed a signed copy of his tract on the seven-year-old Vaniusha.[34] Similarly, one of Koshelev's uncles, Rodion Koshelev, was a mystic with powerful ties at court; he was also one of Russia's leading Freemasons, among whom pietism and Rosicrucian mysticism were widespread in this period.[35] As children, Kireevsky and Koshelev, at least, are unlikely to have been aware that there was any fundamental discrepancy between Orthodoxy and these other forms of piety.

Some prelates of the church had expressed alarm at the spread of heterodox thought among the nobility in the eighteenth century. In the early 1820s, however, Russia's metropolitans began to condemn with increasing urgency the spirit of independent-mindedness that had possessed their flocks. These included the most influential clergymen of the day, such as Metropolitan Filaret of Moscow, and Metropolitan Evgenii of Kiev and Galicia. To be a good Orthodox Christian, they explained in their sermons, was to be a "servant of God," entrusting oneself to him without questioning. Attempting to reason by oneself was futile, for human beings' mental capacities had been irreparably damaged at the time of the Fall by their sinfulness, making "revelation and its clear meaning" inaccessible to them. Far too many allowed "curiosity" to get the better of them and indulged in all manner of speculation about religion, which could only lead to doubt and from there to damnation.[36]

Though hierarchs of the Orthodox Church agreed about the dangers posed by pietism and mysticism, they disagreed as to the proper remedy. Some, including Metropolitan Filaret of Moscow, hoped that a Russian translation of the Bible might be used to bring the nobility back into the Orthodox Christian fold. Filaret played an active role in the translation of sections of the Old and New Testament, which were published in Russian for the first time from 1819 to 1824. Opponents of the Russian Bible, including Metropolitan Serafim of St. Petersburg, believed this would only further encourage freethinking. He rightly emphasized that the Russian Bible Society itself had been founded at the suggestion of Scottish Protestant missionaries who used copies of the Holy Writ in indigenous languages as part of their campaign to spread the Gospel. The notion that laypeople should read and interpret the Bible was, to Serafim, a dangerous Protestant innovation.

An anonymous article titled "Simplicity of Faith" that appeared in an 1824 issue of *Christian Reading* (*Khristianskoe chtenie*), the journal of the St. Petersburg Theological Academy, explained what was so dangerous about the Russian Bible. The educated elites were already accustomed to "thinking up new riddles, new opinions, and new doctrines" when it came to religion and had allowed themselves to become ensnared in "doubts." Laypeople who read translations of the Bible could only fall into greater and greater confusion and error. They must turn to the clergy for explanations instead of attempting to interpret scripture for themselves.[37] The emphasis here was on discouraging the laity from exploring religion on their own and encouraging them to rely instead on the Orthodox clergy as mediators of the divine.

The fate of the Russian Bible was sealed in 1824 when Prince Golitsyn, a key promoter of the Russian Bible Society, was swept from his position as head of the Ministry of Spiritual Affairs and Enlightenment and replaced by the reactionary Admiral Shishkov.[38] Shishkov believed that the society and its translations would "destroy Orthodoxy," because individuals who sought to interpret scripture on their own would inevitably reach false conclusions. Not only would translations "destroy the true faith," but they would also "disrupt the fatherland and produce strife and rebellion." He ordered copies of the Russian Pentateuch (the first five books of the Old Testament) consigned to the flames.[39] It would be another forty years before church and state authorized the publication of a Russian Bible.

Shishkov undoubtedly had the support of some prelates of the church when he equated biblical interpretation with political and social subversion. Metropolitan Evgenii of Kiev, an opponent of the Russian Bible, used much the same language. Drawing on 1 Corinthians 3:18–19, he declared that "faith has always been praised more highly than curiosity in understanding the revealed truths. Reason itself, according to the testament of the Apostles, must submit to faith and be silent, whatever difficulties it may encounter. [. . .] Of course, the wise men of this world [*mudretsy veka sego*] deny this, owing to the weak state of their spirit and to their folly [*buistvom*]." Here, the word *buistvo*, transposed from Church Slavonic into early-nineteenth-century Russian, took on a peculiar connotation. In Slavonic, it means "simplicity" or "ignorance," with connotations of stupidity and folly. In eighteenth-century Russian, however, *buistvo* could also suggest lack of inhibition, daring, and rebelliousness—in short, insubordination. Evgenii explored these connotations when he compared the worldly "wise man" to a "stubborn" son who questions his father, a "stubborn" pupil who doubts the lessons of his teacher, an insubordinate official who calls his superior to account, and a soldier who demands that his officer explain a secret strategy.[40]

An alliance was formed between certain prelates of the Russian Orthodox Church who opposed the spread of the Bible and some state officials who objected to the spread of pietism and mysticism in the highest circles of the nobility, including the court itself. The Russian Bible, it was charged, was the cause of pietists and mystics and would provoke untoward "curiosity," which in turn would create political insubordination with grave social consequences. Curiosity begat doubt, which begat rebellion. There were certainly members of the nobility who approved of these efforts to curb the influence of foreign ideas in the church and at court.

Yet these policies offended other members of the nobility who had, over the previous half century, grown accustomed to choosing their own reading matter and regarded the tracts they read as morally and spiritually edifying. The Wisdom Lovers would have been all the more unhappy given their personal contacts with some of the people involved. Lopukhin's *Interior Church*, which Ivan Kireevsky had received as a boy, was now banned. Alexander Koshelev had to have been shocked to learn that his uncle Rodion was accused of being an "enemy of church and state" and of heading a conspiracy to undermine the Orthodox Church by replacing it with a universal church of brotherly love.[41] Mikhail Pogodin greatly admired Metropolitan Filaret, whose position in the church had been badly undermined.[42]

Soon after Shishkov had the Russian Pentateuch burned, Venevitinov began to study it. The Wisdom Lovers almost never mentioned scripture in their writings, but on this occasion, Venevitinov commented on the Book of Genesis in a manner that would have confirmed all of Shishkov's worst fears. He inserted his comments in a letter to Koshelev in the summer of 1825, one that formed part of an intense correspondence on Schelling's philosophy. Here, Venevitinov explained his views on the purpose of philosophy: to reconcile man and the world, the ideal and the real, thought and feeling. The Book of Genesis, which he described as an "allegory," represented man's relationship to nature and God at a "primitive stage." "Observe how God converses with man eye to eye, how he presents him with all living creatures; and, casting a glance over them, he named them. Notice that primitive man is not surprised by anything in paradise; it is as if he has already attained everything." Philosophy was only born when man became divorced from nature.[43] Quoting an acolyte of Schelling, Johann Jacob Wagner, in an appendix to this letter, Venevitinov outlined the consequences of this separation: man's life had become fragmented, and religion had lost its former purity.[44] Still, the break had been necessary: "Man, in order to become a philosopher, that is, to seek wisdom, was necessarily forced to forget his familiarity with nature, with his own feelings. An infant is not a philosopher."[45] Now, however, philosophy would lead man back to the founding principle, to the harmony and unity of all things. It was not only man who was finding his way to a more perfect state, however: spirit, the Absolute, was undergoing the same development.[46] In this scheme, Christianity was relegated to a place alongside other religions. Christ is mentioned in the appendage on Wagner's philosophy as a figure who, along with Buddha, Moses, and Zoroaster, had attempted to reunite man with nature.[47]

Echoing the tale of the serpent in the Garden of Eden, Venevitinov referred repeatedly to idealist philosophy as the "tree of knowledge," and he evidently was determined to taste its fruits. To "speak about God through higher mathematics" was, he said, the most "dazzling, the most perfect fruit on the tree of human knowledge."[48] He congratulated Koshelev for his embrace of idealism: "The tree of true knowledge [poznaniia] has sunk deep roots in your mind."[49] Venevitinov had to be aware that such comments, together with his references to Genesis as an "allegory" and the "tale of an ancient historian," were out of keeping with the doctrines of the Orthodox Church. He expressed concern that his friend might be "frightened by conclusions, which in the eyes of many would prove atheism."[50] These words should not to be read as a confession of atheism; instead, they underscore Venevitinov's belief that most people were blind to the truth.

Venevitinov's words reflect his elitism and the Wisdom Lovers' easy conviction that they alone were capable of understanding the true nature of the divine. The doctrinal laws of the Orthodox Church were not written for them. Koshelev would emphasize this in his memoirs: "Christian teachings struck us appropriate only for the popular masses, not for us Wisdom Lovers."[51] By "the popular masses," Koshelev did not just mean peasants or merchants but unenlightened members of the elites.

It was not that doctrines of the Orthodox Church were considered wrong; the Wisdom Lovers, like most noblemen of their generation, knew too little of these doctrines to be interested in criticizing them. Nor did they view the Orthodox clergy as unfit representatives of the divine. Rather, the Wisdom Lovers viewed the church's understanding of the divine as one-sided. Inspired by Schelling, they awaited the inauguration of a new phase in world history, the reconciliation between man, nature, and the Absolute, or God, and they hoped to participate in that process. This aspiration was one reason Schelling had such appeal, as an expert has explained: in his writings, "the boundaries between religion and philosophy became fluid."[52]

Odoevsky, Venevitinov, and their friends tended to use the words "God," "the divine," "the Absolute," "eternal," "fundamental," and "founding principle" interchangeably. They were pantheists, who believed that God and the universe are one. In their poetry, they celebrated the mystery by which the divine imbues the world. As romantics, they also believed that nature, humanity, and spirit are in a state of constant transformation and flux, making the ultimate meaning and higher unity of events in the world extremely difficult, if not impossible, to discern and capture. Here was the source of doubt for poets. Poets' struggles as they seek to comprehend and give voice to the infinite greatness of the divine were a major preoccupation in Wisdom Lovers' poetry. Pantheism itself was less interesting to them than the living experience of pantheist poets. This concern about the interaction between thought and life remained characteristic of Russian thinkers throughout the nineteenth century.

Among the Wisdom Lovers, it was Vladimir Odoevsky who gave fullest expression to romantic pantheism in letters and in conversations, as well as in his philosophical writings of 1824–25. In an unpublished manuscript, he noted that the Absolute (God) is "EVERYTHING," using capital letters for emphasis. God is in everything, and "everything is in Him."[53] Odoevsky's words would make as good a definition of pantheism as any: that God is not separate from natural phenomena but is one with them; his spirit imbues them. In late 1824, Odoevsky was prepared to take pantheism to its furthest extreme by denying God any existence independent of the world. Odoevsky's former tutor, Ivan Snegirev, a highly observant Orthodox Christian, was shocked by what he heard when he dropped in on Odoevsky one November morning. "We discussed Schelling's philosophy and older systems, in which there are signs of materialism." Snegirev notes his former student's conclusion: "He says God cannot exist without the world." Snegirev commented to himself that Odoevsky's views were "heresy," more in line with "Spinoza's pantheism" than with Holy Writ. Odoevsky had enlisted Snegirev to serve as censor for his almanac, *Mnemosyne*. After their conversation, Snegirev attempted to back out—unsuccessfully, for Odoevsky's princely title made it difficult for him to refuse.[54]

Odoevsky himself seems to have had difficulties maintaining this degree of commitment to pantheist principles; he did not like to think of himself as an un-Christian or anti-Christian thinker, even if his views directly contradicted the doctrines of the Russian Orthodox Church.[55] One does in fact encounter the idea that God and the world are coeternal in the fourth volume of *Mnemosyne*. There, Odoevsky expounded on idealism in a series of philosophical aphorisms and fragments. However, he packaged this idea—of the coeternity of God and the universe—as if it were not his own, attributing it to the pre-Socratic Greek philosopher Xenophanes instead (indeed, he inserted a footnote to emphasize that these views were not his own). Speaking for Xenophanes, Odoevsky explained that the universe cannot have been created but must always have existed, because nothing can come from nothing; everything that exists must be eternal. There is a God; he is one; he is the principle that unites all things in the world, and he is coeternal with the world.[56] In short, Odoevsky managed to publicize this view but only by pretending that he did not endorse it.

No other Wisdom Lover ever attempted to expound pantheism so fully in print. Indeed, most avoided philosophical prose, choosing poetry instead, perhaps because the expression of ideas through this medium was less precise, allowing for greater equivocation as well as greater distance between author and content. Venevitinov, Shevyrev, and Khomiakov wrote most of their metaphysical poetry in 1826 and 1827, and it became the genre for which the Wisdom Lovers were best known. Russian poets had not previously attempted to use poetry to express philosophical views in this manner.[57]

The Wisdom Lovers believed that poetry was uniquely suited to describe the unity of the world because of its imaginative, creative element. Vladimir Titov explained this in an article published in the *Moscow Messenger* in 1827: the highest purpose of poetry was to express the oneness of creation and to reconcile spirit and matter. The poet was uniquely gifted in this regard on account of his "all-encompassing imagination," which made him "freer to transport himself into all times and all people, and everywhere he discovers that harmony in which his loving heart believes."[58]

Such harmony is found, first and foremost, in nature. In their poems, the Wisdom Lovers strove to convey not only the beauty and grandeur of the universe but the active presence of spirit in it. The following lines in Khomiakov's "Youth" (1827) offer a particularly fine example of this sentiment:

> Звезды в синей тверди
> Мчатся за звездами,
> И в потоках света
> Льется по эфиру

Тайный страсти голос,
Тайное призванье.
И века проходят,
И века родятся,—
Вечное боренье,
Пламенная жизнь.

[The stars in the blue firmament race behind [other]
stars, and in floods of light, there pours through the
ether a secret voice of passion, a secret calling. And ages
pass, and ages are born, an eternal struggle, fiery life.][59]

Everything that happens in nature has meaning because it is imbued
with spirit, and every event contains that spirit and gives expression to
it. The movement of the stars is, to the narrator of the poem, a "secret
confession," and his role as poet is to put this secret into words. In this
way, the poet plays an active role in the life of spirit. He, like any human
being, is but one part of creation, of the spirit that is forever striving to
give more perfect expression to itself.

The poet-narrator's place in creation is unique, for he is the only
creature endowed with the gift of language. Shevyrev highlights this in
his poem "I Am" (1825), in which one man speaks for all of the creatures
on the earth. The words "I am" are represented here as words of worship
in which nature, through humanity, expresses consciousness of its
existence and debt to the Creator.[60] Simultaneously, they reflect the
will of the Creator back on himself, allowing him a moment of self-
recognition. Finally, human speech is synthetic, "reconciling the discord
of the elements." Poets fulfill the same function: by imaginatively
embracing the universe, they unite, or synthesize, the variable elements
within it. A poet should become what Shevyrev called a "voice of
harmony" or what Khomiakov called the "harmonious voice of the
earth." The poet is, or wishes to be, the vessel of the spirit, its priest and
prophet, simultaneously engaging in an act of worship by proclaiming
the greatness of creation while also revealing its purpose to itself.[61]

It is important to note, however, that for the Wisdom Lovers, a poet's
wish to grasp the divine in its infinite variety could never be more than
an aspiration, though it was the aspiration that mattered and that
became the central theme of all their writings. Everything, from the
Absolute, to the natural world, to human thought, is in a continual state
of change. The essence of the divine or Absolute cannot be grasped
because it is still in the process of development: the future holds the

promise of the full and harmonious synthesis of the world's disparate elements; for the time being, spirit can be captured only in the fleeting moment. Odoevsky discussed these issues in his philosophical manuscripts of the 1820s and found that writing was itself a flawed vessel for conveying the truth, because no final word can be issued on any matter. To quote his biographer Sakulin, even the most comprehensive and thorough system of thought could only represent a passing phase; it was "but one of the steps on the infinite ladder to perfection."[62]

The idea of mutability was not, of course, original to the Wisdom Lovers. It was central to all romantic theory. Romantics tended to view the human mind and spirit as fundamentally unstable, divided, and contradictory. Friedrich Schlegel made a virtue of this in his comments on irony: it was the very awareness of the impossibility of understanding an infinitely variable world that pressed the individual to continue exploring it.[63] Poets' awareness that they had no chance of ever arriving at the end of this quest was wholesome; it was the very precondition for embarking on it in the first place.

While the idea of mutability was standard among western European romantics, it was widely repudiated by the Wisdom Lovers' more conservative contemporaries in Russia. An article published by Ivan Davydov, their former teacher, in 1822, titled "Aphorisms from the Contemporary Love of Wisdom" makes for a telling point of contrast. Davydov had recently come under attack by officials in St. Petersburg and was backing away from some of the more radical implications of idealist philosophy. In his article, Davydov emphasized that reason and morality must always accord with the "unchanging laws of religion" and theology. A wise man, he wrote, "must always reason in the same way, that is, justly, and must also always wish in the same way. But what can a constant or unchanging wish consist in, if not in a just wish, in virtue? Everything other than truth, virtue, and the beautiful is subject to change, falsehood, and inconstancy."[64] The views Davydov expressed were quite unlike those the Wisdom Lovers came to defend.[65] As pantheists, they could not accept the idea of "unchanging laws of religion," unless those laws were of the most abstract possible kind, namely, that there is a spirit which is still in the process of development. Such an idea was now rejected by Davydov. Finally, the Wisdom Lovers would have disputed the notion that one "must always reason in the same way." On the contrary, in their writings, the effort to understand the world and all of its mysteries was usually described as a rather messy process, one that involved struggle and doubt.

As Isaiah Berlin noted, German idealism spawned a certain attitude toward the calling of the educated person that remained central to the self-understanding of Russians in the nineteenth century: "The duty of man was [. . .] to understand the texture, the 'go,' the principle of life of all there is, to penetrate the soul of the world (a theological and mystical notion wrapped by the followers of Schelling and Hegel in rationalist terminology), to grasp the hidden, 'inner' plan of the universe, to understand his own place in it, and to act accordingly."[66] What Berlin and many other intellectual historians have overlooked is the centrality of doubt to this process.

Beginning in 1825, doubt became a major theme in the writings of the Wisdom Lovers, an element that drew them into a powerful alliance with Russia's most important young poet: Alexander Pushkin. The group's admiration for Pushkin may have been heightened by the fact that he was Venevitinov's relative, though the two did not become personally acquainted until 1826, when Pushkin arrived in Moscow after years of exile in the provinces. Pushkin found in the Wisdom Lovers a group that was welcoming of and receptive to the most innovative and daring aspects of his recent work: not only his experimentation with romantic poetic forms but his introduction of doubt as a literary theme in works that were published in 1824 and 1825.

Pushkin used doubt in two distinct ways that the Wisdom Lovers would adopt in their writings. One was as a method of questioning that propels individuals forward in their struggle to grasp the higher unity of the world and its meaning. The Wisdom Lovers immediately proved receptive to doubt in this sense. Indeed, Odoevsky had already anticipated the idea in a letter to Titov in the summer of 1823, in which he called doubt "the path to truth," a state of uncertainty that provides the impetus for further speculation. Odoevsky describes the condition as unpleasant (*tiagostneishee*), though there was clearly sweetness to the suffering, the excitement of venturing into new territory.[67] The second way Pushkin used doubt, which he laid out in 1824 but that the Wisdom Lovers only developed in 1826–27, was as a state of spiritual aridity in which individuals lose any sense of their connection to the divine, a ruinous state of despair that may lead to damnation. The dates are significant because of the importance of the events that occurred in the interval between 1825 and 1826: the Decembrist uprising and the ascent of Nicholas I to the throne. These events marked a major turning point both in Russian history and in the philosophical views of the Wisdom Lovers.

Alexander Pushkin presented the concept of doubt in two works that were published in almanacs to which the Wisdom Lovers also contributed poetry. The first was the poem "My Demon," published in *Mnemosyne* in the late autumn of 1824, which described doubt as a source of despair and damnation. The second was a fragment from *Eugene Onegin*, published in the almanac *Northern Flowers* (*Severnye tsvety*) in January 1825, which described doubt in more optimistic terms as a source of endless striving. Pushkin wrote both in 1823, while he was exiled to the south of Russia for having written poetry critical of the government. There, in the heat of the Black Sea, he whiled away his time, plagued by financial straits and wondering when, if ever, his fortunes might be restored.[68]

"My Demon," written in the first-person singular, narrates a youth's fall from enthusiasm and hope to doubt and despair. The narrator's elevated feelings, appreciation of the beauty of nature, ambition, and yearning for love and freedom have left him vulnerable to the insinuations of an evil genius. The impact of their meeting is described in the second half of the poem:

> Печальны были наши встречи!
> Его улыбка, чудный взгляд,
> Его язвительныя речи —
> Вливали в душу хладный яд;
> Неистощимой клеветою
> Он Провиденье искушал;
> Он звал прекрасное мечтою,
> Он вдохновенье презирал;
> Не верил он любви, свободе,
> На жизнь с насмешкою смотрел
> И ничего во всей природе
> Благословить он не хотел.

> [How sorrowful were our meetings! His smile, his magical glance, his venomous speeches—poured a cold poison into the soul; with unremitting slander he tempted Providence; he called the beautiful a dream, he was contemptuous of inspiration; he did not believe in love, in freedom, he looked upon life with ridicule, and he did not want to honor [bless] anything in all of nature.][69]

In the last four lines, the two figures described in the poem, the narrator and the demon, fuse with one another. The narrator himself has fallen into thoroughgoing skepticism; he does not deny the existence of God, but he has lost faith in Providence and beauty, the whole of the higher order that gives meaning to natural phenomena and human life.

Many contemporaries interpreted the demon in the poem in narrowly biographical terms as a real person, Alexander Raevskii, an acquaintance of Pushkin's in 1823 whose outlook was characterized by extreme cynicism. Most scholars, together with the Wisdom Lovers and Pushkin himself, interpreted the poem in more abstract terms as describing the relationship between poetic exaltation and the "demon" doubt, which is not a person but an inner state of mind. Odoevsky was one of the first to remark on the poem, describing it as a characterization "of those incomprehensible feelings, which cool our heart amidst the most fiery enthusiasms."[70] Pushkin agreed, commenting on the poem in February 1825: "In the best part of life, the heart, not yet cooled by experience, is open to all that is beautiful. It is gullible and tender. Gradually, the eternal contradictions of existence give birth to doubts inside it, a tortuous feeling, though temporary. It disappears, having destroyed forever the best hopes and poetic predispositions of the soul. Not without reason does Goethe call the eternal enemy of humanity the *'negating spirit.'* And Pushkin, did he not want his demon to embody this spirit of *negation and doubt*? In a pleasant picture, he sketched out its distinguishing features and sad influence on the morality of our age."[71] Here, Pushkin invokes Mephistopheles in Goethe's *Faust*, "der Geist der stets verneint." Goethe's Mephistopheles is a real demon, though he feeds off Faust's restless dissatisfaction with his scholarly attainments and desperate desire to get to the bottom of the world's mysteries. As one commentator remarked, Faust "is the victim ultimately not of anything external to himself, but of his own titanic aspirations to transcend the limits of humanity, and that means not in the last place the limits of good and evil."[72] What sets Goethe's and Pushkin's works apart is the outcome for the two protagonists: Faust is saved, while the narrator of "My Demon" will most likely be damned. The damage Pushkin's demon inflicts on the narrator's soul appears to be irreparable.[73]

In 1824 and 1825, the representation of doubt Pushkin had to offer in "My Demon" was as of yet too dark for the Wisdom Lovers, who looked instead to his more optimistic representation of doubt in the second chapter of *Eugene Onegin*. His famous novel in verse began to appear in 1825 but was not completed until 1832. The novel contrasts two protagonists. One is Eugene Onegin, a young nobleman who has known perhaps too much of life's pleasures and whose growing embitterment, described in the book's first chapter, resembles that of the narrator in "My Demon."[74] The other is Vladimir Lenskii, recently returned from studies in Germany, who is introduced in chapter 2. Lenskii is an idealist in every sense of the word. He is a "worshipper of Kant," a freethinker, and a poet—young, full of illusions, and passionate about delving into the world's hidden secrets: "The purpose of life was, to him, an alluring mystery. He racked his brains over it and suspected miracles." His inclination to muse, the narrator explains, is fed by doubts. Unlike those described in "My Demon," however, Lenskii's are wholesome, almost playful: "He entertained the heart's doubts with sweet reverie."[75]

Pushkin had never met any of the Wisdom Lovers when he wrote the second chapter of *Eugene Onegin*. Yet they might easily have seen their portraits in Lenskii: the same hair, curling to their shoulders in the romantic style, the same love of poetry and ambition to uncover the mysteries of the universe. On reading these lines, the Wisdom Lovers immediately embraced them as a statement of their own approach to poetry. Nikolai Rozhalin, one of the group's youngest and most erudite members, saw them as an opportunity to summarize the Wisdom Lovers' attitude to poetry and to expound on the virtues of doubt. Adherents of German idealist philosophy, he explained in an 1825 essay, believed that "the essence of Romantic poetry" lay "in the striving of the soul toward the perfect, which is unknown to it, but indispensable to it, a striving that commands every feeling of true poets of this kind." Striving, however, demands that the poet remain aware of the insufficiency of what he has attained so far. Rozhalin referred to this awareness as an "involuntary method, if I may put it this way, of struggle with himself, with his impressions." Only such awareness could give the poet the impetus to develop more fully, allowing him to approach "perfection" in his work. He emphasized, once again, that this was the aim of all romantic poets.[76]

Rozhalin did not indicate in his review article precisely how far these doubts should extend. As a poet strove to embrace the world in its diversity, "struggle with himself, with his impressions" might just prompt him to dig deeper into its mysteries and strive to synthesize more and more of its contradictions. He left open the question whether such struggle might lead to doubts of a deeper kind.

The Wisdom Lovers received a powerful impetus to pursue these themes further when, in September 1826, they made the acquaintance of Alexander Pushkin for the first time. Pushkin had been called to

Moscow from exile by Nicholas I, who was himself staying in the old capital to mark his coronation that month. The Wisdom Lovers were apparently less enthusiastic about the presence of the emperor, however, than they were about Pushkin's visit. Pushkin was delighted by their delight. Though Pushkin had already been established as Russia's foremost poet, his social and political status had been compromised by his exile. Returning to Moscow, he encountered young men who not only appeared to understand and appreciate his works but were influenced by them, developing his poignant theme of the doubting subject in their own poetry and philosophical writings.

Soon, they were planning a joint venture—the *Moscow Messenger*. The journal would feature Pushkin's writings, but the Wisdom Lovers hoped it would do much more: create a reading public that was capable of independent judgment of literary works. Such independence would then allow poets and other writers to express themselves more freely. In "Some Thoughts on a Plan for a Journal" (1826), Venevitinov once again summarized the group's views on the centrality of doubt to the creative enterprise: "The first feeling never creates and is incapable of creating, because it always represents harmony. Feeling only gives birth to thought, which develops in struggle, and that is when, turning once again into feeling, it appears in a creative work." What applied to the individual also applied to society as a collectivity. Society would not develop until it, too, began taking part in the process of truth seeking. Hence, writers must be freed to express a wider range of views, including some that were potentially false. Admittedly, the exposure of readers to "false" views entailed risks, but these were unavoidable and ultimately to the good: "It is easier to act on a mind when it has become partial to error [*pristrastilsia k zabluzhdeniiu*] than when it is indifferent to the truth. False opinions do not maintain themselves forever, and they give birth to others; in this way, disagreement creeps in, and the contradiction itself creates some kind of movement, out of which truth finally arises."[77] The Russian public would become capable, for the first time, of independent judgment, allowing the country to progress and mature. Inspired by Venevitinov, in 1828 Shevyrev labeled the new critical spirit "noble skepticism" (an expression the Wisdom Lovers had never used before and never used again).[78]

Venevitinov's line of reasoning was entirely out of keeping with the ethics of Russian officialdom in the 1820s. Every part of his argument would have struck a man like Magnitskii as faulty, indeed disastrous. To Magnitskii, the truth did not need to "arise": it could be found at any moment in the Russian Orthodox Church. Disagreement and contradiction could only produce chaos and would bring down the empire if given free rein. While Magnitskii himself was no longer heeded after 1826 (some of the enemies he made during the late reign of Alexander I saw to it that he was demoted), the overall tenor of his views remained firmly in place. Indeed, Nicholas I ensured that they were applied with increasing vigor.

Soon after Pushkin's arrival, Venevitinov was forced to leave Moscow: his family had arranged a position for him at the Ministry of Foreign Affairs in St. Petersburg. In the poetry that he wrote during his time in St. Petersburg from November 1826 to March 1827, doubt assumed darker connotations than in earlier writings by the Wisdom Lovers. Venevitinov now drew on the themes that Pushkin had introduced in "My Demon" and recapitulated in chapter 1 of *Eugene Onegin*, portraying doubt as a form of spiritual aridity. The theme of doubt in Venevitinov's poems may be seen as a counterpoint to the pantheist poetry that Khomiakov and Shevyrev were producing in those same years (1826 and 1827). They described the inner lives of poets who gave voice to the higher unity of the world, celebrated the beauty and perfection of nature and its mysteries, and expressed feelings of unity with the Absolute, with God. In Venevitinov's poems, the narrator faced an entirely different set of emotions: indifference to the beauty of nature, lack of curiosity about its mysteries, boredom, and an inclination toward dissipation. These characteristics, it should be noted, also mark the deadly sin of acedia, the "noon-day demon" of early Christian literature, which had been known to render monks incapable of prayer. Doubt made a natural pair to the exalted spirit that the Wisdom Lovers attempted to capture in their poetry; it was a demon that dogged the poet's most sublime hours of communion with God.

Among the first of Venevitinov's St. Petersburg poems was "Life" (1826), a variation on Pushkin's "My Demon." In its opening section, the narrator evokes the typical outlook of the young poet, joyfully exploring life's mysteries and becoming "enchanted" by them. The second section describes how, with the passage of youth, these miracles lose their allure, suddenly appearing as mere "deception." Life's tale is "twice-told"; its riddle only bores us.[79] Like "My Demon," the poem ends without indicating any possibility of salvation.

Other poems that Venevitinov wrote in this period, like "Elegy" and "XXXV," place greater emphasis on the inconstancy of the mind, which relentlessly shifts between inspiration and doubt. The "flame" of inspiration is both a source of exaltation and torture. It illuminates the narrator's quest to explore the universe in its infinite diversity, but the light it casts is deceptive: the flame is treacherous. If he is to survive, the narrator must suppress his "proud" wish to "embrace the world in a single moment" and reconcile himself to those feelings of doubt, which are an inevitable part of the process of artistic creation.[80]

The poet must reconcile himself to doubt, yet he will be damned if he allows himself to sink into despair. Friendship and love can be his only salvation. The status of friend as savior is marked in Venevitinov's "To My Ring" (1827). The narrator of the poem refers to the ring that has been given to him as a gift of "friendship" in the "bitter hour of parting," a "pledge of compassion." Addressing the ring as a talisman, he hopes it will shield him from evil and temptation, including spiritual aridity and "dark hours of doubt," which threaten to overtake him, speeding him toward moral ruin and insanity. The narrator prays that the ring will "revive [my] heart with hope." The warm feelings evoked by the ring are contrasted to the "emptiness" produced in him by spending time in high society.[81]

The same contrast can be found in Venevitinov's poem "Epistle to R[ozhali]n" (1826). There, the narrator describes how his isolation amid St. Petersburg's *grand monde* has heightened feelings of despair, feelings that have grown so strong that he has come to doubt in Providence.

О, если бы могли моленья
Достигнуть до небес скупых,
Не новой чаши наслажденья,
Я б прежних дней просил у них:
Отдайте мне друзей моих.

[Oh, if only prayers would reach the miserly heavens, I would ask them, not for a new cup of pleasure, but former days: return my friends to me.][82]

Both "Epistle to Rozhalin" and "To My Ring" describe an act of prayer. In "To My Ring," it is addressed not to God but to an object and through it to a friend. In "Epistle to Rozhalin," by contrast, the prayer is only half formed: the narrator says he *would* pray "if only" the heavens would hear him. Not only does he express lack of faith that they will hear him but he accuses them of stinginess, suggesting they will refuse to grant his wish even if they do hear. Moreover, by asking them to return his friends to him, the narrator suggests that it is from friendship and not directly from the heavens that he expects to find true relief.[83]

One further noteworthy feature of these two poems is that they fuse an abstract, first-person narrator with Venevitinov himself by introducing autobiographical details. The ring in "To My Ring" really existed: various details have allowed biographers to identify it with one that Princess Volkonskaia, whom Venevitinov greatly admired, gave him on the occasion of his departure from Moscow for St. Petersburg in 1826. The friend "R." in "Epistle" is clearly Rozhalin.[84] These poems were an exception to much of Venevitinov's poetry that, as Lidiia Ginzburg and other scholars have strenuously emphasized, was intended to express philosophical or abstract truths and not experiences that were particular to him as an individual.[85] Presumably, it was the wish to convey the sincerity of friendship that prompted Venevitinov to infuse these poems with autobiographical elements.

The themes that Venevitinov explored in 1826 and 1827 echoed in an important prose work by Stepan Shevyrev, titled "Dialogue on the Possibility of Finding a Single Law of the Beautiful." The "Dialogue" was intended as a programmatic statement for the Wisdom Lovers' new journal, the *Moscow Messenger*, first published in 1827. It is a conversation between two friends, Evgenii and Litsinii, in which the former attempts to reconcile the latter to the experience of doubt as part of the artistic process. "Dialogue" also addresses doubt in both of Pushkin's senses, as an impetus to the quest for knowledge and as a potential source of damnation.

As the title suggests, aesthetics is the main topic of the essay: Evgenii and Litsinii become embroiled in a debate about the doubts that are evoked when one contemplates beauty. Evgenii notes that the contemplation of beauty in art and in nature exalts the soul, but he also finds that during such moments of exaltation, "the soul is exposed to an innumerable series of questions," which the individual must strive to answer. At such moments, Evgenii proclaims, the soul is "burdened" by "secrets" and "questions," which propel him to search deeper: "Look carefully into [your soul]: you will see inside a mixture of dark doubts and clear pleasure; and then, will you not feel inside yourself the desire to solve the mystery?" Evgenii even goes so far as to claim that this is a response that God wishes for the individual: "Tell me, surely the Creator of the world does not contradict laws that He created?" He means that human nature has been created so as to respond to beauty in this way. Evgenii's attitude to doubt corresponds to that of Lenskii as described in Pushkin's *Eugene Onegin* and that of Odoevsky in his 1823 letter to Titov: doubts allow him to dig deeper without calling into question his faith in himself, his mission, and relationship to God.

Evgenii's interlocutor, Litsinii, is suspicious of doubt. The enthusiasm evoked by beauty strikes him as a wholesome feeling, but doubt only creates despair: "Like you, I questioned myself, but as soon as I had stepped into this soulless chaos of dead rules, I felt a kind of cold in my soul, all feeling disappeared, and I was unable to find the answer to any question." As a result, he has decided to avoid such questioning altogether.[86] To Litsinii, "questioning myself" means a great deal more than simply doubting the validity of his impressions; it means stepping into a maelstrom of thoughts over which the individual has very little control. Litsinii's doubts resemble those Pushkin described in "My Demon": they poison the individual, threatening to render him incapable of exaltation and faith in the beautiful. Litsinii feels his only option is to dismiss and avoid rather than confront these thoughts. In this connection, Litsinii's reference to doubt as "soulless" "dead rules" is noteworthy, for it brings to mind the association of doubt with rationalism (as opposed to exaltation and faith). A similar observation has been made about Pushkin's "My Demon" by the literary scholar Robert Reid, who characterizes it as being "about the inability of idealism to resist the assaults of a pessimistic rationalism."[87]

Shevyrev's dialogue, however, reaches a very different conclusion. Evgenii is given the final word: not only can idealism resist the assault of doubt but it must do so if the individual is to gain any insight into the world's many secrets and mysteries. The dialogue acknowledges the temptations and evils that doubt can produce while demanding that they be addressed and expressing faith that they can be overcome. Doubt, then, had been raised to the status of a necessary, inevitable experience that must accompany the search for truth. The contradictions that humankind finds in nature and thought must be acknowledged if they are to be resolved into a higher synthetic principle. Still, doubts may turn into despair, calling into question both humanity's ability to fulfill this role and the presence and beneficence of the spirit that unites all and gives life meaning. Casting about for hope and inspiration to continue the mission, the quester turns not to God but to friendship.

Venevitinov's poems evoked a narrator who found himself isolated and lonely in the city of St. Peter. This was an image that the young man carried over into his correspondence. Writing to Pogodin a few weeks before his death on March 27, 1827, he commented, "I already wrote above that grief has tortured me. Here, in the midst of this cold, empty, and soulless society, I am alone."[88] The assertion that he was "alone" is striking, given how many other Wisdom Lovers were then in St. Petersburg. Odoevsky, Koshelev, Aleksei and Fedor Khomiakov, and Titov had all moved to the imperial capital in 1826 and for the same reasons as Venevitinov: their families had arranged positions for them in the Ministry of the Interior and Ministry of Foreign Affairs. All the while, they maintained an intense correspondence with friends in Moscow.

The perceived isolation that plagued Venevitinov may have been the paradoxical product of the myth of friendship that the Wisdom Lovers had created in Moscow. The strength of that myth can be observed in the memoiristic writings of Koshelev. Looking back at their group in the 1860s and 1870s, he repeatedly emphasized the close bonds that had once united its members. He and Kireevsky, friends since childhood, had shared all of their feelings and thoughts, hiding nothing from one another.[89]

Their Moscow circle had indeed been tightly knit, with its own rules of comportment. The existence of such rules can be observed in the tensions that ensued when members breached them. Khomiakov and Pogodin had, apparently, been teased for their adherence to Orthodox behavioral norms at gatherings with other Wisdom Lovers. In a letter to his mother, Koshelev complained that Khomiakov made "unbearable" company when women were present because he refused to behave in a flirtatious manner.[90] In his diary, Pogodin recorded how, at one of the group's more raucous gatherings, Venevitinov held a knife to his throat because Pogodin refused to drink champagne with the others.[91] Members of the group were expressing their objection to behavior that set Khomiakov and Pogodin apart—however temporarily—from their friends.

The warm spirit of unity proved impossible to transfer to the colder climate of St. Petersburg. The city made a disastrous first impression on Venevitinov, who was arrested immediately on arrival and held by the police for roughly two days on suspicion of conspiracy with the Decembrists. His brief stay in a damp police cell also took a toll on his health, which had been fragile to begin with.[92] Nor could Venevitinov take any comfort in the presence of Odoevsky, who had moved to the city a few months earlier (days before the execution of five leading Decembrists in July 1826). As Venevitinov reported back to Moscow, Odoevsky showed no interest in anyone other than his new wife and her female relatives. His irritation with Odoevsky was shared by Khomiakov and Koshelev.[93] Meanwhile, Koshelev, Kireevsky, and Titov had problems of their own. Noted for their freethinking spirit, they were placed under surveillance by Nicholas's newly formed secret police.[94] It is easy to see, therefore, why the city would strike Venevitinov as "cold, empty, and soulless."

It was not just the city that stood in the way of maintaining the warmth and carefree spirit that once marked the Wisdom Lovers' circle, however. Age, responsibility, and the wish to succeed in life, too, were contributing factors. The life of the Russian nobleman had always been devoted to increasing his family's prestige and serving the state. To be a Faustian truth seeker was not only alien to the mores of the traditional service nobility; it was also increasingly at odds with the highly conservative ideology that appeared at the end of Alexander I's reign and developed further under Nicholas I. That ideology demanded the unconditional subordination of all Russian subjects, including the elites, and left no room for what it called "brazen dreaming."

Every Wisdom Lover responded differently to the pressures that the regime of Nicholas I placed on him. Odoevsky ventured on a highly successful career in the Ministry of Internal Affairs and was soon placed on the committee that would draft Nicholas I's new laws on censorship. Shevyrev and Pogodin became even more closely intertwined with the new regime, helping in the early 1830s to formulate Nicholas I's ideology of "official nationality." Koshelev attempted to pursue a career in the Ministry of Foreign Affairs but was consistently passed over for promotion and eventually retired. Rozhalin left Russia after having attempted suicide. He traveled in Germany and Italy, where he lived the life of a "superfluous man," a stock character in Russian literature from the 1820s onward. In a letter he sent Koshelev from Rome in March 1832, he wrote, "For the longest time, I have done nothing; I do not even have any plans for the future." Mentioning that he needed to return to Russia (for reasons not specified), he noted that "I firmly intend not to do anything [there] either."[95] Rozhalin died of consumption in 1834.

Kireevsky, too, traveled to Germany in the early 1830s, but he had abandoned the mantle of the Wisdom Lover by the time he returned home. Together with Khomiakov, he came to lead a new intellectual movement known as "Slavophilism." They now argued that the truth they had sought as Wisdom Lovers had been fully revealed long ago: in the writings of the early church fathers and the rituals of the Russian

Orthodox Church. Kireevsky wrote, "Every Orthodox person is conscious in the depths of his soul that Divine truth cannot be embraced by consideration of ordinary reason and that it demands a higher spiritual view, a view acquired not through external erudition but through the inner wholeness of existence. [. . .] For him there is no thought separated from the memory of the inner wholeness of the mind, of that focal point of self-consciousness which is the true locus of supreme truth."[96] As the words "inner wholeness of existence" signal, the Slavophiles had not given up on their earlier romantic proclivities entirely, and they continued to mix their religious thought with large doses of philosophy. But doubt could no longer be part of the equation for the Slavophiles.

In the 1830s, every one of the Wisdom Lovers abandoned the ethos that had once united their group. This does not mean, however, that it disappeared. It left its mark on those adolescents who would dominate intellectual life of the 1830s and beyond: Nikolai Stankevich, Mikhail Bakunin, Vissarion Belinsky, Alexander Herzen, and Nikolai Ogarev.[97] These thinkers, whom Herzen would later dub "Westernizers," drew four interlocking conclusions from the writings of the Wisdom Lovers: that the true calling of the educated person was to "grasp the hidden, 'inner' plan of the universe"; that this was the most genuine means of communing with the divine; that German idealist philosophy, particularly the philosophy of Schelling, contained the key to this plan; and that doubt must feature in the entire endeavor—one must doubt one's relationship to the divine and, potentially, the very existence of the "inner plan." Seizing on the notion of doubt, the Westernizers transformed it into a sustaining way of life. As the chapters that follow show, they eventually expanded the notion of doubt to include a questioning of the existence of God, though none in this cohort went so far as to articulate disbelief. That was left to young intellectuals of nonnoble origins, who rejected "noble skepticism" in favor of the positive assertion of atheism in the decades to come.

Observing the increasing "alienation" between segments of the nobility and state in the first half of the nineteenth century, Marc Raeff and Martin Malia each noted that it gave rise to a uniquely intransigent intelligentsia. Having been raised in the belief that they were born to rule, these young men, exiled from the corridors of power and divorced from the Russian people, would indulge in utopian dreaming, which only heightened their sense of impotence, creating revolutionary urges.[98] These characterizations of Russia's educated elites seem overly deterministic when viewed in connection with the Moscow Wisdom Lovers. These young men did rebel against the pressures that the state brought to bear on them, but they did so by forming a community of friends who together looked for a system of thought that would give their lives meaning, on terms that would not be dictated by the state, the church, or high society. Within the community of the Wisdom Lovers, the quest to grasp the higher principle, to struggle with the contradictions in the world and to resolve them, was not a form of escapism but a means of engaging with life at its very core. The emphasis that they placed on struggle and doubt reveals what, to them, were the ultimate stakes of their endeavor: salvation could only be found by continuing to search for the higher, unifying principle. To opt out of this quest, because one either no longer believed that there was a higher truth or did not think such truth was accessible spelled damnation. These were the terms by which future generations of the intelligentsia would judge themselves and one another.

2

Providence and Doubt
Alexander Herzen, Nikolai Ogarev, and Their Friends

I have a special demon—doubt; that is the wound of my soul."[1] In 1832, when Alexander Herzen addressed these words to his intimate friend Nikolai Ogarev, he was barely twenty, but he had already identified the trait that would delineate his remarkable life. Herzen and Ogarev were central figures among Moscow intellectuals in the 1830s and 1840s. After the 1848 revolutions in France and Italy, in which Herzen actively participated, he became a key spokesman in Europe of Russian opposition to the autocracy. Hailed by historians as the father of Russian socialism, Herzen is also regarded as having been tremendously influential in the codification of the type of friendship and commitment to ideals later identified with the intelligentsia.[2] Herzen was not the sole author of those ideals, however. As he emphasized in his famous memoirs, *My Past and Thoughts*, his life and activities were predicated on his friendship and collaboration with Ogarev. The circle of likeminded friends they formed in the 1830s as students at Moscow University was no less important to their intellectual development: it served as the crucible for the articulation of the new ethos of doubt.

Over the years, the content and nature of doubt among the group's members would change dramatically. Doubt was part of the intellectual legacy that romantic youths of the 1830s inherited from the Wisdom Lovers. The Wisdom Lovers had described it as a temporary condition that set in as individuals struggled to solve the world's mysteries, provoking them to continue their search. It was a sign of intellectual and spiritual strength, a mark of belonging to that higher order of people who devote their lives to the service of the truth. The Wisdom Lovers also warned, however, that it could become a permanent state if an individual despaired of ever finding higher meaning. This was precisely what happened to Herzen and Ogarev in the 1840s. For them, doubt became a process that could lead to only one conclusion: there was no higher meaning or guiding principle behind events in the world. Why did this reevaluation of doubt—and faith—become necessary? How did it come about?

Herzen and Ogarev were seven or eight years younger than the Wisdom Lovers and grew up in their cultural ambit. Like so many educated Moscow youths of the 1830s, they found their calling in the quest to uncover the unity that lay hidden beneath the infinite diversity of the world, and, like those others, they turned first to Schelling to help them uncover it. Herzen and Ogarev's Schelling was not, however, the Wisdom Lovers' Schelling. They were less attracted to the pantheist *Naturphilosophie* of Schelling's early years than to his later, quasi-Catholic *Geschichtsphilosophie*. Schelling confirmed Herzen and Ogarev's belief that they and their friends were prophets, chosen by God to show humanity the errors of its past and present and to point it toward a better future. These extravagant claims stood in contrast to their relatively modest social status: Herzen and Ogarev were both sons of noblemen, but unlike the Wisdom Lovers, they did not come from the highest echelons of the nobility.

In these years, their heavy reliance on Christian terms and concepts also set Herzen and Ogarev apart from the Wisdom Lovers. This habit reflected changes in the cultural atmosphere in Russia during the early reign of Nicholas I. Nicholas not only introduced a more authoritarian style of government but also made effusive displays of Orthodox Christian piety the hallmark of his reign, beginning with his coronation in 1826, a ceremony filled with tears and pious rapture. As emperor, Nicholas made the preservation of his subjects' faith and morals his primary mission. The conservative press described him as the embodiment of this Orthodox nation and a father to the Russian people, who required the merciful but firm command of an autocratic leader.[3] Prelates of the Russian Orthodox Church willingly confirmed this image. Metropolitan Filaret of Moscow welcomed Nicholas I to the Kremlin during every state visit, and on these occasions, he gently pointed out the connections that united the tsar with God. In a speech he gave in 1832, for example, Filaret drew on the designation of Jesus Christ as the

"King of Kings" to link Nicholas I into a hierarchy that extended downward from God to Jesus and from Jesus to the tsar: "May the King of Kings [*tsar' tsarstvuiushchikh*] continue to preserve You, both in Your entire Kingdom and in Your most pious family." Filaret also alluded to Nicholas's status as the "soul of the life of the people" and "father" of his subjects.[4]

The official cult of the pious tsar antagonized Herzen and Ogarev, who also regarded the religion of the official church as false and hypocritical. Instead, they would seek a religion of authentic feeling. In 1834, Herzen and Ogarev were arrested and exiled when their letters outlining their commitment to socialism and articulating their vision of a pure, non-Orthodox faith were seized by the Third Section during an investigation of a student circle. This event only reinforced their providential worldview.

Their exalted religious stance proved impossible to maintain when their provincial exile ended and they returned to Moscow in 1839. Most crucial was their introduction to the writings of Hegel. Schelling had offered them a philosophy of freedom that—in their view—justified their oppositional stance toward political authorities and allowed them to live in anticipation of a better future. Hegel's philosophy, they decided, proved that their notion of freedom was a chimera and that the better world "beyond" did not exist. They came to embrace doubt as a permanent state of uncertainty about their relationship with the divine, and they began to wonder whether their lives had any meaning. As Herzen said, doubt was a "heavy cross" they must bear to keep themselves and one another intellectually honest.

Their engagement with Hegel's ideas resulted in bitter disputes with their friends and the complete breakdown of their prior faith. Debates about the immortality of the soul and God became the order of the day among Moscow intellectuals in the 1840s. To participants, these arguments symbolized a communal quest for the truth and were the only meaningful aspect of lives that otherwise seemed utterly trivial.

Alexander Herzen grew up in a mansion on Tverskoi Boulevard in Moscow, less than half a mile from the house where the Wisdom Lovers held their meetings. He was the son of Ivan Iakovlev, a wealthy nobleman who had retired long before from state service and lived comfortably off the income generated by a thousand serfs. A hypochondriac, Iakovlev ensconced himself in his home, where he ruled as a tyrant and was given to making capricious demands. Herzen's mother, Louisa Haag, lived secluded in a separate wing of his Moscow mansion. The daughter of a petty German functionary, she had eloped with Iakovlev. By Russian law, Herzen was an illegitimate child and was not automatically entitled to noble status. He would have to attain it by working his way up to rank 8 (collegiate assessor) of the Table of Ranks.[5] Herzen was their only child, and Iakovlev doted on his son.

Nikolai Ogarev, too, was the son of a loving but tyrannical father, who attempted to police his son's every movement inside and outside of the house. Platon Ogarev, the master of thousands of serfs spread over multiple estates, was even wealthier than Ivan Iakovlev. Like Iakovlev, he was a recluse. He had left state service shortly after the death of his wife in 1815. "Nick" was only two years old when his mother died, and he grew up deprived of the company of other children. This changed in 1826, when the twelve-year-old boy met "Shura" (Alexander), aged thirteen. From then on, the two boys were inseparable.[6]

According to Herzen's cousin Tatiana Passek, who knew them both, the boys' friendship was founded on a "common religion—a heightened interest in the fate of humanity that so ennobles this stage of childhood. [. . .] They regarded one another as destined for something better." On a more immediate level, however, the two bonded over the discovery that they loved the same poems by Friedrich Schiller.[7] Schiller's tragedy *Don Carlos* (1787) was a special favorite of theirs.[8] They aspired to become like Don Carlos and the Marquis of Posa, whose hearts beat as one and who were prepared to sacrifice their lives in the battle against despotism. Posa became the victim of political tyranny, stabbed by the king, whereas Don Carlos became the victim of religious tyranny, killed as a heretic by the Spanish Inquisition. Schiller was no atheist: he preached faith in God and respect for the Bible, but he condemned Christianity (both Catholic and Protestant forms) as a religion of hypocrisy.[9] Schiller's religious views left their mark on Herzen and Ogarev. He also taught them to think of their lives in heroic terms.

When Herzen turned sixteen, his father hired a priest, Father Vasilii (Bogolepov) to prepare him for the newly required scriptural portion of entrance exams to Moscow University. Father Vasilii was but one of a host of tutors who instructed Herzen in languages, literature, history, and mathematics. As a member of the clerical estate, however, he stood even lower on the social scale than Herzen's other teachers. In a letter to his cousin, Herzen described Father Vasilii condescendingly as a man carried away by religious enthusiasm: "I view Vasilii Vasil'evich like a brilliant meteor; I like him, I listen, and I disregard [him] [*je passe* outre]." Herzen offered several reasons for this disregard. Among them were the "relationship of religion to the state," by which he presumably meant the role that the Orthodox Church played in reaffirming the ideology of autocracy and what he called the "mystical" content of Father Vasilii's teachings. Herzen would have liked the priest to concentrate on what he called the "simple" Christianity of the Gospels.[10] Already at this age, Herzen knew exactly what kind of religion he wanted his tutor to be preaching, and it was not the religion of the Russian Orthodox Church.

During his childhood, Herzen seems to have associated Orthodoxy with insincerity. His father, he claimed in his memoir, maintained appearances as an Orthodox nobleman, not wishing to break from the standards of comportment set by the state and elite society, but did not in fact observe any of the rituals prescribed by the Church. Iakovlev considered religion to be "among those necessities for a well-bred man. He said one ought to believe in Scripture without reasoning, because one's mind can grasp nothing here. [. . .] He believed a little bit out of habit, for the sake of propriety, and just in case." A priest was paid to perform services at his mansion, though Iakovlev never attended them.[11]

Orthodox piety was taken more seriously in the households in which Ogarev and Natalia Zakhar'ina, Herzen's first cousin (later his wife), grew up. Prayers were said every morning and night; they were spoken either standing or kneeling before the kiot, a shelf or section of a wall on which icons were displayed, cased in silver and gold. In Ogarev's home, the kiot was in his bedroom, and his father always came there to pray with him before he went to bed; Ogarev later recalled that he had "understood nothing" of these prayers and that the religiosity instilled in him as a child had been entirely "artificial."[12]

In the home where Zakhar'ina was raised, the kiot was located in her aunt's bedroom. Like Herzen, she was an illegitimate child: her mother was a serf, and her father was Ivan Iakovlev's brother. When her father died, Zakhar'ina was raised by an aunt, Princess Khovanskaia, who educated her as a noblewoman but never allowed her to forget her origins. Zakhar'ina appears to have interpreted the prayer ritual as one intended to instill discipline and obedience to her guardian. She later claimed (in an outline for an autobiography) that her aunt's piety had struck her even then as entirely superficial. As she grew older, she wrote, she began to experience "boredom at church and during prayer" and was "naughty instead of reading my prayers." Zakhar'ina responded by replacing the religiosity prescribed by her aunt with her "own form of religiosity." Her true prayers were now addressed "to heaven at night."[13] This form of worship was the only kind the young Zakhar'ina would recognize as sincere.

Indeed, Herzen himself became the object of her worship; a candle was placed beneath his portrait, as before an icon. When she left the room in which she composed her letters to him and walked downstairs into the company of her aunt, she felt as if she were "returning to the heathens from Zion."[14] Writing to him while he was in exile in 1837, she repeatedly emphasized their shared religion. "My friend, your prayer enraptures me! [. . .] I do not speak of the kind of prayer that consists in countless bows and exclamations, *they* will not understand, you understand."[15] Increasingly, their letters expressed a romantic exaltation that united them in a feeling for one another that was more than purely fraternal. They married in secret.

Herzen agreed that prayer should properly be addressed to the heavens, unmediated by prayer books. As he explained in an 1833 essay, human beings always corrupt every object they touch. Only the heavens can be deemed pure: "The sky, the sky—it is pure, it is as it was on the first day of creation. [. . .] Hither, hither . . ."[16] In light of this statement, it is difficult to accept the claim by some of Herzen's biographers that his religion was entirely earthbound or that "religion had touched neither his imagination nor his heart."[17] It is true, however, that this was not Orthodox Christian religion but a romantic religion of feeling, of yearning for the divine.

When Herzen and Ogarev entered Moscow University in 1829, they formed a circle out of a motley assortment of young men. Several did not come from noble families: Nikolai Ketcher was the son of a factory manager. He had recently graduated from the Medical-Surgical Academy and was a practicing physician. Valued for his sincerity, he became the group's moral policeman. Aleksei Lakhtin was the son of a merchant. Vadim Passek had the most exotic background: he had grown up in Siberia, where his father had been exiled for political reasons in the early 1800s and stripped of his property and noble status. The family had been permitted to return to Moscow only in 1824. Later in life, Herzen would remember Passek, who died young, as "a pure and poetic soul" in the image of Dmitrii Venevitinov, the Wisdom Lovers' leading poet who had died in 1827 and who Herzen claimed had been destroyed by the cruel realities of Russian life in the early reign of Nicholas I.[18] Herzen compared yet another friend, Nikolai Satin, to Venevitinov, as well as to

Pushkin's Vladimir Lenskii.[19] Like Venevitinov, Satin had a weak physical constitution. He came from a wealthy noble family and was very well educated, having attended the same boarding school for the children of the Moscow gentry that had educated some of the Wisdom Lovers. His elevated morals prompted Satin's friends to nickname him "Knight" (*Ritter*).

Together with their friends, Herzen and Ogarev ventured into new philosophical territory, beginning with the study of the Schelling's works. At the time, most young men would have learned about Schelling's philosophy through the Wisdom Lovers' publications and metaphysical poetry, which represented an important source of knowledge about Schelling's idealism for the generation of the 1830s.[20] Herzen received his first book by Schelling from his tutor, Vasilii Obolenskii in 1828, shortly before entering Moscow University.[21] Obolenskii also taught at the Moscow Boarding School for the Nobility and had recently published in an almanac alongside Venevitinov, Shevyrev, Odoevsky, and Titov.[22] In their poems and prose, the Wisdom Lovers relayed Schelling's *Naturphilosophie* of the late 1790s and early 1800s, identifying the highest calling of the individual as the quest to uncover the hidden, unconditional principle—the Absolute—that lent order to an infinitely variable universe. Herzen and Ogarev were fascinated by the *Naturphilosophie*, but they came to see their calling elsewhere, in Schelling's philosophy of history. Here, the aim was to uncover the plan that underlay the variability of human history—to identify developments that are in a state of becoming and to make them into reality.

Their Schelling was the author of the *Philosophical Inquiries into the Nature of Human Freedom* (1809), who had turned away from the "Absolute" and toward a providential "God." The increasingly Catholic and mystical religiosity of Germany's romantics had left its mark on Schelling's writings.[23] In the *Nature of Human Freedom*, Schelling creates a philosophy of history that is also a narration of the ways of God. "God is a life," Schelling explains, "not just a being. Yet every life has a destiny; it is subjected to suffering and becoming."[24] The story of God's life is a cosmic drama in three acts: God's creation of the natural, material world outside of himself (past); God's yearning to reunite with that world (present); and his reconciliation with it (future). Human beings play a central role in these developments. Of all God's creatures, they alone are capable of consciousness, of bringing light into the darkness of matter. They are the objects of God's love and the only part of creation capable of returning that love. To love God is to make oneself his vessel in the world. God has given human beings the freedom to choose this fate: each one is entirely at liberty to maintain his or her unique individuality. Indeed, people often prefer individuality over community with God, though in doing so they opt for a life of sin over one of goodness. God suffers such evil because he wishes freedom for humanity. The choice individuals face is not to be predetermined by the dictates of reason; it must be extralogical or extrarational, independent of any force outside of the individual, including the force of reason. In this regard, people are every bit as free as God himself.

Schelling's philosophy of history was grandiose, but it suited Herzen and Ogarev well. In the summer of 1833, Lakhtin and Ogarev engaged in an intense correspondence about the historian's calling: to "define the relationship of the part to the whole," to identify the "dominant idea" that guided peoples at particular times and places, and, finally, to extrapolate conclusions about the "goal of life" itself. "The historian," Lakhtin declared, "must be a prophet. He is truly, decidedly obliged to show me the future of humanity."[25] Ogarev and Herzen soon hatched a plan to found a journal devoted to the philosophy of history together with Satin, Ketcher, Passek, and Lakhtin. The programmatic piece Herzen composed for its first issue in February 1834 accorded philosophy of history first place among the list of planned topics. All contributions to it, Herzen asserted, would be united by a single ethic: to describe the fundamental unity that underlay human life—in politics and in thought—and to trace human development in all of its stages and point the way toward the future.[26]

Herzen and Ogarev not only believed themselves capable of showing humanity its future; they also aimed to participate in the life of God. They would reconcile the divine and the material and thereby bring the future into the present. In their earliest essays, they paraphrased Schelling's ideas, arguing that freedom is the distinctive trait that separates human beings from all other creatures. God has endowed people with the freedom to choose between evil (the immediacy of the material world, "atheistic egoism") and the good (selfless love, the yearning for a life of unity with spirit). The activity of yearning and loving is itself a means of making the brilliant future present, because these activities synthesize the material and spiritual worlds. Indeed, in loving, people elevate themselves to the divine.[27]

The philosophical importance they accorded love may explain why they sought out women as friends and incorporated them into their circle (a gesture that would not have occurred to the Wisdom Lovers in the

1820s). One of them was Tatiana Kuchina, another of Herzen's cousins, who married Vadim Passek. Liudmila Passek, Vadim's sister, was also brought into their circle; she was Herzen's first love. Herzen admired her for inner purity and for her poetic talent, which he saw expressed in her poem "World of Solace," citing it often. The first-person narrator of "World of Solace" describes a turning away from hopelessness and bitter suffering in the material world toward a world of her imagination: "There is an eternal and beautiful world whither I fly!" There, she feels "the whole enchantment of being." It is a world of "eternal love."[28] This was not great poetry, though "World of Solace" does contain important information about what members of the circle envisioned when they spoke of the future, or the better world "beyond." The "beyond" could refer to a better future for humanity in this world, but it could also, as Liudmila Passek's poem vaguely suggests, signify a world of the imagination or heaven and the afterlife. Longing for death was a prominent theme in Satin's poetry as well as in Ogarev's letters.[29] Tatiana Passek spoke so convincingly of her yearning to attain immortality that Natalia Zakhar'ina proposed that they should die together. She was dismayed when Passek failed to respond enthusiastically to this plan.[30] Zakhar'ina completed the circle: she married Herzen in 1838. All of these young people were united by their high-minded commitment to living in anticipation of a better world, convinced that their yearning would itself help to bring that world into being. Whether it was to be understood as a future in this world or in the hereafter, the future would—as Schelling foretold—feature the reconciliation between a loving God and a loving humanity.

Despite Herzen and Ogarev's enthusiasm for Schelling, they were not at all exclusive in their reading habits and were rather unsystematic in their thinking. They were excited when they thought they found confirmation of Schelling's ideas in a very different source: early French socialism, particularly Saint-Simon's "New Christianity," which they discovered around 1832. That system emerged after 1825, when Claude-Henri de Saint-Simon predicted the creation of a world order in which humanity would voluntarily relinquish all disparities in wealth and power, inspired by the teachings of Christ.[31] The influence of French socialism is clearly marked in a letter Herzen wrote to Ogarev in August 1833 describing the role that Christ's life had played in the development of human thought. Until his appearance, humanity had stagnated under the inequality that dominated the ancient world: "Man demanded renewal, the world awaited renewal. And there in Nazareth the son of a carpenter is born, Christ. As the Apostle Paul says, He is destined to reconcile God and man. Try to understand him. Does he, that great interpreter of Christ, not mean that Christ will return man to the true path, for the true path is the path of God? 'All people are equal,' says Christ. 'Love one another, help one another'; that is the immeasurable foundation on which Christianity is based. But people did not understand it. Its first phase was mystical (Catholicism) [. . .]; the second phase was the transition from mysticism to philosophy (Luther). Now, the third, *true, human* [phase] begins, that of the phalanstery (perhaps, S[aint]-Simonism??)."[32] The life span of the state was of limited duration; the great empires of old had sunk into irrelevance; the guiding force of world history was human thought and feeling. The ideas that Herzen expresses here were very much at odds with the ideology of Nicholas I's reign. The letter became the basis for his arrest in 1834 and his five-year exile.

Herzen, Ogarev, and their friends at Moscow University had been inspired by the Wisdom Lovers to study the idealism of Schelling. Yet, responding to the circumstances in which they were raised, they would emphasize different points in the lessons they learned from the German luminary. They felt they had been called on to identify the patterns by which God had made his will known in history, and they already knew his will for the future: the unification of humanity into a single community of love. They would help bring this about. Their modest social stature, they believed, only enhanced the glory of their quest to contribute to the regeneration of humanity.

Herzen, Ogarev, Satin, and Lakhtin were arrested in 1834 along with a group of students who had been caught singing libelous songs about the imperial family. They were not the first students at Moscow University to be arrested in the early reign of Nicholas I. Officials in the Third Section deemed noblemen between the ages of seventeen and twenty-five—"dvorianchiki"—especially dangerous, "the most gangrenous part of the empire."[33] A handful of young men had been dispatched, heads shaven, to the army or hard labor in Siberia between 1826 and 1827. When revolutions broke out in France, Belgium, and Poland, officials grew especially vigilant: Count Benckendorff, head of the Third Section, reported to Nicholas I in 1830 that students at the university and Moscow Boarding School for the Nobility were "imbued with liberal ideas"; they "dream of revolutions and believe in the possibility of a constitutional government in Russia."[34] Six more students were apprehended in 1831, this time under suspicion of conspiracy with revolutionaries in Poland; again, they were dispatched to Siberia.[35]

Ogarev and Herzen had been delighted by the news of the 1830 uprisings in France and Poland, donning tricolor scarves to express their enthusiasm. They were dismayed by the arrest of fellow students, and Ogarev collected donations in support of those unfortunates who were being sent to Siberia. Such gestures did not escape the notice of the authorities. In 1833, Ogarev was placed under the surveillance of the Third Section after he and an acquaintance of his, the minor poet and novelist Vladimir Sokolovskii, were reported for having sung "La marseillaise" on the steps of the Malyi Theater in an inebriated condition.[36]

Nicholas I understood that arrests were not enough to prevent sedition: positive measures must be taken to shape the outlook of young people. Soon after he took power, courses in "moral and dogmatic theology" became mandatory for all students at Moscow University, and scripture became an examination topic for entrance to the university.[37] Still, Nicholas I and his officials were dissatisfied: the proper outlook should be conveyed by every professor at the university, without exception. In an 1832 report to the tsar on Moscow University, Sergei Uvarov, an official at the Ministry of Enlightenment, suggested that three core ideals should imbue all lectures: "Orthodoxy, Autocracy, and Nationality." Only when every professor promoted them could the university be relied on to transform students into model subjects, namely, God-fearing Orthodox Christians devoted to the tsar and to the service of the state. "Orthodoxy, Autocracy, and Nationality" became the summation of the ideology of Nicholas I's reign and of all succeeding Romanov emperors. Nicholas rewarded Uvarov in 1833 by appointing him to head the Ministry of Enlightenment.[38]

In 1834, a group of students was denounced to the police for singing a libelous song about the Romanov family in the street. Vladimir Sokolovskii proved to be author of the lyrics, which circulated widely at Moscow University and were sung to the tune of "God Save the Tsar." Sokolovskii's lyrics lampooned the autocratic ideology of the state that emphasized the idea of the tsar as divinely anointed ruler and ridiculed the idea that God could have chosen that "son of a bitch" Nicholas as emperor. In his song, God took commands from the Romanovs.[39] The Third Section was able to catch students singing the song thanks to an agent provocateur. Herzen, Ogarev, and Satin were not among them, but they were arrested anyway, and officials found sufficient material to demonstrate that they had been "touched by the depraved spirit of the time."[40]

The documents seized by officials consisted mostly of letters. The ones that interested them the most concerned the religious outlook of the circle. Both the correspondence and the interrogation statements of the accused about their missives confirmed that members of Herzen and Ogarev's group disapproved of religious worship as prescribed by the church but saw no difficulty in calling on God and invoking Jesus Christ as the savior of humanity. One such piece of evidence was a letter by Nikolai Satin to Vladimir Sokolovskii written in 1833 about the latter's most recent novel. Satin expressed disapproval of one particular passage of the novel in which the protagonist prays before icons: "Religious feelings are beautiful and lofty, but you vested them in the usual, narrow forms. *Surely, a true poet will not fall onto his knees in front of a block of wood with the face of Nikolai the miracle-worker and the Mother of God painted on it and pray to it and beg forgiveness for his sins? No! He will not seek Divinity here, and his burning prayer will not pour out in words!*"[41] When Satin was interrogated about the letter, he explained that it was more appropriate to pray in nature than to pray in a church or to bow before a *kiot*: "I only wanted [. . .] to express the dreamy thought that for the wide embrace of the true poet's soul, the boundaries of buildings are tight, that he withdraws into nature and there, falls on his knees before omnipresent God, sending up his warm prayers, like a gift of his soul to heaven, and nothing blocks his view."[42]

Sokolovskii, too, was interrogated about the letter, and he offered a different explanation. Satin, he claimed, had meant to say that the poet should address his prayers to Jesus Christ, not to the saints: "There is only one mediator—the Son of God—between God the Father and people. The whole teaching of the New Testament constantly asserts: whosoever wants to receive God in himself must first receive Christ in himself." Such prayer, Sokolovskii remarked, would come naturally to anyone who "knows the laws of Christ, wishes to receive God in himself and thirstily searches for Divinity." Christ, the "God Man," was the obvious addressee for his prayer.[43] Sokolovskii appears to have shared Herzen's preference for what the latter had once called the "simple" Christianity of the Gospels.

Officials of the Third Section were similarly interested in the letter Herzen wrote to Ogarev in 1833 in which he outlined the history of Christianity and predicted the creation of "the third, *true, human*" phase of history, "that of the phalanstery," inspired by Christian Socialism.[44] Interrogated about the letter, Ogarev endorsed Herzen's thoughts. Christ, he explained, had preached an order in which there would be "no Master and no servants." The prophecy that "there shall be one fold and one shepherd" meant that there would be "neither subjugator nor subjugated" but rather that all would follow Christ as one.[45]

Schelling's philosophy, in combination with French Christian social-ism, allowed Herzen, Ogarev, and their friends to imagine themselves as prophets of a future characterized by unity, equality, and love. When, in 1834, they were suddenly arrested and exiled, they could draw on this worldview to provide them with a narrative that gave meaning to the sudden upheaval in their lives. They believed that God had assigned them this fate and labeled their exile a trial or a purgatory (*chistilishche*). Even as they suffered through the miserable insignificance of provincial exile, they were contributing to something greater. Nicholas I and the Third Section might determine where Herzen and Ogarev lived and how they lived but not what they would live for.

Herzen, Ogarev, and other members of their Moscow University circle remained convinced of their great calling throughout the years of exile. This is attested by a letter Ogarev wrote in 1838, the year before they were released: "It is the influence of Providence—after all we are his children, his beloved children. [Providence] has tried us and it is enough now, we have come out of this crucible even more willing to accept the will of the one who sent us."[46]

Throughout their exile, members of the circle were convinced that this feat was possible only because of the support they received from one another. The friends played a number of interlocking roles. Ogarev, Herzen, Ketcher, and Satin watched over one another, confessing their moral missteps and berating each other for them.[47] Women were ac-corded special powers of moral and spiritual regeneration. Herzen told Zakhar'ina she was his moral guide, helping him to overcome tempta-tions; indeed, he said she had transformed him into a better person. Zakhar'ina said the same of him.[48] Ogarev, too, credited his wife, Maria, with his "rebirth."[49] Maria Roslavleva was the headstrong daughter of a Russian nobleman who had gambled away his family fortune. Her father's profligacy made her a social pariah; Ogarev married her in Penza in 1835.

Herzen and Ogarev drew on biblical imagery to describe their rela-tionships. Herzen and Zakhar'ina referred to one another as a "guiding star" or "morning star," as well as calling each other "Christ," "savior," and "angel," as well as "divine."[50] Indeed, Herzen once referred to all of his friends as "divinities, saints in the temple of my heart."[51] The tendency to attach sacred meaning to friendships was common among European romantics of the early nineteenth century.[52] So was the vision of women as guardian angels.[53] Yet friendship gained a significance for Herzen and Ogarev that was unique to Russia. It did not compete with other loyalties and forms of self-identification, such as one's family, profession, class, religion, and allegiance to the state but more or less replaced them. The importance accorded to friendship is partly attributable to the rigidity of society and politics, the uniformity of the model of behavior demanded of members of the educated elite, especially the nobility. There was a special thrill in attachments formed around elective affinities, affinities of thought and disposition. These were attachments that individuals freely chose, regardless of social hierarchy and family connections. In communities of friendship, moreover, a nobleman who preferred poetry to the pursuit of a military or bureaucratic career could maintain some semblance of self-esteem.

Herzen and Ogarev were not the only ones to accord friendship such importance. The circle that included Nikolai Stankevich, Mikhail Bakunin, Vissarion Belinsky, and Vasilii Botkin exhibited much the same patterns. Botkin, for example, referred to Bakunin as a "prophet" and an "angel."[54] The similarities between the two groups only began here: both were deeply influenced by the philosophy of Schelling; both spoke in increasingly pressing terms of the importance and necessity of doubt. By the mid-1840s, both would include the existence of God among the objects of their doubt.[55] In hindsight, the two groups would strike Herzen as so similar that he considered them as participants in the same movement in his memoir (he dubbed them "Westernizers"). At the time, however, Herzen and Ogarev paid no heed to members of the Stankevich circle, most likely because they were intent on viewing their own group as the only island of the saved amidst a sea of corruption.[56]

The circle contrasted the purity of its members to the moral degradation of the nobility, which it referred to as "the crowd." The crowd was stuck in a world of debauchery and material immediacy—the "filthy" here and now. People who belonged to the crowd were "filthy animals," "scum," a "gutter of dirtiness, vileness and sin." They constituted "a collection of random freaks."[57] The great aim of Herzen and Ogarev's circle was to purify this crowd, dissolving the selfishness and egoism of elite society into a unifying spirit of love.

One way to acquire influence over the crowd was to publish poetry and philosophical works as well as fictional and historical writings in Russian journals. Their journal of choice was *Telescope* (*Teleskop*), printed in Moscow. Ogarev's translation of a passage from Schlegel appeared there in 1831, while Herzen's article on E. T. A. Hoffmann appeared there in 1836. Ketcher, too, published numerous translations in it and was a party to a major scandal that erupted in 1836. The journal gained notoriety for printing Petr Chaadaev's epochal "Philosophical Letter," which applied Schelling's philosophy of history to Russia in order to show that Russia had neither a culture nor a history. Ketcher had translated Chaadaev's letter from French into Russian. The upshot of the scandal was that the journal was shut down and its editor exiled to Ust'-Sysol'sk.[58]

Writing was not the only means by which the circle hoped to reach the crowd. Personal example was equally important, though it too held its dangers. The friends might succumb to paralyzing doubts about their ability to accomplish this Herculean task, especially if the "crowd" rejected them. Satin devoted a cycle of poems to these dangers, published in *Telescope* in 1836 under the title "Repentance of a Poet," which one scholar has tied thematically to the late works of Venevitinov.[59] At the time, his friends hailed this as Satin's greatest work. The poem's first-person narrator is a prophet who knows that he is fated to serve humanity, to awaken in his "brothers" a desire to strive toward perfection. The "spirit of love," he hopes, will unite them and kindle a "spark of renewal" inside them. Yet the prophet is coldly received in society. Consumed by doubt, he finds solace among women, whose love renews his strength and his faith in himself. Restored, the prophet announces he will return to the world to sacrifice his life for mankind and thereby enter the kingdom of freedom at God's side.[60]

Inspired by Satin's poem, Ogarev and Herzen wrote about themselves and their mates in similar terms. Herzen sent Zakhar'ina several letters from exile in late 1836 and early 1837 in which he described such doubts. The indifference of the people surrounding him in exile, their "cold breath," had made him vulnerable to the influence of an "evil genius" of doubt, resignation, and despair. His soul cried for meaningful activity, to share his "thoughts and feelings," to "pour out" his "fire," yet "people" were too selfish to respond. Only Zakhar'ina could save him.[61] Indeed, Herzen was certain that faith in God and in Providence was impossible without faith in Zakhar'ina, as he wrote to her in 1837, describing a moment of doubt: "'What will happen to me,' I thought, and my limbs went cold, 'if in many years I say, "Love is youth's enchanting dream, but like all dreams, it does not carry over into adulthood" and I lose love and faith? Then I will experience everything that the fallen angel experienced. Or, even worse, then I will not even feel pangs of conscience, then I will become an animal.' Oh, Natasha, how dark this thought is, the devil slipped it between Christ's name and yours."[62] Though Herzen had worried that he might dismay his sensitive fiancée, she responded by affirming this thought: "Not to love you means that I would not exist, that there would be no God."[63] Their doubts were easily dispelled.[64]

Ogarev too cast his wife in these terms in an autobiographical cycle of poems titled "Crescendo from the Symphony of My *I* in Relation to Its Friends," which he sent Herzen as part of a letter in the autumn of 1836. The cycle climaxed in a section called "Doubt." Doubts had assailed him about his providential calling, owing to the incomprehension of alleged "friends." Maria was the one who had saved him: "I was gloomy, but *She* looked at me, and I met reproach for doubt in that gaze, and once again, I believed in Providence."[65] Herzen would likewise capitalize pronouns in referring to Zakhar'ina and Ogarev a year later: he said he had invested them with everything sacred, all his beliefs.[66]

The group continued to view friendship and love as a means of transforming humanity, a synthetic act that bonded individuals together. Love involved more than just recognizing one's beloved as the "other half of one's soul"; it entailed the creation of a higher, complete, and perfect being.[67] This was an act of world-historical significance: it was the key to the transformation of all estates and nations into a single community. The transformation would begin here, with them. Ogarev promised his wife that "our love will be the foundation of universal goodwill."[68] Herzen, too, viewed his relationships with Ogarev and Zakhar'ina this way: "Does not the life of all of humanity in the end consist in expressing one person, one being, one soul, one will [. . .]? Ogarev and I are superficially completely different people, and this is precisely why we are so closely united. He has the serenity of conviction, a restful thought. I am all activity, and for this reason we express both thought and activity. In this way you, too, will express the unfading, pure principle of humanity, and I the earthly person. Together, we are both an angel and a human being. Imagine all of humanity, united so tightly by love, proffering one another hand and heart, complementing one another, and the great idea of the Creator, and the great idea of Christianity will reveal itself to you."[69] Love was an act of revelation; it offered a means of bringing the future into the present, allowing individuals to orient themselves away from the evils of material immediacy and toward the greater good that awaited them.

So far, the ideas expressed by Herzen, Ogarev, and their friends cohered with the model the Wisdom Lovers had put forward a decade earlier: doubt was a property of exalted youth. It was a momentary temptation that assailed individuals as they set about accomplishing the impossible. For the Wisdom Lovers, that mission had been to grasp the universe in its infinite diversity. For Herzen and Ogarev, it was to remake humankind. More than the Wisdom Lovers, they viewed the nobility as morally bankrupt, unable to see beyond the cultural and ethical boundaries that the state imposed on it. Both groups also assumed that poetry, philosophy, literature, and literary criticism were the means by which society could be renewed and that they would guide it toward a brilliant future.

During their arrest and exile from 1834 to 1839, Herzen, Ogarev, and Satin had no difficulty maintaining faith in their mission. It began to collapse after their release in 1839, when doubt became a major theme in their writings. In these years, doubt seemed to be the only concept that gave their existence meaning.

On their release, a new life began for them as they moved back to Moscow and made new friends. Among their new acquaintances were Vissarion Belinsky, Mikhail Bakunin, and Timofei Granovsky, all members of the former Stankevich circle, whom they had virtually ignored until now. They realized, painfully, that they had not kept abreast of the latest intellectual trends during their time in exile. Moscow's youth had moved on to the philosophy of Georg Wilhelm Friedrich Hegel. Until now, educated Russians had been largely unfamiliar with Hegel's views: his works demanded a high level of philosophical training, which most readers lacked. The same may be said of Herzen and Ogarev. Once they did begin to read Hegel, they found that their earlier beliefs were inadequate, yet they hesitated to adopt his philosophy as their new worldview. Instead, they would proclaim that there is no higher reason behind events in the world. Herzen and Ogarev gave up speaking of friends as "images of divine holiness" and ceased discussing the brilliant future that was to come, dismissing this as a "boyhood dream." Herzen began to think that they had failed to mature during their years of exile; he remarked to Ogarev in 1839 that "neither I, nor you, nor Satin, nor Ketcher [. . .] has attained adulthood [. . .], nor have we [. . .] found beliefs and convictions that we could settle on for our whole lives and that we could then develop, prove, and preach."[70] These feelings seemed to have emerged mainly in response to their study of Hegel.

Nikolai Ogarev. Portrait in pencil by Eitel, 1830s. In Nikolai G. Tarakanov, *N. P. Ogarev: Evoliutsiia filosofskikh vzgliadov* (Moscow: Moskovskii universitet, 1974), 55. (Russian State Historical Museum, Moscow.)

Hegel was best known for *Phenomenology of Spirit* (1807), his first major work. Until its appearance, the differences between Hegel's philosophy and that of Schelling had been unclear; after its publication, the two men (once friends) became bitter enemies. Their conflict centered on the relationship between freedom and reason. For Hegel, freedom is not about making choices; it is what one gains as one comes to understand the ways in which spirit or reason orders the world and guides its transformation. Having recognized that everything of significance in the world belongs to a higher, rational order, one can then identify one's place in that order. Essentially, reason was Hegel's God, and subordinating oneself to God meant subordinating oneself to reason.[71] Faith in a better world "beyond," which the individual might access by choosing the good, was utterly at odds with Hegel's system. There was no basis for such a world in reality.

In Russia, as in Germany, *Phenomenology of Spirit* drew sharply divergent interpretations. The conservative press of the mid-1830s, including the *Journal of the Ministry of Enlightenment*, represented Hegel as an atheist who encouraged political freethinking.[72] Such attacks practically guaranteed Hegel a warm welcome among those readers already sympathetic to German idealism. In 1837, members of the Stankevich circle, notably Vissarion Belinsky and Mikhail Bakunin, began an intensive study of Hegel's philosophy and came to the opposite conclusion: Hegel in no way challenged the existing order but actually underwrote it, calling for "reconciliation with reality." Hegel's philosophy, they believed, legitimated the political, cultural, and social status quo. Extrapolating from his writings, they argued that Russian autocracy was not the result of historical contingencies but the reflection of the progressive development of the "all-embracing Spirit." Only through the state did reason rule over society. The absolute power of the emperor was an expression of the absolute power of reason. It did not make slaves of Russian subjects, for the only true slavery was the individual's subjection to ignorance. As Belinsky explained, freedom is not whim, but the conformity of laws with necessity. In his famous article "Menzel, Critic of Goethe" (1840) he denounced those people who criticized state institutions; incapable of profound thought, they merely adopted an oppositional pose to aggrandize themselves.[73]

Belinsky's views deeply unsettled Ogarev and Herzen. Most immediately, they were concerned about the implications of Belinsky's opinions with respect to their faith in the future, the better world beyond. Ogarev wrote to Herzen in this vein in 1839: "We are of little faith—that is why we suffer. Let Belinsky & Co. say that even if there is an afterlife [*Jenseits*], it is only a fantasy and not knowledge. They are wrong!"[74] Herzen, too, was loath to let go of faith in immortality. As he wrote to Ogarev, he hesitated partly for personal reasons: two of the children Natalia bore in these years had died at birth. Herzen needed to believe in the better future beyond.[75]

Herzen and Ogarev were also concerned about the political implications of Hegel's theories as Belinsky expounded them. In criticizing the autocracy, had they failed to consider the logic that underwrote the formation of the modern Russian state? Many young Russians of their generation felt that Hegel provided a strong justification for the development of a powerful bureaucratic apparatus and were even inspired to devote their lives to strengthening it by joining state service. Hegel's acolytes, graduates of Moscow University, entered the Ministry of Justice and Ministry of Internal Affairs in droves during the 1840s.[76]

During their years in exile, Herzen, Ogarev, and Satin had been required to serve in the civil administration of the provinces. Now that Nicholas I had pardoned them, they must decide whether to continue along this path, and Belinsky's articles pointed straight toward the offices of the Ministry of Internal Affairs.[77] After some hesitation, Herzen took a position in St. Petersburg, though the move was ill fated; he had difficulty overlooking the petty drudgery of his job and the corruption endemic in the bureaucracy. An incautious remark landed him in the offices of the Third Section and back into exile in 1841. He was again pardoned and allowed to return to Moscow in 1842, but his experiences confirmed Herzen's suspicion that there was little rationality in the organs of the Russian state. He resigned from state service in 1842.

Ogarev and Satin, by contrast, immediately opted against service careers and devoted themselves with renewed vigor to the service of the truth. In 1840, they published vigorously in the country's leading journal, *Notes of the Fatherland (Otechestvennye zapiski)*.[78] This did not, however, mean that they had chosen to ignore Hegel. Ogarev was the first to begin studying Hegel's philosophy in 1839. His attachment to the circle's original worldview, he admitted, had been self-indulgent, and he would now follow the truth wherever it led. "Hegel, or Cieszkowski, or Strauss, or the Pope in Rome, I will follow them if only I become convinced that the truth is there."[79] In November 1839, he proudly announced to Herzen that he wished to "reconcile with the world and myself, with God."[80] The result of this reconciliation, however, appears to have been the rapid breakdown of his former beliefs. In October and

November 1840, he again told Herzen that "it is better to renounce a brilliant future than to reside in falsehood."[81] The falsehood he would reject was his calling as a prophet, in the beautiful future he had foretold, as well as in immortality.

Herzen was slower to approach Hegel. Once he did begin reading *Phenomenology of Spirit* in 1841 or 1842, however, he was swept away: "Depth, transparence, carried away by the current of the spirit—*laschiate ogne speranza*—the shores disappear, the only salvation is within one's breast, but now a voice rings out: *Quid times, Caesarem vehis* and fear dissipates. The shore. The beautiful leaves of the imagination have been torn, but the juicy fruits of reality are here. Gone are the Undines, but a full-breasted maiden awaits."[82] The conclusions Herzen reached at this point were almost identical to Ogarev's: people were obliged to pursue the truth, no matter how much it hurt. Reason—the philosophy of Hegel—had revealed to him that there could be no other world outside of the present world, no *Jenseits*. There was a God, and God had a will, but that will was embodied in history as it unfolded according to the logic of reason. There was no point in pretending that there was any-thing more to God or to life: "To maintain one's personal opinion in opposition to the truth—that is narrow-mindedness, egoism, pride."[83]

Natalia Herzen was the last bastion to fall in 1843. Numerous letters she wrote to her close friend Tatiana Astrakova confirm that she con-tinued to believe in Providence and the life hereafter into the 1840s.[84] This faith disappeared at some point in late 1842 or early 1843, when she began to remark on the "stupidity" of her life and "boredom," which she capped with the statement that life itself was "stupid," a "terrible joke."[85] No more comments followed about faith in Providence and the afterlife, in a God who directed their lives, or in a spirit whose development she could assist. Ogarev registered the change in the summer of 1843: "Natasha is a skeptic! I cannot conceive of it."[86] In subsequent years, she continued to write of life as a "game" in which human beings were nothing more than pieces to be moved around and to argue that this "stupid game" was of no ultimate purpose. They had once, she remarked, been prepared to "crucify a person or to mount the cross" in the name of a single word or idea. No longer.[87] She was adamant that she had no regrets about this loss of faith, describing it as an ulti-mately salutary development: "I have parted with many things, including faith in the afterlife, but it has not impoverished me, on the contrary; I even parted with faith in this life, that is with the possibility and neces-sity of doing anything in particular, or anything at all. [. . .] I live more simply, I have abandoned myself to my nature, I trust it more."[88] She lived for the moment, and she urged others to do the same, warning that "there is no future."[89]

Having renounced the brilliant future for which they yearned in previous years, however, Ogarev and Herzen were unable to commit to Hegelianism. Hegel's philosophy destroyed core aspects of their former worldview without making acolytes of them.[90] Even as he claimed to be "reconciling with reality," for example, Ogarev had to admit that Hegel bored him. He had "lost faith in life, in myself," but found nothing to replace it.[91] Further philosophical explorations did little to fill the void. In the summer of 1841, Ogarev was issued a passport, which enabled him to travel to Germany. There, he picked up a copy of Ludwig Feuerbach's recently published *Essence of Christianity* (1841). Feuerbach reinforced Ogarev's sense that there could be no world "beyond"; the *Jenseits* was but a projection of humanity's hopes and desires in this world onto an imaginary place. Love and suffering were not attributes of a god. They were rather qualities of human beings, who must come to understand that there is no intangible, guiding power, spirit, or God directing their destiny but that it is determined by their actions and decisions.

Initially, Ogarev was enthusiastic about Feuerbach's book. On first reading the *Essence of Christianity* he noted how "destructive" it was to Christian faith. "Where should I take my life? Where should I run from suffering? Where is serenity? Where is bliss? There! In that world! But that world is only as good as our imagination makes it. Repulsion from death, the desire to live individually compelled people to build themselves another world and to pin all their hopes on it. But does that world exist—I do not know. I only know that it is uncomfortable in that world. I know that the mind has doubts and the heart suffers." He now attempted to formulate a new religion that would be characterized by "deep respect for reason, love, in a word, for everything that human beings, unable to recognize anything higher in themselves, gave God as attributes." The heart had suffered as a result of his belief in the world "beyond"; it suffered even more as he stripped himself of that faith. As he wrote to his wife in the summer of 1841, "I have become a victim of reason, suffering from bitter truth, but preferring to suffer from truth than to rejoice in falsehood."[92]

Ogarev's Feuerbachian phase did not last long. He soon began to waver on every score. Sometimes, he described utter loss of faith in himself and in life.[93] At other times, he wondered whether loss of faith was tenable, or even necessary, and claimed to have regained faith in Providence, God, and "life," or he said that he "believed" without knowing what to believe in.[94] Ogarev's confrontation with Feuerbach, as with Hegel, had raised more questions than it answered.[95] Doubt was the central theme of all the poems that Ogarev wrote at this time. The nature of this doubt resembled that which the Wisdom Lovers invoked after 1825: a condition that sets in when the seeker of wisdom despairs of ever finding truth. Ogarev's poem "Discord" (1840) describes a state of inner turmoil, marked by an accretion of unanswered questions that pile up and overwhelm the mind, "suffocating" it with "bitter doubts." In a slightly later poem, "Torn Apart" (1841–42), the first-person narrator describes how he had once achieved a sense of the world's unity, beauty, and order but has since succumbed to a sense of disharmony. Having become aware of "contradictions," his heart and soul will not allow his mind to settle on "reconciliation." Comparing himself to Prometheus, the narrator notes that his heart will eternally be eaten by pain.[96]

Herzen and Ogarev came to view the confrontation with Hegel's philosophy as a test of maturity, of one's willingness to accept "truth" when it challenged boyhood dreams. Nikolai Satin addressed this issue most directly. He was feeling all the doubts of which Herzen and Ogarev spoke but sought the reasons for his inability to achieve "reconciliation" inside himself. In letters he sent to Ketcher, Ogarev, and Herzen from 1841 to 1844, he attributed this inability to personal failings, to the failure to grow up, for example: "I am 27, and I still consider myself a boy. I still love to grieve, to watch the moon [. . .] is it not ridiculous?— Ketcher, will I ever mature? Will I be reconciled with life?" In another letter, he wondered whether perhaps he was just weak willed: "I confess that I have sometimes despaired of myself, there are so many doubts in my mind, so many ambiguities and contradictions in my soul [. . .] Believe me, I sometimes think that I will never be able to reconcile myself to life, and truly *ce n'est pas faute de* bonne *volonté, faute de* forte *volonté* perhaps [. . .]."[97]

In his poetic writings of the same period, however, Satin casts the problem in different terms. There, he describes the break with boyhood dreams as a form of betrayal, one that morally compromises the individual, leaving him incapable of embracing a new and better faith. This stands out in "A Fragment from an Overheard Conversation," published in *Notes of the Fatherland* in 1841. In this dialogue, a doctor, apparently representing Ketcher, reproaches an ailing young man for his "anachronistic" inactivity and urges him to "reconcile" himself with life. The sickly young man, apparently representing Satin, responds that he is willing to reason but that his doubts prevent him from reaching a satisfactory conclusion. He must sacrifice his earlier worldview, and yet he is repulsed by the idea of dismissing it as an empty dream. "Torn inside, I want my prior faith back; I cry out, ask that God be returned to me, but reason is firm! The anxious soul is incapable of victory."[98] "Fragment" is a tragedy; the protagonist has given up his former beliefs in the name of truth, only to find that he cannot live without them.

One of Satin's last works, a poem called "The Little Foot" (1842–43), also depicts the turn away from former beliefs as a personal betrayal. The poem can be viewed as an invective response to Herzen's statement in 1842 that, in the absence of the Undines, he would happily settle for a "full-breasted maiden." Satin makes a water nymph, "Ondine," the heroine of his poem, set in the Middle Ages along the Rhine River. Ondine is the daughter of the Rhine god. When a young knight named Walter falls in love with the nymph, he is told that they can only be united if he pledges eternal love and that if he is unfaithful, he must die. Walter consents but soon grows bored and briefly forgets Ondine in the arms of a real woman. By the time he remembers his pledge, it is too late: the young knight is driven insane by visions of his former love and drowns himself.[99] Satin may have intended this as a cautionary tale for his friends: to break with their earlier beliefs and pledges of friendship was a form of betrayal that would not be without consequence. In this regard, Satin proved right: the determination of some group members to leave behind old vows created rifts in their relationships that proved irreparable.

The encounter with Hegelianism had forced Herzen, Ogarev, and their friends to relinquish a worldview that had been constructed around the philosophy of Schelling. Schelling had instilled in them the belief in their freedom to envision a better world and bring it into being. Having abandoned Schelling, Herzen and Ogarev did not become convinced Hegelians. Instead, they embraced an attitude of skepticism. One must let go of cherished beliefs in the name of truth and live for the here and now. What that entailed, morally or philosophically, remained vague.

The loss of faith in the worldview that had defined the circle initially led to a crisis in their friendships. During the years of exile, they had looked to one another in the distance as models of purity. That image had served as a source of guidance to each one, providing the only salvation from the corrupting influence of the "crowd" and doubt. As soon as their common faith and sense of mission had disappeared, the purpose of friendship, too, became unclear. Friendship had never simply been a matter of passing time with people one liked; that smacked of self-indulgence. A new mode of friendship had to be discovered that could fit their new disposition of eternal doubt.

Herzen began to express suspicion about all of his attachments in 1839. He recognized the qualities of sympathy, goodness, and love that had once made Satin and Ketcher such valued friends, but he now criticized them both as lazy and poorly educated.[100] He claimed that Ogarev suffered from "psychological weakness," making him sentimental about anyone he had been close to in the past, regardless of that person's intellectual and moral merits.[101] Herzen did not even spare his wife.[102] Both Ogarev and Satin attempted to defend themselves by arguing that personal sympathy should count for something and by repeating the old moral code: without the support of their friends, they would sink into mindless hedonism.[103]

Yet moral purity was no longer a priority for the group. Hence, there was no need for a moral policeman, the position that Ketcher had always occupied in the group. Ketcher's scolding lost its charm and began to seem excessively judgmental. Herzen called it his "limitation."[104] Natalia Herzen, too, was irritated. She was annoyed by the letters Ketcher sent after he moved to St. Petersburg to join the Department of Medicine at the Ministry of Internal Affairs. She wrote: "What is all this scolding, scolding, and scolding! I'm tired of your [illegible], but surely you can find something to say other than a reproach? I asked you about this and that, and no answers to anything. May God be your judge. You always say, 'Write, write,' but frankly it sometimes seems that you are not interested in what we write."[105]

Other members of the circle, however, found that their exchanges seemed trivial and superficial in the absence of the moralism that Ketcher stood for. Their gatherings seemed to lack intimacy in the absence of his loud, scolding voice.[106] Granovsky's wife, Elizaveta, was among those who missed him: "Wherever you turn, there is such an emptiness, boredom, eternal pettiness. When you think what a person could be and what he makes of himself, then . . . Sometimes it is good when you think about the never-ending movement forward, but you look closer and it seems to be nonsense. After all, progress expresses itself in very few people. [. . .] You will laugh at this stupid dissertation, Ketcher, but these days I run into people in whom that trait embitters me, even more so because I had been close to them before and loved them. But even then, we were not in complete agreement." Granovskaia may have found Ketcher's reprimands reassuring, an easily identifiable sign of concern among people who appeared to have lost a sense of personal connection in the absence of shared convictions. She concluded her letter to him by proclaiming that it might be better to break entirely rather than maintain the pretense of *"good relations"* that were not based on unity of thought. Her disillusionment seems to have encompassed all members of the former group, including Natalia and Alexander Herzen, with whom she and her husband were very close in this period.[107]

On the surface, the group still maintained the distinction between the "circle" and the "crowd." This was noted by the literary critic Pavel Annenkov, who later became famous for his descriptions of the outlook and intimate lives of the "intelligentsia" (he used the word) in his memoirs. A man who belonged to the same milieu as the Herzens and Granovskys (but not a member of their circle), he visited them at the summer home they rented in 1845: "The circle shunned contact with the unwholesome elements lying off to the side of it, and would become disturbed should any, even accidental or remote, reference be made to them. The circle had not withdrawn from the world, but stood apart from it—which was the reason it attracted attention; but precisely on account of that situation, a special sensitivity developed in its midst toward all that was artificial and sham. Any evidence of a questionable sentiment, crafty expression, empty motto, specious assurance was instantly surmised by the circle and, whenever these things showed themselves, they provoked a storm of ridicule, irony, and devastating criticism."[108]

Sincerity was essential to members of the group, but it was not enough to maintain peace and unity. Without a worldview that gave meaning to all the small moments in their lives, their interactions with one another seemed pointless. As Ogarev put it: "Do you know why it is so boring with almost everybody? Because they all cook in their own little kitchen and talk about their very own potato, which doesn't interest anyone."[109] By 1845 Ogarev had come to accept Herzen's view that sympathy or fondness alone could not form the basis of community. "A person who is a stranger in his own family is obliged to break with his family. He must tell his family that he is a stranger. Even if we were strangers to the whole world, we would be obliged to say so. Only a spoken conviction is holy."[110] Agreeing to differ was not an option.

All of these issues were most clearly displayed in an argument that broke out between Herzen and Timofei Granovsky over belief in the hereafter in 1844. Granovsky came from a provincial noble family of modest means. He had studied at St. Petersburg University, where he met members of the Stankevich circle. Identified by the authorities as a promising young man, he was sent to study in Germany on a government stipend. In 1839 he moved to Moscow to occupy a chair in history at the university and soon won fame as a lecturer and public speaker. Herzen and Ogarev befriended him shortly after their return from exile that year, and he joined their circle. The bitter dispute that began in 1844 concerning immortality was not an exchange of opinion over the nature of the soul but a personal conflict over whether a member of their circle was entitled to believe in a better life hereafter.

Had they met a few years earlier, Herzen, Ogarev, and Granovsky would have found that their attitudes were closely aligned. A letter Granovsky sent from Berlin to a friend in St. Petersburg in 1837 shows that he appreciated the importance of doubt and viewed it much as Herzen and Ogarev did in the 1830s—as part of the process by which true knowledge and faith are gained. Describing a moment of crisis in which he had been visited by a "tempting demon," Granovsky defended doubt as salutary: "Do we have the right to trust the negative results of our doubts? No. We can, we must doubt: that is one of the great human rights, but these doubts must lead to something. We must not stop at the first negative answers, but must go further, we must act through the entire, God-given dialectic. To get to the finish, if not to the absolute [end], then as far as we can, that is the rule for all of humanity."[111] Thanks to their doubts, he told his friend, they would attain a superior form of faith, one that was "purified, rational—not at all like that which we inherit from our father or grandfather along with old wigs and garments."[112] Still, there was one "old wig" Granovsky was not able to throw out, namely, faith in the immortality of the soul. When Stankevich died in 1840, he found this faith to be his only source of consolation and yearned to be reunited with his friend in the afterlife.[113] The deaths of Granovsky's two sisters in 1842 and 1843 only reinforced this feeling.

His friends differed in their responses to Granovsky's professions of faith. Ogarev, ever patient with friends, gently reminded him of the need to live for the present.[114] Herzen told him he was being self-indulgent. The argument between Granovsky and Herzen started in June 1844. That summer, Elizaveta Granovskaia was vacationing with the Herzens at a house in the country when she received a letter from her husband containing the following four sentences: "I carry every grief with me for my whole life. For me, Stankevich, my sisters, they die every day all over again. But Herzen is wrong to call this my romanticism. It is the constant, deep mood of my soul."[115] Herzen was shown the letter and sent Granovsky a lengthy, pained response. Herzen, too, had suffered, having by then lost three infant children. Even more painful, however, were the truths about himself and his friends that he had been forced to accept: "*Sober knowledge* is a truly heavy cross." This was a cross he was determined to bear, having turned his back on all illusion. Only a person of "weak character" would refuse. "You are purer, nobler than I, but I do not envy you. Do you know how they reinforce a dam? With mud, it dries, and you can splash as much water as you want."[116]

Granovsky could only defend himself by repeating what Herzen already knew. Until the death of Stankevich and his sisters, he too had been prepared to embrace the truths that reason and philosophy dictated and had had no need for the *Jenseits*. Their deaths, however, had changed everything; he had suffered too much, and Herzen and the others had no right to judge him.[117] These words cut Herzen deeply, and they also hurt Ogarev, implying that doubt was the luxury of those who had not suffered, that the two had experienced no comparable losses. Yet in fact, not only had they faced the deaths of people they were close to but they had embraced this pain, refusing to alleviate it by cultivating illusions. Ogarev put it as follows: "The need to take things as they truly are; we will bear grief as grief better through real love for truth than by inflating ourselves with fantasies. [. . .] This is the epoch of maturity in the individual. In history, it means that a person stands up on his own legs and looks for help neither in *l'inferno* nor in *il cielo*."[118] Ogarev and Herzen welcomed this pain as a product of their search for truth, commitment to reason, and love for humanity. Suffering was a form of love in its own right.[119] Doubt was an act of love, a voluntary sacrifice they made in the name of truth.

The argument over immortality flared up once more in the summer of 1846 in a conversation between Granovsky, Ogarev, and Herzen, bringing all of the elements of the 1844 debate back to the surface. Natalia Herzen summarized the essential points in her diary, sounding a great deal like Ogarev: "There is some need, thirst, to reveal truth in everything, however painful it may be, even if pieces of one's own body get torn off along with a false conviction."[120] Without explicitly naming Timofei and Elizaveta Granovsky, she described her former friends as childlike in their preference for "fairy tales" over truth: "It is difficult for them to give up their prejudices, like the belief in the afterlife. They willingly leave fetters on themselves, they block the road with them and cry over them and over themselves."[121] She, too, admitted that she had lost a great deal. Of everything she and her husband had once had, only Ogarev remained. "The religious epoch of our relations has ended, the youthful exaltation, fantastic faith, respect—it is all over!"[122]

The argument between Herzen and Granovsky is significant for two reasons. First, it shows how central doubt became to the self-perception of Herzen, his wife, and Ogarev in the mid-1840s. Like the Wisdom Lovers, they began by viewing doubt as a state of suspense that would lead the individual toward a better, purer faith, and like them, they understood that doubt could also lead to utter loss of faith and despair. They came to embrace doubt in this latter sense: it was a sacrifice they were prepared to make in behalf of humanity, and it constituted the only meaningful aspect of their lives. Second, the debate with Granovsky elucidates why disputes over matters of faith became a core part of the interactions of members of the intelligentsia. It was an act of resistance to triviality, a sign they were not, as Ogarev put it, sitting in "their own little kitchen and talk[ing] about their very own potato." Their interactions were significant because they were dedicated to the pursuit of truth. Bitterness and acrimony in their relations were only signs of their devotion to this higher cause.

The memory of the bitter dispute between Herzen and Granovsky did not remain confined to its participants, since Herzen went on to describe it in great detail in the first published installment of his memoirs, which appeared in 1855.[123] Nor did he keep to himself the lessons he had drawn. From 1845 to 1847, Herzen repeatedly commented on the individual's moral obligation to accept truth in articles he published in *Notes of the Fatherland* and the *Contemporary* (*Sovremennik*). Ideas were not there for an individual to pick and choose between: a person's thoughts had to be coherent. In the name of coherence—indeed of "science" itself—it was necessary to rid oneself of every idea and belief, no matter how dear, that "is not justified by reason." This was a test of courage: those who failed it would be condemned to "sniveling penitence" in light of their weakness and timidity.[124] These articles found an eager readership among Russian youths who came forward in the late 1850s and who would measure themselves and Herzen's generation against this standard.

The rejection of yearning for a better world "beyond" was but one manifestation of a broader loss of faith—in themselves, in the meaning of life, and in life itself. The Herzens and Ogarev spoke with increasing frequency of their lack of faith in anything. Truth was the only concept they still claimed to believe in. In the mid-1840s, debates among members of Herzen's circle came to include the question of the existence of God. Yet Herzen and Ogarev hesitated to declare disbelief in God, a position that remained taboo within the circle. This reticence became associated specifically with the nobility in the later 1840s.

Herzen made no secret of his doubts about life and its meaning. His friends, he wrote irritably, should stop asking him about the reasons for anything. "To seek a cause connotes a quest for meaning, reason, and believe me: there is no such thing."[125] It seems likely that his skepticism included a rejection of faith in God. Elizaveta Granovskaia implied that Herzen had indeed taken a stance on this matter in conversation in 1844. As she remarked in a letter to her husband, "I do not have the firm negation of God Herzen does."[126] Here, "firm negation of God" may have meant the denial of a providential God; alternatively, it may have meant the denial of the existence of God. One cannot be sure, because Herzen himself did not address the issue in his writings of this time.

Around the mid-1840s, conversations "about God" seem to have become common among Moscow's former idealists. One key participant in these debates was Vissarion Belinsky. Following Herzen, he had dropped his conservative Hegelianism and, like Herzen, he came to renounce faith as a self-indulgent means of comforting oneself.[127] His insistence on addressing this topic in conversation with friends became the subject of legends. Ivan Turgenev recalled their lengthy debates while Belinsky was already suffering from advanced tuberculosis. Turgenev's mind might wander to the subject of dinner, but Belinsky insisted on arguing beyond the point of physical exhaustion: "'We have not yet resolved the question of God's existence,' he once told me with bitter reproach, 'and you want to eat!'"[128]

Satin, too, participated in debates about God's existence and immortality, a required subject for conversation among those who viewed themselves as intellectuals. He wrote to Ogarev from Paris on March 3, 1845, to complain about a mutual friend, Nikolai Frolov, because he refused to engage these questions:

> It seems to me that [Frolov] has engrossed himself in the question of self-development too much and has become distracted from common interests, perhaps because he does not feel he has the right to judge them. But that's nonsense, Ogarev! We all have the right to it, we imbibed these interests with our mother's milk. They are ours. They are the interests of every moment of our life. . . . If we speak of God, of the immortality of the

soul and the social movement, then it is not in order to express our personal opinion or the strength of our dialectics, but simply because these questions touch the most intimate strings of our humanity. Why does Frolov say: "I am not concerned with these questions—I am a *student*"? That's untrue, Ogarev! As if it were possible in our time at our age to be a *student*?[129]

Yet it seems that these conversations were subject to highly specific and peculiar rules of engagement: for all their enthusiasm for debate, members of the circle were uncomfortable with categorical denials of the existence of God. They never went on record as having denied God's existence. There was only exception, Vasilii Botkin, and responses to his misstep confirm the rule. Botkin, an early member of the Stankevich circle, was the son of a wealthy tea merchant from Moscow and had befriended Ogarev and Satin in 1839. In 1845, he was in Paris, where he spent time with Satin and took part in the discussions about God and the immortality of the soul. Botkin, however, displayed too much zeal, and Satin was displeased with him. In his letter to Ogarev of March 3 (the same in which he attacked Frolov for the latter's unwillingness to engage in debates), Satin criticized Botkin for having taken things too far. Botkin had settled on the antithesis without waiting for the synthesis.

Shortly after Satin wrote to Ogarev, Botkin himself wrote to him, describing in dramatic terms the crisis of faith that had culminated in his coming to the conclusion that God does not exist: "The destruction of an entire, previous worldview, the complete, sincere negation of so-called God, the pathetic lot of the human being, subject to the arbitrariness of force and coincidence, the instability, or to be more precise, the disarray of the greater part of our previous moral and pseudomoral dictates—in a word, the complete *Untergang* of everything on which contemporary society is practically and theoretically established—gradually taking over spirit and mind, plunged them into chaos and dislodged them from their normal rut."[130] In writing this letter, Botkin seems to have been aware that its contents might cause offense. He was careful to note that the crisis had passed, though certain phrases in his letter made it clear that he still adhered to some of the conclusions he had reached, referring to God as "so-called" and commenting "thank God (or something else)." He also called for religion to be replaced by philosophy (specifically, Left Hegelianism) and demanded the creation of a new "social morality."[131]

This was the last such letter Botkin would write, however, and his friends neither admired nor imitated his radicalism. Ogarev's reaction to the letter was uncharacteristically judgmental. He wrote to Ketcher about it in a very condescending tone: Botkin was "going to extremes." Referring obliquely to Botkin's non-noble origins, he noted that, as an autodidact, Botkin could not help but be drawn to "empiricism."[132] It took Ogarev several more years to reach Botkin's level of radicalism. In 1848 he called for the "denial of everything mystical"—a phrase that implies the rejection of God's existence.[133] Even then, though, Ogarev did not affirm this specific point. Like Herzen, he confined himself to capacious declarations of unbelief.

In 1847, the year that Herzen was finally granted permission to travel abroad, the Herzens left Russia for the West, having found life in Moscow increasingly stifling. In a diary entry of 1844, Herzen observed the apparent purposelessness of his Moscow existence: "There, we have no real activity or vocation: to exhaust oneself in eternal lamentation, in concentrated sorrow, is not activity. What is there for me to do in Moscow? [. . .] Two or three close friends and a stupid, vile herd. When I look at the poor peasants the blood rushes to my heart. I am ashamed of my rights; I am ashamed that I am partly responsible for the misery of their life."[134] Most likely, he did not realize that with this trip he was leaving forever. After his father's death in 1846, and thanks to his large inheritance, however, there was little to draw him back.

Herzen arrived in western Europe just in time to witness the unrest of 1848 first hand in France and Italy. Writing home about the events that unfolded around him, he remarked that Europe was not in every way superior to Russia, as he had once believed. Indeed, the revolutions only served to buttress his disillusionment: there, too, the Christian moral system had become obsolete; there, too, hope was at an end.[135] Unable to return to Russia, Herzen would devote his life to commenting on events there from abroad. In the 1850s he settled in London with Ogarev, where they established the Free Russian Press, together with the *Bell* (*Kolokol*), a Russian-language newspaper in which they published all the information about the events—political and social—that censorship in Russia repressed. Once again, they could view themselves as servants of the truth, only now, instead of bringing to light the mysterious unity of nature and history, as they aspired to do in the 1830s, they sought to expose the corruption of the Russian state, the abuse of power by officials, and the mistreatment of peasants. In the early 1860s they were even moved to publish revolutionary tracts, some of which they wrote themselves.

In the twentieth century, Herzen and Ogarev would be commemorated as Russia's first socialists, precursors of the revolutionaries of 1917. Each phase in their lives would appear as a stepping stone to the revolutionary abyss. For Martin Malia, Herzen's intellectual development was a dialectical process: it began with a political event, the uprising of the Decembrists in 1826, then veered away from politics into the realm of ideas, specifically German idealism, and finally reached a higher synthesis in the "philosophy of action," which was political, at which point he became a socialist. The Hegelian turn of the early 1840s was, paradoxically, a "revolutionary" turn away from ideas. Herzen was seized by "exasperation with a life of pure speculation" and yearned "for 'deeds' in the real world—and not just action but political action.[136]

Herzen himself observed no such dichotomy between thoughts and deeds or ideas and politics.[137] In the history he wrote of the rise of "revolutionary ideas" in Russia between 1850 and 1851, he would recall the time of Decembrism as one in which revolutionaries were poets and poets were revolutionaries. Venevitinov was placed alongside Ryleev among the martyrs; he was a "youth, filled with the dreams and ideas of the year 1825." Ideas and their expression in poetry and literature were not a means of avoiding action but a form of action. They were real enough that poets would be "killed" for them, as Herzen claimed had been the fate of Venevitinov, Lermontov, Pushkin, and Belinsky (among others).[138]

This heroic view of Russia's intellectuals of the 1820s and 1830s soon conveyed itself to the generation of the 1850s and 1860s. Every student entering Moscow University, or, for that matter, the universities in St. Petersburg, Kharkov, Kiev, and Kazan in the 1840s and 1850s, would seek out a circle in which the eternal questions could be addressed and resolved. Friends would berate one another for their moral flaws and intellectual inconsistencies. Portraits of Herzen and Ogarev became contraband, traded along with copies of their works and seized by the police as evidence of youngsters' revolutionary disposition. To succeeding generations, however, the skeptical position that Herzen and Ogarev maintained began to seem untenable. Doubt, which had been a passing phase for the Wisdom Lovers, became a way of life for the Herzens and Ogarev. It was an activity, a medium through which individuals living under autocracy attempted to recover a sense of meaning for their lives. That meaning, however, failed to impress members of the next generation. They sought firm conclusions to those eternal questions, and God's nonexistence became a first principle.

Part 2

Atheism

3

Atheists of 1849

Katenev's Tobacco Store Circle and Petrashevsky's "Fridays"

One Thursday night in the spring of 1849, at the Golden Anchor tavern in St. Petersburg, a young man named Vasilii Katenev began arguing with another customer and "asserted that there is no God and that religion is invented." Pressed on this point, Katenev again "denied the existence of God" as well as the divinity of Jesus Christ.[1] Speeches of this kind were unheard of in St. Petersburg or anywhere else in Russia at this time, and Katenev's fellows at the tavern were shocked. They warned him several times that he should stop talking because he might be denounced to the police; blasphemy still constituted a crime in imperial Russia.[2] Indeed, an agent of the Ministry of the Interior was present and copied down his words verbatim.

Katenev was only nineteen years old when he made his speech at the Golden Anchor on Vasilievskii Island, a popular watering hole among students. The son of a wealthy merchant, he was registered as an auditor at St. Petersburg University, though he attended lectures infrequently. Katenev had two friends, Petr Shaposhnikov and Aleksei Tolstov, who shared his radical views. They belonged to the same burgeoning social category, the amorphous estate of urban inhabitants (*gorodskoe soslovie*), which itself comprised numerous legal subcategories: merchants, petty traders, artisans, and others. In the mid-nineteenth century, roughly 7 percent of all Russians belonged to this category.[3] Of the three, Shaposhnikov, twenty-eight, was the only one actively engaged in trade. The tobacco store he owned furnished their regular meeting place, and it was located on St. Petersburg Side, a neighborhood heavily inhabited by tradesmen. Tolstov, about twenty-three years old, was a registered student at the university. Tolstov had attracted the attention of the Ministry of the Interior well before Katenev made his speech in the Golden Anchor; as a police agent noted, his "thoughts are extremely free and his manners are wild as can be."[4]

The reign of Nicholas I was a period of marked economic growth, and as Russian industry expanded, so did the number of urban dwellers. Wealthy merchants had long resisted Westernization, but some now began to encourage their sons to attend secondary schools and university and to adopt Western manners of dress, to exchange their bowl-shaped haircuts, full beards, and long cloaks for top hats, a clean shave, and fashionable clothing. Yet sons of merchants and petty traders were met with unease at gymnasia and universities, which they entered in rising numbers. The 1840s were a period of growth at these institutions: enrollments at universities doubled in less than one decade. Nicholas I and his minister of education, Sergei Uvarov, however, were fearful of the consequences. Not only would these young men compete with the nobility for civil service positions, but education itself might exert a corrupting influence on them, introducing an element of instability into Russian society and politics. New measures restricting nonnoble access to gymnasia and universities were instituted in the 1840s, though the administration refrained from banning merchants' sons entirely: practical considerations prevailed.[5] Once they had graduated, Westernized merchants' sons entered the world as social outsiders. They were greeted with suspicion by fellow members of merchant society—these young "gentlemen" were criticized for rising above their station and embracing Western ideas of dubious moral value. When they entered the bureaucracy, they garnered little respect among noble officials.[6] The literary elite, too, regarded them as outsiders who sought upward mobility through education.[7]

All the while, merchants, their sons, and other urban dwellers became the subject of increasing literary attention in the 1840s. Merchants entered the stage as characters in plays by Alexander Ostrovsky. Writers of the "natural school" also painted sentimental portraits of humbler figures: organ grinders, yard keepers, cabdrivers, low-ranking civil servants, and their despairing wives. They were portrayed as vulnerable but gritty survivors attempting to eke out an existence in the imperial capital.[8] Fedor Dostoevsky best captured the humility, resignation, desperation, and vengefulness of St. Petersburg's lowly inhabitants, who oscillated

Petr Shaposhnikov. Photograph, undated. In Vasilii I.
Semevskii, "Petrashevtsy: Studenty Tolstov i G. P.
Danilevskii, meshchanin P. G. Shaposhnikov, literator
Katenev i B. I. Utin. (S portretom Shaposhnikova),"
Golos minuvshago, no. 11 (1916): 21. (Pushkinskii Dom.)

between an attitude of abject humiliation and pride. Whether drunken
reprobates or saints, they were uniformly demeaned in public by their
social superiors. Returning to their hovels to nurse their wounds, they
comforted and abused one another, cursed their fate, and awaited a better
turn of fortune.

Katenev, Shaposhnikov, and Tolstov belonged to the world that the
natural school described, but they were not content to see themselves
as props in someone else's drama. Shaposhnikov liked to venture south
across the Neva River to the theater, but he also dreamed of becoming
an actor and a playwright.[9] Katenev nursed hopes of becoming a novelist.[10] He and Tolstov spoke of founding a journal. Yet all three knew that
they were unwelcome in the society of St. Petersburg's literary elite.
Shaposhnikov, a mere tradesman, would never dream of entering the
home of a nobleman. Katenev and Tolstov, better educated and more

cultured than he, were acquainted with members of the nobility, yet their origins barred them from the salons and literary gatherings that their friends attended. Instead of cultivating a veneer of polish that might, eventually, have allowed them to climb into that world, they displayed their indifference to high society by breaking its rules. Simultaneously, their radical speech marked their rejection of the society of merchants and petty tradesmen from which they had emerged.

The three became the first Russians on record to have said that God does not exist, Russia's first known circle of atheists. Their speech marked a rupture in the Russian intellectual tradition. By the 1840s, religious doubt had come to be seen as a core part of the spiritual life of men and women who regarded themselves as belonging to the intellectual elite. Friday evening gatherings hosted by Mikhail Petrashevsky are a case in point. These events were attended by writers, students, officials, and military officers, all members of the nobility. Many of them harbored sympathy for socialism, and a few disbelieved in the existence of God. God was even discussed at evening gatherings, yet none would come forward during the Friday meetings to deny his existence. Some attendees feared—and rightly so—that their speech could lead them to be denounced to the police. Yet, as this chapter shows, worries about breaking social codes were more important in determining their silence than fear of reprisal by the state. Atheist speech was still unacceptable to members of the nobility. Katenev, Shaposhnikov, and Tolstov, by contrast, did not let such niceties stand in their way. They possessed one atheistic tract by Friedrich Feuerbach, the brother of Ludwig Feuerbach, and by advertising its contents, they could prove that they were not beholden to the laws of Russian society and state.

In 1849, as Katenev and his friends gathered at Shaposhnikov's tobacco store, St. Petersburg was covered with secret agents working for the Ministry of Internal Affairs and the Third Section of His Majesty's Own Chancellery. The revolutions of 1848 had set Emperor Nicholas I on guard against the possibility of rebellion at home. In his first public announcement about events abroad, the manifesto of March 14, 1849, Nicholas proclaimed that France, Germany, Italy, and Hungary had all been taken over by one and the same force: a "wave" of "chaos" and "anarchy" that spread in the same measure as did "insolence" and "madness" among those populations. God would save "our holy Russia," and every Russian subject should join the emperor in exclaiming that "God is with us! Understand this, oh nations, and submit, for God is with us!"[11]

To Nicholas I, the revolutions of 1848 were not only a political problem, but also a religious problem, created in liberal states whose leaders had failed to look after the piety and morality of their populations. Prelates of the Russian Orthodox Church confirmed the view that the rebellions had been caused by impiety. Archbishop Innokentii (Borisov) of Kherson and Tauria attributed the spread of this "storm" to the "temptations of the false, foreign philosophy." In a sermon that was reprinted in all major Russian newspapers, he urged the Orthodox faithful not to succumb to "tempting spirits," evil seducers who had penetrated Russia from abroad.[12] Archimandrite Ignatii (Brianchaninov) of the Trinity St. Sergius Monastery blamed the revolutions on "rationalism"; it dominated educated Europeans, and it would stop at nothing until the reign of Antichrist was at hand. "Teachers of lies" were "flooding" the world with falsehoods.[13] Metropolitan Filaret (Drozdov) of Moscow also warned of "tempters," whose *right hand is a hand of falsehood.*" These evildoers "reeducated" people, using flattery to lead them first into "pleasant vanities, then immodest ones, then alluring ones, then openly sinful ones, and finally seditious and destructive ones," ending in anarchy and "a flood of evil."[14] The flood metaphor, which Nicholas I, too, had used in his manifesto, comes from Psalm 144:7–8: "Deliver me out of great waters, from the hand of strange children; whose mouth speaketh vanity, and their right hand is a hand of falsehood."[15]

In responding to the threat of atheism, prelates of the Orthodox Church could draw on sermons by their predecessors dating back to the 1770s. In the reign of Catherine the Great, sermons delivered at court often commented on the dangers of false enlightenment. "Atheism," and "unbelief," far from being serious philosophical viewpoints, represented nothing but folly and vanity. Archbishop Georgii (Konisskii) of Belorussia and Metropolitan Platon (Levshin) of Moscow devoted numerous sermons to the topic and explained unbelief in several different ways. It took hold when individuals trusted their own capacities of reason unduly and were too vain to see the error of their ways.[16] They also described unbelief as the consequence of sin: people who feared damnation attempted to reassure themselves by rejecting faith in the afterlife and in God. Depravity could also be a consequence of unbelief, however, because people who had despaired of salvation had no reason to restrain themselves.[17]

From the 1790s, sermons had painted the consequences of atheism in increasingly lurid colors. For example, Anastasii (Bratanovskii), valued by Catherine II for his rhetorical skills, represented the unbeliever as a "demonic standard-bearer" and a "living corpse." "The essence of his actions are clear, and they are blasphemy, trampling on faith and doctrine, lack of submission to God, parents and authorities, adultery, debauchery, greed, enmity, jealousy, murder, drunkenness, disregard for future Divine judgment, carelessness, despair, suicide, and so on. The devil, that enemy of God and man from time immemorial, forms these colors."[18] Suicide was often featured as a consequence of unbelief, because the individual who despaired of faith in salvation was said to have no reason left to live. Further, such people found that their ability to cope with adversity was compromised, increasing the likelihood of suicide as well as of alcoholism.[19]

These characterizations found their way into the secular literature of the nineteenth century. The tempter appeared as a stock figure in novels by Faddei Bulgarin and Mikhail Zagoskin (neither of whom were favorably disposed toward the "natural school") in the 1830s and 1840s. The hero of such novels is a naive young man who has arrived in the city and is just beginning to explore worldly pleasures when he meets the agent of his downfall. Seizing on his weakened morals, the tempter encourages his dissipation, urging him to drink, gamble, and risk amorous adventures. Having compromised his victim's moral judgment, he then sets about destroying his faith in God by ridiculing religion and then leads him into a state of utter despair. Zagoskin called him a "demon of our time."[20]

The image of the tempter, articulated by Orthodox clergymen and developed by novelists, helped shape the response of Nicholas I and senior officials to the revolutions of 1848. Ever since the French Revolution, statesmen had imaged that international conspirators were attempting to spread sedition in Russia. By temperament, however, Nicholas I was unusually suspicious. The ideology of pious paternalism he stood for further encouraged officials to look for the enemy in the shape of a tempter, one who fomented disobedience and spread disbelief and immorality among the youth. Ivan Liprandi, the official at the Ministry of the Interior who investigated Petrashevsky and the merchants voiced such ideas in his summary and explanation of the investigation: "I saw how immaturity and impurity of morals were the main culprits in the disturbances that arose in 1848 in France and Germany. There, similar boys, so to speak, directed by the main leaders from behind the scenes, poisoned almost the entire population with their journal articles, speeches and generally with periodical literature, and they aroused the scoundrels to anarchy."[21]

Because Nicholas I was certain that revolutionaries abroad had already organized their agents in Russia, his officials were under pressure to find a plot. The three who most needed to satisfy him were Count Lev Perovskii, minister of the interior, Leontii Dubel't, director of the Third Section, and Dubel't's superior, Count Aleksei Orlov. Each knew that the success of his career hinged on building a case that would lead to many arrests. The more spectacular the charges, the more likely they were to convince the tsar. The Petrashevsky case provided Perovskii and his protégé, Liprandi, with a valuable opportunity for self-advancement.[22] At the height of an investigation that had begun eleven months earlier, Liprandi employed three undercover agents to spy on what he believed was a group conspiring to overthrow the government. One agent, Petr Antonelli, a twenty-three-year-old student at St. Petersburg University, was assigned in January 1849 to ingratiate himself with Mikhail Petrashevsky, a nobleman and low-ranking official at the Ministry of Foreign Affairs, whom Liprandi regarded as the ringleader of the conspiracy. Two other agents were assigned to track Aleksei Tolstov, Vasilii Katenev, and Petr Shaposhnikov. Social boundaries were well policed even in their policing. The rank of the agents was matched to the rank of their subjects: both were merchants. One was Vasilii Shaposhnikov (no relation to Petr), and the other was Nikolai Naumov, an old friend of Katenev's. All three agents provided Liprandi with almost daily reports for roughly two months from March to April 1849. These agents helped convince Liprandi that a dangerous plot was, indeed, being hatched. This conviction, in turn, reinforced the importance he attached to the atheistic speech of the merchants.

At the end of April, when the investigation was complete, it was handed over to the Third Section, which arrested thirty-six people on charges of revolutionary conspiracy. In addition to the young merchants, those arrested included Petrashevsky and the men who had attended his "Fridays." Several military officers and officials, especially from the Ministry of Foreign Affairs, as well as journalists, teachers, writers, and students were incarcerated. All were held in solitary confinement in the St. Peter and Paul Fortress. As the investigation proceeded, a total of 122 people were called into the offices of the Third Section for questioning, from Petrashevsky's doorman to the madam of a brothel that Katenev once visited. No physical torture was used during the interrogations of prisoners, and their testimonies were largely accurate, cohering with one another and with the agents' prior reports.[23]

The stress of imprisonment did, however, take its toll on the prisoners. Katenev suffered more than most. According to a prison doctor, he became immobilized by "a dulling of mental abilities and mental vigor, he is quiet and responds unsatisfactorily to questions, does not show any desires, displeasures, or boredom, stands in one place for days on end and mechanically smoothes his clothing." On August 30, 1849, he was removed, screaming, from the fortress and taken to an insane asylum where he died seven years later.[24] But for his collapse, he would have been among the twenty-one people condemned to be executed by firing squad, a sentence that was commuted in each case to hard labor in Siberia.

Nicholas I and his officials were not alone in their Orthodox Christian understanding of the atheistic and antimonarchical sentiments they discovered among the townsmen. Katenev and his fellows were not troubled by the doubt that preoccupied their noble forbears and contemporaries—their questioning of their ability to access the divine and uncertainty about the existence of a higher meaning in the world. The young commoners struck a tone of defiant confidence when they avowed that God did not exist. Yet their statements showed that they remained deeply concerned, even distraught, about the moral implications of their attack on God. It was one thing to deny God's existence and quite another to separate oneself from preconceptions about atheism that were deeply ingrained in Russian society.

Documents stemming from the investigation and trial reveal that in the year prior to their arrest, Katenev and Shaposhnikov made verbal statements denying the existence of God on numerous occasions. Their radical, antireligious speech was accompanied by radical political statements. They were excited by the events in Europe that had been set off by demonstrations in Paris, where barricades were built and a republic was proclaimed in February 1848.

While crowds were rioting across western and central Europe, Russia remained quiet. Educated society responded only by stepping into St. Petersburg's coffeehouses to read about the latest developments in Russian, French, and German newspapers. Though they were fascinated by the spectacle of upheaval, most members of educated society condemned events abroad as lurid proof of the evils of socialism and liberalism. To some few, however, the upheaval focused attention on the dramatic differences between the freedoms accorded individuals in western Europe and the authoritarian rigidity of the Russian state, which appeared to have succeeded in bringing history to a standstill.[25]

One month after the revolutions broke out, the state intervened to stem the flow of information. On March 26, 1848, editors of Russian periodicals were advised that they could publish news from only one source: German state newspapers, with translations approved by censors in advance.[26]

Katenev and his friends found the events in France, Italy, and Germany electrifying, and with respect to them, the censors' intervention came too late. They refused to believe that these momentous events would pass Russia by altogether. In the spring or summer of 1848, Katenev had a "Republican costume" tailor made to imitate representatives of the French provisional government.[27] He dreamed of creating a republic at home, as did Shaposhnikov and Tolstov. The young merchants exchanged suggestions as to where in the city they could erect barricades.[28] They also pictured themselves and one another as great orators. So clearly did Katenev envisage this role for himself that he invented a story, which he told the agent Naumov, about having made a stirring political speech to some cabmen in Rzhevskii tavern.[29] His friends also testified that he bragged about making a similar speech at a brothel on Sadovaia Street.[30] Katenev imagined nobler vistas, however, describing to Naumov how they would address crowds on Senate Square, next to the Bronze Horseman. "People will listen to us and we will become rich," he promised.[31]

Katenev and his fellows were motivated not just by the glamour of revolution that emanated from abroad, however, but by a passionate and visceral hatred of Nicholas I. They hated him because he demanded both punctilious displays of subordination and popular reverence. According to Richard Wortman, the "scenario of power" that Nicholas I and his officials promoted was that of the monarch as "epitome of the nation." Nicholas was not only to be recognized as emperor but "worshipped" by the Russian people, and that worship was enacted by cheering crowds at his public appearances.[32] Katenev recalled that he had been present on one such occasion in 1843, when he was thirteen. Nicholas had driven past in a carriage, and Katenev had been enraged by the acclamations the emperor received from crowds on the street. At that moment, Katenev said, he "swore on his soul that he would avenge him for it, and take things so far that he, Katenev, too would [be greeted by people] shouting, 'hurrah.'"[33] In the summer of 1848, Katenev staged a miniature confrontation with the emperor, attending a public flogging in his "Republican costume" so that he could stare Nicholas down.[34] Tolstov made a similar gesture. He and a friend went to the theater one evening when the tsar was in attendance and fixed Nicholas with their lorgnettes: if the emperor squirmed in his seat, they told themselves, it meant that he felt "guilty." Nicholas did indeed begin to squirm, and on the basis of that squirm, Tolstov claimed that "the Emperor fears us, and fears us because he feels he is wrong and his conscience is killing him."[35]

By challenging the emperor in these small ways, Katenev and Tolstov were engaging in a scenario of their own: one according to which they, lowly commoners, became bold rebels, capable of standing up to the tsar. By refusing to worship him, they accrued power, undermining the emperor's aura as epitome of the nation. Their violent rhetoric further damaged the sanctity of the tsar. Inspired by the riots in Paris and Vienna, Shaposhnikov and Katenev exchanged a rhyme about the tsar's corpse dangling from a lamp post.[36]

Denials of the existence of God by Katenev and his fellows were the functional equivalent of their verbal attacks on the tsar. Both stemmed from antiauthoritarian impulses. These young townsmen sought to prove that they recognized neither the physical power nor the religious, moral and legal influence of God and the tsar over themselves. God became their target because he was the highest conceivable figure of authority in Russia; as God was the highest authority, he must be challenged in the most radical way possible.

There is no record of how the young men of the tobacco store came to embrace atheism. Katenev, Shaposhnikov, and Tolstov destroyed all of their private papers in anticipation of their arrest (to be precise, Petr Shaposhnikov, who had taken them for safekeeping, burned them).[37] It is known, however, that they owned a handwritten Russian translation of an atheistic tract by Friedrich Feuerbach titled "Man or Christ? To Be or Not to Be? The Religion of the Future" ("Chelovek ili Khristos? Byt' ili ne byt'? Religiia budushchnosti").[38] The German original was one of several short pamphlets written by Friedrich Feuerbach. He wrote *The Religion of the Future* (1843–45) to make his brother Ludwig's ideas accessible to a broader audience. It was perfect for someone like Petr Shaposhnikov, the tobacco store owner, who possessed no formal education.

The merchants' copy of the book opened with the assertion that human beings are completely independent, owing nothing to a "Higher Being." Their salvation depends entirely on themselves. In the past, humanity had invented God and had sacrificed itself to him. People believed they must seek to become like God, but God was a supernatural being, whereas humans were made of flesh. In order to become like God, they attempted to deny their own, earthly nature, a denial that was tantamount to self-annihilation. They must now recognize that reason and human instinct are the only true basis for action, and humanity's natural instinct is to strive for happiness (*Glückseligkeitstrieb*). Humans do not need any instruction from a higher being on this score; they understand and must continue to learn how best to provide for themselves.[39] Commenting on his brother Friedrich's philosophical thought, Ludwig Feuerbach would call this principle "Selbsttätigkeit," literally "action by oneself," or independent and self-motivated action.[40] *The Religion of the Future* was, therefore, a declaration of independence from God, an assertion of human self-sufficiency and "action by oneself."

The merchants, especially Katenev, were extremely enthusiastic about *The Religion of the Future*. Three separate copies of the translated manuscript turned up in their possession when they were arrested. In all likelihood, Tolstov first received the translation from Alexander Khanykov, an acquaintance at St. Petersburg University. He then gave a copy to Shaposhnikov, who lent it to Katenev, who wrote out another copy and gave that to Naumov to "study." Katenev also gave a copy to another friend of his, and when his friend complained that the handwriting was bad, Katenev offered to read it aloud to him. Yet another copy turned up in the possession of Boris Utin, one of Tolstov's friends.[41]

Another work that Petr Shaposhnikov owned was a printed Russian translation of Voltaire's "Poem on Natural Law" ("Poème sur la loi naturelle," 1752). He lent it to one of the police agents and encouraged him to read it.[42] The poem is not atheistic. On the contrary, Voltaire, a deist, repeatedly speaks of a God who created the world and whose will guides the operation of nature. Yet the poem does place great emphasis on human self-sufficiency, and this may explain why Shaposhnikov found it appealing. Humans have been endowed with the capacity to reason in order to understand God and God's will without recourse to church dogma or scripture.[43]

In western Europe, both deism and atheism were very well established by the time Friedrich Feuerbach's tract fell into the merchants' hands. When exactly they first emerged has been the subject of some controversy. Lucien Febvre argued in *The Problem of Unbelief in the Sixteenth Century* (1942) that "unbelief" (defined, broadly, as the rejection of Christian faith) remained "unthinkable" in Europe until certain "mental tools" had been established, tools that were necessary for unbelief to become "viable and fruitful." Among them was a philosophical vocabulary, including the words "absolute" and "relative," "complex" and "adequate." A scientific vocabulary was no less lacking; the modern conception of truth, falsehood, and probability still needed to be established. Modern unbelief, Febvre argued, was predicated on all of these; it did not and could not exist until the seventeenth or eighteenth century.[44]

The Russian case indicates, however, that availability of words and scientific thought were neither necessary nor sufficient to produce atheism. Voltaire's deistic writings circulated broadly in the late eighteenth century; small numbers of enlightenment-era atheistic tracts were also imported. Historians of atheism, most of whom were Soviet, assumed that these tracts would leave their imprint precisely among the population that commanded the right vocabulary—among the great writers and thinkers. These historians did not know what to make of the first men who did publicly deny the existence of God, because the words were spoken in an idiom that thoroughly lacked philosophical sophistication, one in which reasoning was swallowed into half-sentences. As a result, Soviet historians of atheism did not include the merchants in their histories.[45] The problem was not that the evidence was inaccessible.[46] Rather, these merchants did not meet historians' preconceptions of how an atheist should speak and behave.

Katenev, Tolstov, and Shaposhnikov were literate, but they were uncouth, and they were far from erudite. Their reasons for adopting atheism had little to do with sophisticated argumentation and convincing logical proof. Petr Shaposhnikov, for one, probably did not know the meaning of the words "absolute" and "relative." Tolstov and Katenev were better educated than he, but their concerns were roughly the same. These centered on a single pedestrian problem: authority. They wished to cancel out the power of a being who demanded their obedience and was—ostensibly—capable of directing their fate. The supposition that their atheism was motivated by the problem of authority is confirmed by documentary evidence of their conversations.

Petr Shaposhnikov and Vasilii Katenev were most eager to proclaim God's nonexistence. They made atheistic statements on numerous occasions, and they did not confine their words to private conversations. A fairly large number of men frequented Shaposhnikov's tobacco store and joined them on jaunts to local taverns. They included Tolstov, Shaposhnikov's employee Vasilii Vostrov (twenty years old), who boarded at Shaposhnikov's house; Vasilii Pronin (twenty-one) and Aleksei

Mazurin (nineteen), both merchants; and two architects, Larion Shein (thirty) and Alexander Tverskoi (twenty-nine).[47] These men became witnesses to numerous radical speeches, sometimes participating in conversations, sometimes just listening.

Often these talks took place over drink, a fact that some of the merchants would emphasize in their testimonies to the authorities. Vasilii Pronin, for example, testified that at one gathering in the tobacco store, the guests were "not themselves" and that Mazurin "pronounced the words that we have no God" ("U nas netu Boga") and made critical remarks against the state as well.[48] When Mazurin was asked about this event by the interrogators, he answered, "Shaposhnikov truly did say all of this; I was, to my shame, so intoxicated by the punch that I became nauseated, and I remember having said: yes, yes, yes, but I call upon God as my witness that I did it unconsciously."[49] Under questioning, Shaposhnikov, too, represented his and Katenev's atheistic speeches as accidents, uttered in the heat of the moment: "I do not know anything, other than a vexation, expressed godlessly for a minute while drunk."[50] This plea does not seem to have convinced the investigative committee, however. Indeed, Shaposhnikov and Katenev made too many such statements for the excuse of drunkenness to be convincing.

Alexander Tverskoi testified that Katenev denied the existence of God "repeatedly" in his presence. The architect also alleged that Katenev had once said that "there is no God, and man lacks the mind to understand and sympathize with everything that is beautiful."[51] Vasilii Pronin remembered that once, on their way into a tavern together, Katenev and Petr Shaposhnikov had exclaimed in unison that "for them there is no God, but only the universe" (dlia nikh net Boga, a odna vselennaia).[52] Aleksei Mazurin claimed that "Shaposhnikov brazenly opined about God."[53] Under interrogation, Katenev and Shaposhnikov admitted to having made "blasphemous" comments.[54]

These recorded statements are obviously too short to yield much insight into the intellectual content of the speakers' atheism. Two statements, however, do offer some basis for analysis. Andrei Glagolev, a local merchant who was not a regular member of the group, testified that while he was alone with Shaposhnikov, the latter had said, "God does not exist, or is not at all [sic], and if a person does anything, then it is according to his reason" (Boga ne sushchestvuet, ili vovse net, a esli chelovek chto i delaet, to po svoemu razumu).[55] This clearly was an assertion of independence from God: people are capable of self-directed action, which is not limited by the existence of God.

The most complete recorded atheistic speech, however, was the one Katenev made on April 12, 1849, in the Golden Anchor tavern. Naumov reported:

> [T]here was a heated argument between Katenev and some sitting strangers. Katenev asserted that there is no God and that religion is invented and proved this by the Athenian republic, which flourished without faith, not holding to any religion. One of the strangers objected that God created the earth and can destroy it if ever he wishes. Katenev, contradicting him, denied the existence of God and said that it is not in His power to destroy the earth, and that even if this should happen, it would be from a collision with a comet; that instead of the Son of God, there was an intelligent man who, having learned from the Chaldeans, worked a variety of wonders just like Mohamed and others; that in this sense, I too am [a] god, said Katenev. The stranger remarked that Katenev was taking too great a responsibility upon himself.[56]

That Katenev actually said these things cannot be doubted: rumors about it immediately began to circulate in St. Petersburg; three accounts of his speech were included in testimonies by arrestees, and they all tally with Naumov's report.[57]

Two points may be extrapolated from Katenev's speech. The first is the assertion of God's powerlessness: nature is impervious to divine intervention. Katenev affirmed this when he asserted that "the Athenian republic flourished without faith." Human societies can function and flourish despite their unwillingness to worship God, who cannot intervene to punish them for their unbelief. Katenev affirmed God's impotence even more directly when he declared that "it is not in [God's] power to destroy the earth, and that even if this should happen, it would be from a collision with a comet." Natural events are produced by natural phenomena, and there is no God who can intervene in these processes. Even the appearance of Christ on earth was not an act of divine intervention; Christ was "simply an intelligent man."

The second point follows directly from this claim. In the world as Katenev wanted to see it, intelligence was all that mattered. By virtue of his intelligence, Katenev was the equal of any man, including the one who had been proclaimed God. This point is expressed more clearly in another witness's account of his speech in the Golden Anchor. According to that person, Katenev said that "Jesus Christ was simply a teacher, which he, Katenev, could also be."[58] According to yet another witness (albeit one who heard the story at third hand), Katenev claimed that he could easily have worked the same kind of magic tricks as Jesus Christ had he been alive at that time.[59] In all renditions, his speech was slightly bizarre, but in each, the essence was the same: Katenev did not want to let God or Christ stand above him. If Jesus Christ could be a god, so could he.

To Katenev and Shaposhnikov, their atheistic speeches were themselves proof of God's powerlessness. Katenev's interlocutor in the Golden Anchor tavern evidently believed in a God who would punish youths like Katenev for flaunting their infidelity. God could destroy them, just as he could destroy the earth. Denying the existence of God so openly was a direct challenge to a wrathful God, and it was also a gesture that proved Katenev was not afraid. By the same token, it was proof that Katenev was not afraid of the authorities. Several of the people present in the tavern, including the agent Naumov, warned Katenev that he should be silent, yet he brushed them off, telling them that "it was nothing."[60]

The atheism of the men from the tobacco store centered on the problem of authority in two closely connected ways. It was a denial of God's right or ability to set laws for human behavior, and it was an assertion of the rights and ability of "intelligent men" to think and act as they saw fit.

The lowly social status accorded to these townsmen fed their radicalism and increased their willingness to make antireligious statements. Katenev, Shaposhnikov, and Tolstov wished to join the ranks of a company in which there was no place for them. Educated society in St. Petersburg remained strictly hierarchical, and friendship between men of merchant and noble rank was exceptional. Tolstov had some noble acquaintances, however, including Petrashevsky. He sometimes dropped by Petrashevsky's house on Bolshaia Sadovaia Street at the southern end of St. Petersburg, and he must have told Petrashevsky about Katenev and Shaposhnikov, for Petrashevsky visited the tobacco store two or three times, curious to see them.[61] Yet there was never any question of inviting Katenev and Shaposhnikov to Petrashevsky's home, and none of the three was ever invited to the gatherings that Petrashevsky hosted at his house on Friday evenings; they were not *salonfähig*, not presentable.

Usually, Katenev and Tolstov met Shaposhnikov at his tobacco store on Bolshoi Prospect, St. Petersburg Side, north of the Neva River, where they were joined by other men of merchant rank. To those merchants, most of whom were ill educated, the things that Shaposhnikov, Tolstov, and Katenev said were complex and sometimes incomprehensible, but they were nevertheless impressive. These were "learned conversations," as more than one witness put it.[62] The tract by Friedrich Feuerbach, which Shaposhnikov, Katenev, and Tolstov eagerly displayed and distributed, was proof that they were indeed learned, indicating their familiarity with the latest intellectual developments in western Europe. The tract served them as a status symbol.

Atheistic speech could perform the same function. Katenev, Shaposhnikov, and Tolstov had no exceptional qualities other than their boldness, which allowed them to give verbal expression to ideas that others were unwilling to put into words. By verbalizing views that the noblemen of their generation were hesitant to express, the merchants showed that they were not only the equals of other members of the educated elites but in some sense above them. On one occasion when Shaposhnikov (possibly seconded by Mazurin) denied the existence of God, he prefaced his remarks with the statement that his "level of understanding is higher than that of others." He went on to say: "We have no God; the *muzhiks* are all illiterate, beasts," implying that faith in God was a sign of lack of education. He added that "we ought not to live as we do now; we are all equal and should all rule; instead of paying respect to everyone."[63] Atheistic thought melded into a political program, a statement of dissatisfaction with the merchant's lowly social status, powerlessness, and demand that he obey others higher up the social ladder. Shaposhnikov's speech allegedly drew applause from Vasilii Pronin, who shouted, "Bravo! That's right!"[64]

In his testimony to interrogators, Tolstov presented Shaposhnikov's radical speech as a gesture by which the tobacco store owner could prove that he was indeed well educated: "If Shaposhnikov said something liberal, then it was merely out of vanity, the desire to show off his intelligence. He, Tolstov, is almost certain that Shaposhnikov had not been a liberal until they became acquainted, but in Tolstov's presence he spoke freely only so as not to appear ignorant."[65] Shaposhnikov, Katenev, and Tolstov even engaged in competitions to prove who among them was most intelligent and most radical. Katenev told Shaposhnikov to his face that he was a "stupid, sixteenth-century *slavianshchina*," unworthy of living in the same era as the rest of them. Behind his back, Katenev also remarked that Shaposhnikov was "half insane."[66] Meanwhile, Shaposhnikov explained to one of the undercover agents that of the whole group, he alone had the intelligence and "genius" enough to plan a successful uprising.[67]

All three wanted to see themselves as leaders, and they told others that they had power over large groups. Petr Shaposhnikov, for example, bragged about his influence over "important people" to Vasilii Shaposhnikov: "Yes! evil people, lions and tigers come to me, but having seen me—rub up against my legs and then do what I need."[68] Tolstov told Naumov that he belonged to a five-hundred-member group spreading propaganda throughout Russia.[69] Soon thereafter, Katenev boasted to Naumov that he led a club of Lamartinists who met off Nevskii Prospect on Friday evenings.[70] This was empty bragging, but it was a form of posturing that allowed him to "show his daring," as Katenev explained under interrogation.[71]

The competition to prove who was most daring and most powerful led Shaposhnikov, Tolstov, and Katenev to threaten physical violence against one another. Petr Shaposhnikov is alleged to have told Naumov on one or two occasions that he would murder Katenev and Tolstov. "Petr will destroy those scoundrels, but he will save you if you just listen to him."[72] In a moment of anger, Katenev likewise told Naumov that he would poison and stab Shaposhnikov and Tolstov.[73] Such specific threats were matched by statements of a general eagerness to shed blood. According to Naumov, Vostrov said he would "kill with pleasure," without specifying whom.[74] Similarly, Katenev told Naumov that he was desperate for blood: "I thirst for blood [. . .], and I thirst to such a degree that I am prepared to go into a barber's to see two cups of blood; in this frame of mind I even challenged myself to assassinate the emperor and proclaimed my challenge in the shop of Petr Grigor'ev [Shaposhnikov] in front of him and Tolstov, who laughed at me."[75]

Katenev, Tolstov, and Shaposhnikov were uninhibited in their speech. To them, intelligence was not a matter of displaying one's erudition and command of philosophical reasoning so as to impress one's interlocutor. Rather intelligence was measured by the radicalism of the spoken word, and it was important for the speaker to show that he was unafraid of his interlocutor. Radical speech, the merchants believed, entitled them to power. They had read about radicals in western Europe who acquired power by making speeches, and they would do the same. It did not matter to them that in St. Petersburg their behavior might make a bad impression on others, who would condemn them as immoral. Shaposhnikov, Katenev, and Tolstov had no rejoinder to such a claim; indeed, they readily admitted that their behavior was immoral.

The merchants operated within an Orthodox Christian worldview that equated atheism with depravity. Any Russian who explicitly denied the existence of God in the 1840s would necessarily be assessed as morally degenerate. Because no one had yet stepped forward to articulate disbelief in the existence of God, however, there was also no one to prove that one could lead a good life in the absence of faith in God. On the contrary, Katenev and his friends seemed, by their outrageous behavior, to enact the direst of predictions about the consequences of atheism that circulated so widely in Russian society. Petr Shaposhnikov expressed his self-loathing to his friend, Vostrov. He said he was revolted by conversations he had with Katenev and Tolstov and that he burned a notebook of his own writings, commenting that it was "frightful."[76]

Drunkenness, one of the vices that Anastasii (Bratanovskii) had warned against, was prevalent in the group. The merchants were partial to punch and Madeira, and they were often intoxicated. Katenev drank heavily, and some of Shaposhnikov's associates were known even to their own friends as alcoholics.[77] Alexander Tverskoi was frequently referred to as "the drunken architect Alexander Mikhailovich" and Larion Shein as "an unfortunate, wretched drunkard."[78] Tverskoi and Shein were, according to the testimony of Shaposhnikov's landlord, sometimes drunk even before they got to Shaposhnikov's place, as were some of his other guests, such as Pronin and Vostrov.[79]

Despair, another sin against which Orthodox clergymen had warned, was also displayed by members of the group. The merchants sometimes admitted that they were disgusted by their own words and behavior. Katenev told Naumov, "I sense that in all my life I have done nothing good, but strived toward evil deeds; my father, mother and whole family repudiate me. I feel death approaching, which cannot occur in any other way than through the gallows or the axe. It is distressing to look at our surroundings."[80] In statements about himself to other people, Katenev intentionally cultivated the image of a "fallen man." This stands out especially clearly in his conversations with Grigorii Danilevskii, a student from the nobility whom he had befriended at a konditerskaia (coffeehouse and pastry shop) in December 1848 and who shared Katenev's dream of becoming a writer. Danilevskii had not known that Katenev came from a merchant family when they first met, yet Katenev soon began both to emphasize his connections with members of Russia's lower orders. Danilevskii testified that Katenev told him, "Shortly before the time I met you, I led the very lowest of lives in the company of one woman [. . .] and I even went to such places where only the wish to get to know the way of life of the lower class could lead me, namely to simple eating houses."[81] This allusion to knowledge about the lower orders may have been a standard one in this period, but Katenev added to it a nuance of his own moral baseness.[82]

In the weeks before his arrest, Katenev began to speak of death and suicide. Yet again, his speech conformed to the image of the atheist promoted by Orthodox clergymen. Not only did he tell Naumov that he expected to be hanged or beheaded but he also talked of suicide in the wake of his speech in the Golden Anchor. When he heard that rumors about the incident were circulating around St. Petersburg, he worried that he had been denounced to Leontii Dubel't, director of the Third Section.[83] Katenev told Naumov that he planned to commit suicide in Dubel't's office in case he was called in: "Kotenev [sic] also told me that he is taking the two best pistols from Ivan Vasil'ev and ordered him to prepare several bullets and a pound of powder, which the latter, indeed, promised to provide him soon. When I asked him, what is it all for? Kotenev answered: 'so that the pistols will always be ready, and when they send a paper from Dubel't for me, then I will appear before him with the pistols and if they arrest me, then instead of an answer, I will kill myself.'—'Look here,' Kotenev continued, 'if I disappear for three days or so, then you tell all [our] acquaintances that I killed myself at Dubel't's.'"[84] He spoke about acquiring a weapon on another occasion as well.[85] Katenev's bad relations with his parents, his despair and suicidal statements, and his drinking all accorded with the stereotype of the atheist that had been promoted by clergymen of the Russian Orthodox Church as well as in novels by Bulgarin and Zagoskin.

Under arrest, Katenev, Shaposhnikov, and Tolstov were encouraged not only to confess their crimes but also to explain how it was that their intellectual development had taken this turn. The narratives they produced drew heavily on Orthodox Christian assumptions about the origins and consequences of unbelief. Katenev, for example, attempted to manipulate the tempter theory to his benefit, explaining that his morals had been weakened by sin, which led to blasphemy, and from there to further sin. In this condition, he had succumbed to the influence of a tempter, Petr Shaposhnikov, who utterly destroyed his faith: "Katenev confessed to blasphemy, explaining that he, Katenev, possessing neither fundamental principles nor convictions, led a debauched life. He did not recognize the Christian religion and became even more debauched and immoral from the company of the tradesman, Petr Shaposhnikov. Turning him, Katenev, away from the Christian religion,

[Shaposhnikov] gave him the moral law by Voltaire and a manuscript notebook titled "The Religion of the Future" to read. He, Katenev, copied [the notebook] out and gave it to Naumov to read."[86] Apparently, Katenev was not aware that in his testimony he cast himself in the roles of both victim *and* tempter (passing on the books he received from Shaposhnikov to Naumov).

Tolstov produced a similar narrative for the police, but he did so to much greater effect, because he was pardoned as result of his confession and avowals of regret.[87] He informed his interrogators that, a few years before he met Shaposhnikov and Katenev, around 1845, he had experienced a crisis of faith, connected to what one would now call an existential crisis. Questions about the meaning of life, Providence, and creation led him to despair: "Why do I live? What awaits me? Is there a future? Is life worth the effort? If there is a God, then where is his mercy? To create a person and force him to suffer. If he is not, why torture oneself, is suicide not better?" At this point in the narrative, Tolstov drew on literature to illustrate his point, though without naming his sources. Paraphrasing Pechorin in Lermontov's *Hero of Our Time* (1840), he noted that his was "not the kind of despair which people cure with the barrel of a pistol" but "was a cold, impotent despair."[88] He then continued in his own words, "I started to drink and drank brutally." He also noted a change in his emotional life, quoting Pushkin and Lermontov, "At first I was embittered, then I became sullen."[89] He crowned all this with a further literary reference: "My fellows jokingly called me Hamlet." Tolstov made no effort to smooth over the sinfulness of this phase of his life, describing it as marked by loss of innocence and a slide toward criminality. Eventually, he claimed, he regained faith, even if this was not the end of his struggle with unbelief.[90] Tolstov had effectively composed a bildungsroman for the investigators, one that was not only dramatic but recognizable as a narrative of sin and penitence.

In their testimonies, Katenev, Shaposhnikov, and Tolstov all played up the Christian image of the unbeliever as desperate and depraved while expressing regret for their falls. Katenev and Shaposhnikov clearly did not just adopt this narrative strategy for the benefit of the investigators. Prior to their arrests, it seemed as if they had wanted to act out the faithful Christian's worst nightmare. For seventy years, prelates of the Church had disseminated an image of the unbeliever as one who denied the authority of his parents and social superiors and who would stop at nothing to sow discord in society. That image had served to discourage educated Russians from claiming atheism as a legitimate proposition.

In 1848 it evidently began to lose its efficacy as a deterrent, even as it continued to define social preconceptions of what it meant to be an atheist. Indeed, for Katenev and his friends, the stereotype of the atheist as speeding toward destruction had acquired an allure that church prelates could not have anticipated. Ill repute, however, could do little to damage Katenev and Shaposhnikov's chances of social advancement. In this regard, they had nothing to lose: the elite society of educated people to which they might have liked to belong would not have accepted them in any case.

In December 1849 the state issued a brief report of the investigation and its verdict, condemning twenty-one men to death. This report represented Shaposhnikov and Katenev as part of a wider conspiracy, led by Mikhail Petrashevsky, to overthrow the state and institute anarchy. Petrashevsky, they claimed, had invited young men to his home on a regular basis for the purpose of inciting them to violence, and "blasphemy" had been one of his chief "weapons."[91] The regular gatherings referred to in this report did take place. They were Petrashevsky's "Fridays"; he began hosting them in 1845, and they were usually attended by ten or twenty men. The setting produced a very different tenor of conversation than the one observed at the tobacco store and Golden Anchor tavern. There is no evidence that anyone ever denied God's existence at Petrashevsky's assemblies.[92] Indeed, the testimonies gathered by investigators show that defending atheism was taboo. These statements reinforce the thesis that educated members of the nobility were not yet ready to countenance atheism in the 1840s. By insisting that atheism had been promoted at the meetings (thus contradicting their own evidence), officials showed how important it was to them to represent atheism as an integral part of political opposition.

Almost all the guests who attended Petrashevsky's Fridays were in their late twenties and early thirties, almost all were members of the nobility, and almost all held university degrees. Most of them were at the beginning of their careers; their incomes were modest, and some still depended on financial help from their parents.[93] They viewed the Fridays as an opportunity to exchange political gossip, to complain about the corruption and ineptitude of state functionaries, and to exchange opinions on the necessity of political and social reform. They also shared with Petrashevsky an enthusiasm for the writings of the French socialists. This was not the strident, atheistic socialism of Karl Marx, who did not gain adherents in Russia until the 1870s, but the quasi-Christian socialism of Charles Fourier. The spirit that guided Petrashevsky's guests was, according to Nicholas V. Riasanovsky, one of "naïve optimism." In the early part of the nineteenth century, Fourier had observed the gross inequalities that recent economic developments had brought about and argued for the creation of a society in which all human needs, material and emotional, could be fulfilled. More equal access to education, sustenance, and labor was called for, he claimed. It should be noted that Fourier was no atheist. By working toward "the rehabilitation of men," he claimed to be "completing" the work of Jesus Christ.[94]

As Fourierists, most of Petrashevsky's guests regarded a program of political and social reform as fully compatible with religious faith, and Fourier's system as essentially religious.[95] They were prepared to countenance criticism of the Russian Orthodox Church insofar as it promoted subordination to the political and social status quo. Yet calling into question the divinity of Christ or the existence of God does not appear to have been acceptable to them. If the term "atheism" was ever used in general company on a Friday night, it would only have been put forward as an intellectual possibility, though not one that anyone was planning on adopting.[96] Petrashevsky appears to have found the tone of these conversations insufficiently radical, especially when it came to religion. He himself probably did not believe in God and solicited lectures on religion from two regular guests, apparently hoping that they would speak in a critical spirit. Both lectures were unsuccessful.

Petrashevsky turned first to his old classmate from the Alexander Lyceum, Nikolai Speshnev.[97] A wealthy and mysteriously taciturn twenty-eight-year-old, Speshnev was usually reserved at Petrashevsky's Fridays. He sometimes implied that he held radical ideas about religion and society but generally kept his associates guessing as to what they were. When asked to comment on Speshnev's views in detail under interrogation, his fellows found themselves unable to do so.[98] Most likely this was because Speshnev was a master of equivocation. In letters he sent to the Polish writer Edmund Chojecki, for example, Speshnev described the contemporary debate in western Europe over the compatibility of atheism and Christianity with socialism. Speshnev himself, however, took no position. Atheism was a stance that one *could* take and that could serve socially progressive causes. Yet he also noted that one could be Christian while maintaining equally progressive social views.[99]

In the winter of 1847, Speshnev promised that he would lecture on the relationship between religion and society "from the point of view of the communists."[100] This was to be a bold and daring speech, judging by a manuscript that the police found when they arrested Speshnev, which included an explicit denial of the existence of God. It also called for revolutionary violence: "As long as our poor Russia has existed, there has only been one possible means of communication—verbal. [. . .] Since we are left with nothing but the spoken word, I intend to use it without any shame or conscience, without any disgrace, to disseminate socialism, atheism, terrorism, everything, everything good in this world, and I advise you [to do] the same."[101] When it came time to make his speech, however, shame and conscience got the better of Speshnev. Witnesses testified that Speshnev had skirted around the issue of religion and talked about metaphysics in terms that were incomprehensible.[102] Under interrogation, Speshnev told the police that he had chosen to speak neither about philosophy nor about religion, because he "consider[ed] these questions to be somewhat delicate" and that it was "generally not [. . .] entirely decent to make speeches in the society of practical strangers."[103] The lecture appears to have been unsuccessful, not because it sparked too much controversy but because Speshnev lost courage even before he began to speak.

Next, Petrashevsky invited Felix Tol, a regular guest at the Fridays, to deliver a lecture on religion and its origins.[104] Aged twenty-six, Tol was a teacher of Russian literature at St. Petersburg's Main Engineering School and was one of the few nonnoble guests to attend Petrashevsky's Fridays. The lecture he gave on March 11, 1849, was a blend of anthropology and religious history and drew heavily on the ideas of Ludwig Feuerbach.[105] Tol claimed in his testimony under arrest that he had toned the lecture down considerably because he was "afraid" of how his words might influence his audience.[106] In his lecture Tol *implied* that the major world religions, including Christianity, were an invention, and that their value was to be determined by the uses to which their inventors put them.[107]

The lecture provoked enormous controversy and was received very differently by different listeners. Antonelli claimed that it was titled "On the Uselessness of Religion with Regard to Society" ("O nenadobnosti religii v sotsial'nom smysle"). Its central point, he asserted, was that the creators of organized religions acted out of self-interest (*iz vidov*) rather than faith. Further, religion did not improve human morals, because it relied on fear, not personal conviction, to coerce people into behaving well.[108] Other witnesses understood the speech as an analysis of religion rather than a criticism. Alexander Maderskii noted that Tol had spoken of religion but that his comments had no pertinence to Christianity.[109] Those who did confess that the lectures had an antireligious component emphasized that they had argued with Tol. Pavel Filippov claimed to have contradicted him, asserting that the founders of religions were believers.[110] Tol's assertion that fear lay at the root of religious feeling sparked the most controversy. Several members of the audience were committed to the view that love, enthusiasm, and respect had been the emotional sources of religion.[111] Finally, others in the audience denied that the lecture contained any antireligious or anti-Christian implications. They were offended by the suggestion that they could have listened to an antireligious lecture impassively. Alexander Balasoglo insisted under interrogation that the "expressions attributed to Tol" (by which he seems to have meant Antonelli's claim that the speech was about the "uselessness of religion") were "slander." Had any speakers attempted to claim that religion was unnecessary in his presence, he, Balasoglo, would certainly have challenged them.[112] Whatever their interpretation of Tol's lecture, however, it seems that no one endorsed it. Subsequently, Tol was condemned to death precisely for having given this speech.[113] In this way, Petrashevsky's guests showed they were not receptive to anti-Christian thought and were not particularly tolerant of anti-Christian speech. They reacted negatively to Tol's lecture, while Speshnev and Petrashevsky himself did not dare give lectures on the subject in the first place.

Vissarion Belinsky's letter to Gogol, which Fedor Dostoevsky read aloud at the gathering on Friday, April 15, 1849, by contrast, prompted a very favorable response. Belinsky corresponded with Gogol in the summer of 1847 regarding Gogol's controversial and extremely conservative *Selected Passages from Correspondence with Friends* (1847). There Gogol sought, among other things, to justify the institution of serfdom by claiming that noble landholders had a duty to God to protect the morality of their peasants. Belinsky attacked Gogol for celebrating the "gloom of autocracy, Orthodoxy, and the pseudofolk style." Though his famous letter has widely been taken as a testimony of his atheism, it fell far short of any such definitive statement.[114] Arguing with Gogol, Belinsky denied that the Orthodox Church had anything to do with Christianity, or at least, with the teachings of Christ. Instead, Belinsky insisted that true love of Christ could only mean sympathy for the suffering of others and thus the condemnation of serfdom.[115] By all accounts,

Dostoevsky's reading was greeted with great enthusiasm. One witness testified that the audience had been especially pleased by the passage in which Belinsky disputed the piety of the Russian people.[116] Criticism of the church, then, was acceptable and even welcome, though denying the existence of God was not. Belinsky's letter took on a status similar to that of *The Religion of the Future* among the men in the tobacco store: countless copies were made, and Dostoevsky read it out on numerous occasions.[117]

Certainly, Petrashevsky's Friday evening gatherings promoted views that were hostile to Nicholas I and his doctrine of "Orthodoxy, Autocracy, and Nationality." Yet the view that they were being used to promote atheism can in no way be supported by the conversations and debates that took place at the gatherings. The guests were evidently receptive to socialist views, particularly a quasi-Christian socialism, but not to the critique of religion as such.

Despite this lack of evidence, Liprandi persisted in promoting the view that Petrashevsky was a corrupter of youth, and he succeeded in convincing his superiors that this was true. Much of his case rested on evidence that he was able to gather about Petrashevsky's activities outside of the Friday evening gatherings, and here he found ample material. The case that Liprandi built not only serves to explain how officials could be convinced that Petrashevsky represented a threat to the state but also why his fellow noblemen would be hesitant to participate in conversations that were explicitly atheistic.

Petrashevsky came to the attention of the Ministry of the Interior in 1845. Only in 1848, when Ivan Liprandi was appointed to investigate him, however, did the state make significant headway in gathering evidence against him. Among this evidence were reports about Petrashevsky's earliest days as a pupil at Russia's most prestigious school, the Alexander Lyceum at Tsarskoe Selo, which he attended in the 1830s. At that time, the school was under the directorship of General Fedor Gol'tgoer, who imposed a regime of unusually harsh discipline.[118] Petrashevsky soon became noted for his disobedience. By the time he graduated, he was on record as a "freethinker."[119] Indeed, Petrashevsky himself claimed that the conflict with Gol'tgoer had contributed substantially to his rebelliousness: anger and resentment led him to read forbidden books and associate with "scoundrels" at his school.[120]

Petrashevsky also drew unfavorable attention from the authorities while studying law at St. Petersburg University in 1840–41. He grew a beard and cultivated a "free" manner of speaking. Indeed, the opinions he expressed were so radical that fellow students began to avoid him, mistaking him for an agent provocateur. As a result, it was alleged, he began to talk in a more circumspect manner to fellow students.[121] He also began lending out foreign literature to them and soon amassed a substantial library of foreign books, including books by French socialists as well as French philosophes and German Left Hegelians.[122] Then, in 1844, it came to light that Petrashevsky had invited three boys from the Alexander Lyceum to his quarters and encouraged them to criticize Christianity and the social order. In the report concerning this incident, Petrashevsky's status as the schoolboys' "tempter" was duly noted: "It turned out that they had been inveigled into associating [with Petrashevsky] by the vainglorious fragrance of new ideas, which Mr. Petrashevsky used to entice their minds." Officials from the school took the matter quite seriously: two boys were expelled, the third was flogged and subsequently died, and the school's headmaster even attempted to have Petrashevsky banished from St. Petersburg.[123]

After his arrest in 1849, further damning evidence about Petrashevsky as a "tempter" came to light. Two men testified that he had approached them individually, trying to turn each away from religion: Alexander Maderskii, a well-educated young man of lowly social origins who boarded at Petrashevsky's house, and Konstantin Timkovskii, a pious young official who had attended the Friday evening gatherings a handful of times.[124] A freed serf who boarded at Petrashevsky's house between 1843 and 1845 also told the agents in 1849 that Petrashevsky and other boarders (about four men) sometimes used to "laugh at religion" and said they did not "recognize God."[125]

Not only did many of Petrashevsky's acquaintances testify against him; some even expressed extreme contempt. Nikolai Grigor'ev, a regular guest at the Fridays, spoke of Petrashevsky in terms that verged on hatred. He referred to him as a "teacher and corrupter" (*uchitel' i razvratitel'*). Grigor'ev had found Petrashevsky repulsive at their first meeting, and his worst fears had been confirmed: "That accursed man corrupted and ruined all these wonderful young people; they were his pupils, and I was theirs."[126] During the trial, various rumors about his behavior also entered the record. According to one of these tales, dating to the mid-1840s, he had once entered Kazan Cathedral wearing a dress and stood among the women until he was noticed by a police officer.[127] Dostoevsky noted under interrogation that Petrashevsky's reputation was bad without entirely endorsing that condemnation himself: "Lots of people talk about his eccentricities and strangeness—almost everyone who knows or has heard of Petrashevsky—and they even draw their conclusions about him based on them. I heard the opinion expressed several times that Petrashevsky has more wit than judgment."[128]

Petrashevsky thought of himself as someone who was indifferent to public opinion. In private notes that the police seized on arresting him, he observed that the voice of "social opinion" should not be confused with "the voice of truth" or "the voice of God." It was, in fact, the "voice of falsehood," or error (*zabluzhdeniia*).[129] He wrote that he had only contempt for people who sacrificed their commitment to social reform out of fear that it might tarnish their reputation.[130] Still, the condemnation of others appears to have pained Petrashevsky well before his arrest:

> There is nothing more dangerous and even fatal than to express an opinion that is not compatible with social [opinion], [nothing more dangerous] than a brave, open, noble rebellion against the terrible hydra of bias, prejudice, and superstition—sanctified, deified through the longevity with which these have been inculcated by the ignorant majority of society, . . . and a bitter fate is often the lot of the man who, like the preachers in the first centuries of Christianity, is so bold as to convince righteous heathens of the worthlessness of the objects they worship, who is so bold as to call their idols idols rather than gods, [. . .] and he, like the disciples of the true Christ, [. . .] will be accused of preaching godlessness, he will be publicly cursed as an atheist and will be imprisoned as Antichrist, joining the throng of holy people . . .[131]

Petrashevsky had ridiculed Christ on some occasions. Here, however, his feelings of personal rejection prompted him to compare himself with Christ.[132]

Even for a rebel like Petrashevsky, condemnation appears to have been difficult to bear. Under interrogation, he tried to justify himself to the police in various ways. He attempted in June 1849 to compose a narrative of sin and penitence of the kind Tolstov wrote (though he cannot have known of Tolstov's testimony). In this deposition, he described the crisis of faith he had endured in 1840 or 1841, explaining that it had been prompted by the realization that there was no higher "wisdom" in the world than natural law (thereby implying—but not explicitly saying—that he lost faith in God). This had led him to recognize the "insignificance of my person in the face of nature," and he ceased to believe in freedom of the will, which he called a "proud dream." During that time, he said, he became indifferent to life and became obsessed with the idea of committing suicide: "For three months in a row, a loaded pistol lay by my side. [. . .] For three months, I settled the question for myself."[133] This statement was as close as Petrashevsky ever came to identifying himself as an atheist.

The pain of rejection only became stronger in prison, as Petrashevsky faced not only the agent Antonelli's denunciations but also those of his erstwhile associates. The strain led to a mental breakdown around July 1. His testimony on that day shows that he felt he had been terribly betrayed by Timkovskii and others who accused him of undermining their faith and by the trial committee, which was, he said, subjecting him to a "moral trial." His testimony on this day ran to numerous pages, in which he compared himself to Socrates, who "sacrificed himself" (by drinking hemlock); declared the entire trial to be a witch hunt; admitted that he had lied to the investigative committee about having attended confession and communion two years earlier; proclaimed that all of his testimonies had been false; and announced that he was committing "juridical suicide" because he had "lost the right to exist."[134] Petrashevsky's breakdown was surely a natural response to two months spent in prison, most of which were passed in solitary confinement and under extreme psychological stress. His disturbing testimony engrossed those officials who read it. Some saw it as just another manifestation of his impertinent audacity. Dubel't, the director of the Third Section, however, wanted to show it to the tsar, perhaps because it so eloquently illustrated preconceptions about the disturbed mentality of an atheist.[135]

Petrashevsky's testimony may further be used to illustrate something altogether different: the very real danger involved in expressing antireligious thought in imperial Russia. This was perilous not only in the sense that the speaker could be denounced to the authorities at any time—even years after the event—but also on a more intimate level, because of the humiliating moral condemnation and contempt that the speaker might encounter in the persons he confided in.

Humiliation was a prominent theme in Russian literature of the 1840s, including in the fiction of Fedor Dostoevsky, who often attended Petrashevsky's Fridays and was one of the men condemned to death in 1849, largely for having read Belinsky's letter to Gogol. The death sentence was commuted to hard labor in Siberia. During the 1840s, Dostoevsky was an acute observer of the manner in which Russia's hierarchies influenced the mental and spiritual condition of the many people living in St. Petersburg, especially its petty functionaries, and he was particularly interested in the problem of humiliation. On his release from exile, he published *Notes from the House of the Dead* (1860–61), in which he described a pattern of moral self-destruction to which many prisoners were prone: "It is as if, having once overstepped a line that was sacred to him, he is already admiring the fact that there is nothing sacred left to him; it is as if he is being urged to overstep any kind of lawfulness and authority and to take pleasure in his unbridled and limitless freedom, to revel in that sinking of the heart that comes from horror, which he cannot but feel toward himself." A wounded sense of dignity, Dostoevsky argued, could be caused by some sort of injury or insult, though it might also be the result of undignified misbehavior. Once he sensed freedom in that misdeed, the humiliated individual was on a slippery slope. He might feel a kind of ecstasy in inflicting further indignity and humiliation on himself.[136] Dostoevsky's theory helps to explain Petrashevsky's self-destructive prison testimony as self-inflicted humiliation by someone who had already been thoroughly humiliated. The theory can also be applied to Katenev, Tolstov, and Shaposhnikov: these townsmen, offended by their own social insignificance, had been driven by the need to show that they were, indeed, "low," which led them to flaunt their worst character traits. Having once overstepped a line that was sacred to them, they admired the fact that there was nothing sacred left to them and yet were at the same time horrified by it. Their professions of atheism, drinking, whoring, self-reproach, recrimination of others, and threats of violence and suicide were all part of the same process of self-gratifying self-destruction.

The year 1849 represented a turning point in Russian intellectual history. It was at this time that young people first stepped forward to articulate the idea that God does not exist. Born into the estate of merchants and petty traders, they broke from its ranks by embracing Western education and radical Western ideas to assert their place in Russian intellectual life. Their words were made possible by the availability of education through gymnasia and universities to people from outside the nobility, the promise of participating in a new literary culture, and the model of public speech provided by revolutionary events abroad. They directed their brazen speech not only at fellow townsmen, but at a state that, having opened educational institutions to them, resented their presence and at noble intellectuals who gazed at them with fascination but refused to recognize them as equals.

The merchants understood that the extremity of the views they verbalized was their only claim to significance. Petr Shaposhnikov expressed his thoughts on the matter this way to the agent Vasilii

Shaposhnikov: "Look here, my friend. In every person, there is a strength [*sila*], and that strength signifies various attributes of the soul. For example, in all of Pushkin's works, you can see the soul of someone who is good, who loves all that is beautiful and tender, and so on. Yet in Nikolai [*sic*] Pugachev, there is also a force of soul, but it is expressed in deeds: to hang, to kill, to destroy everything beautiful."[137] Shaposhnikov believed that he, too, had a "force of soul" and that it lay in his willingness to speak. It was the radical nature of his speech that brought him attention: first from the students Katenev and Tolstov, who regularly visited his tobacco store, then from the nobleman Petrashevsky, and finally from the tsar himself.

Katenev, Shaposhnikov, and Tolstov could afford to be daring because they were unwilling to settle for the modest prospects that their social status afforded them. Shaposhnikov must have realized that no one would let him enter the stage as an actor or playwright: he was too poorly educated.[138] Katenev and Tolstov were sufficiently well integrated into the Westernized world of the elites to reject the possibility of becoming merchants; they found their access to the literary world was limited, however, and they had no ambitions to pursue a government career. By contrast, Petrashevsky, Speshnev, and Tol were not so free; their dependence on reputation seems to have kept them from expressing atheistic views.

The state did its best to prevent the attitudes of Shaposhnikov and Katenev from spreading to other sectors of Russian society. Together with Petrashevsky and his associates, they were placed in solitary confinement in the St. Peter and Paul Fortress and tried by a military tribunal, guaranteeing that their depositions would remain secret. Most educated Russians learned only that they had uttered blasphemies and that their fate was one to be avoided. There were rumors, however, that spread among young people in St. Petersburg. Nikolai Chernyshevsky, the son of a priest, who had come to St. Petersburg to study, must have heard about the merchants through his classmate Alexander Khanykov, who was a friend of Aleksei Tolstov and an acquaintance of Petrashevsky. It was partly under Khanykov's influence that Chernyshevsky came to embrace atheism. This step was facilitated by the fact that atheism was no longer uncharted territory in Russian society. The townsmen had shifted the idea that God does not exist from the unspeakable to the spoken.

When Chernyshevsky became a journalist in the second half of the 1850s, he would seek to undercut the negative moral associations that accompanied atheism by constructing a new, non-Christian system of ethics. In this task, he was joined by Nikolai Dobroliubov, a fellow priest's son. Commoners, like the merchants, would explicitly repudiate the "noble skepticism" of the generations that preceded them. As journalists, Chernyshevsky and Dobroliubov set themselves a further goal: to discredit autocracy as an institution and prove that it was up to the intelligentsia to define the future development of the nation. To them, atheism was no longer a form of depravity but a necessary first step for any member of the intelligentsia who wished to save the country from historical insignificance. As the next three chapters demonstrate, however, young people in the 1850s and 1860s remained heavily influenced by Orthodox Christian patterns of thinking, which shaped their assumptions about what it meant for an educated person to play an active role in Russian society.

4

Atheism as the Predicate for Salvation
Nikolai Chernyshevsky and Nikolai Dobroliubov

I n the late 1850s and early 1860s, two priests' sons, Nikolai Chernyshevsky and Nikolai Dobroliubov, became Russia's two most influential
journalists. They were also the first to claim in print that God does not
exist. Belief in an omnipotent, infinitely merciful being harms people,
they argued, by lulling them into a state of torpor and passivity. Censorship prevented them from declaring "there is no God," as the St. Petersburg merchants had done to their peril only a few years earlier. Yet
when Chernyshevsky expounded on the ill effects of faith in an "imaginary humanlike being" who controls the natural world and described a
fantasy world in which all human needs would be met, his readers
knew exactly what he had in mind.[1]

The clergy into which Chernyshevsky and Dobroliubov were born
was a closed estate in Russia, and sons of clergymen who entered the
secular world encountered many of the same difficulties as the merchants' sons. Divorced from their own community, they were, at best,
treated with polite condescension by noble members of the literary
world into which they sought entry. Chernyshevsky and Dobroliubov
discovered this firsthand when they began to write for the *Contemporary*.
This journal had long been an important cultural institution in Russia.
Founded by Alexander Pushkin in the 1830s, it had attracted the literary
critic Vissarion Belinsky and Alexander Herzen in the 1840s, along with

such influential writers as Lev Tolstoy and Ivan Turgenev. The *Contemporary* had stood for a liberal politics in the 1840s and early 1850s. In the late 1850s and early 1860s, Chernyshevsky and Dobroliubov transformed it into a radical organ, edging out established contributors. Their articles were read with tremendous enthusiasm by a young audience that included students at Russia's schools, seminaries, and universities. Chernyshevsky and Dobroliubov turned first to literary criticism to attack the ideology of autocracy and the norms of what they regarded as an unjust society. Literary critics, they wrote, must become the mouthpiece of society, expressing its dreams and aspirations.

The view Chernyshevsky and Dobroliubov articulated, namely that the well-being of the country rested in the hands of educated society, not the state, and that it was the moral duty of every educated Russian to direct the country toward a better future, was the ethos of the intelligentsia, and it was only after their crucial intervention that the word came into widespread use. Aspects of this ethos had been elaborated by earlier generations, beginning in the 1820s, when the Wisdom Lovers made it their task to create a readership capable of literary and philosophical judgment. Yet Chernyshevsky and Dobroliubov went much further. They not only encouraged independent judgment—literary, social, and political—but also provoked enormous controversy by asserting that educated society would not assume its responsibility until it had renounced faith in God. To their young acolytes, this proposition became an article of faith.

Nikolai Chernyshevsky and Nikolai Dobroliubov both renounced faith in God at a young age, in their late teens or early twenties, and both experienced this renunciation as a grave spiritual crisis. Chernyshevsky, born in 1828, was the son of an archpriest from Saratov. Dobroliubov, eight years younger, was born in Nizhnii Novgorod in 1836, and he, too, was the son of a priest. Though each had his particular reasons for rejecting religious belief, they shared one common motivation: both wished to overcome their past. They did not want to deny their origins as priests' sons but rather to prove to themselves that they could determine their own intellectual development as adults without being limited by their early education.

As priests' sons, Chernyshevsky and Dobroliubov received extensive training in theology. Orthodox Christian patterns of thinking would leave a lasting mark on both and manifested themselves in their writings long after they had rejected faith in God. Yet the pair never emphasized their close familiarity with Russian Orthodox theology, and, unlike advocates of atheism in the west, they never explicitly entered into debates with theologians in the many articles they wrote. Though they were Russia's first journalists qualified to carry out such debates in print, they evidently felt that theology was not the platform on which they wished to do battle with God.

The clergy comprised roughly one percent of the total population of European Russia in the mid-nineteenth century. Governed by its own proud ethos, this estate had its own hierarchies, in which priests stood firmly above deacons and sacristans. It also possessed its own educational institutions, reserved for the sons of clergymen. Seminaries were largely the domain of sons of priests, and the most talented among them were designated for Russia's theological academies, which were intended to produce prelates for the Orthodox Church, as well as teachers for its seminaries.[2]

As sons of well-educated priests, both Chernyshevsky and Dobroliubov received the best education available at a seminary. Russian Orthodox theology rapidly developed during the first half of the nineteenth century, and Russian seminaries were reformed in an effort to improve the quality of education.[3] Chernyshevsky and Dobroliubov were instructed in Latin and Greek, biblical history, holy writ, biblical hermeneutics, dogmatic theology, Orthodox Church history, and the history of liturgy, and they passed these courses with the highest marks.[4]

Study at a theological academy, however, held little appeal for either Chernyshevsky or Dobroliubov. Chernyshevsky felt that only St. Petersburg University could do justice to his abilities: he had excelled not only in theology, Greek, and Latin but also in history and mathematics at the seminary in Saratov. He had also studied enough French and German to pass the entrance exams to the Historical-Philological Faculty at St. Petersburg University, where he enrolled with his parents' blessing in 1846. Dobroliubov, too, dreamed of studying at that university and was devastated when his father denied his request. His parents, who could not afford to pay for his studies without a stipend, wanted him to enroll at a theological academy instead, yet Dobroliubov was convinced that such an education would doom him to a life of insignificance. As he confided to his diary: "You are fated to pass through life unnoticed, and upon your first effort to pull yourself out of the crowd, circumstances crush you, like a worthless worm . . . and you shall do nothing, you shall be incapable of doing anything, regardless of all your self-confidence, and this has reminded me of Lermontov's bitter poem: Don't believe, don't believe in yourself, young dreamer! [*Ne ver', ne ver' sebe, mechtatel' molodoi!*]"[5] Unpersuaded, his parents sent him to St. Petersburg to take the entrance exams for the Theological Academy, but on arriving in the capital in 1853, he enrolled at the St. Petersburg Main Pedagogical Institute instead.

The St. Petersburg Main Pedagogical Institute welcomed priests' sons with open arms, offering full tuition, unlike many other educational institutions, which denied them entrance. The institute aimed to produce future teachers, men who would exhibit the highest possible morals, to whom the schoolchildren of tomorrow could safely be entrusted. The pious sons of clergymen were considered perfect recruits. To protect their morals, a tight disciplinary regime was established under the directorship of Ivan Davydov, who, in the view of some students, was excessively given to professions of piety and love for the tsar.[6] Students were obliged to attend early morning and evening prayers, and staff kept a close watch to ensure that they did not leave the building and even monitored conversations in the refectory. The curriculum included lessons in catechism, dogmatic theology, "practical" or moral theology, biblical history, and the history of the church.[7] The obligatory nature of these lessons, combined with the generally oppressive regime at the school, may have diminished their appeal in students' eyes.

Students at St. Petersburg University were accorded far greater freedom, but they, too, were obliged to attend lectures in theology. These lectures do not appear to have been of a very high quality, for the university evidently experienced difficulties in locating suitable instructors. Theologians were trained in the academies, run by the Orthodox Church and exclusive to sons of clergymen. Professor Andrei Raikovskii, a graduate of the St. Petersburg Theological Academy, delivered them in the 1840s in a style that was said to have been "dry" and "cold" and in a manner that "did not accord with the high level of university studies."[8] Chernyshevsky must have attended these lectures, yet he never commented on them in his diaries. Subsequently, when his works were attacked by theologians employed at Russian universities and spiritual academies, he would declare that he did not consider them worthy intellectual adversaries.[9]

University professors in Russia in the 1840s and 1850s evidently failed to convey the sense to students that theology was a vibrant and developing discipline. This situation may be contrasted with the status of theology at universities in western Europe, where it still held prestige as the queen of the sciences in the middle of the nineteenth century.

Many of the Left Hegelians, including David Friedrich Strauss, Ludwig Feuerbach, Bruno Bauer, and Max Stirner, had studied theology alongside philosophy at the University of Berlin and the University of Bonn. They hoped for university careers, using the pulpit to transform theology as a discipline by reconciling theological and philosophical reasoning. Strauss's *Life of Jesus* (1835–36), which marked the opening salvo of the Left Hegelian movement, was a work of careful biblical exegesis in two densely researched volumes. Strauss had set out to salvage the true, historical figure of Christ amid the mythic elements in the Gospels, but instead he demonstrated that this task was unrealizable: Christ was a mythic figure. Around 1840, Ludwig Feuerbach and other Left Hegelians went one step further, denying the existence of God and pronouncing themselves atheists. *The Essence of Christianity* (1841) was the most influential of these works. Feuerbach did not dismiss theology but turned it into a weapon in his attempts to undermine religious faith in his readers. Theology remained an obsession for other Left Hegelians, too. As Arnold Ruge wrote of Bruno Bauer, "He negates theology in its entirety, he hates the theologian as such; he persecutes them dreadfully, but he does so with the fanaticism of theology."[10]

The same could not be said of Chernyshevsky and Dobroliubov. Thanks to their clerical background, Chernyshevsky and Dobroliubov possessed the requisite skills to fully understand and reproduce the Left Hegelians' methods and lines of argumentation in an Orthodox context, but they declined. Documentary evidence shows that Chernyshevsky read Feuerbach and Strauss during the religious crisis that led to his loss of faith from 1849 to 1853. Dobroliubov is known to have read Feuerbach's works in 1855 or 1857, shortly after his loss of faith. Yet Feuerbach's influence appears rudimentary in articles the duo wrote for the *Contemporary* in the second half of the 1850s and the early 1860s. They were prepared to repeat certain key ideas, such as the view that God is a product of the human imagination, without entering into the philosophical and theological arguments that Feuerbach adduced to prove his claims.

Apparently, Chernyshevsky and Dobroliubov viewed their theological training as a burden, as a body of knowledge that had been inculcated in them without their consent. At the time they reached adulthood, they self-consciously set out to overcome what they thought of as intellectual limitations placed on them by this legacy. The contours of their loss of faith are worth recounting in detail because of the tremendous influence these two men would exert in Russia during the second half of the nineteenth century and more particularly because they applied lessons drawn from their own experiences to the Russian reading public as a whole.

Chernyshevsky's religious crisis, which began one day in November 1848 when he was accosted by another student while putting on his coat in the cloakroom at St. Petersburg University, was motivated by his fear that the religious beliefs with which he had been raised were holding back his intellectual development. The student who accosted him, Alexander Khanykov, was an acquaintance of Aleksei Tolstov and had visited Petr Shaposhnikov's tobacco store two or three times. A member of the nobility, he was also a regular guest at Petrashevsky's Fridays. In November 1848 he approached Chernyshevsky in the hopes of making a new convert to Fourierism. He spoke at length and with enormous enthusiasm, overwhelming the latter with his zealousness. As Chernyshevsky remarked, Khanykov's words testified to his "fervid, passionate conviction of the truth, and his faith that it must be spread, that every person who recognizes it must become its apostle." Yet Khanykov's ardor also made him nervous, and this nervousness prompted sharp self-reproach. Contrasting himself to the young nobleman, Chernyshevsky remarked sadly that "my cowardice and indecisiveness and inability to abandon those previous conceptions that have ingrained themselves in me force me to remain in the same situation."[11]

Chernyshevsky's encounter with Khanykov took place at a crucial juncture in his life. As late as September 1848, just over two years after having left home, he was still relatively confident about his Orthodox faith. He reassured himself of this in his diary: "I must say that, in essence, I am definitely a Christian, if by that one means faith in the title of Jesus Christ as divine [*verovanie v bozhestvennoe dostoinstvo Iisusa Khrista*], that is, [I believe] in the way that all Orthodox people believe, that he was God and suffered, and was resurrected, and created miracles; in sum, I believe in all that."[12]

At the same time, Chernyshevsky was an avid reader of all journals, Russian and foreign. He eagerly consumed the poetry and prose of Mikhail Lermontov and Nikolai Gogol, as well as that of Alexander Herzen and Vissarion Belinsky.[13] He also perused foreign newspapers available at St. Petersburg's coffeehouses. Volf's café and confectionery on Nevskii Prospect, a famous meeting place for Russian writers from Pushkin and Lermontov to Dostoevsky, was one of his favorite haunts. Chernyshevsky's interest in foreign events became especially intense in

1848, and he found that his sympathies were with the revolutionaries. The French socialist Louis Blanc was a special favorite. Like the young merchants in the tobacco store, Chernyshevsky began to compare himself to his heroes. He felt a sudden calling to do something extraordinary and believed he had it in him to become a "remarkable man."[14]

Unlike the tobacco store merchants, Chernyshevsky did not dream of rabble-rousing oratory. He took a more contemplative approach. He wished to "move forward the history of humankind somewhat with regard to its worldview," to become a "servant of the times," apparently by becoming a writer. What exactly his field of endeavor would be he was not yet sure, though he listed Hegel, Plato, and Copernicus as models. Measuring himself against these great men, however, Chernyshevsky was painfully aware of how little he had to show for himself so far: "My life is as stagnant as a swamp [*moia zhizn' techet v bolote*]." By his age, he observed with regret, Louis Blanc had already become the head of a party.[15] That Chernyshevsky's meeting with Khanykov came at a particularly painful time helps to explain why their encounter would prompt him to remark on his "cowardice and indecisiveness." This sense of personal stagnation also had other important consequences: Chernyshevsky would later identify stagnation as a problem that plagued the nation as a whole.

Chernyshevsky's concern about his inability to abandon his "previous conceptions" also had another source, however: the writings of Alexander Herzen. Shortly before he left Russia, Herzen had published some of his most influential articles, which appeared in *Notes of the Fatherland* and the *Contemporary* in 1846 and 1847. These made a very deep impression on Chernyshevsky.[16] The articles reflected Herzen's recent rejection of faith in divine Providence and the immortality of the soul. Though he could not address these issues in print, Herzen did explain the principle that underlay his decision: the individual's moral obligation to doubt, to subject his beliefs to searing criticism and reject them if they did not accord with truth. Herzen defended the bravery of those intellectuals who proved willing to "draw the final conclusions from their own principles." They did not hesitate, even if it would entail giving up some long-cherished belief. Those who did hesitate were "timid" and untrustworthy. "He who has *not* torn *everything* out of his chest that is not justified by reason is not free and may go so far as to reject reason *entirely*."[17] Chernyshevsky was afraid that he must be numbered among the timid.

Khanykov did not succeed in converting Chernyshevsky into a Fourierist, yet he did force his reticent acquaintance to ruminate on the problem of personal change. In at least one private conversation, Khany-kov made no secret of his critical attitude to Orthodox Christianity and even stated that he did not believe in the existence of God.[18] Chernyshev-sky's response was to become increasingly uncertain whether he main-tained his religious faith because it was in fact superior to other systems of thought or whether he was simply unwilling to abandon his former beliefs—indeed incapable of doing so. To test himself, he devised a hypothetical scenario, according to which Christianity would collapse, in the same way that paganism fell in Roman times and was replaced by Christianity. This imagined situation allowed him to explore his potential response. Would he, who was so "timid," have the courage to accept a "new messiah" and a "new religion"? He admitted he was attached to his old faith and wondered whether to take this as a sign of "weakness" and "stupidity." On this occasion, he seemed to think he could resolve the issue by appealing to the Orthodox idea of divine Providence: if religion collapsed, that meant God wanted it to. "May it be done as pleases God" (*Chto ugodno [B]ogu, to da budet*).[19] The thought did not assuage his fears, however, and Chernyshevsky remained concerned about his inability to change.

In March 1849 Khanykov lent Chernyshevsky a copy of Feuerbach's *The Essence of Christianity*. As Chernyshevsky picked up the book and carried it home, he worried, once again, about his intellectual inflexibility. Would Feuerbach overturn his convictions, or would he "remain with practically the same beliefs," even though he sensed their inadequacy?[20] The result was, for the time being, stasis. *The Essence of Christianity* argues that God and religion more generally are products of the human imagi-nation. God is nothing but an image in the mind that human beings have developed on the basis of their feelings, wishes, and needs. Dis-satisfied with their inability to gratify their physical and emotional needs, they have projected them onto a higher being, one in whom all of these needs are fulfilled and one whom they believe to be capable of intervening to satisfy them on earth or in heaven. God is thus a "fantastic" being, an "illusion"—he is "everything" in the human imagination, but "nothing in truth and reality."[21]

Shortly after having begun to read *The Essence of Christianity*, Chernyshevsky was prepared to admit that human beings had projected their essence onto God, but he was not yet ready to accept this as proof that God does not exist independently of human imagination.[22] In the summer of 1849 he observed with regret that he still believed in God but noted that he did so primarily because of his pious upbringing—"that is, according to concepts that have grown to form part of my life." He believed "out of habit," and was therefore uncertain whether his faith in God had the strength of conviction.[23]

His religious beliefs now became the test through which to measure his "cowardice," and for the time being, they confirmed his worst fears.[24] In January 1850 he repeated that he believed *only* because he lacked the "firmness and decisiveness" necessary to reject his habitual faith. Had he the "courage" to stand by what he thought "in theory," he would stop believing and become a follower of Feuerbach.[25] Chernyshevsky confronted the following difficulty: in order to change, one has to believe one can change. But how does one acquire belief in one's ability to change? In later years, he would present this as a key problem for the intelligentsia as a whole.

At some point, Chernyshevsky did change, though it is difficult to say when this occurred. In the autumn of 1850 he commented in his diary that he was now "almost completely" dedicated to Feuerbach.[26] In 1851 he noted that he had defended the views of Feuerbach and David Friedrich Strauss in conversation with some acquaintances (he did not, however, go into any detail as to the nature of their influence on him in this diary entry).[27] By 1853 it seems clear that he had renounced faith in God.[28]

His new outlook, specifically Feuerbach's idea that God is a "fantastic being," found expression in Chernyshevsky's master's dissertation, "The Aesthetic Relation of Art to Reality," which he wrote in the autumn of 1853. The thesis was principally intended as an attack on the philosophy and aesthetics of Russian romantic idealism, which represented art and nature as imbued by spirit, or the divine. Into the pages of his thesis, Chernyshevsky wove a critique of religious beliefs. Human beings, he wrote, have invented "a humanlike being" (God) to rationalize the intervention of natural forces in their lives, which are unpredictable and painful and result in privation. To explain this unpredictability, they imagine a reasonable being who controls the world, and they compensate for the world's imperfections by using their imaginations to construct a better one, where all their needs will be met.[29] Essentially, Chernyshevsky represented God and heaven as products of human fantasies that developed out of a desire for safety and comfort, though censorship prevented him from expressing this view so bluntly.

Chernyshevsky anticipated that at the university, his examiners' poor knowledge of German philosophy would blind them to the dissertation's radical implications. Yet his supervisor, Professor Nikitenko, hesitated to approve it, delaying the defense for one and a half years until the summer of 1855. At the defense, Chernyshevsky's tone was combative. He had embarked on the thesis in the hopes of pursuing an academic career. By the end of the disputation, though, it was clear that he would not be recommended for a teaching position at St. Petersburg University or, for that matter, at any other university.[30] His chastisement did not come as a disappointment. He viewed the abandonment of his religious faith as a test of personal strength, proof that he was not beholden to his upbringing. The possibility of conflict with the authorities offered a further opportunity to test his courage. His friend Alexander Khanykov had been apprehended by the Third Section in 1849 shortly after having handed Chernyshevsky his copy of *The Essence of Christianity*. Alexander Herzen, whom he so greatly admired, had been arrested on more than one occasion. As Chernyshevsky proudly proclaimed in 1853, he fully expected to share Herzen's fate.[31]

Chernyshevsky's ambitions went much further, however. He hoped that he could not only separate himself from his religious background, thus freeing himself to embark on a new future, but also help Russians do the same by goading them into the admission that their country had stagnated and that they needed to change. He would do so as a journalist, contributing articles to the literary journal the *Contemporary*.

At the time Chernyshevsky was embarking on his career as a journalist, Dobroliubov was still a student at the St. Petersburg Pedagogical Institute, undergoing his own crisis of faith. His doubts had begun the year after he arrived in St. Petersburg, and he subsequently celebrated his renunciation of belief as the moment in which he first managed to overcome the limitations of his past. It was a "feat of self-definition."[32] Like Chernyshevsky, Dobroliubov had become familiar with the writings of Belinsky and Herzen before he arrived in the capital.[33] Indeed, he had dreamed that studying at St. Petersburg University would allow him to become acquainted with writers and journalists. Unlike Chernyshevsky's crisis, however, Dobroliubov's loss of faith does not appear to have been connected to the aspiration to imitate models prescribed by his intellectual heroes but was prompted by events in his personal life: the deaths of his parents in 1854.

In some secondary literature, Dobroliubov's loss of faith has been dated to 1853. Scholars have cited the diaries he kept that year, in which he commented on his "coldness," as evidence of his slide toward atheism.[34] This is most likely a misreading: diary keeping was prescribed for priests and their sons because it was believed to offer a "daily mirror for clergymen's souls, providing [. . .] an opportunity to identify existing imperfections and the means of correcting them."[35] The character trait Dobroliubov was most concerned about was acedia (sloth), a cardinal sin in Orthodox theology that was usually rendered into Russian as "dejection" (*unynie*) or "numbness" (*beschuvstvie, nechuvstvie*).[36] These were, incidentally, also traits that Chernyshevsky criticized himself for in his diary.[37] During Lent of 1853, Dobroliubov displayed a classically Orthodox Christian understanding of the problem, lamenting that his heart was "callous [*cherstvo*] and cold toward religion" and criticizing himself for being too feckless to revive it "with the warmth of prayer."[38] So concerned was Dobroliubov that he began keeping a separate Lenten diary (titled "Psikhatorium") to track his moods. Archetypal signs of acedia presented themselves in this context. He noted that vanity and pride distracted him when he tried to pray; he was lazy about going to church and was bored while there.[39] The same "laziness" and "coldness," he wrote, even infused his act of penitence: the record he kept of his sins in his diary. The voluminous pages he devoted to minute self-analysis were not, apparently, enough.[40] Concern about these traits continued to haunt Dobroliubov even after he had lost faith; indeed, he would attribute them to almost everyone he knew, including the Russian reading public as a whole.

It was only after his parents' death that Dobroliubov began to express disbelief in core doctrines of the Orthodox faith, as confirmed by his letters to friends and family. Initially, the news of his mother's death in childbirth in March 1854 evoked feelings of self-recrimination, the suspicion that Dobroliubov had broken her heart by enrolling at the Pedagogical Institute against his parents' wishes.[41] Only one month later, at Easter, he noted in a letter to his father that he had difficulty celebrating the resurrection of Christ: "Twelve times a day, in the morning and at night, before lunch and dinner, I hear: 'Christ is risen from the dead,' but often that sacred song seems like bitter and brutal mockery of my circumstances."[42] Arriving home for the summer, he apparently found his faith revived, as he wrote to one of his classmates.[43] This faith was uprooted by a further blow in August 1854, when his father died of cholera. Instead of guilt, Dobroliubov now felt anger: his parents had left behind eight orphaned children, together with substantial debts.

Efforts by his former seminary teacher to comfort him by appealing to God's wisdom and Providence made him angry.[44] His relatives urged him to take comfort in the teachings of the Church, the doctrines of immortality and Providence, yet these again struck him as "mockery." At Easter 1855, he wrote to his relatives with great bitterness, noting that he would not be celebrating Christ's resurrection.[45]

With time, the experience of suffering and loss of faith became a source of pride for Dobroliubov. By December 1855 he was prepared to represent them to himself as invigorating. These developments, he wrote in his diary, had enhanced his ability to act and set him apart from and above his contemporaries:

> As the son of a priest, who was brought up according to the strict codes of Christian faith and morality, [. . .] who managed, notwithstanding all the circumstances, to arrive at the conviction that some of the principles that were inculcated in me since early childhood were false, and did so using my own reason [, . . .] I now feel that I, more than anyone else, have the strength and the capability to take action. . . . "I myself was once what you are, sirs," I will say to my pitiful associates, "here is the story of my life. . . ." [. . .] A terrible misfortune, the death of my father and mother, befell me. But it only convinced me of the ultimate justice of my cause, in the nonexistence of those phantoms, which the Eastern imagination invented for itself, and which is thrust upon us by force, against common sense. It [the misfortune] embittered me against that mysterious force, which one so boldly calls good and merciful.[46]

Suffering, Dobroliubov claimed, had had a liberating influence on him. Until then, he had been "tied up," condemned to immobility by "phantoms." Having recognized their nonexistence, he was now not only free to think but also to act.

Some scholars have attributed Dobroliubov's crisis of faith, particularly as expressed in this diary entry, to the influence of Ludwig Feuerbach. Yet there is no clear evidence to suggest that Dobroliubov had read Feuerbach at this point.[47] More likely, he derived the view of God as an imaginary "phantom" from Chernyshevsky's master's thesis. Chernyshevsky was at this point attracting attention as a critic at the *Contemporary* and had published a review of his own thesis in that journal, in which he repeated his assertions about the troublesome nature of the human imagination.[48] Dobroliubov must have looked up to Chernyshevsky as a priest's son whose success in overcoming the limitations of his religious upbringing represented a triumph.

Poems that Dobroliubov wrote over the following two years display a radicalization in his thought. His parents' deaths, more particularly that of his father, had set him free, and his verses now identified this freedom with liberation from God. When Dobroliubov lost his father, he also lost faith in the beneficent "benefactor" he had been taught to believe in as a child. In the poem "The Benefactor" (August 1856), he describes how, as a child, his "impotence" had made the idea of a God (the benefactor) seem comforting. God had failed to intervene at the crucial moment (his father's death), however, and the result was loss of faith in a provident, beneficent God. Dobroliubov describes this loss of faith as a physical act of liberation that allows him to move freely for the first time:

> Теперь я сам могу идти неутомимо
> И действовать—не как его покорный раб,
> Не по его таинственным приказам,
> Чрез сотни уст дошедшим до меня,
> А как велит мне собственный мой разум,
> Как убежден я сам, при полном свете дня.

> [Now I myself can proceed tirelessly / And act not as a beholden slave, / Not according to mysterious commands / Conveyed to me through hundreds of mouths, / But as my own reason orders me, / In accordance with my convictions in the bright light of day.][49]

A year later, in August 1857, Dobroliubov went so far as to "bless the sad hour" when his father had died, because it had freed him from his childish ways and motivated him to become an active agent in the world.[50]

Dobroliubov's abandonment of his prior religious faith became a test of personal strength, just as it had been for Chernyshevsky. It was proof that he could overcome his past, as well as transcend the limitations of birth by an act of will, by choosing a new belief system for himself. In a letter to a friend, Dobroliubov called renunciation of faith a "feat" (*podvig*) (note, however, that "feat" is a very Christian word).[51] Like Chernyshevsky, he, too, wished to believe that he was out of the ordinary and entertained the possibility that he was "called upon by fate" to change the course of history.[52] He, too, would turn to the *Contemporary* as the forum in which he would make his contribution to humanity. Dobroliubov was already submitting articles to the journal in 1856, a year before he graduated from the Pedagogical Institute.

Dobroliubov and Chernyshevsky first met in April 1856, when the former submitted an article on Russian literature in the reign of Catherine II to the *Contemporary*.[53] Through their meeting and subsequent friendship, each man gained a powerful ally. Dobroliubov saw in Chernyshevsky the son of a priest who had managed to break into the world of Russian journalism, still strongly dominated at that time by noblemen. Chernyshevsky saw in Dobroliubov a talent who would alleviate his professional isolation and help undermine the power of the noble faction at the journal, who looked down on him for his lowly clerical origins.

Chernyshevsky had begun submitting literary reviews in 1853 to *Notes of the Fatherland* and the *Contemporary*, both revered journals that had published Alexander Herzen before he emigrated and Vissarion Belinsky before he died in 1848. Both periodicals continued to be staffed by Western-oriented liberals who had come to prominence in the 1840s. Even before they learned Chernyshevsky's name, they took notice of the unusual tone of his reviews, which were more stridently critical than they were deferential. Matters came to a head in the summer of 1855, when Chernyshevsky published his dissertation, "The Aesthetic Relation of Art to Reality," and reviewed it (anonymously) in the June 1855 issue of the *Contemporary*. The dissertation and review sparked howls of protest by fellow contributors, who were offended by the excessive confidence of an uncouth priest's son who dared to make bold pronouncements on matters of aesthetics. Ivan Turgenev, Alexander Druzhinin, and Lev Tolstoy would refer to him in their correspondence as "pakhnushchii klopami" (bedbug stinker). In early July 1855 Turgenev announced his intention to "persecute" and "destroy" Chernyshevsky and wrote to one of the journal's principal editors, Ivan Panaev, to complain about him. Turgenev, together with Dmitrii Grigorovich, Druzhinin, and Tolstoy, satirized Chernyshevsky in a short play they composed and privately performed. The play became public when Grigorovich published it in the September 1855 edition of the conservative journal *Library for Reading*.[54] Amid these scandals, Chernyshevsky did not lack entirely for defenders. The editors of the *Contemporary*, Ivan Panaev and Nikolai Nekrasov, backed him, yet they simultaneously attempted to conciliate his detractors.

Tensions with noble staff members at the *Contemporary* must have fueled Chernyshevsky's resentment toward the nobility. It would express itself in his characterization of noblemen as weak and lacking energy (the very qualities he had recently assigned to himself) and their doubt as an expression of that weakness. His resentment must also have made him more enthusiastic about the prospect of cooperating with Dobroliubov. In 1857, when Dobroliubov graduated from the Pedagogical Institute, Chernyshevsky sought and secured permission for him to remain in St. Petersburg as a staff writer for the *Contemporary*, thus waiving the requirement that Dobroliubov serve for several years as a teacher at some provincial school. Chernyshevsky also became a friend and mentor to Dobroliubov, offering him advice on the care of his seven orphaned younger siblings, counseling him on his health and love life, and lavishing him with praise and encouragement when he was prone to self-doubt. Writing to Dobroliubov during a brief period of separation, he remarked that both were unusually high-minded, unusually "noble, or heroic, or something like that." Dobroliubov should not blame himself if he could not keep up the high level of heroism at all times. Both held themselves to impossibly high standards. They tried to be "angels, Christs and so on." Whatever his flaws might be, Chernyshevsky was sure that Dobroliubov was the superior of the two: "You are better than I; I am convinced of it like $2 \times 2 = 4$," and both were "very good people."[55] The relationship was based on more than mutual sympathy and admiration, however; the two worked closely together at the *Contemporary*, achieving a true intellectual symbiosis. So closely was their outlook aligned that readers had difficulty distinguishing their reviews.

Despite their evident closeness, this was not a friendship that conformed to the model of attachment that characterized noble circles of the 1830s. Indeed, Chernyshevsky and Dobroliubov explicitly rejected that model.[56] Chernyshevsky commented on this in a review he published on Ogarev's poetry in 1856. There, he drew attention to poems Ogarev dedicated to his friends in the 1830s and noted that the loyalty, selflessness, and sentimentality Ogarev exhibited in them, though admirable in their way, not only seemed outmoded but were now defunct.[57] Chernyshevsky might have added, however, that Herzen and Ogarev were themselves partly responsible for this shift in attitude; in the mid-1840s they had come to think that friendship was not viable in the absence of shared conviction. He learned this from no lesser a source than Herzen himself, because relevant parts of Herzen's memoir — describing the collapse of his circle and friendship with Granovsky — had appeared in 1855 in his own journal, the *Polar Star* (*Poliarnaia zvezda*), which was smuggled into Russia and undoubtedly read by Chernyshevsky.[58] The first installment of Herzen's memoir certainly raised his stature in Chernyshevsky's eyes. It helped define his friendship with

Dobroliubov as a partnership in ideas that could be harnessed to promote their cause in journalism. Herzen's memoir may also unwittingly have encouraged the pair to assume that Herzen's contemporaries of the 1840s did not deserve the same respect.

In the second half of the 1850s, Chernyshevsky and Dobroliubov would attack the generation of the 1840s with increasing vigor, rejecting their doubt as a sign of the weakness of all members of their estate. It is difficult to say whether this was a reaction to the disdain with which Chernyshevsky in particular had been treated by staff writers at the *Contemporary* or whether it was principally a product of fundamental ideological differences. Either way, the rift only deepened, until the two found themselves exchanging harsh words with their former idol, Alexander Herzen. Surely, neither Chernyshevsky nor Dobroliubov could have undertaken a debate with so many influential opponents without one another's support. Neither would they have been so bold in attacking the existence of God. Their cooperation and friendship was based partly on mutually held convictions, but their friendship also gave them the courage to articulate those convictions.

Between 1855 and 1862, the articles Chernyshevsky and Dobroliubov wrote for the *Contemporary* brought them both fame and admiration among reform-minded Russians, as well as notoriety and opprobrium among conservatives. Together, they transformed the *Contemporary* into a mouthpiece of radical social criticism, quickly making it Russia's second-largest journal, with four thousand subscribers.[59] They promoted the view that the quality of all writing, including fiction, poetry, history, and natural science, was to be determined by its political and social relevance. Journals must educate readers and encourage them to directly take part in the cultural, social, and political transformation of their country. In this way, Chernyshevsky and Dobroliubov sought to turn the readership into an active, "conscious" political and social force. Educated Russians must stop believing in higher authorities and take the future of their country into their own hands. This could only be accomplished, however, if they separated themselves from their past and stopped believing in the "superstitions" and "nanny's tales" that had been inculcated in them as children. Chernyshevsky and Dobroliubov were prescribing to their readers their own intellectual development. To make their claims more convincing, they drew on the history of Russian literature and literary criticism, inscribing themselves into a venerable tradition.

Chernyshevsky and Dobroliubov gathered influence with unusual speed, and political circumstances facilitated their rise. Nicholas I died unexpectedly in 1855, leaving the country in turmoil. In the wake of the 1848 revolutions, the state had grown ever more conservative and repressive. The years from 1848 to 1855 were subsequently remembered as the "dark seven years," a time when, according to Alexander Herzen, intellectual development ceased owing to the crippling sense that life and thought were utterly meaningless.[60] In 1853 Nicholas I embroiled Russia in the Crimean War, which quickly devolved into a series of humiliating defeats. St. Petersburg society attributed these defeats not only to the ineptitude of the military leadership but also to the authoritarian style of governance that Nicholas had cultivated and to the country's economic and technological backwardness. When Alexander II (reigned 1855–81), Nicholas I's son, came to the throne, there was consensus among educated Russians that he must issue a comprehensive package of social reforms and do so quickly. Chernyshevsky and Dobroliubov thus encountered a readership receptive to the view that Russia must either change dramatically or collapse. The crucial question was who should initiate change.

Chernyshevsky and Dobroliubov were not among the large majority of Russians who believed that Russia's autocracy was capable of issuing the necessary reforms. To them, this was not because Alexander II lacked the right personal attributes but because of the very nature of the monarchical state. In the first major articles that Chernyshevsky and Dobroliubov published at the *Contemporary* between 1855 and 1856, they strongly implied that statesmen were not in a position to grasp the will and needs of the nation they led. Even the most skilled and enlightened monarch was incapable of fundamental intervention in the life of a society. Change could not be legislated from above; it could only come from the intelligentsia, which must make society recognize that its habits were detrimental to its well-being.[61] These comments were addressed to a readership whose most enthusiastic element was comprised of young people, students from the nobility. But they were also aimed at seminarians who stood to benefit most from the decline of the old order.

Change must be initiated by writers, not statesmen. Literature, Chernyshevsky boldly stated, is "immeasurably more important than almost everything that one places above it." It had "ruled over people's minds and mores" and had directed "their aims in life." It remained the "most powerful of forces acting upon the development of our social life." Writers must live up to the moral obligations that influence brought with it by proposing solutions to all the major questions facing Russia—educational, political, juridical.[62] The highest calling of writers, whether they were novelists, poets, or journalists, however, was to "guess the needs of society," as Dobroliubov put it in 1856, or to articulate its hidden wishes.[63] At any given time and in every nation, there was a consensus—unconscious and unarticulated—concerning the path its development must take. The function of writers was to put that consensus into words, to become the mouthpiece of society and thereby make it conscious of its own wishes. The function of readers was to hold writers to this high standard.[64]

Chernyshevsky and Dobroliubov inserted their claims about the function of literature and its relationship to society and state into articles on the history of literature in the eighteenth and early nineteenth centuries. By couching these claims in a historical context, they could circumvent the strictures of censorship while simultaneously situating themselves in a tradition that their readers were familiar with and respected. In this regard, Chernyshevsky's series *Essays on the Gogol Period in Russian Literature* was most significant, celebrating Gogol as the first writer to "awaken in us the consciousness of ourselves." The real hero of the *Essays*, however, was Belinsky, whose name was still forbidden by censorship at the time Chernyshevsky began to publish them. Chernyshevsky celebrated Belinsky for drawing attention to the writer's moral obligation to serve humanity; writers could not in good conscience pursue art for art's sake. He also paid tribute to Herzen, another name then forbidden by censors. Drawing material from the first, published segment of Herzen's memoirs, Chernyshevsky praised "Ogarev and his friends" for introducing the ideas of French "utopian" writers, that is, the Christian socialists, in Russia.[65]

Implicit in Chernyshevsky's praise for Belinsky and Herzen was an attack on other members of their generation for having abandoned the mission these two men had laid out for them. Belinsky had died in 1848 and, as Chernyshevsky's readers well knew, Herzen had left in 1847. Since then, Chernyshevsky claimed, nothing of any significance had happened in Russian literature.[66] In pointing out this flaw, he drew on the Orthodox conception of acedia, the sin of listlessness, numbness, and sloth. The late 1840s and early 1850s had been marked by torpor. Russians had grown drowsy, succumbed to the temptation to take a little snooze, and developed the "excessively long habit of sleeping."[67] Such listlessness, as Chernyshevsky provocatively suggested in the

1858 "Russian Man at a *Rendez-vous*," displayed itself in even the most secular of settings: in the "cowardly," "limp," and "hesitant" behavior of the heroes of Russian romantic fiction toward beautiful women. The amorous protagonist's "worn-out weakness of character" paralyzed him the moment he was asked to put theory into practice.[68]

In this regard, members of the nobility were especially disadvantaged. Their upbringing had prepared them only for flaccid inactivity as adults, and social influences further discouraged independence of thought and activity.[69] They had been raised by caretakers who filled their minds with "superstitions," "nanny's tales," and "childhood lore" and thereby encouraged an overactive imagination in their charges.[70] While Chernyshevsky mocked the Russian man for his lack of manliness, he acknowledged the difficulties entailed in renouncing the habits and beliefs one had been raised with. "We cannot tear ourselves away from those prejudices [. . . and] petty conceptions, which have been inculcated in us by the society that surrounds us." Those conceptions bred an inactivity that was threatening to become harmful. Russians justified their inactivity by claiming that all their dreams for a better future were nothing but a "mirage" and that their fear of impending danger was nothing but a "bogeyman." Meanwhile, they continued to nourish the fantasy that someone else would intervene to save them.[71]

To excuse their shortcomings, Chernyshevsky claimed, the men of the 1840s invoked the sacrifices they had made while struggling to free themselves from old ways of thinking. The paralyzing doubts that had resulted from this struggle were merely a symbol of their inadequacy, their incapacity to cast off the legacy of their childhood and youth. The younger generation was tired of hearing their complaints and excuses: "It may be that many of us are now prepared to hear different speeches, in which the torture of inner struggle might not speak so loudly." It was time for a "new spirit to chase away Mephistopheles."[72]

Chernyshevsky's remarks prompted pained rejoinders from men of the 1840s. Pavel Annenkov, who now stepped forward as their representative, charged that Chernyshevsky had failed to recognize the contributions they had made to the development of Russian thought. It had taken a great deal of energy to challenge the status quo. "All their energy—and they had had a lot of energy—was exhausted as they constructed a special world of moral, guiding rules and tried to find in that construction the complete satisfaction of one's spiritual needs." The possibilities of choice and action Chernyshevsky presented to his readers were unrealistic. It was easy to act without asking oneself what one was doing or why. Self-confidence was a sign of "spiritual poverty, not of a rich nature." The "more limited the compass of a person's understanding, the fewer options there are for him in life, the easier it is to choose a path."[73] Observing these debates from abroad, Alexander Herzen would weigh in on the side of Annenkov. Chernyshevsky and Dobroliubov were wrong to ridicule the men of his generation for their inactivity. Belinsky and Granovsky alike had no action plan, no road map; all they had was a "demon," and that was all any decent man could have had in Nicholaevan Russia. In the 1830s and 1840s, there had only been one alternative to becoming a conflicted, torn, inactive—superfluous—man, and that was a government stooge.[74]

The reprimand he received from Herzen horrified Chernyshevsky, who traveled to London to talk to him in person. The visit and the content of their conversations were not recorded and remain unknown, but the result was a deepening of the rift between them.[75] Dobroliubov was most unmerciful in his assessment of the current role being played by the men of the 1840s. In "When Will the Real Day Come?" (1860), he likened them to a toothless squirrel holding a nut. "Those people understand where the root of evil lies, and they know what is to be done. [. . .] But—they lack the strength for practical activity; they pounded themselves to the point that their nature somehow became overstrained and grew weak."[76]

A year later, in "The Downtrodden People" (1861), a review of Dostoevsky's works, Dobroliubov reflected further on the problem of inertia. There was, he admitted, a natural human tendency to remain passive and to ground this passivity in faith: "They say, it is gratifying for man to have someone behind him who takes care of him, who thinks and decides for him, who arranges his whole life, all of his actions and even his thoughts. They say that this is consonant with man's natural inertia, with his need to give himself up selflessly to someone, to supply the soul with some kind of a model and a master, under whose dominion he might calmly sleep."[77] More clearly than any other, this passage points to faith in a higher power as the source of sloth and inertia—of acedia. For too long, Russians had justified their impotence and suffering by convincing themselves that their dejection and humiliation accorded with some divinely ordained scheme and that their acceptance of it made them "saints in the kingdom of heaven." The bitter fact was that by accepting their lot, they had willingly entrapped themselves.[78]

One striking aspect of these assertions is how strongly reminiscent they are of Herzen's position in the 1840s. Herzen had argued that his friends must renounce faith in Providence and the immortality of the soul as comforting beliefs that had no basis in reality. There is no higher meaning in life, Herzen said, though he hesitated to state that there is no God. In the late 1850s, Herzen had also begun to entertain hopes about the status of Alexander II as reformer; perhaps this Romanov would succeed in bringing to Russia the changes it so desperately needed, including the liberation of the serfs.[79] To Chernyshevsky and Dobroliubov, these were misplaced hopes, easily attributable to bad childhood habits of putting one's faith in a redeemer. To their minds, faith in the monarch and faith in the phantom, God, were indistinguishable.

Calling on educated Russians to renounce their faith and break from their past, Chernyshevsky and Dobroliubov clearly drew on their own experiences as young men. The rejection of faith in a higher being— God—was the key element that would enable educated Russians to overcome their lethargy and timidity. For the first time, they would become conscious of their wishes and needs, allowing them to take an active role in the transformation of their country.

In urging their readers to give up faith in God, Chernyshevsky and Dobroliubov did not limit their journalistic writings to literary criticism but also promoted a blend of philosophy and science, drawn from the mid-nineteenth-century German materialists. The rise of materialism is often assumed to have been a causal factor in loss of faith during this period.[80] Yet the loss of faith that Chernyshevsky and Dobroliubov underwent as young men was not precipitated by the discovery of materialism. Nor did they subsequently become consistent adherents of the materialist worldview. They did, however, make extensive use of materialist theories in justifying the stance that there is no God and in arguing that ethical behavior is not contingent on faith in God. In this way, they could counter the Orthodox Christian assertion that atheism is a product of depravity and must lead to despair and suicide.

The three writers Chernyshevsky and Dobroliubov drew on most heavily were Carl Vogt, Jacob Moleschott, and Ludwig Büchner. All three had been trained in natural science at German universities in the 1830s. From the mid-1840s to mid-1850s, they wrote popular scientific works that fused chemistry and physiology with politics and socialism. Sympathetic to the uprisings of 1848, they were convinced that the science of the human organism would prove that all human beings were innately equal.[81] Their most strident and controversial claims, however, were directed against the existence of God. Physics and chemistry showed that there could be no such thing as a supernatural, incorporeal being that intervened in the natural world; there could be "no force without matter."[82]

The theories advanced by Vogt, Moleschott, and Büchner cohered well with the Feuerbachian theory of God as a product of the human imagination, which Chernyshevsky and Dobroliubov promoted. This was no coincidence, as Feuerbach had also been a major source of inspiration for the German materialists. What the materialists provided Chernyshevsky and Dobroliubov was a detailed psychological explanation of how the human brain could malfunction in such a way as to produce religious beliefs. For example, there were people who claimed to have experienced the supernatural firsthand. Such impressions were the product of an unhealthy organism: physical illness, along with ascetic practices such as depriving the body of nourishment, could lead a person to experience auditory and visual hallucinations.[83] The influence of culture and education also had an important role to play. People who had been encouraged to give the imagination free rein in childhood, for example, were more inclined to be superstitious as adults.[84] In cultures where scientific knowledge was not available, such beliefs were given undue credence, giving rise to false assessments of the operation of the natural world. Natural phenomena became "dark forces," and dark forces became gods. False beliefs then confirmed the assumption that human beings were powerless, which discouraged people from undertaking the kind of independent-minded inquiry that would have disabused them of their mistaken assumptions. Entire societies would then settle into a state of "indifference," "passivity," "vegetation," "stagnation," and "hostility to change."[85] Religious believers were doomed to stagnate.[86]

Vogt, Moleschott, and Büchner supplied Chernyshevsky and Dobroliubov with a ready-made set of arguments and scientific examples through which they hoped to dispel faith in the supernatural among their readers. Dobroliubov made this explicit in an article published in 1859, though he couched his assertion in the characteristically obtuse language that was supposed to disarm censors: "Ever since the spread of what is now commonly known as the truth, namely that force is an inevitable attribute of matter, and that matter can only exist for our perception to the extent that it manifests some kind of force, ever since that time, we have considered all those Ormuzds and Ahrimans entirely superfluous."[87]

Such assertions could not convince every reader that God is a superstition; in Germany, Ludwig Büchner conceded that religious belief would continue to flourish "for decades, possibly even centuries," despite the tens of thousands of copies that his book *Force and Matter* sold.[88] Materialism did, however, allow Chernyshevsky and Dobroliubov to portray the question of the existence of God as a contemporary problem to which there were new and contemporary answers. In this way, it became easier to portray those educated Russians who did not accept their conclusions as relics—people out of touch with "what," Dobroliubov claimed, "is commonly known as the truth."

Chernyshevsky and Dobroliubov would also draw on the works of Vogt, Moleschott, and Büchner in advancing their theory of a non-Christian ethics, a theory that subsequently came to be known as "rational egoism." Its essential content was that conceptions of good and evil are not innate categories in the mind but describe human preferences. "Good" describes experiences that bring people pleasure, while "evil" describes experiences that cause them pain. This theory has been traced to a large and diverse number of philosophical sources, especially English utilitarianism.[89] The contribution of materialism was to reinforce the view that human perceptions of pleasure and pain are not arbitrary: they are physiologically conditioned and thus subject to the laws of nature. A person familiar with these laws is in a good position to assess actions and practices based on the extent to which they conform to physiological need. In this way, individual needs and wishes can be balanced against the needs of community for the purposes of establishing which practices will allow a maximum number of individuals in a community to flourish. Though scholars dubbed this theory "rational egoism" (implying that ethical decisions were to be made on the basis of calculation), Chernyshevsky and Dobroliubov both assumed that the natural instincts of a healthy adult could serve as reliable guides in forming judgments, provided that the minds of those adults were not cluttered by "superstitions" and "prejudices."[90]

Both Chernyshevsky and Dobroliubov understood this ethical system to contradict the teachings of the Orthodox Church, according to which all human beings are created by God with innate knowledge of good and evil, which are absolute categories.[91] These conceptions of good and evil were, to them, artificial and arbitrary inventions that human beings had imposed on one another. Materialism was, therefore, an important component of their antireligious writings. It allowed them to deepen their attack on faith in the existence of God by providing a scientific basis for their claims. They also drew extensively on materialism in advancing a new, non-Christian ethics. It should be emphasized, however, that neither of the two was entirely consistent in adhering to the letter and the law of materialist theories, as became especially clear in 1860 and 1861, when Dobroliubov began to make use of words such as "sacred" and "divine" to describe humanity in his literary reviews.

In 1860 Dobroliubov published "A Ray of Light in the Kingdom of Darkness," a review of Alexander Ostrovsky's play *The Storm* (1860), perhaps the most widely read of all his articles. Here, Dobroliubov argues that any healthy individual must instinctively understand the falsehood of Orthodox ethical conceptions. Ostrovsky's heroine, Katerina Kabanova, is a pious young woman who commits suicide when she comes into conflict with her own religious beliefs after having betrayed her husband with another man. Significantly, her piety is not subject to question in Ostrovsky's drama: "More than anything, I loved to attend church! It was just as if I was entering paradise; I saw no one, and time stood still, and I did not hear when the service ended. It was just as if it all happened in a single second."[92] Dobroliubov transforms Katerina into a disillusioned rebel. Her "strong mind" and instinct for love have shown her that the religious beliefs with which she has been raised, including Orthodox ethics of sin and virtue, are untrue. She has always been too independent to fully accept church doctrine.[93] The immense suffering she experiences on realizing that she cannot act on her feelings of love, however, allows her to see how dark and nightmarish the world of the church truly is:

> As before, she seeks refuge in religious practice, by attending church, in edificatory conversations; but even here she cannot recreate her previous impressions. Crushed by her daily work and by her eternal servitude, she is no longer capable of the clarity with which she once dreamed of angels, singing in a cloud of dust, lit by the sun; she cannot imagine those heavenly gardens with their appearance of imperturbable serenity and joy. Everything around her is somber, frightening, everything exudes coldness and some kind of insuperable menace: the saints' faces severe, and the liturgical readings are threatening, and the tales of the pilgrims are monstrous. . . . In essence, they are all as they were before, they have not changed at all; she is the one who has changed: she no longer has the

inclination to invent ethereal visions, and that vague sense of bliss she used to imagine, which used to give her pleasure cannot satisfy her anymore. She has grown up, gained strength. [*Ona vozmuzhala*].[94]

Katerina's loss of faith is not the result of a reasoned decision—she is rather driven to it by instinct, by a capacity for powerful emotion that compels her to rise above "ordinary prejudices."[95] Once again, Dobroliubov equates loss of faith with maturation. Five years earlier, he had attributed his own rejection of belief in God to suffering, to the "terrible misfortune" of his parents' deaths. That experience had not only allowed him to turn his back on childhood beliefs, but it also gave him confidence in his "strength and capacity to take action." By 1860 he had come to view this as a normative experience, one that every strong-minded person should be capable of.

Dobroliubov's readers would subsequently note that there was a contradiction in his thought. In 1859 he had indicated that improved education and scientific knowledge were key components in unmasking the falsehood of religion. In "Ray of Light in the Kingdom of Darkness," published the next year, he accorded great powers of insight to Katerina, a thoroughly uneducated provincial woman. The contradiction may in fact represent a shift in Dobroliubov's thinking over the course of this short time. As a journalist, he now wanted to change his readers by both enlightening them with scientific truths and opening their eyes to the squalor that surrounded them. Writing to a friend in March 1860, he explained that he now aimed to "torture" his readers by exposing them to the full measure of "dirt" in their surroundings, to produce disgust in them, thereby prompting them to "jump up with agitation and utter: '[. . .] I don't want to live in this mire anymore.'"[96]

In 1861 Dobroliubov continued to insist on personal responsibility for independent thought in "The Downtrodden People," but he distanced himself even further from his earlier materialist approach. He noted that the true source of human liberation lies in a "divine," "sacred" spark that all people possess but that lies buried beneath their ignorance and humiliation. Mr. Goliadkin in Dostoevsky's *The Double* might feel that his humiliation had turned him into an old rag, yet he remained, he thought, a rag with feeling and ambition, however meek. The "downtrodden people" are, as Dobroliubov pointed out, "those people, who truly seem to have been turned into a rag; who only in some filthy repository manage to preserve the remnants of something human, inaudible, entirely meek, and yet making itself felt at times."[97] Dobroliubov claims

Nikolai Dobroliubov. Photograph, Naples, 1861. In Nikolai A. Dobroliubov, *Polnoe sobranie stikhotvorenii*, edited by Boris Ia. Bukhshtab (Leningrad: Sovetskii pisatel', 1969), between 160 and 161.

that this divine spark manifests itself in the recognition, however momentary, that they are not protected and cared for by a benefactor; they are rather dirty, naked, neglected, and their poverty is an unbearable insult. Makar Alekseich in Dostoevsky's *Poor Folk* exhorts himself to take courage, yet lack of a decent pair of shoes makes his heart sink: "'Just guess what boots I will wear to the office tomorrow! That is the rub, little mother. And it is just that kind of thought that can destroy a man, completely destroy him.' [. . .] Amid such worries," Dobroliubov adds, "man feels to what level he has been debased, to what extent he has been insulted by life. At that very moment, he addresses bitter reproaches to that, on which, it seems, he so sweetly reposes at other times."[98]

Dobroliubov wished to think that all human beings, whether educated or not, were capable of making the same discovery that he had made as a young man. The scientific argumentation of the Büchners and Moleschotts might only be necessary for the educated few whose privileges had protected them from the experiences and sentiments that ordinary Russians encountered every day.

Despite Dobroliubov's grim assessment of Russian realities, he and Chernyshevsky remained optimistic about the country's near future. In writings of the early 1860s, both spoke of a new generation that would soon become the dominant force in Russian society: the "new people." These people would be entirely free of the prejudices that the generation of the 1840s—as well as Chernyshevsky and Dobroliubov—had to struggle to rid themselves of. Dobroliubov describes how easily intellectual development would come to the new generation: "Slowly but surely, from childhood on, they have been soaking up those concepts and goals that the best people of earlier days had to fight, doubt, and suffer for in their mature years."[99]

Chernyshevsky made the "new people" the heroes of his enormously influential novel *What Is to Be Done?* (1863). The defining characteristic of its heroes is their self-confidence—the ease with which they make decisions and their immunity from doubt. In an early manuscript of the novel, the narrator even voices puzzlement about this characteristic in Vera Pavlovna, the central figure: "Verochka, there is something [. . .] that is strange [. . .] to the majority of people who have never met people like you: why have you neither hesitation nor doubt?"[100] The reason Vera and her friends never hesitate is because they are not prone to Orthodox Christian prejudices about virtue and vice. They act on the basis of "egoism," following their inclinations, trusting their feelings as guides to action. Unlike her friend Lopukhov, a natural scientist, Vera does not even need books to tell her that egoism is the proper basis for decision making. She seems to grasp this, too, instinctively.[101]

Though Chernyshevsky attempted to paint his "new people" as entirely free from the burden of a Christian upbringing, his novel is riddled, as Irina Paperno points out, with Christian symbolism and biblical allusions:

> The very title of the novel, *Chto delat'?* [, . . .] recalls the episode of the baptism in Luke (3:10–14) and the question that "the multitude that came forth to be baptized of him" asked of John: "What shall we do?" (*Chto zhe nam delat'?*). [. . .] The new men—"men of goodness and strength, justice and ability," as they are introduced to the reader—are seen as the apostles of a new creed, a new and improved Christianity. "You are the salt of the salt of the earth," the author says of them, reinforcing the words that Christ addressed to his disciples in the Sermon on the Mount. [. . .] Petrovna, the landlady of the newlywed Lopukhovs, impressed by the chastity of their marriage ("as if they were brother and sister"), takes them for members of a religious sect.[102]

Chernyshevsky wrote *What Is to Be Done?* in prison; he was arrested on suspicion of revolutionary conspiracy in July 1862 and held in St. Peter and Paul Fortress for almost two years. When he was finally sentenced in May 1864, he was pilloried in Mytinskaia Square with a sign on his chest that read "State Criminal." According to Paperno, his punishment was considered a "mock crucifixion" by his contemporaries. Thus, even Chernyshevsky's most ardent supporters continued to understand his life and writings in Orthodox Christian terms. Desacralization in Russia, Paperno claims, did not involve the disappearance of Christian concepts but rather their reinscription in the domain of "the daily life of ordinary men"; educated Russians had simply reversed "the spheres of the sacred and profane."[103] Russian atheism of the nineteenth century was not secular.

What Is to Be Done? was the last work that Chernyshevsky published in his lifetime. The unexpected success of the novel prompted the authorities to decide that he should never be allowed to publish again. Nor could Dobroliubov carry on his legacy: he was already dead, having succumbed to tuberculosis in November 1861. Their followers were therefore left to figure out for themselves the implications of these two men's writings.

The fact that Orthodox concepts play such an important role in their last works demonstrates the difficulty of the task that Chernyshevsky and Dobroliubov had set for themselves and for their contemporaries. They argued that educated Russians must turn away from the "nanny's tales" and "superstitions" they had been taught in childhood. That was the precondition that would allow them to attain self-consciousness and the freedom to become active participants in the transformation of their society. In order to facilitate this departure, Chernyshevsky and Dobroliubov promoted materialist explanations of the operation of nature and the human mind along with an avowedly non-Orthodox system of ethics. They hoped this would liberate educated Russians from the self-loathing that had troubled members of the tobacco-store circle, who had been unable to overcome the sense that their atheism was both a consequence and cause of moral depravity. Chernyshevsky and Dobroliubov also hoped to liberate the intelligentsia from those crushing doubts that had assailed members of Herzen's generation and led to inactivity and resignation.

The injunction that educated Russians divorce themselves from the beliefs inculcated in them as children also posed new problems, however. Did Chernyshevsky and Dobroliubov really mean that the individual must abnegate not only belief in God but also every part of the Orthodox Christian legacy as well? Or was it acceptable to draw on elements of that heritage (such as the biblical allusions that Chernyshevsky made such heavy use of in his novel)? Their adepts, among them radical students in rural Russia, appear to have answered this second question in the affirmative. Anticipating a peasant revolution in the countryside, these young men would interpret the impending cataclysm in Orthodox religious terms: to them, revolution spelled apocalypse.

Dobroliubov and Chernyshevsky also claimed that all human beings must learn to act independently by relying on their instincts and inclinations to guide their actions rather than on authorities or inherited beliefs. This proposition was not only radical but thoroughly untested. It implied a kind of individualism that had never existed in Russia's highly communitarian society. It also placed a heavy burden on individuals, who must invent and build a life on the basis of those inclinations. Dmitrii Pisarev, the literary critic who succeeded Chernyshevsky and Dobroliubov as Russia's leading radical journalist, would experiment with this idea, attempting to live his life in accordance with it. Pisarev also came far closer than they would to creating a secular code of behavior for his readers.

Readers of the *Contemporary* could thus draw two radically different conclusions from the writings of Chernyshevsky and Dobroliubov. One was that they were meant to devote themselves, in communitarian fashion, to the salvation of Russia, drawing heavily on Orthodox conceptions as they did so. The other was that they were supposed to live a life of total independence, stripping their minds of all preconceptions and attempting to discover a new set of principles and way of life on their own. The denial of the existence of God, therefore, did not put an end to the search for truth and meaning that lay at the heart of intelligentsia life. Rather it only heightened it and opened new questions for subsequent generations to debate.

Part 3

Two Modes of Living
without God

5

Atheism and Apocalypse

Revolutionaries in the Provinces,
1856–1863

In provincial towns of the Russian Empire, from Kharkov and Kazan to Viatka and Perm, a revolutionary movement developed with extraordinary rapidity during the late 1850s and early 1860s. This movement was predicated on the conviction—widely shared among educated Russians—that the empire stood on the brink of an abyss and that continued poverty among Russia's serf majority would lead to mass violence. Revolutionaries hoped such violence could be transformative, leading to the creation of an egalitarian, constitutional, democratic state, ruled along federalist lines by representative assemblies. In those assemblies, as the revolutionaries foresaw them, it would be the *narod* that would predominate, former serfs in their bast shoes and long tunics.

The student revolutionaries who first came forward in the provinces in 1856 were not atheists. One such group, a circle in Kharkov, was largely composed of noblemen, most of whom considered themselves Orthodox Christians, and they felt that rebellion was fully compatible with their religious beliefs. Indeed, they expressed their convictions in a vocabulary heavily imbued with biblical allusions. Above all, they represented the impending revolution as the Apocalypse, a day of reckoning on which evildoers would be destroyed and the Russian people saved.[1] Apocalyptic speech continued to dominate revolutionary propaganda in the provinces during the early 1860s, in Perm and Kazan, even as revolutionaries themselves came to embrace atheism and to argue that faith and revolution were incompatible.

Student radicals had been anticipating a large-scale peasant uprising since 1856. The failure of this eagerly anticipated event to take place undermined faith that the Apocalypse would come to fruition by God's will. The revolution would only be successful if the population as a whole abandoned its belief that God would provide and came to understand that it must provide for itself through self-motivated action. That atheism was a precondition for successful revolution would remain a widely held assumption among Russian revolutionaries in the early twentieth century and became a central component of the ideology of the Soviet state.

The young revolutionaries who came to promote atheism in the provinces were characterized by their modest social origins. Sons of priests, of deacons and subdeacons, of provincial school teachers and petty officers, almost none of these young men came from noble families. They found their point of entry into the revolutionary movement at Russian universities, where they arrived from the far-flung corners of the provinces, sometimes on foot, ill-kempt, uncouth, and impoverished. In the early reign of Alexander II, Russian universities grew markedly in size, though their social composition did not change: sons of priests and other commoners remained well below 50 percent of the total student population.[2] Students from impoverished families were recognizable on campus for their worn-out student uniforms. By the early 1860s, however, they were not entirely unwelcome, at least not in the radical circles that had grown up in the last half decade. To signal their closeness to the people and disapproval of official norms of comportment, radical youths of all origins cultivated an unkempt appearance, often incorporating elements of peasant dress.[3] Their circles embraced young provincials of obscure origins, offering them a new sense of identity. Participation in the radical movement allowed these commoners to feel that they could contribute to a higher cause, that they could assist in remaking their nation. Apocalyptic rhetoric expressed their faith that Russia was about to be transformed; atheist rhetoric expressed their conviction that this event would be wrought by human hands.

Seminarians in particular read articles by Chernyshevsky and Dobroliubov, fellow *raznochintsy* and sons of priests from the provinces, with rapt attention.[4] Chernyshevsky and Dobroliubov did not invent the rhetoric of revolution as apocalypse. The two journalists did, however, articulate the view that atheism was an essential component of taking charge of one's life—and the fate of the nation. As revolutionaries in the provinces composed their broadsheets, combining religious rhetoric with calls to abandon faith in God, they inserted Chernyshevsky and Dobroliubov's ideas into them.

These young men not only composed revolutionary tracts but also walked into the countryside to disseminate them among the peasants, evidently believing that they would be receptive to the words of fellow commoners. The lowly social status and provincial background of these young men, most of whom were born and died in obscurity, facilitated their assumption that they could easily reach out to and influence the peasant population. They may also have believed that their heavy use of biblical allusions would heighten the appeal of the material they distributed. They held fast to these beliefs, even when the peasants proved wholly unwelcoming to them and their publications.

Apocalypse" is a word that evokes fear and hope in the mind of many Christians, and it especially did for Orthodox Russians—conservatives and radicals alike—in the later 1850s. For the earliest student revolutionaries, the sense of apocalypse was bred by the feeling that the autocracy had betrayed the Russian people. Opposition to autocracy had risen in 1848–1849. The outbreak of the Crimean War in 1853, however, heightened students' feelings of nationalism and betrayal. By 1855, when Nicholas I died, it was clear that Russia would lose the war, and that his son, Alexander II, could do little to improve the situation.

Beginning in 1856, Russia's student revolutionaries in the provinces began to argue that the betrayal perpetrated by the autocracy was much worse than defeat in war, that it in fact consisted of centuries of exploitation of the Russian people, particularly of the serf population. Popular discontent, they now hoped, would provoke a massive uprising that would fundamentally alter the political and social landscape of Russia. Small peasant disturbances had, indeed, already occurred in 1854 and 1855, as various rumors circulated among peasants, such that they would be liberated in the event of a British and French victory or that those peasants who enlisted in the war effort would be rewarded with freedom. These tensions in the countryside convinced not only revolutionaries but also conservatives and liberals that a large-scale uprising was about to take place. The well-known liberal jurist Konstantin Kavelin, for example, commented in 1857 that "all signs point toward a frightful cataclysm in the future, apparently soon, although it is impossible to predict what form it will take and where it will take us."[5]

To the political elites, it was clear that this cataclysm could only be averted in one way: by emancipating the serfs. As state officials began to deliberate on the terms of the emancipation, this event, too, took on apocalyptic meaning in the eyes of educated Russians. Liberal supporters felt the emancipation held promise for the "resurrection" of the country. It would, they hoped, inaugurate a "new life" for Russia.[6] Some state officials clearly shared this view. Easter, the celebration of Christ's death and resurrection, had always been a time to contemplate the Last Judgment at Christ's Second Coming. The imperial state often planned important events to coincide with it. Alexander II signed the emancipation into law on February 19, 1861 (the sixth anniversary of his reign), but officials chose the first day of Lent, March 5, 1861, to announce the emancipation and its terms to the peasants.[7]

Radical revolutionaries, too, hoped for a "new life" for the country, but they viewed the emancipation as a palliative measure, one that might itself provoke an uprising. Some radicals pinned their hopes on peasant sectarians and Old Believers, whom they thought most likely to revolt. Emerging out of the schism in the mid-seventeenth century, Old Believers viewed the Romanov state as evil and had participated in several major uprisings during the seventeenth and eighteenth centuries. Convinced that the Apocalypse was at hand, they identified Tsar Alexis Romanov as Antichrist, and they would later say the same of his son Peter.[8] Millenarian expectation among sectarians began to peak once again toward the middle of the nineteenth century.[9] Radicals hoped this trend would produce one last popular rebellion that would sweep the Romanovs from power.[10]

Just as the state decided to announce the emancipation to the serfs on the first day of Lent, so radicals chose the period between Lent and Easter to distribute revolutionary broadsheets announcing the impending collapse of the state and transformation of the country. Their own expectation of revolution always peaked at this time. Easter brought to mind Judgment Day, on which an old, corrupt society would be swept away or disappear in a pool of blood. Those who were prepared would be reborn into the "new people" and would inhabit the kingdom of heaven on earth. This, at least, is what revolutionaries promised in a series of proclamations produced in Kharkov, Perm, Kazan, and other provincial towns in and after 1856. Their sense of mission was preserved even as students turned away from faith in God.

Apocalypse" (*apokalipsis*) literally means "revelation," or the unveiling of God's intentions to humankind. Apocalyptic texts purport to be based on visions revealed to a prophet by God. The revelation includes an eschatological representation of the past and shows that history, after having passed through various stages, will soon come to an abrupt end. At that time, a "New Jerusalem," the kingdom of heaven on earth, will come into being, where people will enjoy eternal life. The New Testament specifies that these events will be accompanied by much tribulation, softened by two appearances of the Messiah. At his First Coming, Christ ties up his adversary (Antichrist, or Satan) and establishes a kingdom that lasts a thousand years (Revelation 20:2). At his Second Coming, Christ unleashes his adversaries for 1,260 days, or three and a half years (Revelation 12:6). Humankind then falls under the sway of false prophets and of a wicked man (or ruler) who claims to be God (or Christ himself) (2 Thessalonians 2; Revelation 13:7, 19:19–20). At this point, the Messiah makes his final appearance, the epiphany. Having vanquished his enemy, he will judge the living and the dead, who are to be resurrected, and the new order, a "new heavens and a new earth," will be brought into being (Revelation 21:1).

Scholars have noted that apocalyptic writings have usually been produced in times of extreme political and social crisis.[11] Their function has been to unite the faithful and to point to God's intervention—the imminent arrival of the avenging Messiah and the advent of a new kingdom—as a way of conveying hope. As H. H. Rowley explains in *The Relevance of Apocalyptic*, "It was of the essence of Biblical prophecy to use prediction not primarily for the sake of unfolding the future, but for the bringing home of the message of God to the men who first received it. [. . . The apocalyptists'] purpose was essentially practical, to proclaim a great hope to men and to call them to a great loyalty and watchfulness."[12] The time when the new kingdom would be created was never spelled out but always remained a vague "soon."

Apocalyptic passages in the Bible have long provoked speculation. Whom did the prophets have in mind when they warned of Antichrist? In the Book of Revelation, he is identified as a political and military ruler (13:7, 17:10–12, 19:16–18), perhaps a Roman emperor, though theologians supposed he might also be a Jew or a Muslim. In 2 Thessalonians 2:3–4, 8–10, Antichrist is identified as a sinful man—possibly an apostate from within the ranks of the church, who would put himself forward as God and be worshipped by misguided Christians.[13]

The timing of the Second Advent also remained the subject of conjecture. Was Christ's first kingdom still at hand, or had the 1,260 days of the reign of Antichrist begun? These questions were left open in the New Testament. The apostles Peter, James, John, and Andrew acted with characteristic impertinence when they asked Jesus Christ to specify when exactly "this will be" and what signs to look for (Mark 13:4). It was for God to know these things; people must wait, pray, and watch. The role of the just and faithful in the Apocalypse was not to act, not to take up arms themselves, but to suffer persecution.

While the faithful vigilantly waited for the Second Coming, one course of action remained open to them: that of remaking themselves into "new people" in the image of Christ. This was their only hope for salvation. The new people are mentioned in the Pauline Epistles of the New Testament: Ephesians 2:15, 4:22; Colossians 3:9–10; 2 Corinthians 5:17; and Galatians 6:15. Here, the terms "new man" and "new people" (sometimes also referred to as "new creatures") refer both to Christ and to those who live in his name. They remake themselves by "casting off" the "old man" (or old Adam) and "putting on" the "new man" (Christ), thus becoming "new people." This transformation has been interpreted as an apocalyptic image in some recent Protestant theology. The appearance of the new man is what initiates the collapse of the old world and the creation of the new kingdom.[14]

The Russian Orthodox Church forbade speculation about the timing of the Apocalypse.[15] In theological tracts, sermons, and epistles, the Russian clergy of the mid-nineteenth century dwelt on the importance of the Last Judgment, emphasizing that salvation would come only through God's mercy, not human volition. Little was said about the creation of the new kingdom that was to follow the day of reckoning.[16] Nor did clergymen of the mid-nineteenth century say much about the "new man" and "new people" in connection with the Second Coming of Christ.[17] Theological textbooks noted that people can become sanctified, "reborn" and renewed in Christ, by cleansing themselves of sin (for example, in baptism), but emphasized that this only happens through God's merciful intercession.[18] Ignatii (Brianchaninov) noted that one becomes a new man only by subordinating oneself completely to God, learning to suppress one's will.[19] Filaret (Drozdov) said much the same: every person's soul contains the seed of a new man, but it can only grow if one turns away from the world and the ways of the flesh, suppresses one's pride, and cultivates humility. Most important, it is not up to the individual to choose to be reborn. One can hope and prepare for the transformation, but only God can make it happen.[20]

Chernyshevsky and Dobroliubov's use of the concept of the "new people" in their writings of the early 1860s was, of course, very different from nineteenth-century Orthodox usage; they clearly did associate the advent of the "new people" with the salvation of Russia and emphasized that becoming a new person was a matter of human volition. Dobroliubov introduced the term to refer to the rise of a young generation, energetic and free of doubt, whose emergence would inaugurate the transformation of Russia.[21]

The concept of the "new man" was also developed by Nikolai Pomialovskii, a fellow priest's son, in fictional works he published in 1861. Some of these appeared in the *Contemporary* and were wildly popular among the radical youth. Pomialovskii's hero, Molotov, is a "new man," born into poverty, whose difficult childhood makes it relatively easy for him to "discard the old life" and open a "new, moral world." The rejection of religious beliefs is part of the process: "Even now, he remembers what moral tortures and doubts it cost him to [realize] the truth that it is not Elijah the prophet who produces thunder. Nothing came easily now, no new beliefs [replaced the old ones . . .]. Moral labor brought Molotov benefit: he learned not to believe in authority and the old ways. [. . .] He became accustomed to doing things for himself [*samodeiatel'nost'*], to being able to dismiss false opinions."[22] The key phrase here is "doing things for himself" (*samodeiatel'nost'*). Independence becomes possible because Molotov learns "not to believe" in the religious dogmas he had been taught.

The concept of "new people" took on its fullest apocalyptic connotations in Chernyshevsky's famous novel, *What Is to Be Done? Tales of the New People* (1863). Here, Chernyshevsky repeatedly emphasizes that the new people are not gods but rather entirely human.[23] Yet he also refers to them as a "sign of the times" (*znamenie vremeni*) (Matthew 16: 3–4) and saviors of humanity. "Six years ago, nobody saw these people; three years ago, they were despised. Now . . . but it does not matter, what they think of them now; in a few years, a very few years, they will call to them: 'Save us!' [*Spasite nas!*]." The new people, Chernyshevsky prophesied, would have to come at least twice, for at their first appearance, humanity persecutes and curses them. Only after their second appearance will the rest of humanity transform itself in their image: "Then, there will no longer be a separate type, because all people will be of that type."[24]

To students in Russia's provincial towns, these promises were alluring. Yet they appear to have discovered the value of apocalyptic rhetoric well before Dobroliubov and Chernyshevsky began to speak of the "new people." The biblical Apocalypse spoke to students' assessment that the country they lived in was irredeemably corrupt. Radicals felt that peasants must share their view, and they produced their own apocalyptic broadsheets and pamphlets to drive that message home. Year after year, however, the uprising they awaited did not come. Ultimately, an entirely human blueprint came to replace belief in a divine plan for transformation. There was no God, only a people that needed saving. Student radicals would become their apostles and redeemers.

The first young people to announce the apocalyptic revolutionary message appeared in Kharkov in April 1856. They were faithful Orthodox Christians, mostly students from noble families, who prepared a special surprise for the city's inhabitants on Easter Sunday. That morning, the people of Kharkov awoke to find that their town had been plastered with some fifteen to twenty-five copies of a mock imperial manifesto. Announcing the disastrous terms of Russia's defeat in the Crimean War, the manifesto (purportedly signed by Alexander II) thanked Russian subjects for allowing themselves to be exploited and duped by the state.

The broadsheet had been composed by two students at Kharkov University—Nikolai Raevskii, enrolled at the Physical-Mathematical Faculty, and Mitrofan Muravskii, a student at the Law Faculty.[25] The two were an unlikely pair in both social background and disposition. Raevskii, a wit from a very wealthy noble family, died of tuberculosis in 1858 at the age of nineteen. Muravskii, of petty gentry origins, was a fanatical Orthodox Christian believer and went on to a long career in revolutionary circles, where he came to be known as "Father Mitrofan." The friends who helped them copy and post the manifesto were even more diverse. Petr Zavadskii, an ardent Ukrainian nationalist, was the son of a priest and studied medicine; his housemate Petr Efimenko was also a Ukrainian nationalist. The son of a military officer, Efimenko studied at the Law Faculty. Iakov Bekman was a nobleman and, like Efimenko, a student of law. This highly heterogeneous group was united by two common sentiments: a sense of contempt for the Russian state, which had been defeated in the Crimean War, and a shared longing for revolution, which they understood in apocalyptic terms.

The group's apocalyptic leanings were displayed in the way they went about distributing the manifesto. It was posted on the eve of the Orthodox celebration of Christ's resurrection, and they made the connection to Easter explicit. They stuffed one copy into an envelope and threw it into a mailbox, intending for it to be found by officials. The envelope was marked: "Christ is risen! Truly he is risen! But the truth is still being resurrected [*voskresaet*]."[26] The words on the envelope showed that the manifesto was to be interpreted as a "resurrection of the truth." The body of the manifesto, however, insisted that Christ himself needed to rise again. "Christ, the eternal embodiment of the truth," was being "sold and crucified" while Russia slept. Specifically, he was being sold and crucified by clergymen of the Orthodox Church, who lent ideological support to Alexander II and his policies.[27] The message was that Russia had fallen away from the true faith; the clergy as represented here could be seen as the false prophets of 2 Corinthians 11:4 and Acts 20:29–30. Waking up to find the manifesto on Sunday morning, the people of Kharkov must also have remembered warnings in the New Testament that at his Second Advent, Christ would come "like a thief in the night," unnoticed by his inattentive flock (1 Thessalonians 5:2; Matthew 24:43; Mark 13:36; Luke 12:39; 2 Peter 3:10; Revelation 3:3, 16:15).

Apparently, this first gesture did not satisfy the group's zeal. One month later, in May 1856, they posted about four copies of a second parody around Kharkov University. This broadsheet, a mock advertisement for a "historical drama" was entirely written by Muravskii.[28] If anything, it was more explicitly apocalyptic than the manifesto had been, as can be seen in its opening lines, which refer both to the millennium and to the triumph of light over darkness:

> By the will of God [Izvoleniem Bozhiim]
> For the benefit of humanity
>   Toward 1862, the thousand-year anniversary of Russia, if the people awake soon, the inhabitants of the Russian land will accomplish [the following]:
>   The Emancipation of Russia from the heirs of Batu [Khan], or
>   The Triumph of the light of freedom over the darkness of autocracy.

The drama's central protagonists were "preachers of truth," the "people," "patriots" and "chosen Russians," who would do battle against "persecutors of truth" and "enemies of the fatherland." The performance was set to begin "at any time of day and night." As the playbill advertised, it would take place in three acts: act 1 would depict the humiliating peace treaty of 1856, act 2 the destruction of autocracy, and act 3 freedom in Russia.[29]

The mock manifesto and the parodic playbill constituted an attack on the Romanov monarchy and on the Russian Orthodox Church as an institution that supported the monarchy. To repeat, however, the group did not reject faith in God. Rather its members firmly believed that

Orthodox Christianity was contrary to monarchy. Its members were outraged by Alexander II's attempts to cloak himself in the mantle of Orthodoxy.[30] They also believed that Orthodoxy was incompatible with serfdom, which they strongly opposed.[31] As Orthodox Christians, group members believed that the events they prophesied would not occur as the result of human initiative but by the will of God: "Izvoleniem Bozhiim." This was one point that authors of later apocalyptic texts would explicitly deny; faith in Providence, they would argue, could only prevent the necessary events from occurring.

No major uprising took place in the months after May 1856. By January or February 1857, for reasons that are not entirely clear, members of the group had lost their enthusiasm for conspiratorial activity.[32] The circle fell apart in 1858, and several of its members moved to Kiev. In 1860 they were arrested and exiled; a second series of arrests took place in 1862, and they were spread even further apart: to Vologda, Samara, Arkhangelsk, Onega, Olonets, Viatka, Kursk, Shadrinsk, and Dorpat.

They continued to understand their activities in Orthodox Christian terms. The most important of these efforts was their participation in the "Sunday school" movement, a program to bring literacy to Russian peasants and workers, which began in 1859. Petr Zavadskii was one of the first to become involved. As he testified to the Third Section after his arrest in 1860, his aim was not only to spread literacy but also to improve the people's knowledge of Orthodoxy: "Simple people need to know Christian doctrine, but they do not know it." The liturgy, he added, was of little help: "they all go to church and stand there and listen, but many do not understand what is being declaimed."[33] The version of Orthodox theology Zavadskii and his friends planned to teach (and probably did teach) in these Sunday schools was not the one that authorities wanted disseminated.

When the state began to impose severe restrictions on Sunday schools in the early 1860s, members of the Kharkov group interpreted this as part of the apocalyptic battle, and they were not the only ones to do so. In March 1861 Apollinarii Pokrovskii, a leader of the movement in Moscow (unconnected to Muravskii and his friends) remarked that the authorities were trying to prevent the "dawning of the new life of the people."[34] Temporarily, such persecution raised Muravskii's hopes: "Persecution [. . .] will only make things come to a head more quickly [*goneniia* [. . .] *vedut k uskoreniiu razviazki*]."[35] Yet the events he anticipated did not come to pass.

Orthodox thought was a central part of the revolutionary propaganda of Muravskii, Zavadskii, Bekman, and Efimenko in the later 1850s. At this point, they were not only believers but also viewed the use of Orthodox Christian concepts in their writings as something that might attract a popular audience. Old Believers were one target group, but the friends set their sights on other people(s) as well. They were angered by the spread of Polish culture among Ukrainians, and even more so by the spread of Catholicism in Little Russia. Once the revolution broke out, they promised they would convert Ukrainians back to Orthodoxy.[36] Muravskii was also in favor of converting the non-Christian peoples of the Russian south.[37] Neither last nor least, the Orthodox themselves needed to be taught the true meaning of their own religion.

When members of the circle were arrested and exiled in 1860, however, it became clear that participation in the revolutionary movement necessitated difficult choices of allegiance, as can be observed in the case of Mitrofan Muravskii, the Kharkov group member who remained most strongly committed to Orthodox Christianity.[38] He was also the one who fared the worst in prison and during the early years of exile, sinking into depression and alcoholism following his release from prison. In 1861 he remained in contact with his former friends and reassured them that their letters were an important source of moral support; their correspondence had the power to "raise" one another "from the dead."[39] Yet the relief can only have been temporary. Muravskii suffered enormously from a sense of despair. In the late 1870s he told a young radical that he had been crushed by the failure of the Apocalypse to materialize, devastated when, as he put it, the trumpets that were to herald the day of the Last Judgment "did not sound." As a result, he said, he took to drink. If this account is correct, Muravskii's crisis would have taken place in the early 1860s.[40]

Though his friends did not know it, Muravskii had more practical reasons to slip into despair. Under interrogation in 1860, he had given the prosecutors much valuable information about the activities of the Kharkov circle.[41] What is more, his strong Orthodox convictions had been central to prosecutors' success in extracting information from him. Muravskii spent his first days under interrogation steadfastly asserting his innocence and that of his friends, even when prosecutors produced incriminating evidence against him. It was only after they had arranged for a priest to meet with him that Muravskii's story changed. Following the

priest's admonition, he made a full confession to the authorities, implicat-
ing himself as well as his friends.[42] His guilt might explain why Muravskii
was so relieved to receive mail from his former associates in the early
1860s: the letters showed that his friends had not guessed his betrayal.

It would be easy to attribute Muravskii's confession to personal
weakness, but such a judgment would be precipitous. Solitary interviews
between priests and detainees became a standard technique for extracting
confessions in the mid-1860s. The institutionalization of such procedures
had much to do with the dramatic increase in the number of people
arrested and exiled for political conspiracy, beginning in June 1862.[43]
The growing frequency of arrests also meant, however, that the behavior
of suspects also grew more routinized, as participants in the revolutionary
movement established their own procedures for managing interrogations. This most likely included a set response to any priest.[44] Arrested
in 1860, however, Muravskii was caught unprepared. He knew only
what every Orthodox believer was told—that it was a cardinal sin to lie
to a priest and to ignore the priest's exhortations.

Loyalty to the canons of the Orthodox Church had become difficult
to reconcile with conspiratorial activity and would remain so as long as
priests remained loyal to the state. More important, the failure of the
uprising to materialize posed a problem, making it difficult to maintain
simultaneously faith in God's Providence and in the Apocalypse as a
peasant uprising. Those who continued to use apocalyptic rhetoric
began to argue that radicals, together with the people, must take matters into their own hands.

Though Chernyshevsky and Dobroliubov began to articulate atheistic
ideas in the pages of the *Contemporary* in the later 1850s, it was only in the
early 1860s that they found expression in revolutionary proclamations
produced by provincial radicals. The activities of Petr Efimenko, a
founding member of the Kharkov circle, help clarify how this shift took
place. The growth of radical networks in Russia enabled Efimenko and
others to make contact with counterparts in Moscow and St. Petersburg, facilitating the spread of ideas. This diffusion was further aided by
underground associations that made journals and books increasingly
available in the countryside. The available texts included authorized
publications, such as the *Contemporary*, as well as contraband writings,
such as the pamphlets and journals published by Alexander Herzen in
London and a translation of Feuerbach's *Lectures on the Essence of Religion*,
lithographed by students in Moscow. Efimenko and his associates

would draw on all of these as they began to produce revolutionary proclamations containing antireligious content. While they continued to describe revolution in apocalyptic terms, they would insist that the rejection of divine Providence was essential for anyone wishing to take part in the revolutionary movement. The anticipated uprising would never take place if Russians waited for the trumpets of the Last Judgment to sound.

Petr Efimenko was born in 1835, the son of a low-ranking and impoverished officer in Tokmak, Berdiansk district (present-day Zaporizhzhia, Ukraine). The parish of Tokmak is known to have been home to a large population of radical sectarians, whose mood was increasingly rebellious and whose millenarian expectations were high.[45] Efimenko appears to have been considered the Kharkov group's expert on sectarians; at any rate, Iakov Bekman, a leading member of the circle, hoped that he would infiltrate the Old Believers by passing himself off as a priest.[46]

Instead, Efimenko drifted away from Orthodox faith. In 1858 he left Kharkov to study in Moscow, where he stayed for a brief time and made contact with a fresh set of people, the "Vertepniki," who espoused both French socialism and German Left Hegelianism. Under arrest in 1860, Efimenko recalled one meeting in particular, at which the group's leader read a "short article from Feuerbach" in the midst of a debate on miracles.[47] The "article" was most likely a chapter on miracles from Feuerbach's *Lectures on the Essence of Religion*, the most explicitly political of his works, produced for German students during the uprising of 1848.

To Feuerbach, the belief in miracles, like belief in God, is partly a product of human feelings of dependence (*Abhängigkeitsgefühl*) on nature. People are especially prone to look for miracles in times of crisis, when they want their physical needs to be met. The sick long to be healed, the hungry long to be fed, and they all wish to believe that all their pain could be instantaneously eradicated by some being. Belief in God and belief in a king, according to Feuerbach, go hand in hand; they are products of the human fantasy that events in nature and in the world at large can be made subject to the will of some being. They dream of how God or kings might pass all sorts of laws and annul them again as they see fit. The desire for such a lord is unhealthy, because it is based on the mistaken belief that everything in life is subject to will. Some things cannot be changed. And yet, in reality, people are self-motivated (*selbsttätig*) and must provide for themselves. The idea of God strips people of their independence and *Selbsttätigkeit* by creating the illusion that he is the one who provides for them.[48] This was the illusion that Russia's atheists of the early 1860s would seek to dispel.

Efimenko did not begin to put the lessons he had learned that evening in Moscow into practice until after his arrest in 1860 and release into exile. He arrived at his place of banishment, Perm, in July 1860. Soon thereafter, he wrote to Muravskii to declare his break from Christianity. His letter began with complaints about the general despondency and lack of initiative of radicals in Perm. Then, rather awkwardly, he noted that "right now, I am mainly studying Christianity, and have come to such conclusions as will seem strange to you, namely that, in my opinion, it is immoral in the highest degree."[49] Efimenko did not specify here exactly what he deemed immoral about Christianity, but his subsequent writings suggest that he based this judgment on the view that Orthodox Christianity bred passivity.

The most important of these writings was an apocalyptic tract, "The Epistle of Kondratii the Elder," which Efimenko assisted in composing. The document was produced just before the emancipation of the serfs was signed into law on February 19, 1861, and it was designed to incite a major peasant uprising. Specifically, it was aimed at Old Believers living in the Ural Mountains, near Perm. It urged them to stop paying taxes, disobey the boyars, or nobility, and refuse to serve in the army. It also encouraged readers to destroy the institutions of autocracy and bureaucracy and form a representative government.[50] Efimenko's partner in writing the epistle was Aleksei Morigerovskii, a teacher at the Perm Seminary, just under thirty years old.[51] Students at the seminary served as copyists, producing at least eight replicas of this long manuscript. Owing to the group's premature arrest, the tract was never distributed. Most likely, the only people who read it were those who produced it and the tight circle of their friends.[52]

The text was inspired by a pamphlet printed in London by Alexander Herzen.[53] That pamphlet, titled *Visions of the Holy Father Kondratii*, by the émigré Vladimir Engelson, was advertised as the work of an Old Believer priest. Published during the Crimean War in 1854, it called on Russian Old Believer soldiers to lay down their arms.[54] The *Visions* are written in a combination of Russian and Old Church Slavonic and are suffused with biblical language, including the language of Apocalypse: Nicholas I is Antichrist, a sinful man who, pretending to be God, encourages all kinds of wickedness.[55] The pamphlet in no way seeks to undermine faith in God; indeed, it contains two commandments ostensibly dictated to Father Kondratii by God.[56]

Morigerovskii and Efimenko's Perm "Epistle" is three times the length of Engelson's *Visions*. Unlike its model, the tract does not claim to be based on a divinely inspired vision. Still, it too makes heavy use of Church Slavonic words and contains numerous references to the biblical prophets, citing the Book of Daniel, the Book of Revelation, and the Epistles of St. Paul chapter and verse. Announcing that "the time is at hand" (*vremia, bratiia moia i sestry, prispelo*), the Perm epistle urges its readers to take action "to create the kingdom of God on earth" (*vodvoriaite na zemle Bozhie tsarstvie*).[57] As in *Visions*, the emperor (now Alexander II) is represented as Antichrist, the wicked man of 2 Thessalonians 2, who cloaks himself in the mantle of God. Alexander/Antichrist has taken away his subjects' freedom, their will, and their reason, offering them a stultifying "peace" instead.

Despite its heavy reliance on biblical authority, "The Epistle of Kondratii the Elder" also sets out to undermine readers' religious faith. Indeed, Efimenko and Morigerovskii couch their injunctions against faith in biblical terms. Citing 2 Thessalonians 2:10–11, the authors warn that people whom Antichrist deludes into believing falsehood will perish.[58] Their first, "new commandment" is "do not believe" (*ne ver'te*). Individuals should rely only on their own reason and reject any belief that is not supported by their reason. They should accept nothing on faith but should engage critically with what they are told. This message fits the document's wider emphasis on self-reliance. There is no reason to hope for a better life in the hereafter; all should work to ensure their happiness in the here and now.[59]

Looking back at the text in light of this directive, one notices that, for all of its apocalypticism, it does not actually discuss the Second Coming of Christ. Jesus is mentioned only twice: once as a personal inspiration to "Father Kondratii" and once as a historical figure.[60] Even the Gospels are referred to as "the book, called the Gospels" (*kniga, imenuemaia Evangelem*).[61] Christ's crucifixion is noted but not his resurrection. He is to play no role in current events. The creation of the kingdom of heaven is emphatically to be brought about by human hands, not by God. As the authors repeat three times, its creation "depends" on the actions of their readers: "Your deeds, your life [*zhitie*] alone will be responsible for establishing the kingdom of God on earth. Clothe yourselves in the full armor of justice [*oblekites' vo vseoruzhie pravdy*], and patiently establish the kingdom of God on earth." As the authors explain, "the voice of the people is the voice of God." This was truly to be a kingdom without a king: no Messiah would rule over the new earth. Sacrifice and martyrdom would be the province of human beings, who must now die in the name of their kith and kin.[62]

The message of self-reliance that Efimenko and Morigerovskii put forward in their tract was based on several sources. Feuerbach, whose ideas Efimenko had been exposed to in Moscow, must have been one. Efimenko may also have been reacting to lessons learned by the Kharkov group in 1856: if one waited for the Second Coming of the Messiah, one might wait a very long time indeed. By rejecting faith in God and the Messiah, revolutionaries hoped they could make the Apocalypse happen themselves. Even then, however, these young men had no way of knowing whether their will and efforts would be sufficient to bring about the outcome they hoped for. A certain kind of faith continued to be necessary, even if it was not Orthodox Christian faith. Apocalyptic rhetoric now signified hope and belief in the coming transformation of the country by the revolutionaries themselves. This is why it remained a core part of their propagandistic writings even after they professed to have given up belief in God.

Beginning in 1861, student revolutionaries decided they must do more than produce pamphlets if the peasant uprising was to come about. That year, students at Kazan University walked into the countryside in an effort to foment peasant rebellion. These self-proclaimed apostles were of modest backgrounds—sons of deacons and petty merchants. They hoped that their unpretentious origins would enable them to communicate their apocalyptic hope to the peasants. Yet walking out into the countryside was, as they quickly learned, a dangerous undertaking with little promise of success. The apostles must have regarded their mission as an end in itself.

To understand the students' growing radicalization, one must bear in mind the political and social tensions occasioned by the proclamation of the emancipation of the serfs. Not only did the terms of the emancipation appear ungenerous to the freed serfs, but they would not begin to go into effect for another two years. As radicals had predicted, peasant disappointment led to numerous rebellions. These events only confirmed the perception, already established among all members of the revolutionary intelligentsia, both noblemen and *raznochintsy*, that the state was incapable of reforming the country.

It was not the emancipation itself that radicalized students, but the state's brutal response to the peasant rebellions that broke out during Lent of 1861.[63] The Spassk district in Kazan province was one area where disturbances became especially intense during early April. Peasants there were convinced that they had been lied to about the emancipation: the nobility had thwarted the tsar's true intentions by suppressing the announcement of key passages of the edict. In Bezdna, a village in Spassk, an Old Believer peasant, Anton Petrov stepped forward to announce that he had obtained a copy of the emancipation edict and would read the key passages aloud. Thousands gathered to hear him. Soldiers had been dispatched to disperse them, and when on April 12 they were ordered to shoot, they killed more than one hundred unarmed peasants.[64] It did not take radicals long to make out the meaning of these events; they were already prepared to view the fallen peasants as martyrs in the apocalyptic struggle.[65]

Student radicals were not alone in interpreting the Bezdna massacre this way. Alexander Herzen, too, represented the events in overtly apocalyptic terms in a report he published on the event two months later in the *Bell*: "But you, my hapless Old Believer-brothers, you who have suffered much, [. . .] preserve in your memory the day of the new passion—April 12. The time of Biblical persecutions is at hand. You know from the *Lives of the Saints* what massacres of the Christians the emperors undertook—and you know who triumphed. But triumph does not come without faith, and it does not come without deeds. Be strong in spirit, and remember the cry of the fallen martyrs of Bezdna, Freedom! Freedom! [*Volia! Volia!*]"[66] While glorifying the fallen, Herzen drew attention to a problem that troubled every person who sympathized with the revolutionary cause: unless peasant rebellions were coordinated into a wider event that toppled the Romanov regime, the deaths of individual peasants would be for naught.

The same issue was raised when students at Kazan University, together with students at the Kazan Theological Academy, organized a requiem for the dead peasants of Bezdna.[67] The requiem was to take place on Lazarus Saturday, April 16, the day before Palm Sunday, the beginning of Passion Week.[68] Members of a group called the "Circle" (*Kruzhok*) took the initiative in organizing this event.[69] They requested that the university's most popular lecturer, Afanasii Shchapov, make a speech at the requiem. Shchapov, who was also a professor at Kazan Theological Academy, was popular among students at the university because in his lectures on history, he openly displayed sympathy for peasant democracy.[70] His oration would become the climactic event of the requiem, and it confirmed and further encouraged the students' apocalyptic interpretation of events.

Shchapov's address was so successful that students in Kazan celebrated him as an "apostle of freedom" and sent a copy of his speech to friends in Perm.[71] It called for a countrywide insurrection, concluding with the words: "Long live the democratic constitution!"[72] Such radicalism on the part of a professor was unprecedented. As befit a requiem, Shchapov's address was full of references to Christ, and this aspect of the speech, too, proved memorable.[73] Jesus Christ, Shchapov explained, was a "Mythical Democrat," or rather a "Democrat who has until now been mythical." Passion Week was about to begin, and people would worship him for his sacrifice, but they failed to understand what he truly was.[74] Jesus Christ had lived in the Roman Empire, had preached "communal-democratic freedom," and as a result, he was "nailed to the Cross, and appeared a universally redeeming sacrifice for freedom." The peasants who were killed in Bezdna were also Christs.[75] They were "prophets" and martyrs, or "redeeming sacrifices" (*iskupitel'nymi zhertvami*), for the freedom of the Russian people from despotism.

Like the Perm "Epistle," however, Shchapov's speech referred to Christ only as a man, not as God.[76] Indeed, the speech undermined Christ's stature as resurrected God, noting that Christ had "appeared" after his death but only as a symbol, as a "universally redeeming sacrifice for freedom." Shchapov also hailed the fallen peasant, Anton Petrov as a "prophet," yet in Shchapov's rendition, he was a prophet without a vision and without a God to reveal that vision. Nowhere in the speech did the word "God" appear. The events in Bezdna had not been God's will; they were rather the result of actions taken by the peasants in Bezdna.

Shchapov's words were directed to the dead, whom he addressed as "you," as if they could hear him. The first sentence was "Friends, who have been killed for the people!" Yet the beneficiaries of their deaths were "us"—Shchapov and his audience, who had been galvanized to political action by the peasants' sacrifice. "*You* were the first to interrupt *our* sleep, you destroyed it by your initiative."[77] He then identified this state of sleep as "doubt," doubt in the ability of the people to take political action. Like Chernyshevsky and Dobroliubov, therefore, he represented doubt as a form of acedia, which prevented people from acting in accordance with their convictions. As a result of his speech, Shchapov was arrested on personal orders of Alexander II, which only increased his stature in the eyes of his student admirers.[78]

The massacre of peasants in Bezdna, therefore, further radicalized those students already opposed to the autocracy and strengthened their sense of apocalypticism. The peasant uprising had begun, and a battle was at hand between the forces of darkness and those of light. Unless the students could transform isolated incidents into a countrywide insurrection, however, peasant blood would have been spilled without purpose. Young revolutionaries must now be prepared to sacrifice their own lives if necessary. Their response was to walk out into the countryside to communicate with the peasants directly.

On hearing of the massacre in Bezdna, participants in the Kazan circle not only organized a requiem but dispatched two students to Spassk to engage personally with the peasants. Both were studying at the Faculty of Medicine.[79] One of them, Mikhail Elpidin, was the son of a deacon from the Laishev district (which bordered on Spassk). The other, Samuil Klaus, was a teacher's son from Saratov.[80] Both were arrested on April 18 after Klaus had approached an officer on the street in Bezdna asking to see Anton Petrov.[81]

Despite this disappointing result, yet another participant in the circle, Arkadii Biriukov, a student at the Historical-Philological Faculty in Kazan set out into the countryside a short while later. He walked on foot in the hopes of a chance encounter with peasants, and though he did encounter them, he found they were unwilling to talk to him, though he was by no means a city slicker himself. He was the son of a subdeacon from the village of Petropavlovskoe, in the Shchadrinsk district of Perm province. The peasants were evidently frightened by the prospect of more state reprisals and did not wish to bring danger on themselves by speaking to strangers.[82] Even so, Biriukov did not consider resigning himself to the idea that the revolution was not about to happen.

In the wake of these unsuccessful missions, Elpidin and his friend Ivan Umnov, the son of a tradesman from Riazan' province, set about composing revolutionary proclamations. Umnov, who was older than Elpidin and the students, occupied a special position in the group: he had spent time in Saratov and knew Chernyshevsky personally. The proclamations that Elpidin and Umnov helped compose were specifically addressed to a peasant audience and could be handed out by students in the countryside even if they did not manage to engage peasants in conversation. They were titled "I Bow to the Orthodox People" (1861) and "Long Have You Been Oppressed, Brothers" (1862).[83] Despite the heading of the first leaflet, both were sharply antireligious as well as antimonarchical. The people must cease to hope that the tsar would come to their aid. It was only in fairy tales that the tsar cared about the people. Nor was it any use to pray to God. God might help the peasants in their sacred cause, but they must start to rely on themselves: "One must think for oneself, using one's own mind, setting one's matters to right by one's own strength. Enough. We used to live according to the mind and will of other people. We lived a dog's life, but no good came of it."[84]

There is much less biblical language in these proclamations than there had been in Shchapov's speech. Yet the second proclamation, composed in the fall of 1862 and printed illegally in 1863, did include a lengthy extract from the First Book of Samuel, in which Samuel prophesies the reign of evil kings.[85] The document urges peasants to keep their hopes for freedom alive. Now might not be the right moment for an uprising, but there would come a time when their brothers, the students (referred to here as *kaftanniki*, because of the peasant garb they donned on their travels), would send the people word that they should "arise for the sacred cause." Then, peasants would make their views known, and they would finally "live without sorrow," in true freedom.[86]

The idea at the core of these two proclamations was the same message of self-reliance expressed in the Perm "Epistle." Like the authors of that manuscript, Elpidin and Umnov had both been exposed to Chernyshevsky's and Dobroliubov's articles in the *Contemporary* and, most likely, to Feuerbach's *Lectures on the Essence of Religion*. Mikhail Elpidin had almost certainly read Feuerbach. When he was arrested, the authorities found a document he had written titled "The Teachings of Buddha" ("Uchenie Buddy") sewn into his mattress. The text consisted of a series of bulleted points, each denouncing holy writ and the Orthodox faith as a series of lies: "Joshua [*Iisus Novin* [*sic*]] stopped the sun: nonsense. [. . .] Man is guided by reason. [. . .] Man is capable of being moral without any faith in mysteries. [. . .] People are taught superstitions since childhood. [G]od did not create man, but man [G]od, [and] even [endowed him] with a gray beard [*Ne [B]og sotvoril cheloveka, a chelovek [B]oga, da eshche s sedoi borodoi*]."[87] The idea that man had created God was one that Feuerbach often repeated. Elpidin explained under interrogation that he associated these ideas with the teachings of "German philosophers."[88] He probably had Feuerbach in mind.

The attacks Elpidin and his Kazan friends leveled against the tsar in their proclamations cohered with Feuerbach's attack on God. If God was a human invention, then so was the merciful tsar, to whom the peasants looked for their freedom. That tsar was a figment of their imagination. The proclamation "I Bow to the Orthodox People" notes that "the good-natured Tsar-father exists only in fairy tales."[89] The political claims that the group put forward in their proclamations were therefore also claims about religion, and the moral they drew from these applied equally to the tsar and God. The group came closest to expressing this thought in "Long Have You Been Oppressed, Brothers": "Enough, brothers, of comforting yourselves with nonsense, enough of relying on such a sovereign. You will say: whom should we rely on, then? Rely on yourselves, brothers, may you obtain freedom for yourselves and by yourselves."[90] (In these sentences, "rely on" could also be translated as "hope in"—the Russian verb is *nadeiat'sia na*.)

The moral, then, was one of self-motivated action, what Pomialovskii had called "samodeiatel'nost'," and Feuerbach "Selbsttätigkeit." Action was now becoming central to the radicals' code of honor in Kazan. Ivan Krasnoperov, the son of an impoverished deacon from the village of Ikskoe Ust'e (present-day Tatarstan), emphasized this in a letter he wrote to his cousin Egor Krasnoperov, a seminarian in Viatka, in February 1863. "Generally speaking," he wrote, "it is indecent [*neblagorodno*] for youths to sit around with their hands folded at the present time." He urged his cousin to "spread his convictions among the seminarians."[91] Ivan Krasnoperov's emphasis on self-motivated action had religious as well as political implications. He, too, was an adept of Feuerbach, whose *Essence of Christianity* was one of two books he took with him when he left the seminary in Viatka on foot to enroll at Kazan University in September 1862.[92]

Participants in the Kazan circle hoped that peasants, even if they refused to speak to the students, might prove receptive to these broadsheets. Student revolutionaries may also have hoped that the rhetoric of Apocalypse and biblical references in their leaflets might lend them greater authority with their intended audience. It would appear, however, that peasants were merely confused by the documents, which proved utterly ineffective as propaganda. This miscalculation on the part of the authors confirms the supposition that apocalyptic rhetoric appealed first and foremost to the students themselves.

Students' revolutionary fervor peaked again in the spring of 1863, when they set out once more from Kazan into the countryside to distribute their revolutionary leaflets. That spring, the terms of the emancipation of the serfs, announced in 1861, were supposed to enter into effect. Now at last, students believed, peasants would rise up to claim their land and freedom, and Apocalypse continued to structure their thoughts about this event. As Krasnoperov wrote in his memoirs, he and his friends were overcome by apocalyptic expectation at this time: "We whole-heartedly believed in the coming kingdom of light and freedom and devoted ourselves entirely to that current."[93] Krasnoperov's roommate, Konstantin Lavrskii, certainly felt this way. Lavrskii was a priest's son from the town of Gorbatov near Nizhnii Novgorod and a student at Kazan's Historical-Philological Faculty. Three weeks before Easter, Lavrskii wrote to a friend: "All have the fast-approaching great deed [skoro griadushchee velikoe delo] in their hearts and minds. [. . .] Here, a noise from beneath the earth can be heard, and the eruption of a volcano is being prepared. Anyone who has had his ears opened, or who has very good hearing has started preparing for that eruption." He concluded his letter: "Easter is coming soon. [. . .] Not long now, not long now, and there will be a festivity on our street, too."[94]

The students were unaware that their trips into the countryside were receiving a powerful impetus from outside Russia: in January 1863, a massive uprising broke out in Poland. In early February, in the first week of Shrovetide, a Polish agent in Kazan met with Krasnoperov, Lavrskii, Biriukov and a few others. Without revealing he was a Pole, he tried to convince them that the Russian uprising was about to begin. The students should participate.[95] The Polish plan was to organize a revolt in Russia that would serve as a diversion for Russian troops attempting to put down the disturbance in Poland, a fact that they hid from students in Kazan. Polish agents urged students to circulate copies of a false manifesto they had printed, in which "Alexander II" declared a new peasant emancipation. Peasants were granted "complete free-dom" and land and were released from all obligations to the nobility. The manifesto further declared the creation of a representative body to which every district would send deputies. Peasants should prepare to defend their new rights by force, since the nobility was likely to oppose the tsar's will.[96]

The agents further hoped that students would participate in an armed uprising in Kazan itself. These plans, as the students themselves realized, were of dubious merit. If the peasant rebellion remained confined to Kazan, then peasants would once again be gunned down to little effect.[97] Some students were apprehensive about bloodshed in any form, hoping for a bloodless rebellion.[98] Moreover, they objected to the Poles' false manifesto in principle: it reinforced the notion of a benevolent tsar, which the students wished to undermine. Further, they disliked the idea of lying to the peasants. A few Kazan students took the agents' money to finance their journeys into the countryside but declined to distribute the manifesto, disseminating their own revolutionary proclamations instead.[99]

Given the circumstances, it is remarkable that participants in the Kazan circle agreed to cooperate with the Polish agents at all. The Poles were unknown to them, and the Kazan students appear not to have trusted them. Some of the students who journeyed into the countryside did not know each other very well either; a few even disliked one another. What united them were not bonds of sympathy but bonds of belief—shared hopes for Russia and shared expectations of themselves. The danger of the mission they undertook may also have increased its appeal.

In the months of March and April 1863, about ten students set out in different directions, a few dressed in peasant garb. The three main participants in these journeys were in their twenties, somewhat older than the average student. They had mixed expectations of what they would find, and they knew by this point that the peasants might prove inhospitable. Mikhail Elpidin, twenty-eight, had already been to Bezdna in 1861 and had been expelled from the university as a result. Arkadii Biriukov was then twenty-three and had also been expelled for failing to appear at an exam in early 1863. He, too, had already been to the rural areas and had found peasants uncommunicative. Ivan Orlov was either twenty-two or twenty-five, the son of a clergyman from the Kudara-Zabaikalskaia region in Siberia, an auditor at the Medical Faculty at Kazan University. Elpidin and Biriukov were friends, but Orlov disliked both of them.

During their journeys in the spring of 1863, they did not find the peasants any more receptive. Biriukov went to the countryside three times in the spring of 1863. On his first trip, the only book he took along was a heavily annotated copy of the Gospels.[100] While the peasants proved happy to hear him read from the book, they were largely unwilling to engage in conversation. On his second trip, Biriukov went to Spassk. Not only did the peasants refuse to speak to him; they also would not allow him to sleep in their houses and threatened to turn him over to the police. To add insult to injury, he was robbed along the road. He swore he would never go again.[101] Yet he could not resist; his third trip was to Kungur in the region of Perm. This time, he took along proclamations and a book of "Old Believer poems," as well as extracts from an Old Believer text titled *Mirror for the Inner Spiritual Person*. The extracts included wording that denounced the tsar as Antichrist and the bishops and archbishops as his minions: "The Christian high clergy established the throne of Satan instead of the throne of Christ; Antichrist, the proud spirit, the enemy of [G]od, sits on it."[102] It is not clear whether Biriukov found any peasants or workers to whom he could read these. He stopped in the home of a priest, and the two quickly became embroiled in a heated argument over "theology." The priest attempted to beat Biriukov before denouncing him to the police, whereupon Biriukov was arrested.[103]

Unlike Biriukov, Elpidin did not suffer physical harm, but his attempts to make contact with the peasants fared little better. His route took him to his home district of Laishev, which bordered on Spassk. There, he sought to distribute copies of "Long Have You Been Oppressed, Brothers," pressing several into the hands of a local merchant, who in turn gave them to some peasants. The merchant and peasants were soon denounced and arrested (the police were very thorough: a copy of the proclamation was found hidden in an icon case in a peasant's home). Elpidin was not only unable to distribute the broadsheet effectively but, as interrogations by the Third Section proved, the proclamation itself was thoroughly incomprehensible to a peasant audience. The extract from the Book of Samuel turned out to be most confusing, because peasants were unable to identify Samuel as a biblical figure. One, who had heard the proclamation read aloud, testified that "from what was read, I understood that it is necessary to pray to God, that some Tsar Samuel wants to send us a new freedom, different from the one our sovereign, Alexander Nikolaevich gave us." Another testified that "from what was read I seem to remember that it was written by the unfaithful Tsar Samuel, who seems to be asking us for help."[104]

Ivan Orlov, who headed north, could distribute only two copies in the first five days of his trip. As he awaited fresh horses at a coach station on the road to Viatka in the village of Kliuchevoi, Nolinsk district, he produced a sealed envelope containing printed material and handed it to an illiterate coachman. The coachman, Denis, was instructed to find a peasant who was literate, have him open the envelope and read the contents aloud before an assembly, which should then follow the instructions carefully. Denis did indeed hand the envelope to a literate peasant, but when the recipient saw the contents of the proclamation it contained, he immediately burned it.[105] Orlov further complained that on the road he mainly came across Cheremis, Votiaks, and Besseriakhs, few of whom seemed to know any Russian.[106] From Viatka, he moved on to Perm. Stopping along the way in the town of Okhansk, Orlov drank some vodka with a seminarian (from Perm) and then handed him a small stack of proclamations. The seminarian made no guarantee that he would be able to give them away; his reticence was understandable given that he had been badly beaten a year earlier when he tried to agitate among some workers.[107] The seminarian did not distribute the broadsheets but left them in the town square. There they were found by the police, who quickly arrested him.[108] Orlov himself was arrested a few weeks later in a village not far from Kazan.

The advent of Easter, which fell that year on March 31, did little to dispel the enthusiasm of group members for such trips, for several more now set off into the countryside. They had little more luck than their predecessors. Among them was Nikolai Dernov, another priest's son, who walked northward to Nolinsk in Viatka province together with two other students. Under interrogation, Dernov testified that he deposited two proclamations in peasant houses before throwing the rest into the forest.[109]

These missions into the rural regions were clearly not based on any reasoned calculation that they would be successful. Elpidin and Biriukov, who had already been to the countryside in 1861, had known enough to predict that they would encounter great difficulties, and their experiences were no secret to their friends. If, during their first ventures to distribute revolutionary broadsheets, students expected an immediate response in the form of an uprising, this cannot have remained their expectation for long. Success, therefore, was not the motivating factor. Instead, the students appear to have been propelled by a sense of moral obligation and, perhaps, a sense of adventure.[110] When Biriukov left for Spassk in early March 1863, his close friend, Konstantin Lavrskii wrote to another friend that Biriukov was walking "in the footsteps of Christ" and that he might never return ("edva li uspeet vorotit'sia"). He seemed more excited than worried.[111]

The people who went on these missions came to be known as "apostles."[112] In the Christian tradition, an apostle is a messenger from God.[113] Christ was such a messenger, and so were his closest followers, the twelve whom he sent to convey the news of his resurrection. In the New Testament, the term was usually reserved for those followers who had seen Christ after his resurrection, that is, those to whom Christ had "revealed" himself, thereby entrusting them with a special mission. The message of the apostle was therefore about the "revelation" he had seen (the Greek word being *apokalipsis*), namely, that Christ had been resurrected and that he would come again.[114]

Members of the circle understood the word in its Christian sense, as can be seen in a letter of recommendation that Krasnoperov wrote for Ivan Orlov to take with him on his travels to Viatka: "In light of the things that must come to pass for the general good, this man has taken upon himself the role of an apostle-preacher, a role that is beautiful and useful in the highest degree. I ask that you receive this apostle joyfully and carry out those responsibilities that he will lay upon you. The time is drawing near; the old world is about to end, and Russia will awake from its slumber. I believe that you are taking a direct part in this matter." Borrowing the last sentence of Shchapov's speech, Krasnoperov concludes, "Long live the democratic constitution!"[115]

The letter not only designates the messenger, Orlov, as an apostle but also anticipates the message that Orlov has come to convey: the time is near, the old world is about to go under, and a new Russia is about to be created. The words are drawn from the first paragraph of the Book of Revelation: "The Revelation of Jesus the Messiah, which God gave him to show to his servants the things which must soon come to pass. [. . .] Blessed is he who reads, and those who hear the words of the Prophecy and hold fast the things which are written in it; for the time is drawing near."[116] The phrasing of the letter's first sentence ("in light of the things that must come to pass") and the penultimate one ("the time is drawing near") are directly drawn from this source, as is the message that the reader should "hold fast to the things that are written in it."[117] Once again, however, the content of the apocalyptic message is not Christian in any strict sense. The letter makes it clear that the messenger (Orlov) is not an emissary of Christ or anyone's emissary in particular: he has "taken the role of the apostle-prophet upon himself"; he is a self-activating apostle, something decidedly at odds with the Orthodox Christian tradition. God has no role in this, and neither the letter writer nor the messenger has been inspired by an epiphany.

Krasnoperov was arrested and interrogated about this missive by the Third Section, and he attempted to play down its significance. When he said that "the time is drawing near," he claimed, he had merely meant that a "new life" would begin in Russia once the emancipation had taken effect.[118] Perhaps he thought these words would reassure his interrogators, convincing them that he supported the terms of the emancipation, but they were certainly ambiguous.

Krasnoperov, Orlov, and their fellow students had proven themselves capable of taking action, but their actions did not produce the intended results. The democratic constitution did not materialize, and again, there was no peasant uprising. By May 1863, all of the "apostles" had been arrested, together with their friends, and the Poles had been arrested too. Five of the Poles were executed by firing squad. Orlov was read the same sentence, though it was commuted to fifteen years of hard labor in Siberia; he was freed five years later. Krasnoperov served four years of a twelve-year sentence of hard labor. Elpidin was sentenced to five years of hard labor but escaped and emigrated to Switzerland, where he began to publish Chernyshevsky's collected works. Biriukov served four years of hard labor, during which time he became an alcoholic. Lavrskii was sentenced to seven years hard labor. He and Elpidin were the only ones to continue their revolutionary activities: the others sank into oblivion. They had wished to match the death of the Bezdna peasants with a martyrdom of their own, and in this regard, they were successful.

In the early 1860s, it became clear that young people could not maintain allegiance to the Orthodox Church and to the revolutionary movement simultaneously. This, at least, would appear to follow from the experiences of Mitrofan Muravskii, whose unwillingness to part from Orthodox Christian loyalties forced him to betray his friends in prison, leading to years of depression and alcoholism. Only decades later, as a handful of Orthodox priests embraced the revolutionary movement, did this change.

Though Muravskii came from a family of the petty gentry, many of the student revolutionaries who became active in the early 1860s were of clerical origin. Elpidin, Biriukov, and Krasnoperov were sons of priests, deacons, and subdeacons who had attended seminaries in provincial towns such as Viatka and Perm. Their Orthodox upbringing made the language of Apocalypse comfortingly familiar: it allowed them to express their dissatisfaction with a regime they regarded as thoroughly corrupt and to express hope in thoroughgoing change. The worldview they developed also created new modes of interaction and a new sense of community, as personal sympathies now mattered less than common commitment to a cause. Apocalyptic rhetoric also served to imbue their risky undertakings with a certain kind of glory, allowing young men of very obscure origins to view themselves as participating in a battle of epic proportions.

These young men did not see the need to choose between professing atheism and expressing their hope for revolution in apocalyptic terms. On the contrary, atheism appears to have facilitated their continued faith in the revolutionary apocalyptic rhetoric. If the peasant uprising had not yet occurred and the battle for the new world had not yet begun, then this must be because they had been mistaken in relying on Providence to set this train of events into motion. The revolution would begin once Russians had dispensed with faith in God. Here, atheism served revolutionaries as an ethic of self-reliance, one they drew from the writings of Feuerbach as well as those of Chernyshevsky and Dobroliubov.

Collectively, the revolutionary youth of the early 1860s developed one answer to the question of how one might live without God: it was a communitarian model, which offered young men in the provinces the hope that they might participate directly in the political and social transformation of their country. Rejecting faith in God was the first, necessary, step in this process, both for the individual and for society as a whole. Though this vision made little impression on the peasants to whom student radicals addressed their propagandistic leaflets, it did inspire succeeding generations of revolutionaries. As is well known, writings by Bolsheviks from Luncharsky and Bogdanovich to Bukharin and Preobrazhenskii abound with the phrases "new people" and "new earth."[119]

6

Doubt after Atheism

Dmitrii Pisarev

Dmitrii Pisarev is remembered for the enormous influence his
writings exerted over succeeding generations of Russian youths
from the 1860s on. His articles, said to have been the "Code of Laws"
and "Koran" for many young radicals, were passed around well into
the 1890s by students at Russia's universities and secondary schools in
"dilapidated tomes of his collected writings along with ancient copies
of *Russkoe slovo*," the *Russian Word*, where his work had appeared.
Young people, it was said, turned to them for answers to all of their
"unanswered questions," great and small.[1]

It is ironic that Pisarev would be remembered as an oracle, because
the core message he sought to convey was that individuals must liberate
themselves from any and every such guide. By advocating atheism,
Chernyshevsky and Dobroliubov had thrown open the question of how
people were to construct meaning and codes of behavior in the absence
of God. The answer Pisarev proposed, and for which he became famous,
was that individuals must live by and for themselves; they must learn to
think and to live according to their own impressions, tastes, and inclinations. Indeed, they must dispense with any and all principles and ideals,
orienting themselves entirely in the present without the benefit of hope
in the future. In advancing this individualistic view, Pisarev rejected the
communal ethic of sacrifice cultivated by members of the revolutionary
intelligentsia, as well as the ethics of friendship and cooperation that
had become dominant among its members.

Pisarev readily admitted that the individualistic code of thought and
behavior he proposed would be difficult to sustain. In 1862, amidst

increasingly vigorous efforts by the state to curb radicalism, Pisarev was arrested and held in solitary confinement for more than four years. During this time, even he would reject his "nihilist" views. People, he now felt, needed something to believe in, something to live and hope for. They were called on—morally required—to make sacrifices for the good of humanity, which would only be possible if they permitted themselves to embrace this higher cause with "fanatical" devotion. After his release from prison, Pisarev's thought underwent one final transformation. Rejecting radical "fanaticism," he came to embrace "doubt" as the only legitimate stance a person could take.

His writings sparked enormous controversy not only among liberals and conservatives but among radicals, some of whom regarded them as a threat to the revolutionary movement. Pisarev, they claimed, undermined his young readers' commitment to the people's cause by encouraging them to pursue their personal inclinations instead.[2] His harshest critics would claim that Pisarev's individualistic worldview was nothing but the product of his idiosyncratic psychology.[3] They found ammunition for their claims in Pisarev's own writings: in one autobiographical piece, Pisarev had noted that the philosophical and moral prescriptions he issued in the *Russian Word* in the early 1860s had partly been formed in response to an early mental breakdown in 1859, at the age of nineteen.[4] Pisarev's interest in psychology was not purely autobiographical, however: it was the product of new currents in Russian literature and journalism. As Lidiia Ginzburg noted, psychological prose arose in the mid-nineteenth century out of romantic concerns with the tensions between "dream and reality, the ideal and the real." In later decades, Turgenev, Dostoevsky, and Tolstoy would develop the romantic conception of the divided soul toward a more multifaceted representation of the human mind.[5] In journalism, especially radical journalism, interest in psychology was further the product of a preoccupation with science and materialist explanations of the operations of the mind.[6] A concern for Chernyshevsky and Dobroliubov, psychology became a major preoccupation for Pisarev.[7] Fascinated by the confrontation between the ideal and the real in the human mind, Pisarev drew both on literature and on popular science in elaborating his psychological views. Psychology was one of the central grounds on which he would frame his critique of belief in God.

One of the most attractive features of Pisarev's writing was the confidence and ease with which he invariably expressed his views. Yet this display masked fundamental doubts about himself and his relationship to his readers, as well as to the people to whom he was closest. The only question about which he never expressed any hesitation was the non-existence of God.

To understand the extremism of the positions Pisarev advanced, it is necessary to appreciate the pressures exerted on him. Some of these were social. Pisarev came from a provincial noble family of declining fortunes. He was born in 1840 on his parents' country estate, Znamenskoe, in the province of Orel, yet, owing to his family's straightened circumstances (partly the result of his father's gambling habit), his parents were forced to sell their home when he was ten. They then moved to Grunets, a smaller house on their last remaining estate, located on the border between Orel and Tula. Though Varvara Pisareva worked hard to make this gentry nest hospitable, it was riddled with discord: bitter arguments with her profligate husband and insipid brother, the writer Andrei Danilov (a frequent guest), repeatedly erupted.[8] The persistence of family scandals must have facilitated Pisarev's later rejection of his noble roots.

Early on, the family took enormous pride in the talents of their precocious only son, who they hoped would restore the family fortune by pursuing a brilliant career as a civil servant. Shortly after selling Znamenskoe, his parents sent the eleven-year-old Mitia to St. Petersburg to live with relatives so that he might receive a solid education. There, he attended the Third St. Petersburg Gymnasium, his student fees being paid by a wealthy uncle. The Third Gymnasium was known as one of the cheapest in the capital city; it prepared young noblemen of modest means for teaching careers, imposing a strict regime on students and requiring large amounts of rote memorization. Initially, Pisarev's St. Petersburg aunt wondered whether this regime might be too strict: "How can you expect that in your twelfth year, you should be able to bear such hard and constant labor? That would mean demanding the impossible of nature."[9] The boy was undaunted.

Pisarev exceeded his relatives' expectations by graduating with a silver medal at the age of sixteen. While his St. Petersburg cousins trained to become military officers, Pisarev enrolled as one of the youngest students at the Philological-Historical Faculty of St. Petersburg University, where he made a highly favorable impression on his professors. It was at this time that he began to argue with his relatives, and he also started to show indications of psychological distress. Already in 1857, he displayed signs of what doctors diagnosed in 1859 as "melancholy."

He noted in his diary: "I got up like a sensible person at 8 o'clock. I started to get dressed and suddenly froze in the same position, fell to thinking, and then, having picked up a little knife, cut my finger, and lay down again." It was not the first such incident.[10]

When Pisarev enrolled in 1856, years of turmoil at St. Petersburg University were about to begin. As in Kharkov and elsewhere, the death of Nicholas I in 1855, combined with Russia's defeat in the Crimean War in 1856, called into question the spirit of discipline and obedience that had characterized Nicholas' reign. The petty authoritarianism of university regulations led to the first displays of insubordination by students, who started wearing mustaches and smoking on campus. As they became more self-assertive, organizing their own funds for the support of impoverished classmates and their own printed journals, they clashed with university authorities. These scuffles led to large-scale demonstrations that culminated in the closure of the university for two years in 1861.[11]

In 1856 and 1857 Pisarev eagerly attended gatherings to discuss the creation of a newspaper. There, Alexander Herzen's London journal, the Bell (Kolokol), was read aloud (one of the student journals, Kolokol'chik, came to be named after it). Yet Pisarev's position was hardly that of a firebrand: the views he defended in debates over how stridently students should demand new freedoms were moderate.[12] Nevertheless, his uncle was displeased that he was participating in the gatherings at all and accused him of having become a "Saint-Juste en miniature." Pisarev left his uncle's home and moved in with a new friend he had met at one of the meetings, Nikolai Treskin.[13]

Pisarev then joined a student circle, all of whose members hailed from noble families: Leonid Maikov was the younger brother of the famous poet; Petr Polevoi was the son of a well-known literary critic; Alexander Skabichevskii came from an undistinguished noble family, as did Nikolai Treskin. In some ways, this group imitated the student circle Alexander Herzen had described in My Past and Thoughts: it was tightly knit, with strict rules of comportment. Writing about these years in their memoirs, Skabichevskii and Polevoi would strongly emphasize the group's "despotism"—moral and intellectual. According to Skabichevskii, the circle insisted that its members devote themselves to their studies while maintaining highly ascetic and Christian morals; they were to perfect themselves, to become "the embodiment of the ideal of true Christianity." By their standards, Pisarev seemed too worldly, "despite the fact that he wore a Christian cross." Not only did he insist on playing billiards and cards; he also professed love for a woman, Raisa Koreneva.[14] This was Pisarev's first cousin, who had been raised by his parents at Grunets and to whom Pisarev was passionately devoted.

As a student, Pisarev inhabited two worlds that stood in conflict with one another. One, the world of the nobility—of his circle—seemed to be reenacting a bygone era in which noblemen cleaved to one another and pursued glory within state institutions. The other world was that of the radical movement, marked by student confrontations with the authorities, demands for civic engagement, and the dream of changing the world through journalism. As a student, Pisarev seems to have hovered uncomfortably between the two.

In the winter of 1858 Pisarev began to write literary reviews for the *Dawn* (*Rassvet*), a small, liberal journal. Later, in the autobiographical account he wrote in 1863, he claimed that his decision to write for the *Dawn* caused a rupture with his friends, who expected a brilliant professorial career of him and felt that journalistic writing was an unnecessary distraction. According to his account, they upbraided him for his decision, warning him that he would become "like Dobroliubov," whom they apparently despised for his lowly social origins and radicalism. Thereupon, Pisarev said, he became his own agent. For the first time, he learned to think independently, calling into question all of his previous beliefs.[15] Pisarev was not being entirely truthful here: his friends cannot have disapproved so strongly of his journalistic efforts, because at least two of them, Treskin and Skabichevskii, submitted work to the *Dawn* as well.[16] It was within the framework of the group, therefore, that Pisarev undertook his first ventures as a journalist. It was also within the group that he began to develop his distinctive outlook, including his anti-religious stance.

Pisarev's religious upbringing was that of a typical Russian nobleman. His parents, just like his St. Petersburg relatives, punctiliously adhered to the Orthodox calendar, fasting and attending church on holy days.[17] In the evenings, they also read devotional literature, largely in French, which was the language of conversation in both families. Such heterogeneous reading habits formed a core part of the hybrid religious culture that had characterized noble families since the eighteenth and early nineteenth centuries. One work the Pisarevs especially cherished was *Méditations religieuses*, a multivolume collection of no explicit confessional orientation. Pisarev described these readings as "elevated" and "beautiful."[18] The nondenominational spirituality of his early religious reading helps explain why, when Pisarev subsequently wrote about the dangers of religion, he spoke in general terms, not just about Russian Orthodoxy.

Religiosity became the subject of debate in Pisarev's circle in 1858, when Alexander Skabichevskii underwent a crisis of faith. Pisarev joyfully reported to his cousin Raisa Koreneva that he, Treskin, and Skabichevskii spent hours discussing the latter's doubts.[19] Skabichevskii was not the only one who wavered: by the summer of 1859, Pisarev and Treskin had lost faith in Orthodoxy and in God. That summer, they traveled to Grunets together, where they made it their task to convert Koreneva and Vera Pisareva, Dmitrii's fifteen-year-old sister, to atheism. When Vera revealed her newfound unbelief to her mother, Varvara Pisareva was horrified and demanded an explanation from her son. He responded as follows: "As far as the religious convictions [of Vera] are concerned, Mama, do not be distressed. They are correct and will lead her neither toward immorality, nor toward apathy. She will be a kind and intelligent woman. And God, if he indeed exists, cannot make any claims on our convictions. Can all of us, who do not believe [neveruiu-shchie], Treskin, Raisa, Verochka and I, be worse than believers? Our moral convictions are firm and strict, because they are founded on thought. And what, besides moral convictions does a person need from the domain of religion?"[20] Judging by the letter, Pisarev and Treskin had been reading recent editions of the Contemporary, where Chernyshevsky and Dobroliubov argued for the possibility and legitimacy of a non-Christian ethical system.

Though the tone of Pisarev's letter to his mother was playful, his break with the Orthodox faith was accompanied by growing irritation over the pressures to which his mother and friends subjected him. His love for Raisa Koreneva, whom he hoped one day to marry, stood at the center of tensions with his mother, who disapproved of their plans and actively interfered to prevent them from seeing one another by sending Koreneva to live with other relatives. In response, Pisarev announced to his mother that he had attempted to reduce his emotional dependence on other people, so that he would become indifferent to their feelings about him. He referred to this impulse as the beginning of his new theory of egoism.[21] Soon, these experiences would find their way into Pisarev's published work.[22]

His friends noticed a change in behavior. Polevoi, for example, remembered that Pisarev stopped speaking to his friends about personal matters in the fall of 1859.[23] He was also confrontational with them. He accused Treskin, for example, of attempting to exert undue influence over him: "I, my dear, am not being sentimental with you; I am not enacting a novel about the raptures of friendship, but yet my love for you is stronger than yours for me. That is because I value you for yourself, as you are, not more, not less. But you want to make something or another of me, and in me, you love the product of your own creation."[24]

During the late autumn of 1859, the symptoms of melancholy he had begun to display in earlier years worsened considerably, and the Treskins, who were very fond of him, saw no other recourse than to commit him to a mental hospital, which they did in the early winter. By the summer of 1860, he appeared to have recovered and graduated from St. Petersburg University with a silver medal. The fact that Pisarev became mentally ill in 1859 should not detract from the importance of the ideas he developed that year. That date marked a turning point in Pisarev's intellectual life: it was the year in which he gained confidence in his journalistic abilities, articulating for the first time some of the ideas that became central to the worldview he espoused at the *Russian Word*. It was also the year that he lost faith. These developments took place while Pisarev was amid friends. It was only later, at the time he began to write for the *Russian Word*, that the situation changed. His radical journalism did not suit his noble friends, nor did they suit him any longer.

In reviews that Pisarev wrote for the *Dawn* in 1859, he began to develop the critique of religion for which he later became famous, arguing that religion destroys human beings by holding them to impossibly high standards. He did not initially couch these criticisms in terms that were utterly opposed to religion; the *Dawn* was a journal addressed to girls, their mothers, and governesses, and it could not afford to appear overtly antireligious.[25] Pisarev, therefore, confined himself to the observation that authors of spiritual tracts must bear the frailties of their readers in mind when instructing them. Over time, he developed this view further, drawing on the writings of Chernyshevsky and Dobroliubov, as well as German materialists, whose works he reviewed in the *Russian Word*. All the while, however, the charge that religion makes "impossible demands" on believers remained central to his writings.

In reviews of religious literature that he wrote for the first five editions of the *Dawn* in the spring of 1859, Pisarev warned that authors of spiritual tracts must not demand great feats of self-sacrifice; such commands would only discourage readers, frightening them and shaking their confidence.[26] In other reviews, he added that such stringency could easily backfire, encouraging young people to repress all sincere religious feeling and put on fake, hypocritical displays of piety instead.[27] Christian writers who demanded too much of their readers might unwittingly encourage the perversion of faith.

In his reviews of literary works, published in the fall of 1859, however, Pisarev went further, arguing that Christian morality itself might prove detrimental to the individual. "If we shall demand the impossible of ourselves, if, in the name of a misunderstood letter of moral law, we shall always [. . .] waste our energy on entirely unnecessary feats of humility and self-sacrifice, then we shall simply torment and exhaust ourselves. [. . .] Owing to our voluntary and fruitless sufferings, we shall allow our own reasonable happiness [*razumnoe schastie*] to slip from our hands, and [we] will cloud the happiness and calm of people close [to us]. [. . .] Fanatical striving toward an unrealizable goal, standing above humanity, leads to the weakening of moral strength."[28] Catholic moralists in particular, he claimed, condemned tendencies in people that are entirely natural, impulses and inclinations that appear spontaneously and are not subject to choice ("the most inevitable manifestations of feeling, the pursuit of enjoyment and pleasure that is entirely natural in youth").[29]

To forbid people to act according to their natural tendencies is not only cruel, Pisarev argued, but destructive to their very being, canceling sides of the personality that are constitutive of a person's nature. In advancing these views, Pisarev appears to have been inspired by articles written by Chernyshevsky and Dobroliubov for the *Contemporary*. They argued for the recognition of inclinations that belong to the physical constitution of the human organism, drawing on the writings of German materialists and Ludwig Feuerbach. They also posited that religion is a "fantasy," a product of an overactive imagination, one that lulls people into a state of listlessness and torpor, convincing them that they cannot fulfill their own needs and comforting them with the idea that their poverty and humiliation are part of some grand scheme. Pisarev, too, promoted this view, arguing that religion encourages people to cultivate escapist fantasies instead of working to improve the world around them.

His distinctive claim was that the torpor that the believer succumbs to is far from comforting: religion makes every believer miserable. Pisarev commented on this aspect of religion in one of his final reviews for the *Dawn*, an article-length critique of *A Gentry Nest* (1859) by Ivan Turgenev, whose works played a central role in Pisarev's formation as a critic. In Pisarev's review, Turgenev's heroine, Liza, serves as a cautionary example. As a child, she had been left in the charge of a thoroughly uneducated and pious nanny, whose "burning religious sentiment" became "the most important element" in her upbringing. Liza's imagination becomes "grossly overdeveloped," and she proves utterly incapable of controlling her thoughts. Her ideals, instead of prompting reflection, haunt her like "phantoms." She ends up not only torn between conflicting inclinations but utterly unable to orient herself among them. A battle she can neither understand nor resolve flares up inside her, and she withers under the strain. In the end, Liza punishes herself by entering a monastery, a "feat of self-abnegation" that condemns her to the life of an "eternal, voluntary martyr."[30]

Though people turn to religion as a source of comfort, it is in fact a source of pain. This was the observation that Pisarev added to Chernyshevsky and Dobroliubov's critique of religion: individuals never can achieve the perfection they imagine is possible and suffer for it.

Pisarev developed these criticisms further as he began to write for the *Russian Word*, submitting his first article shortly after his graduation from St. Petersburg University in 1860. He turned to this journal at a time of financial need, when it appears he would have been willing to work for any publication that would pay him.[31] The *Russian Word* was still an obscure journal. Its editorship had just been passed to Grigorii Blagosvetlov, a priest's son, who was known to hold radical sympathies. By working for Blagosvetlov, the young nobleman subordinated himself to a *raznochinets*, signaling his disregard for questions of social prerogative that had been so contentious at the *Contemporary* in the late 1850s. The old social hierarchies would not be preserved on the new stage of radical journalism, even as its actors remained self-conscious about their origins.[32] The cooperation between Pisarev and Blagosvetlov proved highly fruitful for both: Pisarev was free to develop his views on the relationship between the individual and society, as well as to advance a more extensive and thoroughgoing critique of religion, its origins, and deleterious effects. On the strength of Pisarev's articles, Blagosvetlov's journal became a major institution in the radical community, competing successfully against the *Contemporary* for the loyalties of their young readership.

The critique of religion Pisarev continued to develop at the *Russian Word* during the early 1860s was partly based on views that Chernyshevsky and Dobroliubov had publicized: religion was a product of ignorance. Like them, Pisarev also appealed to the authority of German materialists, whose works he reviewed several times and used to buttress claims against the existence of immaterial forces—and by extension, God.[33] Faith in supernatural powers arose among "primitive" peoples whom the forces of nature filled with awe. They deified these natural forces, endowing them with human qualities, and bowed before them with childlike naïveté.[34] The world of faith was primarily a world of imagination; people tended to embroider the images of their deities, inventing elaborate stories about them, along with rituals of worship.[35] Because belief in supernatural beings was a result of ignorance, it would become superfluous and disappear once scientific knowledge advanced and spread.[36]

Ignorance might have been the source of religious beliefs, but misery further encouraged them. Pisarev showed that this had been especially true at the time Christianity arose, a period he analyzed at length in articles about the rise of stoicism and pagan philosophy, which he had studied intensively while writing his thesis for St. Petersburg University. In the first century A.D., life in the Roman Empire was, according to Pisarev, marked by "betrayals, denunciations, and torture." When "the aristocracy was transformed into a crowd of flatterers and informers, and religion into a muddled set of superstitious rituals," the "best" people found they had no choice but to "retreat into themselves."[37] The turn inward involved a turn toward religion; people sought explanations for why there was so much evil in the world and looked for ways to cope with it. Society was so corrupt that it proved nearly impossible to maintain one's ethical standards in relation to other people, yet the believer could always maintain them in communion with God.[38] Religion provided an imaginary world into which unhappy people could retreat. Pisarev captures their reasoning as follows: "I am unhappy here, it is stifling, difficult, it hurts to breathe, and so I will at least find relief in that eternally light, eternally quiet and warm atmosphere, which my imagination creates, and which cannot be penetrated either by grief, or by cares, or by the groans of those who suffer."[39]

Having conjured up an imaginary world in their minds, however, people became overwhelmed by it, forgetting that it was their own creation. This was the point that interested Pisarev most and constituted the distinctive feature of his writing on religion. The fantasy world became a world of phantoms that began to exert power over the individual's mind. As an example, Pisarev points to the religious beliefs of the Pelasgians, a prehistoric tribe in Greece: "Thus, for example, the Pelasgian established his primitive religion and fell in the dust before the creation of his own thought. His hallucination was blindingly brilliant; criticism was too weak to destroy the dream. The struggle between the phantom and man was uneven, and man bowed his head and felt he was pushed down, pinned to the earth."[40] The battle that the Pelasgians had begun lasted to Pisarev's day. Time after time people succumbed to their own "phantoms" and "hallucinations" and proved utterly helpless to defend themselves. The ideas, ideals, and fantasies that the discontented person cultivated in his or her imagination could all too easily take on a life of their own.[41] Far from providing a source of comfort, they became a further source of distress.

Pisarev's core claim against religion, then, was psychological: religion is a set of delusions that torments people. In elaborating these claims, Pisarev drew heavily on the vocabulary of psychiatry. He referred to a person with an overdeveloped imagination as a "psychically sick" person, suffering from a "morbid condition" (*boleznennoe sostoianie*).[42] He used the term "hallucinations" to refer not only to religious visions but also to the concepts and ideals that religious believers claimed to have faith in. Indeed, any person who attached great meaning to abstract concepts could be accused of hallucinating.[43]

Religious people could not distinguish between dream and reality and treated the ideals they had invented as if they constituted absolute law. Though it should have been obvious that this was impossible, believers spent a lifetime trying to live up to their ideals.[44] The same was true of most philosophers. "Blinded by the brilliance" of their ideas, they allowed abstractions to become "phantoms" that ruled them. What had begun as a dream turned into an unceasing nightmare.[45] Pisarev proffered Plato as an example. Caught up by his theoretical interest in the idea of forms, Plato came to believe that the beautiful images he conjured up in his mind were real. Plato's intelligence captivated other people, who adopted his theories as if they were their own, and subsequently came to be haunted by the same visions. In this way, Plato's philosophy became a "religion."[46]

Religion was a dream that people spent their lives chasing after or, worse still, might sacrifice their lives for: "Trifling with a dream is dangerous; a broken dream can make a calamity of life; chasing after a dream, one can yawn away a whole life, or sacrifice it entirely in a fit of mad inspiration."[47] Far from offering people comfort and security, then, religion condemned them to self-flagellation.

Religion, according to Pisarev, also provoked the most painful form of doubt. By arguing that doubt was an inevitable feature of the religious experience, Pisarev introduced an important innovation. In the 1820s, romantic youths, the Wisdom Lovers, had celebrated the troubled truth seeker, locked into a state of inner turmoil. To them, doubt was a sign of election—not the experience of every Orthodox Christian but reserved for those who would not content themselves with the mundane beliefs of the "crowd." It was a precondition for the discovery of higher truths and superior faith. By the 1840s, Russian intellectuals had come to see doubt as thoroughly at odds with religious belief: it initiated a loss of faith that could not be reinstated. Now, Pisarev made doubt the permanent condition of all human beings, believers as well as nonbelievers.

Whereas nonbelievers embraced doubt as a healthy state of mind, religious believers suffered doubt involuntarily. For them it was a torturous state of inner turmoil that was entirely unproductive. Religion bred deep-seated uncertainty about oneself and the world. People not only turned to it looking for comfort but for metaphysical certainty, and here again, it disappointed them. Precisely because the imaginary world did not accord with reality, because it placed demands on the individual that could not be realized, and because it increased personal misery, religion unleashed internal battles that could not be won.

Pisarev had already drawn attention to the way in which the incompatibility between the ideals promoted by religion and the physical constitution of the human organism could produce doubt in the religious believer in his 1859 review of Turgenev's *A Gentry Nest* for the *Dawn*. In articles for the *Russian Word*, he continued to point to the ways in which religion produced doubt, now explaining it as a result of the discordance between the teachings of religion and the natural world. The religious believer necessarily inhabited a "dream world." That, according to Pisarev, was the condition of faith. Yet any halfway intelligent person was bound to notice that there was a "grayish world of reality" outside of that dream world.[48] Even if the believer chose to disregard the real world, he or she would find it a constant source of irritation. Formally, faith admitted no doubt: precisely because the dream world was a mere figment of the imagination, a house of cards, the entire edifice would collapse if even one element of it were called into question. The believer could not acknowledge his or her doubt; instead he or she attempted to avoid it by withdrawing further and further into the world of faith. The resulting state was one of increasing inner pain and turmoil.[49] The only way out was to abandon faith entirely.

Pisarev's claim that doubt was an inevitable part of the religious experience marked a crucial moment in modern Russian thought. Doubt, in the sense of inner turmoil, had for the first time become a characteristic of religious faith, not the lot of some few believers who chose to question religion. Doubt was the fate of any believer.

Pisarev's reassessment of doubt also marked an important departure from the views of Chernyshevsky and Dobroliubov. They had rejected doubt as self-indulgent hesitation. They further argued that belief in God should be replaced by faith in humanity: the replacement of one faith with another was the hallmark of the "new people," whose confidence in humanity and in the future would allow them to save Russia and the world at large. Pisarev argued that people must wean themselves from faith entirely by communing with the "powerful spirit of criticism and doubt."[50] They must be vigilant so as to avoid assigning too much meaning to abstract concepts, thus escaping the temptation to raise them to the level of ideals. People must learn to live without any ideals at all. Pisarev referred to this vigilant stance variously as "skepticism," "egoism," and "materialism."[51]

By "skepticism," Pisarev meant a way of life that was lived "by pure negation." The skeptic must refrain from believing in anything whatsoever. Skeptics must focus their minds entirely on the present; they must live without aims and therefore without hope for the near future. They are "people of the present" who anticipate nothing. They "do not rush about, do not look for anything, do not seek [career] placements, do not yield to any compromises, and they do not hope for anything."[52] For Pisarev, the ideal person is thoroughly modest and passes unnoticed. Such a person may believe in a better future, but that lies far in the distance, generations from now, too far off to permit the comforting anticipation of success.[53] This is a life without emotional commitments, "without active struggle, and without passionate attachments." It requires that one "believe neither in oneself, nor in other people, nor in an idea." Such a state can be maintained only by "significant sobriety of mind and unusual strength of character." Pisarev admitted that "very few people are capable of putting up with such a sad view of life" but insisted that the adoption of such a view was essential if one was "to preserve one's mental independence amid the chaos of ignorance, force, and prejudice."[54]

As Pisarev claimed, conventional morality undermines not only mental independence but the very individuality of the person. What people generally think of as morality is simply one person's arbitrary opinion imposed on others. Pisarev explained: "We allow our neighbor to have his own taste with regard to an appetizer or a dessert, but woe unto him if he expresses an independent opinion about morality."[55] Yet ideas about ethics are no more transferable from one person to the next than tastes in food. The only possible way to fully internalize others' views is to "annihilate one's own personality" first. Precisely for this reason, Pisarev argues that the full adoption and integration of someone else's views into one's own outlook is impossible. Those views would remain a "chip off of the other person" (*skolok s drugoi lichnosti*) without ever becoming one's own.[56]

One should neither act according to other people's rules of behavior nor organize one's own behavior around long-term goals or guidelines that one sets for oneself. Instead, one should act according to "the inclination of a feeling" or act "as living feeling inclines one."[57] Following inclinations means "being oneself," a state in which "every feeling might manifest itself freely, without control and invented constraints [imposed] from outside."[58] In "Bazarov" (1862), Pisarev's celebrated review named for the hero of Turgenev's *Fathers and Children*, he found various ways to describe this thing that was supposed to represent the wishes of the self: being "guided by his immediate inclination," "taste," "personal taste," "calculation," "personal calculation," and even "personal caprice." Bazarov also embodied Pisarev's other ideals: a materialist who could deem only such things true as were empirically verifiable, Bazarov rejected faith in anything supernatural, including the immortality of the soul, along with principles.[59] Bazarov also rejected ambition, stating that he had none. Having sworn off all aims, he showed no interest in the pursuit of a brilliant career. The future was one of the unknowns he refused to speculate about.[60]

What makes "being oneself" an ethical stance is that it is natural, and what is natural is good.[61] Pisarev was adamant about this in his early articles for the *Russian Word*. By nature, people are kind and loving beings. The artificial demands that other people place on them, or that people take from others and place on themselves, are what make them aggressive and destructive: "By nature, man is a very good creature, and if [we] do not sour him with contradictions, [if we] do not train him [like a circus animal], if we do not demand [that he perform] unnatural conjuring tricks of a moral type, then he will develop the most loving feelings toward the people around him."[62] This insistence on "being oneself" explains why Pisarev attached such importance to the concept of "egoism." He saw it as the guarantor of happiness, confidence, and certainty: "Egoistic convictions, placed on the lining of a soft and good nature, will make you a happy person, not heavy for others and pleasant to yourself. It will be easy to bear life's vicissitudes, and disillusionment will be impossible, because there will be no illusion."[63] Egoism, therefore, is the key to personal and social harmony. Reading such passages, one is reminded why Pisarev's views have been called "intellectually immature."[64] The stance that scholars associate with immaturity, however, had to be invented. Its genesis lay in romanticism, which, as Ginzburg remarked, centered on the quest to create an integral representation of the individual's inner life by exposing the tension between "dream and reality, the ideal and real."[65] Pisarev's writings centered on this tension, and he sought to resolve it early in his career by drawing on materialism to banish the ideal.

Pisarev argued that every human being should be given every possible freedom to construct a life that accords with his or her inclinations, that people have a right to be themselves. That presumption came to be so widely held in the West during the twentieth century that few people now recognize it as an intellectual position with a genealogy. It was not yet an established proposition for Pisarev and his contemporaries, however. Nor was Pisarev blind to one obvious problem associated with this theory: individuals, if they are to act on their inclinations, must have some way of knowing which of those inclinations express their real selves, as opposed to those that society has designated as desirable. The question—whether in fact any individual's inclinations are true expressions of the natural self or whether they are merely learned preferences—would remain an important concern for him.[66] In the early 1860s his only solution to the problem was to encourage his readers not to accept advice and prescriptions about how to live from other people. All people who are, "in the strict sense of the word, egoists by conviction" will "worry only about themselves and submit themselves only to their bent of feeling, without creating artificial concepts of ideals and duty, and without interfering in others' affairs."[67] Pisarev also sought to reduce the influence of society on the individual by encouraging readers to become emotionally self-sufficient, so that the opinions of others would matter little or not at all.

Pisarev had begun to display suspicion about the influence that people exert over one another in 1859. This became more than a personal stance toward his mother and friends, however; it also entered his written work that year. He began to regard emotional attachments to other people as a sign of personal weakness, a lack of self-sufficiency, which expressed itself in the need to turn to other people for emotional support. In his 1859 review of Goncharov's *Oblomov* for the *Dawn*, he excoriated Goncharov's hero for his dependence on other people, noting that "weak characters always require moral support and are, for that reason, always prepared to open themselves [to others]." By contrast, Pisarev saw Stolz, Oblomov's friend—and later rival in love—as strong because he only expressed his opinions when he thought it appropriate.[68]

Pisarev's admiration for strong and silent men only increased in the following years. He came to describe lack of intimacy as a sign of intellectual greatness as well as inner strength. Once again, Bazarov in Turgenev's *Fathers and Sons* embodied this virtue. As an exceptional man, Bazarov can find no equal in society, so he does without friends: "He needs no one [. . .] he loves no one."[69] A few years later, in 1865, Pisarev identified the same qualities in Rakhmetov in Chernyshevsky's *What Is to Be Done?* Rakhmetov never wastes time on unnecessary conversations, because he "does not depend on the people who surround him."[70] Pisarev acknowledged, however, that this isolation was partly involuntary. The more intelligent the man, the more devoted he is to his work, and so the less likely it is that others will understand him and the less likely it is that he will want to communicate his thoughts to them. Pisarev returned to this notion in 1867. "Intellectual titans," he claimed, "have no time and no one to love; they live in eternal isolation. [. . .] [T]hey cannot share their hopes, joys, worries, and fears with anyone."[71] They are entirely self-sufficient, and they are alone.

The praise Pisarev accorded men who "loved no one" may again be understood in connection with his personal life. Between 1858 and 1862, he continued to hope that Raisa Koreneva would marry him—he could not forget those "enormous, greenish eyes" that gleamed "devilishly."[72] Koreneva made and broke off engagements at least three times before marrying another man. Pisarev contributed to their troubled relations by his displays of self-sufficiency. As Koreneva noted in a letter to his mother in 1862, his veneer of toughness had grown so pronounced as to make intimacy with him impossible: "Mitia is cold, callous, and harsh. He is so full of himself that he cannot put himself in the place of others. He is never afraid of and does not take care to avoid wounding them and making them suffer. As for him, he is covered in armor; you won't even find an Achilles heel on him. He sees this invulnerability as his strength, and he is satisfied with it, proud of it, pokes everyone in the eyes with it, and he treats those who do not have such armor with contempt. He does not value people at all, so long as he has partners for card games."[73]

Koreneva observed that Pisarev's behavior drove away friends, including herself. But when Koreneva became engaged to another man—an officer—in March 1862, Pisarev lost his equanimity entirely.[74] He repeatedly insulted his rival in the hopes of provoking a duel. When these tactics proved ineffective, he turned to more extreme measures. In early May, Pisarev disguised himself as a coachman, donning a peasant coat and fake beard, and intercepted Koreneva's fiancé at a train station, planning to humiliate him in public by striking him with a whip. The police intervened in the ensuing brawl and forced him to participate in a formal reconciliation with his adversary. As he subsequently admitted, the habits of a nobleman were hard to break.[75]

According to Pisarev's theory and self-image, his "egoism" should have made him immune to such utter loss of composure. In the short term, however, the experience did not lead him to question his system of thought but to shore up self-sufficiency ever more strongly. His declaration that "intellectual titans have no time and no one to love" testifies to his continuing suspicions about love and intimacy. The self had a great deal of work to perform, according to Pisarev's views of the early 1860s. Literally, one was supposed to live for the self. It needed to be buffered from the rest of the world; every piece of information, every thought or idea had to be carefully scrutinized before a person could incorporate it into his or her worldview. Other people had to be kept at arm's length, lest they undermine the individual's vigilant stance.

Pisarev's commitment to this outlook was sorely tested when he was arrested in the summer of 1862 for writing a political tract. Thanks to his mother's desperate campaign of petitions, imploring the authorities to allow Pisarev to continue writing in prison on account of his fragile mental health and the family's straightened economic circumstances, Pisarev was eventually permitted to continue submitting articles to the *Russian Word*. Two years into his confinement, however, he abandoned what had once been key commitments. In 1864 he began to couch his theories in the quasi-Orthodox language he had previously eschewed. In 1865 he also jettisoned his former endorsement of egoism in order to promote socialist views, arguing that educated people are morally obliged to seek the means to eradicate poverty and suffering. Fusing these two tendencies, he now praised "fanatical" faith in socialist convictions. The shift in his thinking and writing proved temporary; after his release from prison in the late autumn of 1866, his ideas changed again as he returned to his previous views on doubt. Nevertheless, his use of religious rhetoric in these years is noteworthy. It suggests that religious terminology still came easily to writers even when they had vowed to wipe their minds clean of every trace of their religious upbringing. It further suggests that the state's heavy-handed policies encouraged such rhetoric.

In 1864 and 1865 Pisarev's writings came to resemble the articles, pamphlets, and broadsheets of revolutionaries. He had shown little interest in political matters until the spring of 1862, when the Ministry of Internal Affairs closed the *Russian Word*, along with the *Contemporary*, for several months. At the urging of his acquaintance Petr Ballod, he wrote a short tract expressing support for Alexander Herzen and his London publication, the *Bell*, as well as for the revolutionary movement (without, at this point, changing his rhetorical style).[76] The tract was the basis of Pisarev's arrest and conviction. From the ages of twenty-one to twenty-six, he was held at the St. Peter and Paul Fortress in St. Petersburg, which was generally reserved for political prisoners. He saw almost no one for more than four years, apart from his interrogators, his mother, and his editor at the *Russian Word*, Grigorii Blagosvetlov. Yet he and inmates in adjacent cells could, at times, communicate by a kind of Morse code, spelling out words by rapping their knuckles against the walls of their cells.[77] Pisarev evidently came to identify himself with them, which would explain why he now embraced socialism and began to imitate the revolutionaries' quasi-Christian rhetoric.

Influenced by his confinement, Pisarev also wished to establish a closer emotional connection with his readers on the outside. Somewhere in the provinces, he told himself, was a young man—younger than himself—who needed his help. That boy craved knowledge and experience of the world, he needed advice, and Pisarev could offer it: "And so, when I see that reader in my mind's eye, I am overcome with the most burning desire to bring him as much benefit as possible, to tell him all the good things that I might possibly say."[78] This desire to connect with his reader may have prompted the use of religious language to heighten its emotional appeal.

Pisarev's first impulse in prison was to continue promoting his former theories. If anything, he emphasized the value of self-sufficiency even more strongly. The self, he asserted, could become one's "best friend," and self-cultivation should be the individual's chief task.[79] One must "become the complete master [*polnym khoziainom*] of one's inner world" and achieve "unlimited autocracy over one's inner world." This activity should constitute a person's "highest pleasure." People should also cultivate "self-respect," or "respect for the human dignity inside themselves." This self-respect could easily grow to the point of self-worship, or passionate self-love, and there was nothing wrong with this as long as the person was vigilant about what the self actually stood for.[80] Words such as "dignity" and "worship" already mark a departure from his earlier writings.

More striking is Pisarev's inclusion of religious language in his discussion of the effects that the study of science and the exercise in empirical observation would have on the individual. The individual would undergo a transformation as he or she struggled for self-mastery that resembled the formation of the "new man." Pisarev recommended that, in order to sharpen their minds and anchor their thought processes more firmly in the empirical world, people should spend time honing their skills of observation. Engaging in scientific experiments is, according to Pisarev, the most effective means. He highly recommended the dissection of frogs, Bazarov's favorite pastime. The spectacle of the frog, legs pinned to the dissection tray, would afford observers new mental clarity: all thoughts about things that were not empirically verifiable would vanish from their minds: "Looking at a dissected frog, it would be abstruse to go into raptures and talk in phrases, of which you only understand a tenth." Yet Pisarev did go into raptures, making a messiah of the crucified amphibian: "It is precisely here, in the very frog, that the salvation and renewal of the Russian people is located."[81]

Those individuals who engaged in scientific study, moreover, would be transformed in a manner that went well beyond the acquisition of better mental habits. Study would "create anew [*peresozdat'*] the entire character of the individual personality." Such transformations, he remarked, constituted "miracles" of a "very natural" kind.[82] Drawing on the parable from the Gospels, he declared that the individual's thoughts would become a "clear," new "wine"—not a new wine that had been poured into an "old wineskin" but new wine in a new skin.[83] Pisarev was gesturing here at the rhetoric of the new people and the meaning attached to it by Chernyshevsky and Dobroliubov, as well as revolutionaries in the provinces. Following their conceptions, he prophesied that once members of the educated minority had created themselves anew, the re-creation of the world, and of all the "concepts, habits, and institutions of the greatest human societies," would follow naturally.[84]

All the while, Pisarev continued to argue that religion and science are incompatible, and that science, if allowed to flourish, will always drive away belief in the supernatural.[85] The proposition, promoted by

German materialists, that the study and practice of natural science are incompatible with religious faith and will eliminate belief in God had already been articulated by Chernyshevsky and Dobroliubov. Yet what applied to God did not apply to the "miracle" of the transformation of humanity and the reign of justice on earth. Had they been forced to account for this discrepancy, Pisarev and his colleagues might have explained that what needed to be abolished was hope for salvation in the afterlife, not hope for the improvement of people's material living conditions.

Socialism tinged Pisarev's articles of 1864, but socialist ethics became the dominant theme of his prison writings in 1865. Egoism continued to mean the pursuit of individual interest and pleasure, as well as the rejection of the status quo, particularly social norms of thought and behavior that stunted personal development. Yet Pisarev now emphasized just as strongly that the material goods to be enjoyed must be distributed equally in society.[86] The individual should not value his or her well-being and pleasure more highly than the good of society as a whole.

Pisarev did not entirely cast off his previous commitment to the individual as someone who ought to pursue pleasure. Working to improve the living conditions of the impoverished masses should constitute a pleasure. Yet this pleasure was now the only kind Pisarev thought the individual should pursue; the cultivation of such indulgences as listening to refined music, reading great works of literature, or eating well, which benefited only the individual, were luxuries inappropriate to members of a society where poverty was endemic. People must devote as much time as possible to helping others, providing for the basic physical needs of the masses, ending hunger, and curing illness.[87] Indeed, by 1867 Pisarev came to believe that commitment to the welfare of the poor ought to override basic instincts, such as the instinct for self-preservation.[88]

More importantly, Pisarev now urged his readers to embrace socialist principles as articles of faith. They should view themselves as "people of passionate conviction, whole people, knowing and believing people."[89] Unlike the "old man" (*vetkhii chelovek*), full of self-doubt, the "new man" of Russia was marked by faith in himself. "Superior people" of this kind possessed a "burning faith" in a "brighter future" and in the sacredness of human nature. Cultivating such belief was the key to achieving that brighter future.[90] In this way, Pisarev briefly adopted

Chernyshevsky and Dobroliubov's denigration of doubt, contrasting the faith of the new people with the doubt and hopelessness of the old Adams, who had allowed themselves to be overwhelmed by past disappointments. To Pisarev, faith meant two related things: the hope for a better future and the commitment to a sacred idea. It ceased to bother him that "believing" in a great and "sacred" idea or truth might take a person beyond the immediate realities of the here and now.[91] People ought to be critical minded, yet amid all their criticism, they needed something to believe in.

The most essential ideals were least likely to be realized in the present, and it became all the more necessary for people to cultivate faith in their ultimate triumph. In this regard, Pisarev believed there were lessons to be learned from the history of religion. In "The Historical Ideas of Auguste Comte" (1865), he found that the supernatural beliefs of the most "primitive" societies had given them a distinct advantage. When people were at their weakest and most vulnerable, living under the most dispiriting circumstances, it was only their fetishistic beliefs that gave them the courage to act, and to do so with an enviable degree of self-confidence. Pisarev concluded: "Weakness consists in the inability to act on nature; and strength in the ability to hope and, by means of these fantastical hopes, to maintain one's moral courage, for which, in a given period of development, no other real source of support may be possible."[92]

While arguing that radicals could draw positive lessons from religious "fanaticism," Pisarev was not urging them to revert to the belief in supernatural forces. He continued to claim, as Chernyshevsky and Dobroliubov had before him, that belief in gods had resulted from ignorance of nature and had bred in people an unnecessary conviction of their helplessness. Human beings would only adopt an active, positive attitude toward themselves and their ability to order their lives once they had given up faith in God.[93] In other words, the "faith" that Pisarev called for in prison was predicated on atheism. People must believe in their ability to resolve the most intractable economic, social, and political dilemmas, and this would only be possible once they had rejected any and all belief in the supernatural.

After his release from prison in 1866, Pisarev subjected his views to one final revision. In 1864 and 1865 he had urged readers to embrace "faith" in socialism and to believe in the possibility of creating a better future. He continued to argue that poverty in Russia was a problem that needed urgently to be addressed, yet he also began to warn against "fanatical" attachment to any idea. Returning to the position he had adopted at the very outset of his career in 1859, he emphasized the inevitability and necessity of doubt.

Pisarev was released from prison about six months after the fateful day in April 1866 when a deranged student radical, Dmitrii Karakozov, had attempted to assassinate Alexander II, hopeful that the violent death of the tsar might inspire a revolt. The Karakozov attempt provoked another wave of government repression, during which time both the *Russian Word* and the *Contemporary* were shut down. It also divided the radical community over the question of the legitimacy of violence. Some historians have claimed that Karakozov's attempt caused Pisarev to back away from support for revolutionary violence. In particular, they point to "The Struggle for Life," a review of Dostoevsky's *Crime and Punishment* (1866), which Pisarev wrote in March and April 1867 and published in the new radical journal, the *Cause* (*Delo*).[94]

From its very first installment, which appeared shortly before the assassination attempt, *Crime and Punishment* was regarded as a commentary on the radical movement.[95] After the assassination attempt, Dostoevsky's novel came to be seen as a commentary on Karakozov. According to Claudia Verhoeven, the problem that Karakozov brought to the attention of his contemporaries, one that was recapitulated in *Crime and Punishment*, was "the individual use of violence to *force* the birth of an idea that, at its core, crowns the subject sovereign."[96] Pisarev, however, rejected such violence. Step by step, Pisarev analyzed the path by which Rodion Raskolnikov came to act on an elaborate scheme he thought would relieve his desperate poverty, help his family, and save humanity: the murder of a pawnbroker and theft of her possessions. Extraordinary people, Raskolnikov told himself, are entitled to commit murder when humanity stands in the way of progress. Pisarev observed that Raskolnikov's thoughts and plans made no sense: violence is not a means by which world history can be sped up to facilitate progress.[97]

More important, Pisarev now rejected the "fanaticism" that he had recently urged on members of the radical community; single-minded devotion to higher ideals was unhealthy. Ever the materialist, he argued that Raskolnikov's ideas were the product of an unhealthy organism, of hunger and desperation. In his weakened physical state, Raskolnikov had allowed his imagination to get the better of him; he had fallen prey to his own "damnable dream," which had "bewitched" him.[98] Here, Pisarev drew on ideas he had articulated in the early 1860s, when he warned readers that ideals could become "phantoms" that slipped from the individual's control.

In considering the significance of Karakozov's assassination attempt as a causal factor in Pisarev's change of position, it should be noted that his review was written a full year after the event. Articles he wrote in the intervening months did not deny the value of faith. The word "fanaticism" still held a positive valence in one article he wrote late in 1866 or in early 1867. Here, he dubbed Russia's radicals "new puritans" on account of their "passionate convictions" and "faith." He also expressed limited support for the use of violence, even if his stance toward it became more ambivalent.[99] Other developments, then, must have accounted for his gradual rejection of violence and radical fanaticism. Difficulties he encountered upon reentry into St. Petersburg society played an important role.

One particularly valuable document in this regard is a letter Pisarev wrote to Ivan Turgenev in March 1867, at the very time he was working on "The Struggle for Life." Turgenev had written to Pisarev to ask him how he and members of his "circle" had responded to Turgenev's latest novel, *Smoke* (*Dym*), in which Turgenev criticized the radical movement. Pisarev responded that he had no circle: "I do not see and do not know any of those whom they [. . .] call my supporters." Without endorsing Turgenev's representation of radicals, he noted that "I myself deeply hate all idiots in general and I especially hate those idiots who pretend to be my friends, confederates, and allies." Again, Pisarev did not feel such contempt for all radicals: he mentioned that he respected many of his colleagues but added that the ones he respected most were not to be found in St. Petersburg. Pisarev also noted that prison had taken its toll on his health and that following his release, he had found it difficult to write.[100]

In speaking of "idiots who pretend to be my friends," he most likely had in mind his former editor, Blagosvetlov, who had been one of the few people Pisarev had seen in prison. Now, the two had become embroiled in personal conflicts over Pisarev's place in Blagosvetlov's new publishing ventures, leading them to sever all connections. Reintegration into St. Petersburg society also meant face-to-face contact with figures in radical society who had, for years, existed only abstractly in his mind. The earnest young readers he had imagined while confined to the St. Peter and Paul Fortress were now in evidence everywhere around him. He smiled when, during a rare visit to the offices of the famous radical editor Nikolai Nekrasov, a girl approached him asking him to

Dmitrii Pisarev. Photograph, 1865. In Iurii Korotkov, *Pisarev* (Moscow: Molodaia gvardiia, 1976), between 288 and 289.

autograph a large photograph she had obtained of him.[101] Generally, he avoided radical gatherings.

By 1868 the rejection of "fanatical faith" had become a core element of Pisarev's journalism, and he did not confine his criticisms of fanatical faith to radicalism. In "The Old-Time Gentry" (1868), a review of the first three volumes of Lev Tolstoy's *War and Peace*, he turned his attack on the supporters of Russia's autocracy, using the patriotism of Nikolai Rostov, a young officer in the Napoleonic Wars, as his prime example. Rostov is generally prone to idol worship: "Ideals, idols, and authorities spring up from the ground like mushrooms before his feet at every step." His veneration of Alexander I, however, approaches "fanaticism." Rostov, Pisarev commented, resembles the high priest of some primitive religion, willing to sacrifice himself simply to prove his love for his god: "Ablaze with an all-consuming and blinding love for their godhead, these priests are often driven by their love to such extremes, to such monstrous and unnatural feelings, that their godhead could only feel insulted, indignant, angered were it to discover their existence."[102]

Like any religious believer, however, Rostov cannot entirely blind himself to the incongruity between his faith and reality. The emperor has shortcomings. Having experienced the ghastly conditions of life at the front lines of the war, Rostov is horrified to discover, when he reaches the imperial court, that it—and, by implication, the emperor himself—are utterly indifferent to the suffering of Russian soldiers and civilians. Yet Rostov's faith prevents him from drawing the necessary conclusions. Instead, he is pained by the doubts that nag him and condemns himself for having them. As Rostov explains to fellow officers after having drunk some wine, "If we were to start passing judgment and reasoning, then soon nothing sacred would remain. We would wind up saying that there is no God, there is nothing at all." Instead of settling on this thought, Rostov declares that "our business is to fulfill our duties, to fight, and to not think," whereupon he orders another bottle.[103]

Pisarev contrasted Rostov's response with that of the "experienced person." Human life entails a series of disappointments; as people mature, they become steadily more disillusioned with the ideals and beliefs they grew up with in childhood. After each successive disappointment, the individual seeks to rebuild a worldview from the ruins of the old one. But what remains after each disappointment becomes smaller and smaller, until all that is left is dust running through one's fingers. It is only when we realize that all of the "thoughts and feelings" that have been inculcated in us are false that we can begin to attain a solid under-standing of the world surrounding us.[104]

Pisarev's insistence on the importance of doubt denotes a partial return to his early criticism of religion. Yet his late articles also demon-strate a reversal of his earlier contentions in one key regard: he now argued that love for another person constitutes the highest and only real good: it is the one emotional need that nothing else can replace.[105] In his review of Dostoevsky's *Crime and Punishment*, Pisarev even suggested that Raskolnikov could have avoided committing his crime had he spent more time in the company of friends. They would have comforted him, helped him materially, and even helped him see the nonsensical nature of his theories and plans.[106]

This shift, as historians have universally agreed, can be attributed to a development in his personal life: Pisarev fell in love. It was in his mother's apartment, soon after his release from prison, that he met Maria Markovich, better known to her readers by her Ukrainian penname, Marko Vovchok, another cousin, who now became the center of his life. Markovich was Pisarev's cousin thrice removed, and he had known her since he was a boy. She was absent from Russia between 1859 and 1866, when she returned to St. Petersburg. Within a year of having met her, Pisarev felt he could not live without her, declaring that he was "entirely hers" and would be willing to change every aspect of his character to please her. She was his "divinity," his "goddess."[107]

Just as in his theory, Pisarev's worship of Markovich could only lead to disappointment: she did not entirely return his love. When Pisarev drowned while vacationing with her at a lake in the summer of 1868, many suspected suicide.[108] One might expect that Pisarev's turn from fanaticism toward doubt would have alienated his radical followers, but this was not the case. His funeral became a major public event, attended by hundreds of participants in the radical movement; weeping devotees threw themselves on his coffin, mourning the loss of yet another writer who had died too young. Turning this thought on its head, Nekrasov would remark that Pisarev had died just young enough to be remembered without reproach.[109]

Pisarev's defense of doubt placed him within the tradition of noble doubt of the 1830s and 1840s. After his death, Herzen himself would claim Pisarev—and Bazarov, the hero of Pisarev's famous article—as his "prodigal sons." Herzen defined Pisarev's "nihilism" as "complete freedom from all those ready-made concepts, from all those inherited obstructions and rubble, which prevent the Western mind from walking forward, upright." This movement, Herzen asserted, had begun in the 1840s, among his own generation. Pisarev's nihilism was "nothing new"; he had simply articulated it with much more clarity and energy than the men of the 1840s had managed to do.[110] Herzen's words about Pisarev were, of course, an apologia for his own contributions to Russian intellectual life, which he felt had not been adequately appreciated by members of Pisarev's generation.

Herzen was not entirely wrong in putting himself forward as an inspiration to Pisarev. His London journal had been among the first oppositional publications that Pisarev came into contact with when he became a student in 1856. The small circle he joined in 1857 had been formed in imitation of Herzen's Moscow circle. The revolutionary tract for which Pisarev was arrested in 1862 was written in defense of Herzen against conservative detractors. Yet Herzen's legacy was not something that Pisarev ever addressed in his writings, however tangentially. Why not? Some answers are obvious: Herzen stood for a noble heritage, which had been more of a hindrance than a help to Pisarev at the time he was trying to establish himself as a journalist. At that time, Dobroliubov and Chernyshevsky were the dominant—present—figures in Russian journalism, in relation to whom he had to position himself as a writer. Herzen was no longer in Russia, and he was a nobleman of the old school, one who would never recognize that these priests' sons, too, were his children. Pisarev, by contrast, belonged to a younger generation of noblemen who were beginning to find that they could no longer afford to observe such distinctions. There were many young noblemen of Pisarev's age—including his university friends—who found this regrettable. One reason why radical readers found Pisarev's "realism" so compelling was his willingness to turn his back on "old prejudices" and to embrace new ideas, regardless of the social origins of the people who promoted them.

His readers also found Pisarev's writings inspiring for the answer they provided to one essential question—how to live in the absence of God. The individual, he argued in the beginning and end of his career, must stare bravely back into the void created by the abnegation of ready-made answers. Pisarev opened "Heinrich Heine," one of his last important articles, with the observation that "there are many good books in the world, but these books are good only for those who know how to read." Any good reader, however, knows that no book contains the answer to the one essential question: "How to live?" ("Kak zhit'?").

That is the dilemma that even the best readers must work out for themselves, and here, he proposed no resolution.[111]

Pisarev's skepticism about the value of books focuses attention on the broader question that stands at the center of this book: why did educated Russians attribute such importance to the question of the existence of God, and why did they turn away from faith in growing numbers? The historian demands tangible answers to such questions, and this book has attempted to provide them by pointing to the particularly tense relationship between writers and an autocratic state, to the influence of Western thinkers, to the influence of social hierarchies within Russian educated society, and to the inner dynamics of debate within the intelligentsia. For every individual, however, the reasons were also always personal. Pisarev was a young nobleman swept up by the radical movement. Yes, he was deeply influenced by his predecessors in Russian journalism—Herzen, Chernyshevsky, and Dobroliubov foremost among them. But he was also a young man struggling to come to terms with personal difficulties: the domineering behavior of his family, relatives, and friends; his disappointment in his lovers; and the contradictions in his own system of thought during his years in solitary confinement.

What was God to him? Another source of misplaced hope, and a being, he suspected early on, who would never resolve his doubts.

Conclusion

The October Revolution of 1917 cast a long shadow backward, flattening the intellectual landscape of nineteenth-century Russia and draining it of its more nuanced colors. Amid all the attention that was paid to the intelligentsia in light of the revolution, historians lost sight of one important aspect of its life: the mode of questioning—rather than dogmatic exposition—that leant meaning to the lives of its members.

In the twentieth century, Russian intellectual historians were preoccupied with political and social thought, with rising objections to autocracy and growing disapproval of serfdom, which lead to the emergence of liberal and socialist opposition in the later nineteenth century. To them, the "accursed questions" were primarily material in nature; problems of religious belief occupied a position that was marginal at best. This book has argued that the political, social, and religious were not separate spheres in Russian intellectual life of the nineteenth century. The accursed questions were eternal questions, not only because they were difficult to answer, but because beliefs about the transcendental were woven into them. The manner in which the problems of the existence of God, the immortality of the soul, and the very proposition that human life has a higher meaning were resolved played a central role in defining the identity and allegiances of members of the intelligentsia.

Russian intellectual historians wrote little about doubt and loss of faith among their subjects. When they did broach the topic to discuss atheism, they tended to treat it as a discrete phenomenon—as an abstract proposition that emerged out of the interaction between individuals and books imported from the West. Thus, for example, it was often argued that atheism arose as a consequence of materialist scientific and philosophical conceptions. To some extent, nineteenth-century memoirs were complicit in creating this picture. Thus, Longin Panteleev recalled that a Russian translation of Büchner's *Matter and Force* hit St. Petersburg "like a bomb," so that "the remnants of [our] traditional beliefs were torn apart at once."[1] Similarly, Alexander Herzen recalled in *My Past and Thoughts* how he was transformed after picking up a copy of the *Essence of Christianity*. "Having read the first pages, I leapt with joy. Down with the masquerade costume, away with insinuation and allegories; we are free people [. . .] we do not need to drape truth in myths!"[2] Such anecdotes are as misleading as they are appealing if one takes them as statements about how loss of faith occurred. Letters and diary entries Herzen produced at the time he claimed to have read the *Essence of Christianity* furnish a very different picture; indeed, none of them suggest that the book made any such impression. Rather, one finds gradual shifts in opinion, plenty of doubt, and not joy, but pain.

Ideas are unlike bombs in that they strike only when the ground has already been prepared. In imperial Russia, this preparation took place largely in conversation. Even books such as the *Essence of Christianity* were recommended and passed on between friends in the context of conversations. Such exchanges were influenced by habits and norms of interaction between educated people, norms that developed over decades and that made the eternal questions a mandatory topic of discussion. Expressions of doubt and disbelief were informed by the close relationships between the participants, delimited by concerns of reputation and social status, and spurred on by political developments. Individuals also responded to events in their lives—to death, betrayal, and imprisonment, as well as to love, friendship, and release from prison and exile— as each sought to formulate a world view that fit these experiences.

Members of the intelligentsia not only insisted on debating the eternal questions, but demanded that the practices of daily life must conform to the principles they held. Their social habits must reflect their beliefs, or lack thereof. In his memoir, Herzen recounts how his friend, the literary critic Vissarion Belinsky, flung down his dinner napkin and stormed out of a dinner party when his host admitted that he served Lenten fare "for the benefit of the servants."[3] Belinsky objected to the patronizing attitude his host took toward his servants, and, indeed, to the very fact that his host had servants. Most importantly, however, he was enraged by the complacent observation of an Orthodox ritual in the absence of faith. Herzen admired Belinsky not only for his outrage, but for having left the party—for acting on his principles.

The social nature of doubt and atheism stands out in the canonical novels of the Russian nineteenth century. Thus, in Tolstoy's *War and Peace* (1865–69), Pierre Bezukhov and Andrei Bolkonsky could assure themselves of their friendship only after spending a short eternity debating the immortality of the soul under a starry sky, and the results they reached became Bolkonsky's reason for living.[4] In Dostoevsky's *Brothers Karamazov*, discussions and arguments in which the brothers share their thoughts about the existence of God and the meaning of the life of Christ serve as rare moments of intimacy between men who are different in almost every other way. Ivan Karamazov's famous legend, the "Grand Inquisitor," appears in the novel not as a pamphlet but as an unwritten story one brother shares with another.[5]

The *roman russe* was Russia's most influential export item at the end of the nineteenth century. According to Owen Chadwick, these novels were so widely read because they addressed what was perceived to be the inadequacy of Westerners' agnosticism. They "met a need of the moment. A Paris jest of the time ran that the Russians were revenging themselves for the burning of Moscow by Napoleon Bonaparte."[6] Positivism, so influential in France, Britain, and Germany at this time, stood for a "calm acceptance of the world" and its inherent order, yet this calm covered over "some ultimate point of truth about the human predicament": imperfection, and the awareness of that imperfection, as a feature of human nature.[7] Russians, embodied in the novels of Dostoevsky and Tolstoy, symbolized disorder: they were tormented by the questions they had not answered, by their own insufficiency and their inability to provide for themselves and one another. They could not find the answer to the question, how to live? Indeed, the narrator of Dostoevsky's *Notes from Underground* wondered whether the acceptance of any answer might not mark a cowardly act of capitulation.[8]

Those young people who were integrated into the revolutionary community of the early 1860s attempted to resolve these questions by dedicating themselves more vigorously to the Russian peasantry. They lived in hope of radical transformation and redemption, terms that they borrowed from the vocabulary of Orthodox Christianity. The presence of Christian conceptions in the absence of God did not trouble them. Others, however, were troubled. Dmitrii Pisarev was foremost among them. To him, living without God was a task of total personal reinvention, a process in which all conceptions, preferences and priorities were to come from within the individual. Pisarev was indeed so strident as to insist that faith in God could not be replaced by faith in any other kind of principle. The task he set his readers was one he attempted to realize in everyday life. Under arrest, his radical experiment proved unsustainable. This book ends with Pisarev, not because he was representative and not because he was successful, but because he most fully explored the implications of what it might mean to live without faith—in God, or in anything whatsoever. His problem was the legacy of atheism to the modern world.

Pisarev's death in 1868 did not spell the end of the diverse intellectual developments described in this book. In the late nineteenth and early twentieth century, doubters and atheists continued to argue with themselves and one another. Among them were atheists who searched for new forms of belief and doubters who sought new philosophical grounds on which to revitalize Orthodoxy. The populist Alexander Malikov invented an atheistic religion he called "Godmanhood," in which God was to be denied so that the god in man could be recognized. Meanwhile, the philosopher Vladimir Soloviev reinvented Russian Orthodoxy by placing the concept of human divinity, or Godmanhood, at its center.

Lonesome individuals continued to seek truth and meaning inside themselves, even as friendship circles remained essential to the life of the intelligentsia. Mikhail Gershenzon argued that doubt, not messianic faith, was the only intellectual method by which eternal questions could be answered and that individuals must broach this task alone. Lev Tolstoy cultivated his fields while urging his followers to embrace mutual love. Zinaida Gippius and Dmitry Merezhkovsky made platonic love and intellectual communion the basis of their new religion, the "Third Testament." Socialists created a cult of people, though many argued that human need would only be fulfilled when religion was abandoned. Viktor Chernov, the leader of one of Russia's most violent revolutionary organizations, viewed himself as one of the "new saints" in a "new, secular religion."[9]

In October 1917, atheism became a central tenet of Soviet ideology, a fact that has generally been attributed to the influence of Marxism on Vladimir Lenin and his associates. If anything, Lenin was more ardent in his insistence that religion be eradicated than Marx, Engels, and their followers among the German Social Democrats.[10] The difference has sometimes been attributed to the intellectual legacy of the Russian intelligentsia, from which Lenin inherited the view that the destruction of faith in God was a predicate (not a consequence) of successful revolution.[11] Ever since the 1860s, atheists in the Russian revolutionary

community had argued that abandonment of faith i
step in taking control of one's own destiny and the d
nation. This attitude cannot but have influenced the
in Russia, particularly for Lenin, who was so aware Russia .
ary tradition. There was another reason, however, why atheism w
central to Bolshevik ideology, namely, habits of thought. By the early
twentieth century, the existence of God had been firmly established
among members of the intelligentsia as the question without which
the struggle for the salvation of humanity could not be resolved.[12] This,
ultimately, was Lenin's aim—to create heaven on earth—and it could
not be accomplished without overthrowing God.

Nikolai Berdiaev, who emigrated in 1922 to become one of the most
prominent critics of the Soviet Union in the West, would identify the
October Revolution as Russia's long-awaited Apocalypse. He insisted
that Soviet atheism and communism were in large part products of
intelligentsia traditions, most notably the intelligentsia's egalitarianism
and "aversion to capitalism," its "striving after an integrated outlook
and an integrated relation to life," its "denial of spirit and spiritual
values," and "a well nigh religious devotion to materialism." The revolution itself, he claimed, was a product of the millenarianism inherent in
the Russian soul.[13] Berdiaev's works were not only a comment on but a
reflection of the intelligentsia's tendency to view every area of political
and social life in the light of religious problems. His writings proved
remarkably popular among Western audiences. Arguably, this was because Western readers recognized in Berdiaev what they already knew,
or thought they knew of Russia, from the *roman russe.*

Members of the intelligentsia could be dogmatic, but it was not
dogmatism that most impressed their readers. Rather, it was the refusal
to settle for the practical, but temporary, solutions to problems that the
world offered them. The insistence on addressing and continually re-
addressing the eternal questions arose out of a perceived need to knock
up against the boundaries of what was possible. Those individuals
who denied God acted out of a sense of their own inadequacies, and in
continuing to deny him, they kept him ever present.

Notes

Introduction

1. Dostoevskii, *Brat'ia Karamazovy*, 14:212–13.

2. Ibid., 14:65.

3. Russians adopted these terms from Catholic and Protestant apologetic tracts. In the West, as in Russia, theological and philosophical attacks on "atheism" preceded the spread of atheism proper. The scholarly literature on the development of Christian apologetics has centered on France. See Kors, *The Orthodox Sources of Disbelief*, and Monod, *De Pascal à Chateaubriand*. On the development of the literary image of the atheistic philosophe, see Wade, *The "Philosophe" in the French Drama of the Eighteenth Century*.

4. Dostoevskii, *Besy*, 10:94. Capitalization of "God" follows the 1871 Russkii vestnik edition. For a comment on this episode, see Paperno, *Suicide as a Cultural Institution in Dostoevsky's Russia*, 129, 143–46, and Frank, *Dostoevsky: The Miraculous Years*, 481–83.

5. Confino, "On Intellectuals and Intellectual Traditions in Eighteenth- and Nineteenth-Century Russia," 118. (He adds the caveat that this might not be unique to Russians: Karl Mannheim had said exactly the same of German intellectuals.) Other scholars, too, have commented on the Russian intelligentsia's ruthless logic; see Malia, "What Is the Intelligentsia?" 1, and Berlin, *Russian Thinkers*, 125.

6. For example, Georges Florovsky faulted Mikhail Gershenzon in 1926 for dwelling on "the fleeting minute" rather than tracing continuities in the development of ideas over time. "In every system of ideas he tries to find [. . .] that individual blend of passions and affinities, habits and wishes, which conditions the uniqueness and inimitability of a given personality. This is why he lays such value on private documents, which contain the fleeting minute [. . .], where the breath of life still lives and is warm. It is the fleeting moment that attracts him—moments of anguish and anxiety, of struggle or restless quest; and as a contrast he lovingly reproduces also minutes of calm, of delight,

and moments when the spirit is once more whole" ("Michael Gerschensohn," 318).

7. Lovell, "Biography, History, and Finitude," 249, 253.

8. Chaadaev, "Lettres philosophiques adressées à une dame," 92, and Aizlewood, "Revisiting Russian Identity in Russian Thought," 38–39.

9. Abrams, *Natural Supernaturalism*, 378–83.

10. Berlin, *Russian Thinkers*, 128–29.

11. Walker, "On Reading Soviet Memoirs," 330. Numerous important studies have emphasized the importance of the circle, yet they continued to insist on the dominance of charismatic leaders in Russian intellectual history: Gershenzon, *Istoriia molodoi Rossii*, 2:85–86; Kornilov, *Molodye gody Mikhaila Bakunina*, 103–7; Malia, *Alexander Herzen and the Birth of Russian Socialism*, 65–66; Riasanovsky, *A Parting of Ways*, 283–85, and Brown, *Stankevich and His Moscow Circle*, 10–13.

12. John Randolph has recently remarked on and critiqued this line of inquiry in *The House in the Garden*, 4, 13.

13. The position I take contradicts the thesis advanced by Raeff in *Origins of the Russian Intelligentsia*. Raeff claims that the "alienation" between nobility and state that produced the intelligentsia was a product of mid-eighteenth-century state reforms that gave the nobility too much freedom from state service.

14. This has been convincingly demonstrated in a groundbreaking study by Elena N. Marasinova: *Psikhologiia elity rossiiskogo dvorianstva poslednei treti XVIII veka*.

15. Marker, *Publishing, Printing, and the Origins of Intellectual Life in Russia*, 96–97. This is the leading study on this topic, documenting the emergence of a literary life independent of the state during the later eighteenth century. Marker expresses ambivalence in his conclusions, however: "Most writers and translators continued to exist simultaneously in both the intellectual and the political spheres of public life, at least through the first half of the nineteenth century, in part because the market could not yet support them as professional journalists or writers." For the *literator*, "literature and service were either part of a single moral endeavor or were, at the worst, complementary activities. By the end of Catherine's reign, the leading writers were coming to look ever more like full-fledged intellectuals, albeit ones who, for the most part, continued to serve" (233).

16. Randolph, *The House in the Garden*, 33–39, 45–46, 61. For similar reasons, Wladimir Berelowitch has argued that Russia could offer no equivalent to the French salon in the eighteenth century: gatherings took place in the homes of powerful noble families in the late eighteenth century, but guests were either relatives or political clients of the hosts, and everyone imitated the manners and conversation cultivated at court ("La vie mondaine sous Catherine II," 102–6).

17. I argue this, despite the well-known corrective by Gregory Freeze, who demonstrated that in the wake of Peter's reforms, the church maintained a higher degree of institutional autonomy from the state than once recognized ("Handmaiden of the State?"). For other perspectives on Peter's religious policies, see Cracraft, *The Church Reform of Peter the Great*, and Zhivov, *Iz tserkovnoi istorii vremen Petra Velikogo*, 34–68.

18. On the centrality of Orthodoxy to the Romanovs' ideology of autocracy, see Smolitsch, "Die Stellung des russischen Kaisers zur orthodoxen Kirche in Russland vom 18. bis 20. Jahrhundert." Smolitsch notes that "Christian ruler" was the term of choice under Peter the Great, whose successors, including Catherine the Great, emphasized their status as "Orthodox Christian" monarchs (142, 145, 146).

19. According to the law code of 1649, heretics and blasphemers were to be burned at the stake, though they were seldom sentenced to death in the eighteenth century (Grekulov, *Pravoslavnaia inkvizitsiia v Rossii*, 20–25). While Peter the Great demanded less extreme forms of punishment, he expanded and reinforced the codes for blasphemy and heresy. His policies mirrored practices in western European states in the early eighteenth century, but exceeded them in extent; see Cabantous, *Blasphemy*, 84.

20. Smilianskaia, *Volshebniki, bogokhul'niki, eretiki*, 207–8.

21. As Richard Wortman has noted, the coronation as a ceremony that sacralized autocratic monarchy was based on western European as well as Byzantine models (*Scenarios of Power*, 1:27–29). On the coronation in Russia, see also Smolitsch, "Die Stellung des russischen Kaisers zur orthodoxen Kirche in Russland vom 18. bis 20. Jahrhundert," 155.

22. Thomson, "The Corpus of Slavonic Translations Available in Muscovy," 195. Muscovy's theological poverty is a point of universal consensus in histories of the Orthodox Church. See, for example, Meyendorff, *The Orthodox Church*, 90–91, 96–97, and Schmemann, *The Historical Road of Eastern Orthodoxy*, 225–27, 319–20.

23. Florovskii, *Ways of Russian Theology*, vol. 1, chaps. 4–5. Though Florovsky's work is widely considered to be tendentious, it remains the most deeply researched and authoritative study on Russian theology and its development in the modern age. It should be noted that theological developments in the eighteenth and nineteenth centuries in Russia have been gravely understudied.

24. Freeze, *The Russian Levites*, 210.

25. Raeff, *Origins of the Russian Intelligentsia*, 153, 233n9.

26. Freeze, "Handmaiden of the State?" 82.

27. Zhivov, "Marginal'naia kul'tura v Rossii i rozhdenie intelligentsii," 42; Manchester, *Holy Fathers, Secular Sons*, 42–44, 51–58.

28. Marker, *Publishing, Printing, and the Origins of Intellectual Life in Russia*, 61–65.

29. For an insightful discussion, see Martin, *Romantics, Reformers, Reactionaries*, 144–47, and Rothe, *Religion und Kultur in den Regionen des russischen Reiches im 18. Jahrhundert*, 75–85.

30. Marker, *Publishing, Printing, and the Origins of Intellectual Life in Russia*, 209.

31. Voltaire's reception in Russia is more fully discussed in my "The Rise of Unbelief among Educated Russians in the Late Imperial Period," 8–21.

32. Raeff, *Origins of the Russian Intelligentsia*, 112, 118, 135.

33. Soviet historians took great pains to catalog and describe every eighteenth-century atheist manuscript they could find (mostly translations of Western works). They found only a handful but persisted in claiming that

many more had circulated in the eighteenth century. Shakhnovich, "Novyi pamiatnik russkogo svobodomysliia XVIII veka," 742. To explain the lack of remaining copies, they asserted that the majority had been destroyed, though they could provide only anecdotal evidence of such destruction. See, for example, Persits, "Russkii ateisticheskii rukopisnyi sbornik kontsa XVIII–nachala XIX v.," 362–64n14.

34. Pomeau, *La religion de Voltaire*, chap. 2.

35. Kors, "The Atheism of D'Holbach and Naigeon," 274, 278–83, 297–98. Kors has argued that seventeenth-century debates between Aristotelians and Cartesians over proofs of the existence of God were a major source of the rise of atheism in the eighteenth century. This is more fully discussed in Kors, *The Orthodox Sources of Disbelief*, chap. 8.

36. Febvre, *The Problem of Unbelief in the Sixteenth Century*. See especially the final three chapters.

37. One of the most thorough critiques is Wootton, "Lucien Febvre and the Problem of Unbelief in the Early Modern Period." Febvre, Wootton argues, "imagined that he had found in sixteenth-century France not a civilization almost as sophisticated as his own but a primitive tribe, incapable of sequential thought" (727). See also Edwards, "Religious Faith and Doubt in Late Medieval Spain," 21. For a compelling defense of Febvre's approach, see Schröder, *Ursprünge des Atheismus*, 21–27.

38. Here, I especially have in mind Kors, *D'Holbach's Coterie*.

39. See, most notably, Turner, *Without God, Without Creed*, especially chap. 6. On the relationship between science and atheism in the nineteenth century, see Hecht, *The End of the Soul*.

40. Shlapentokh, *The French Revolution in Russian Intellectual Life*, 84.

41. Riasanovsky, *A Parting of Ways*, 111–14.

42. The question of what kinds of books should be subject to synodal approval was highly contentious; see Marker, *Publishing, Printing, and the Origins of Intellectual Life in Russia*, 219–24, and Kotovich, *Dukhovnaia tsenzura v Rossii*, 3–4.

43. Papmehl, *Freedom of Expression in Eighteenth Century Russia*, chaps. 6–7; Skabichevskii, *Ocherki istorii russkoi tsenzury*.

44. Monas, *The Third Section*, 134, 173. Monas admits that censors' decisions could be unpredictable (137).

45. For many years, historians argued over the composition of the group, debating whether it was mainly comprised of noblemen or of nonnoble commoners, the *raznochintsy*; whether it included only participants in the revolutionary movement, a subculture that emerged in the 1860s, or else included all educated members of Russian society. One highly influential article in this regard is Leikina-Svirskaia, "Formirovanie raznochinskoi intelligentsii v Rossii v 40-kh godakh XIX v." Daniel Brower carries forward this approach in "The Problem of the Russian Intelligentsia." The treatment of intelligentsia as a sociological category has been called into question by Otto Wilhelm Müller in *Intelligencija*; he concludes that the term was an "empty slogan." Recent studies, notably Elise Kimerling Wirtschafter's, tend to agree that the "insistence on treating the intelligentsia in sociological terms creates serious problems in

interpretation" (*Structures of Society*, 126). See also Manchester, *Holy Fathers, Secular Sons*, 4–5, and Engelstein, *Slavophile Empire*, 4–7.

46. Early in the twentieth century, Ivanov-Razumnik famously defined the intelligentsia in this way (*Chto takoe intelligentsiia?* 1). Alan Pollard has traced this notion to the 1860s, when Russian journalists, beginning with Ivan Aksakov, started to identify the intelligentsia as the "consciousness of the nation" ("The Russian Intelligentsia," 13–16). Nathaniel Knight makes this point more forcefully in "Was the Intelligentsia Part of the Nation?" 743. The definition Knight offers of "intelligentsia" as "a collective representation or ethos" (738) is similar to mine. The only adjustment I would make to this definition is to suggest that the word "intelligentsia" should refer not just to the ethos but to the people who applied it to themselves.

47. A good example is Shelgunov, "Beskharakternost' nashei intelligentsii."

48. Gershenzon, "Creative Self-Consciousness," 58, 67.

49. Berdiaev, "Philosophical Verity and Intelligentsia Truth," 6; Bulgakov, "Heroism and Asceticism (Reflections on the Religious Nature of the Russian Intelligentsia)," 22–23; Semen Frank, "The Ethic of Nihilism (A Characterization of the Russian Intelligentsia's Moral Outlook)," 135–37; Struve, "The Intelligentsia and Revolution," 120. Struve insisted that atheism was the core feature of the intelligentsia, though he did not view it as a form of religion: "The spiritual birth of the Russian intelligentsia, in our use of the word, took place when progressive Russian intellects accepted Western European atheistic socialism" (120).

50. Berdiaev, *The Origin of Russian Communism*; Berdiaev, *The Russian Idea*.

51. Some of the key works in this tradition are Voronitsyn, *Istoriia ateizma*; Kogan, *Ocherki po istorii ateisticheskoi mysli XVIII v.*; and Persits, *Ateizm russkogo rabochego*.

52. See, for example, Confino, "On Intellectuals and Intellectual Traditions in Eighteenth- and Nineteenth-Century Russia," 134.

53. Gershenzon, "Creative Self-Consciousness," 67. The language in the untranslated text is more evocative. See Gershenzon, "Tvorcheskoe samosoznanie," 104–5.

54. Gershenzon, *Istoriia molodoi Rossii*, 2:82–84.

55. The literature, particularly on the Slavophiles and Dostoevsky, is so extensive that only a few of the many notable titles can be named here: Gershenzon, *P. Ia. Chaadaev*; McNally, *Chaadayev and His Friends*; Walicki, *The Slavophile Controversy*; Engelstein, *Slavophile Empire*; Riasanovsky, *Russia and the West in the Teaching of the Slavophiles*; Müller, *Russischer Intellekt in europäischer Krise*; Scanlan, *Dostoevsky the Thinker*; Cassedy, *Dostoevsky's Religion*; and Pattison and Thompson, *Dostoevsky and the Christian Tradition*.

56. Vissarion Belinsky, Mikhail Bakunin, and other members of the highly influential Stankevich circle left behind a rich written record but I discuss them only in passing in chapter 2, which is devoted to the circle of Herzen and Ogarev. This difficult decision was motivated by the consideration that their intellectual development was in so many ways similar to that of Herzen and Ogarev that a full chapter would only have replicated the findings of chapter 2. Fundamental studies on the Stankevich circle are cited in that chapter.

Chapter 1. Forbidden Fruit

1. Koshelev, "Moi vospominaniia ob A. S. Khomiakove," 345.
2. Pogodin, "Vospominanie o kniaze Vladimire Fedoroviche Odoevskom," 52–53.
3. In this chapter, I use "he" and "man" as a generic term for any person, reflecting the exclusivity of the Wisdom Lovers' orientation toward other men as thinkers. Though the Wisdom Lovers were acquainted with and related to highly educated women, these women were not invited to participate in their group, nor did they read or discuss philosophical or poetic works by women. Women in Russia did not become members of intellectual circles until the 1830s; see chapter 2 of this book.
4. Belinsky often praised Dmitrii Venevitinov in the literary criticism he wrote between 1835 and 1841. He did not hesitate to list Venevitinov alongside Pushkin, Zhukovsky, and Griboedov as a writer of exceptional talent. See, for example, "Russkaia literatura v 1840 godu," 4:409, and "Russkaia literatura v 1841 godu," 5:562. Herzen remembered Venevitinov as an opponent of the state. Herzen, "Du développement des idées révolutionnaires en Russie," 7:75, 77, 93.
5. Two other factors may have been important in discouraging the study of the Wisdom Lovers. One is that historians tended to assume that Hegel was a more important influence in nineteenth-century Russia than Schelling, and the result of that was that Schelling's reception in Russia was, for many years, understudied. A second factor was that the problem of doubt itself never became a topic of scholarly interest, as intellectual historians, especially in the Soviet Union, were largely interested in finding manifestations of atheism.
6. Literary historians generally agree that romanticism entered Russia only in the mid-1810s, though they note that some members of the literary establishment continued to defend the aesthetic norms of the Enlightenment well into the 1820s. For a discussion of the periodization of Russian romanticism, see Mersereau, "Romanticism or Rubbish?" 7, 9.
7. Setschkareff, *Schellings Einfluß in der russischen Literatur der 20er und 30er Jahre des XIX. Jahrhunderts*, 33.
8. Koshelev, *Zapiski*, 14.
9. Snegirev, Apr. 29, 1824, July 12, 1824, and Sep. 2, 1824, in "Dnevniki" [Diary], 399, 409, 426.
10. Bulgarin, *Ivan Vyzhigin*, 1:88. The novel was originally published in 1829.
11. Lotman, "The Decembrist in Daily Life," 135–36.
12. Vladimir Odoevsky's half brother, the Decembrist Alexander Odoevsky, criticized Vladimir's idealist writings; see Tur'ian, *Strannaia moia sud'ba*, 85–86, 91–92. Other Decembrists, however, were interested in reading Schelling's works; see Kanunova and Aizikova, *Nravstvenno-esteticheskie iskaniia russkogo romantizma i religiia*, 118–19.
13. Lotman, "The Decembrist in Daily Life," 101–4, 137.
14. Koshelev, *Zapiski*, 16. The most detailed and balanced account of Wisdom Lovers' reactions to the Decembrist uprising can be found in Maimin, *Russkaia filosofskaia poeziia*, 8–11. See also Tur'ian, *Strannaia moia sud'ba*, 108, 90–91.

15. Smith, *Working the Rough Stone*, 181–82. Needless to say, there were pockets in Russian elite society, especially in the officer corps, that were indeed very hostile to Alexander I and his policies. Otherwise, the Decembrist uprising would not have taken place.

16. See Sukhomlinov, *Issledovaniia i stat'i po russkoi literature i prosveshcheniiu*, 1:185, and Koyré, *La philosophie et le problème national en Russie au début du XIXe siècle*, 46–87, esp. 50–51, 72–73.

17. For an account of the impact of romanticism on idealism, see Beiser, *The Romantic Imperative*. On objections to Schelling's philosophy in Germany, see Bréhier, *Schelling*, 167–68, 208, 212–13.

18. Sukhomlinov's study offers the most complete account of these investigations. Not every professor was made subject to them, however. Vellanskii and Pavlov, for example, appear to have been left alone because they ostensibly taught natural sciences, not philosophy. Why exactly some professors suffered while others did not, however, needs to be investigated further.

19. Qtd. in Sukhomlinov, *Issledovaniia i stat'i po russkoi literature i prosveshcheniiu*, 1:263.

20. Sukhomlinov, *Issledovaniia i stat'i po russkoi literature i prosveshcheniiu*, 1: 256–57. This argument was emphatically not idealist but was most likely drawn from Friedrich Heinrich Jacobi. See Beiser, *The Fate of Reason*, 47.

21. Setschkareff, *Schellings Einfluß in der russischen Literatur der 20er und 30er Jahre des XIX. Jahrhunderts*, 12.

22. In a diary entry of February 19, 1824, Snegirev recorded a conversation with a student who had just returned from St. Petersburg: "They respect and envy us there. Magn[itsky] said that he forestalled the revol[ution] by fifty years!!" ("Dnevniki ," 392).

23. Feoktistov, *Materialy dlia istorii prosveshcheniia v Rossii. I. Magnitskii*, 154, 198; Setschkareff, *Schellings Einfluß in der russischen Literatur der 20er und 30er Jahre des XIX. Jahrhunderts*, 16.

24. See the anonymous "O religii kak osnove istinnogo prosveshcheniia," 1:8–12.

25. "Manifest 13 iiulia 1826 g.," 17:252–53. On changing images of the Decembrists in the Russian press following December 14, 1825, see Gotovtseva and Kiianskaia, "Dvizhenie dekabristov v gosudarstvennoi propagande."

26. Even before he organized the Wisdom Lovers, Odoevsky had started publishing short stories celebrating the "strange man" in Russian society as one who persisted in the pursuit of knowledge amid an elite that had condemned itself to ignorance.

27. Materialism figures in some Soviet accounts; see, for example, Virginskii, *Vladimir Fedorovich Odoevskii*, 16–18. Venevitinov as well as Koshelev have been called skeptics; see Piatkovskii, *Kniaz' V. F. Odoevskii i D. V. Venevitinov*, 130, and Kamenskii, *Moskovskii kruzhok liubomudrov*, 11, 79. Venevitinov's relationship to the church is characterized as "indifferent" by Wytrzens (*Dmitrij Vladimirovič Venevitinov als Dichter der russischen Romantik*, 97–98).

28. For an example of the firm believer camp, see Riasanovsky, *Russia and the West in the Teaching of the Slavophiles*, 35, 40. The pantheist character of Khomiakov's poetry is emphasized in Maimin, *Russkaia filosofskaia poeziia*, 53–63.

29. Kirichenko, *Dvorianskoe blagochestie*, 146–55. He quotes a father instructing children how to read scripture not "solely for knowledge, but as a guide into the life eternal" (*ne dlia uvedeniia tokmo, no dlia putevodstviia v zhizn' vechnuiu*) (148).

30. Florovskii, *Ways of Russian Theology*, 1:189.

31. Rothe, *Religion und Kultur in den Regionen des russischen Reiches im 18. Jahrhundert*, 75–85.

32. Martin, *Romantics, Reformers, Reactionaries*, 144–45.

33. Khomiakova, "Vospominaniia ob A. S.," 52–53.

34. What exactly is meant by "austere piety" in literature on Vasilii Kireevsky is unclear. It is said, for example, that he bought up copies of works by French encyclopedists in Moscow for the sole purpose of destroying them. This did not automatically make him a strict adherent of Orthodox religiosity, however. See Koliupanov, *Biografiia Aleksandra Ivanovicha Kosheleva*, 1.2.3–4; Peterson, "Rasskazy i anekdoty," 361fn3; and Liaskovskii, *Brat'ia Kireevskie*, 4.

35. Pypin, *Religioznye dvizheniia pri Aleksandre I*, 115.

36. Filaret [Drozdov], "Slovo v den' Blagoveshcheniia Presviatyia Bogo-roditsy," 64–65; "Slovo v den' sobora sviatago arkhistratiga Mikhaila," 25–26; and "Beseda iz pritchi o plevelakh," 237–39; Evgenii [Bolkhovitinov], "Slovo 23. v nedeliu 7. po piatidesiatnitse," 207.

37. "Prostota very," 215–16, 223.

38. Attacks on the Bible Society were made possible by ministerial infighting that led to the fall of Prince Golitsyn. Golitsyn had been the major patron of the Bible Society. See Florovskii, *Ways of Russian Theology*, 1:194.

39. Zacek, "The Russian Bible Society and the Russian Orthodox Church," 434; Florovskii, *Ways of Russian Theology*, 1:198.

40. Evgenii [Bolkhovitinov], "Slovo 7. v nedeliu sv. Apostola Fomy" and "Slovo 8. v tuiuzhde nedeliu sv. Apostola Fomy," 1:47, 62–63.

41. On Lopukhin, see Kotovich, *Dukhovnaia tsenzura v Rossii*, 485fn5. On Koshelev, see Pypin, *Religioznye dvizheniia pri Aleksandre I*, 216. His accuser was Fotii (Spasskii), archimandrite of Iur'ev Monastery.

42. Barsukov, *Zhizn' i trudy M. P. Pogodina*, 1:169, 220.

43. Venevitinov to Koshelev, mid-July 1825, in Venevitinov, *Stikhotvoreniia, Proza*, 350.

44. Venevitinov, "O matematicheskoi filosofii," 238–39.

45. Venevitinov to Koshelev, late July 1825, in Venevitinov, *Stikhotvoreniia, Proza*, 354.

46. Ibid., 353, and Venevitinov to Koshelev, mid-July 1825, in Venevitinov, *Stikhotvoreniia, Proza*, 349.

47. Venevitinov, "O matematicheskoi filosofii," 239.

48. Venevitinov to Koshelev, ca. July 20, 1825, in Venevitinov, *Stikhotvoreniia, Proza*, 352.

49. Venevitinov to Koshelev, mid-July 1825, in Venevitinov, *Stikhotvoreniia, Proza*, 349.

50. Ibid., 351.

51. Koshelev, *Zapiski*, 15.

52. Setschkareff, *Schellings Einfluß in der russischen Literatur der 20er und 30er Jahre des XIX. Jahrhunderts*, 2.

53. Odoevskii, "Opyt teorii iziashchnykh iskusstv," 2:164.

54. Snegirev, Nov. 18, 1824, and Dec. 11, 1824, in "Dnevnik," 535, 543.

55. In his philosophical manuscripts of 1824 and 1825, he frequently wrote of the necessity of faith in God, or the "Absolute." One of the manuscripts is titled "On the Error of Wrong-Headed Philosophers, Who Deny Revelation." Here, Odoevsky paraphrased extracts from Voltaire's *Philosophical Dictionary* and apparently planned to refute Voltaire's arguments. He left the section that was to be devoted to his refutation blank, however ("Zabluzhdenie lzhemudrstvuiushchikh filosofov, otvergaiushchikh Otkrovenie," papers of Vladimir F. Odoevskii, RNB, f. 539, op. 1, pereplet 31, ll. 41–44 ob).

56. Odoevskii, "Sekta idealistiko-eleaticheskaia (otryvok iz Slovaria istorii filosofii)," 173–77.

57. Usok, "Filosofskaia poeziia liubomudrov," 112; Ginzburg, "Opyt filosofskoi liriki," 198–200, 210.

58. Titov, "O dostoinstve poeta (teoriia iziashchnykh iskusstv)," 232–33.

59. Khomiakov, "Molodost'." In order to facilitate the reader's understanding of the poem, I have translated the words without adhering to the poems' line breaks. This is my procedure throughout.

60. By choosing to speak of a creator, Shevyrev was backing away from the more extreme pantheistic stance that Odoevsky had taken in 1824. If God is the creator of nature, then he is in some sense separable from it. Over the following years, Shevyrev moved further and further away from pantheism and came closer to an explicitly Orthodox representation of God.

61. Shevyrev, "Ia esm'." Cf. Khomiakov, "Poet," 73. Both poems are discussed in Usok, "Filosofskaia poeziia liubomudrov," 113–15.

62. Sakulin, *Iz istorii russkogo idealizma*, 1:329.

63. On the divided and contradictory nature of mind and personality in romanticism, see Huch, *Die Romantik*, 112–41. Schlegel's view of irony is captured in his statement that "Ironie ist klares Bewußtsein der ewigen Agilität, des unendlich vollen Chaos" (qtd. in Immerwahr, "The Subjectivity or Objectivity of Friedrich Schlegel's Poetic Irony," 177). Romantic irony could be carried to different extremes. Some scholars present it as if it eclipsed faith in truth or the transcendental sphere entirely. See, for example, Greenleaf, *Pushkin and Romantic Fashion*, 39–49. This understanding of irony goes well beyond what the Wisdom Lovers had in mind.

64. Davydov, "Aforizmy iz nravstvennogo liubomudriia," 211, 206. Davydov published this article under the pseudonym "Memnon."

65. Odoevsky nevertheless continued to praise Davydov. See Bielfeldt, *Selbst oder Natur*, 278.

66. Berlin, *Russian Thinkers*, 120–21.

67. Odoevsky used both the words "doubts" (*somneniia*) and "uncertainty" (*nereshimost'*). Portions of the letter are reproduced in Sakulin, *Iz istorii russkogo idealizma*, 1:134. Sakulin explains that the term remained important to him into the late 1820s, when he "praised [*vospevaet*] the sweet 'suffering of doubt'" (1:330).

68. Lotman, *Pushkin*, 84–90; Maimin, *Pushkin*, 60–79.

69. Pushkin, "Moi demon," 11–12. Pushkin was dissatisfied with the version that appeared in 1824, emended it slightly, and subsequently published it as

"Demon." The emended version is better known, and can be found in Pushkin, *Polnoe sobranie sochinenii*, 2.1.299.

70. Odoevskii, "Eshche dva apologa," 35.

71. Pushkin, "[O stikhotvorenii 'Demon']," 11:30, 301. In the manuscript, Pushkin first wrote, "It needs to believe" (*emu nuzhno verit'*) instead of "It is gullible and tender."

72. Mason, *Goethe's Faust*, 176–77.

73. The differences between Pushkin and Goethe are discussed at greater length in Vatsuro, "K genezisu pushkinskogo 'Demona.'" Vatsuro analyzes the debt Pushkin owed to Mme de Staël's *De l'Allemagne* (1813) for his interpretation of *Faust* (130).

74. Мне нравились его черты, / Мечтам невольная преданность, / Неподражательная странность / И резкий, охлажденный ум. / Я был озлоблен, он ургюм. (Pushkin, *Evgenii Onegin*, 6:23). Lotman pointed out the direct connection, both in the time of composition and in theme, between these and subsequent lines of *Eugene Onegin* and "My Demon" (*Pushkin*, 581–83).

75. Он забавлял мечтою сладкой / Сомненья сердца своего; / Цель жизни нашей для него / Была заманчивой загадкой, / Над ней он голову ломал / И чудеса подозревал. (Pushkin, *Evgenii Onegin*, 6:34). See also Lotman, *Pushkin*, 592. As Lotman notes, Lenskii's enthusiasm for Kant can be viewed as a criticism of St. Petersburg's reaction against idealism, for which Pushkin had as much contempt as the Wisdom Lovers.

76. Rozhalin, "Nechto o spore po povodu Onegina (pis'mo k redaktoru Vestnika Evropy)," 26–27, 29–30. This essay was published under the pseudonym "I. R———in." Rozhalin's authorship is confirmed in Masanov, *Slovar' pseudonimov russkikh pisatelei, uchenykh i obshchestvennykh deiatelei*, 3:17.

77. Venevitinov, "Neskol'ko myslei v plan zhurnala," 131, 130.

78. Shevyrev, "Obozrenie russkikh zhurnalov v 1827 godu: Moskovskii telegraf," 81–82.

79. Venevitinov, "Zhizn'," 42. The reference to Shakespeare (the "twice-told tale") is intentional; Venevitinov was then discovering Shakespeare's works through the translations of August Schlegel.

80. Venevitinov, "Elegiia," "XXXV."

81. Venevitinov, "K moemu perstniu."

82. Venevitinov, "Poslanie k R[ozhali]nu," 44.

83. Ibid.

84. His friends viewed "To My Ring" as autobiographical. The end of the poem calls for the narrator's friends to place the ring on his finger when he dies. When Venevitinov died, his friends did place Volkonskaia's ring on his finger.

85. Ginzburg, "Poeziia mysli," 51, 62, 63. She returned to this point in *Tvorcheskii put' Lermontova*, 86–87. This is also the position taken by Maimin, *Russkaia filosofskaia poeziia*, 47. One problem they do not address is that members of the Wisdom Lovers saw these poems as autobiographical. Fedor Khomiakov, who lived with Venevitinov in his last month, described his poems as a kind of diary (*zhurnal*) (Khomiakov to Khomiakov, Dec. 3, 1826, in Venevitinov, *Polnoe sobranie sochinii*, 398).

86. Shevyrev, "Razgovor o vozmozhnosti naidti edinyi zakon dlia iziashch-nogo," 509–12.

87. Reid, "Lermontov's Demon," 199.

88. Venevitinov to Pogodin, Mar. 7, 1827, in Venevitinov, *Stikhotvoreniia, Poeziia*, 399–400.

89. Koshelev, *Zapiski*, 12.

90. Qtd. in Koliupanov, *Biografiia Aleksandra Ivanovicha Kosheleva*, 1.2.150.

91. In his diary, Pogodin noted that Venevitinov had been uncharacteristically "bestial," egged on by some friends. Pogodin had been trying to observe an Orthodox fast. See Barsukov, *Zhizn' i trudy M. P. Pogodina*, 2:134.

92. Mikhail Venevitinov, "K biografii poeta D. V. Venevitinova," 122–23.

93. On tense relations between Odoevsky, Koshelev, Venevitinov, Rozhalin, and Kireevsky in St. Petersburg, see Koliupanov, *Biografiia Aleksandra Ivanovicha Kosheleva*, 1.2.99, 119–21.

94. Lemke, *Nikolaevskie zhandarmy i literatura*, 41, 68–70.

95. Qtd. in Koliupanov, *Biografiia Aleksandra Ivanovicha Kosheleva*, 1.2.124. On the origins of the "superfluous man" in Russian literature and the Wisdom Lovers' contribution to it, see Udodov, *M. Iu. Lermontov*, 519–25.

96. Qtd. in Engelstein, *Slavophile Empire*, 134.

97. Ivanov-Razumnik, "Obshchestvennye i umstvennye techeniia 30-kh godov," 1:249; Kornilov, *Molodye gody Mikhaila Bakunina*, 112–17, 130; Brown, *Stankevich and His Circle*, 61.

98. Raeff, *Origins of the Russian Intelligentsia*; Malia, *Alexander Herzen and the Birth of Russian Socialism*. Malia writes that idealism "is a 'method' that admits of no permanent enigmas, which leaves no areas of uncertainty or doubt. It is, in short, a device for people who cannot afford to face reality as it is and yet who are in a hurry to make the world over in the image of the heart's desire, a short cut to understanding and to an illusive feeling of mastery over experience" (93).

Chapter 2. Providence and Doubt

1. Herzen to Ogarev, Aug. 2, 1832, in Herzen, *Sobranie sochinenii*, 21:22.

2. On Herzen as the inventor of Russian socialism, see Malia's classic study, *Alexander Herzen and the Birth of Russian Socialism*. For a recent investigation of Herzen's role in the history of the formation of the Russian intelligentsia, see Paperno, "Intimacy and History."

3. Riasanovsky, *Nicholas I and Official Nationality in Russia*, 120; Wortman, *Scenarios of Power*, 1:285, 335.

4. Filaret [Drozdov], "Rech' Blagochestiveishemu Gosudariu Imperatoru Nikolaiu Pavlovichu, pred vstupleniem Ego Velichestva v Uspenskii sobor," 3:206–7.

5. Malia, *Alexander Herzen and the Birth of Russian Socialism*, 201.

6. One year, Herzen secretly reset all the clocks in the mansion one hour earlier on New Year's Eve so that he could escape to be with Nick at midnight (Herzen to Tatiana P. Kuchina, Dec. 31–Jan. 1, 1829–30, in Herzen, *Polnoe sobranie sochinenii*, 1:47–48).

7. Passek, *Iz dal'nikh let*, 1:271.

8. Malia, *Alexander Herzen and the Birth of Russian Socialism*, 49–50.

9. Schiller, "Vorrede zur ersten Ausgabe der 'Räuber,'" 2:9. See also Schiller's poems in volume 1 of the *Gesammelte Werke*: "Rousseau," "Zuversicht der Unsterblichkeit," "Tabulae Votivae: Mein Glaube," "Das eigne Ideal." See also Fricke, *Der religiöse Sinn der Klassik Schillers*, 91–102.

10. Herzen to Kuchina, Oct. 1828, in *Polnoe sobranie sochinenii*, 1:29–30.

11. Herzen, *Byloe i dumy*, 8:54.

12. "I prayed every morning and evening, unaware of what I was doing, I bowed to the ground before the *kiot* and diligently read the necessary prayers from a thick prayer book, without understanding a thing I read" (qtd. in Passek, *Iz dal'nikh let*, 1:276).

13. Passek, *Iz dal'nikh let*, 1:282; Natal'ia A. Herzen, "Kopiia predsmertnoi zapiski, napisannoi karandashom," 118–19. See also Zimmerman, "Natalie Herzen and the Early Intelligentsia," 256.

14. Miliukov, "Liubov' u 'idealistov tridtsatykh godov'," 132.

15. Zakhar'ina to Herzen, Dec. 24, 1837, in Herzen, *Sochineniia A. I. Gertsena i perepiska s N. A. Zakhar'inoi*, 7:409. See also Zakhar'ina to Herzen, Apr. 14, 1837, and Apr. 27, 1837, in *Sochineniia A. I. Gertsena i perepiska s N. A. Zakhar'inoi*, 7: 264, 275.

16. Herzen, "Den' byl dushnyi," 1:55.

17. Labry, *Alexandre Ivanovič Herzen*, 27; Malia, *Alexander Herzen and the Birth of Russian Socialism*, 168. See also Florovskii, "Iskaniia molodogo Gertsena," 400–401.

18. Herzen, *Byloe i dumy*, 8:143–44. On Venevitinov, see also Herzen, "Du développement des idées révolutionnaires en Russie," 7:75, 77, 93.

19. Herzen, *Byloe i dumy*, 10:317.

20. Malia, *Alexander Herzen and the Birth of Russian Socialism*, 39; Labry, *Alexandre Ivanovič Herzen*, 77–78. Herzen's biographers suppose that he was familiar with *Mnemosyne* and the *Moscow Messenger*, but due to the paucity of primary sources, they cannot pinpoint which articles Herzen and Ogarev read.

21. Labry, *Alexandre Ivanovič Herzen*, 68. The title of the book is unknown.

22. Obolenskii contributed to *Severnaia lira na 1827 god*. Despite his connections and erudition, he did not make a favorable impression on Herzen, who described him as a poorly dressed pedant to Kuchina (Herzen to Kuchina, Oct. 1828, in *Polnoe sobranie sochinenii*, 1:29).

23. While scholars have often remarked that Herzen and Ogarev read Schelling beginning in 1828, they have not pointed to *Philosophical Inquiries into the Nature of Human Freedom* as an influence. Most likely, this is because the title of this work does not appear in any of their writings. Yet it corresponds much more closely to their worldview in the 1830s than works by Schelling with which scholars are more familiar, such as the *System of Transcendental Idealism*.

24. Schelling, "Philosophische Untersuchungen über das Wesen der menschlichen Freiheit," 4:295.

25. Lakhtin to Ogarev, June 28, 1833, in Lakhtin, "Pis'mo," 294.

26. Herzen, "Programma i plan izdaniia zhurnala," 1:59. The document was cosigned by Nikolai Sazanov and Nikolai Satin; Ogarev, Ketcher, and Lakhtin were also involved.

27. Herzen, "O meste cheloveka v prirode," 1:17–18. See also, more notably, Ogarev, "Profession de foi," 2:119–21, 126. Though, as Gershenzon suggests, Ogarev wrote "Profession" for his wife, Maria (112), the inspiration may have come from Herzen's "Plan for a Journal." There, Herzen had called for a "profession de foi" to organize the journal around a single philosophical worldview.

28. Herzen to Ogarev, June 24–27, 1833, and Herzen to Zakhar'ina, Aug. 5 and Aug. 12 or 19, 1833, in *Sobranie sochinenii*, 21:14, 25. Herzen also cited it in "Den' byl dushnyi" (55) together with the refrain from Goethe's "Mignon": "Dahin, dahin / Möcht ich mit dir, o mein Geliebter, ziehn."

29. Satin, "Umiraiushchii khudozhnik," 2:425; Ogarev to Herzen, June 7, 1833, in "Iz perepiski nedavnikh deiatelei," *Russkaia mysl'* 9, no. 7 (1888): 5; Ogarev to Herzen, Aug. 29, 1835, in Ogarev, *Izbrannye sotsial'no-politicheskie i filosofskie proizvedeniia*, 2:273–74.

30. Zakhar'ina to Herzen, Mar. 18, 1838, in *Sochineniia A. I. Gertsena i perepiska s N. A. Zakhar'inoi*, 7:526.

31. On Saint-Simonism, see Kolakowski, *Main Currents of Marxism*, 1:189–90. Labry explains how Herzen and Ogarev could combine Schelling and French socialism (*Alexandre Ivanovič Herzen*, 139–40).

32. Herzen to Ogarev, Aug. 7 or 8, 1833, in *Sobranie sochinenii*, 21:23, emphasis in original.

33. Nasonkina, *Moskovskii universitet posle vosstaniia dekabristov*, 127.

34. Brodskii, "Moskovskii universitetskii blagorodnyi pansion epokhi Lermontova (iz neizdannykh vospominanii grafa D. A. Miliutina)," 5.

35. *Istoriia Moskovskogo universiteta*, 1:208–11.

36. Mervaud, *Socialisme et liberté*, 58–61, 65, 92–93; Malia, *Alexander Herzen and the Birth of Russian Socialism*, 134–35.

37. Labry, *Alexandre Ivanovič Herzen*, 93. Petr Ternovskii was hired to teach this course in 1827. His textbook (*Dogmaticheskoe izlozhenie ucheniia very provoslavnoi tserkvi*), which was said to have been rather unscientific, was used for theological instruction at the university. On Ternovskii, see Filaret [Gumilev], *Obzor russkoi dukhovnoi literatury*, 487.

38. Zorin, *Kormia dvuglavogo orla*, 343.

39. Sokolovskii, "Russkii imperator," 2:368. The poem's last four lines read: "Manifest chitaia, / Szhalilsia tvorets, / Dal nam Nikolaia, / Sukin syn, podlets."

40. Qtd. in Monas, *The Third Section*, 127.

41. Satin to Sokolovskii, Nov. 29, 1833, documents of the Third Section, GARF, f. 109, 1. eksp., 1834, op. 9, d. 239, ch. 1, lit. A, l. 53, emphasis in original. The documents seized are in a file titled "O litsakh, pevshikh paskvil'nye pesni."

42. Interrogation of Nikolai Satin, Oct. 15, 1834, documents of the Third Section, GARF, f. 109, 1. eksp., 1834, op. 9, d. 239, ch. 1 lit. A, ll. 433 ob.–34.

43. Interrogation of Vladimir Sokolovskii, Aug. 20, 1834, documents of the Third Section, GARF, f. 109, 1. eksp., 1834, op. 9, d. 239, ch. 1 lit. A, ll. 36–37.

44. Herzen to Ogarev, Aug. 7 or 8, 1833, in *Sobranie sochinenii*, 21:23, emphasis in original.

45. Interrogation of Nikolai P. Ogarev, Aug. 20, 1834, documents of the Third Section, GARF, f. 109, 1. eksp., 1834, op. 9, d. 239, ch. 1 lit. A, l. 58-ob.

46. Ogarev to Herzen, late Apr. 1838, in *Izbrannye sotsial'no-politicheskie i filosofskie proizvedeniia*, 2:292–93. Herzen likened his time in exile in Vladimir to the forty days of Christ's temptation in the wilderness (Herzen to Zakhar'ina, Nov. 29, 1837, in *Sobranie sochinenii*, 21:237).

47. Satin's letters to Ketcher are especially striking in this regard; they are unpublished and housed at the manuscript division of the Russian State Library in Moscow (RGB). See, for example, the following: "Sometimes I feel radiant, very radiant; it seems to me that conviction and Faith are overcoming all boundaries. At these moments I am strong, happy, I look boldly into the future . . . But there are other moments, heavy moments of a gambler, when I feel I need support, and only in friendship do I see such support. [. . .] Who does not doubt his strength when he finds himself alone?" (Satin to Ketcher, first half of 1836, papers of Nikolai Kh. Ketcher, RGB, f. 476, kart. 5185, no. 33, ll. 22 ob.). See also Ogarev to Ketcher, Dec. 27, 1835, in *Izbrannye sotsial'no-politicheskie i filosofskie proizvedeniia*, 2:274–75, and Herzen to Ketcher, Sept. 10, 1837, in *Sobranie sochinenii*, 21:206.

48. Herzen to Zakhar'ina, Apr. 30, 1837, June 18, 1837, and July 6, 1837, in *Sobranie sochinenii*, 21:166–67, 176, 182; Zakhar'ina to Herzen, Nov. 12, 1835, Dec. 16, 1835, Nov. 17, 1836, and Feb. 15, 1837, in *Sochineniia A. I. Gertsena i perepiska s N. A. Zakhar'inoi*, 7:42, 52, 179, 227.

49. Ogarev to Ogareva, in Gershenzon, "Liubov' Ogareva," 3:256.

50. "Savior," "Christ," and "angel": Zakhar'ina to Herzen, June 8, 1836, in *Sochineniia A. I. Gertsena i perepiska s N. A. Zakhar'inoi*, 7:99; Herzen to Zakhar'ina, Aug. 16, 1836, Mar. 29, 1838, and Nov. 1, 1836, in *Sobranie sochinenii*, 21:92, 341. "Divine": Zakhar'ina to Herzen, Sept. 24, 1835, Dec. 16, 1835, and Jan. 29, 1836, in *Sochineniia A. I. Gertsena i perepiska s N. A. Zakhar'inoi*, 7:35, 51, 61–62; Herzen to Zakhar'ina, Apr. 30, 1837, in *Sobranie sochinenii*, 21:166–67. The star image had originated in letters by Zakhar'ina to Herzen, June 3, 1835, Nov. 26, 1835, and Jan. 2, 1836, in *Sochineniia A. I. Gertsena i perepiska s N. A. Zakhar'inoi*, 7:15, 47, 56. In his letters, Herzen called Zakhar'ina "little star," "morning star," and "guiding star" (Dec. 11, 1836, Sept. 6, 1836, Nov. 1, 1836, and June 18, 1837, in *Sobranie sochinenii*, 21:127, 96, 113, 176).

51. Herzen to Zakhar'ina, June 25, 1835, in *Sobranie sochinenii*, 21:43.

52. Lankheit, *Das Freundschaftsbild der Romantik*, 96–97, 113, 129, 133–34.

53. See, e.g., Corbin, "Backstage," 569.

54. See Botkin to Bakunin, Oct. 15, 1838: "My rebirth is fused with you, because you were the *first* to introduce me to the ideas that dropped the blindfold from my eyes. I entered a free sphere of being, where for the first time my spirit sighed freely and easily, wearied by the meanderings [. . .] of reason and all sorts of doubts" (Botkin, "Pis'ma k M. A. Bakuninu," 96, emphasis in original). See also Botkin to Bakunin, Oct. 28, 1839: "Bless me, my friend, for my new life. You were a prophet and an angel, you annunciated the Spirit and Truth to me" (Botkin, "Pis'ma k M. A. Bakuninu," 121).

55. On the philosophical development of the Stankevich circle, see Randolph, *The House in the Garden*, 146–271; Pustarnakov, *Filosofiia Shellinga v Rossii*, 330–42; Brown, *Stankevich and His Moscow Circle*, 94–117; and Schultze, *Wissarion Grigorjewitsch Belinskij*, 50–57, 107–63, 176–209.

56. In his memoirs, Herzen claims that the two groups were united as "Westernizers" in opposition to the "Slavophiles" in the 1840s. In the 1830s, however, according to Herzen, the two groups had not joined together because Herzen's circle was fundamentally "political," whereas Stankevich's circle was too "philosophical." This statement has been taken at face value in scholarly literature, beginning with Kornilov, *Molodye gody Mikhaila Bakunina*, 107. It should be remembered, however, that Herzen wrote his memoir at a time when he wished to disassociate himself from his earlier idealist views; as an opponent of autocracy, he rather wished to cloak himself in the mantle of the Decembrists. There is little evidence that in the 1830s Herzen viewed politics and philosophy as separate; why in the early 1850s Herzen came to think that they were fundamentally at odds with one another is a subject for a separate study.

57. Ogarev to Herzen, 1837, "Iz perepiski nedavnikh deiatelei," *Russkaia mysl'* 9, no. 9 (1888): 6; Herzen to Zakhar'ina, Dec. 5, 1836, in *Sobranie sochinenii*, 21:123; Ogarev to Ketcher, end of 1836, in *Izbrannye sotsial'no-politicheskie i filosofskie proizvedeniia*, 2:284.

58. Levin, "N. Kh. Ketcher," 2:530.

59. Kiseleva-Sergenina, "N. M. Satin," 2:418.

60. Satin, "Raskaianie poeta," 2:430–31, 445.

61. Herzen to Zakhar'ina, Dec. 12, 1836, and Jan. 9, 1837, in *Sobranie sochinenii*, 21:127, 134.

62. Herzen to Zakhar'ina, July 6, 1837, in *Sobranie sochinenii*, 21:182.

63. Zakhar'ina to Herzen, Aug. 18, 1837, in *Sochineniia A. I. Gertsena i perepiska s N. A. Zakhar'inoi*, 7:332.

64. The passage ending in "the devil slipped it between Christ's name and yours" continues: "But I looked at your soul and was comforted. No, disappear, hellish thought. Your soul is inseparable from love. Love is such that it is impossible to imagine her without love toward me" (Herzen to Zakhar'ina, July 6, 1837, in *Sobranie sochinenii*, 21:182).

65. Ogarev, "Crescendo aus der Symphonie meines Ichs im Verhältnisse zu seinen Freunden," 1:41, emphasis mine.

66. Herzen to Ketcher, Sept. 10, 1837, in *Sobranie sochinenii*, 21:206.

67. Zakhar'ina quoted Satin's views on this subject: he longed for "a person whose soul harmonizes" with his "and who forms, so to speak, the second half" of himself (Zakhar'ina to Herzen, Apr. 28, 1836, in *Sochineniia A. I. Gertsena i perepiska s N. A. Zakhar'inoi*, 7:87).

68. Ogarev to Ogareva, [1836], in Gershenzon, "Liubov' Ogareva," 259.

69. Herzen to Zakhar'ina, Apr. 10, 1837, in *Sobranie sochinenii*, 21:159–60. Two years later, Ogarev offered the same idea to his wife in a simplified form (Gershenzon, "Liubov' Ogareva," 276).

70. Herzen to Ogarev, Nov. 14, 1839, in *Sobranie sochinenii*, 22:53.

71. Hayner, *Reason and Existence*, 66–67, 97–98; Laughland, *Schelling versus Hegel*, 59, 141–43.

72. Labry, *Alexandre Ivanovič Herzen*, 210–11. Hegel was also attacked in the conservative journal *Library for Readers* (Jakovenko, *Geschichte des Hegelianismus in Russland*, 7–8).

73. Belinskii, "Mentsel', kritik Gete," 3:392; Jakovenko, *Geschichte des Hegelianismus in Russland*, 50–52.

74. Ogarev to Herzen, [1839], "Iz perepiski nedavnikh deiatelei," *Russkaia mysl'* 9, no. 11 (1888): 8.

75. Herzen to Ogarev, Feb. 20, 1841, in *Sobranie sochinenii*, 22:100.

76. Wortman, *Development of a Russian Legal Consciousness*, 226–28.

77. Ogarev to Herzen, Mar. 6, 1840, in *Izbrannye sotsial'no-politicheskie i filosofskie proizvedeniia*, 2:307–8: "About service, I completely agree with you. There the most important task is to comprehend the general spirit of the age and the most important question which must be resolved at the current moment and to work toward resolving it. [. . .] About Menzel, we will talk another time. [. . .] We must first clarify for ourselves the idea of the state."

78. Ogarev published thirty-three poems in *Notes of the Fatherland* between 1840 and 1844, a record that is all the more remarkable given that he published nothing before 1840. Herzen, who had last published an article in 1836, now submitted numerous pieces to *Notes of the Fatherland*, including fiction. Satin also contributed poems to the journal, and Ketcher published translations there.

79. Ogarev to Herzen, [1839], "Iz perepiski nedavnikh deiatelei," *Russkaia mysl'* 9, no. 11 (1888): 4.

80. Ogarev to Herzen, [Nov. 6, 1839], in *Izbrannye sotsial'no-politicheskie i filosofskie proizvedeniia*, 2:302.

81. Ogarev to Herzen, Nov. 8, 1840, in *Izbrannye sotsial'no-politicheskie i filosofskie proizvedeniia*, 2:312.

82. Herzen to Andrei A. Kraevskii, Feb. 3, 1842, in *Sobranie sochinenii*, 22:128. Both quotes are misspelled in the Soviet edition.

83. Herzen, diary entry, Nov. 18, 1842, in *Sobranie sochinenii*, 2:243. See also diary entries of Oct. 26, 1842, and Dec. 22, 1842, in *Sobranie sochinenii*, 2:236, 253.

84. Herzen to Astrakova, Apr. 18, 1841, Dec. 17, 1841, and Mar. 23, 1842, in Natal'ia A. Herzen, "Pis'ma T. A. Astrakovoi," 603, 605, 608.

85. Herzen to Astrakova, Oct. 22, 1842, and ca. Jan.–Mar. 1843, in Natal'ia A. Herzen, "Pis'ma Astrakovoi," 611, 612.

86. Ogarev to Herzen, June 17, 1843, "Iz perepiski nedavnikh deiatelei," *Russkaia mysl'* 11, no. 3 (1890): 8–9.

87. Herzen to Ogarev, [Dec. 1846], in *Russkie propilei*, 1:239–40. Herzen to Astrakova, Jan. 9, 1848, early Oct. 1849, and Oct. 9, 1849, in Natal'ia A. Herzen, "Pis'ma Astrakovoi," 637, 653, 654.

88. Herzen to Astrakova, Dec. 6, 1849, in Natal'ia A. Herzen, "Pis'ma Astrakovoi," 656.

89. Herzen to Tuchkova, ca. 1847–48, in *Russkie propilei*, 1:242.

90. Here I side with Shpet, *Filosofskoe mirovozzrenie Gertsena*, 7. I disagree with Labry and Malia, who argue that Herzen did become fully "Hegelian," at least for four or five years from 1843 to 1847 (*Alexandre Ivanovič Herzen*, 221; *Alexander Herzen and the Birth of Russian Socialism*, 228). Dmitrii Chizhevskii indicates ambivalently that Herzen became a Hegelian "without adopting Hegelian formulations or Hegelian schemata" (*Gegel' v Rossii*, 195).

91. Ogarev to Herzen, Nov. 8, 1840, in *Izbrannye sotsial'no-politicheskie i filosofskie proizvedeniia*, 2:312.

92. Ogarev to Ogareva, [July 20, 1841], [July 22, 1841], and [July 27, 1841], in *Izbrannye sotsial'no-politicheskie i filosofskie proizvedeniia*, 2:317–18.

93. Ogarev to Herzen, Nov. 8, 1841, in *Izbrannye sotsial'no-politicheskie i filosofskie proizvedeniia*, 2:312; Ogarev to Botkin, Mar. 16, 1843, in Ogarev, *O literature i iskusstve*, 197. Herzen spoke of "blind skepticism" in a letter to Ketcher (Dec. 2, 1843, in *Sobranie sochinenii*, 22:160).

94. Ogarev, "Tuman upal na sneg polei," 1:143; Ogarev to "friends," Sept. 17, [1843], "Iz perepiski nedavnikh deiatelei," *Russkaia mysl'* 11, no. 8 (1890): 7.

95. "One must save the will, otherwise every moral principle disappears. There is a demand for personal immortality. There is faith in reconciliation with these questions. But now I am in chaos. [. . .] Generally, there is faith in the ability to resolve even these problems, but up to now nothing has been resolved. Meanwhile the need for a solution is becoming more palpable with every hour. [. . .] One needs great strength to live. And one must live. Suicide is impossible. That would require even more weakness. Faith in life and resignation: that is my slogan. But resignation is hard . . . *Dahin, dahin*" (Ogarev to Satin, Dec. 27, 1841, in *Izbrannye sotsial'no-politicheskie i filosofskie proizvedeniia*, 2:329).

96. Ogarev, "Razlad," 1:97; Ogarev, "Razorvannost'," 1:146.

97. Satin to Ketcher, Oct. 7, 1841, and Dec. 1841, papers of Nikolai Kh. Ketcher, RGB, f. 476, d. 35, l. 8 ob., 13 ob. As late as 1844, we find Satin exclaiming that he could not and did not wish to reconcile himself. See Satin in a postscript of Ogarev's letter to Herzen and Granovskii, June 12, 1844, "Iz perepiski nedavnikh deiatelei," *Russkaia mysl'* 11, no. 9 (1890): 11.

98. Satin, "Otryvok iz podslushannogo razgovora," in Satin to Ketcher, Oct. 7, 1841, papers of Nikolai Kh. Ketcher, RGB, f. 476, d. 35, l. 9. The identification of Satin and Ketcher with the characters in the sketch is made clear in another letter: "Here you see the continuation of our conversation. I know you will scold me for it" (Satin to Ketcher, Oct. 7, 1841, papers of Nikolai Kh. Ketcher, RGB, f. 476, d. 35, l. 9 ob).

99. Satin, "Nozhka." The poem was not published in Satin's lifetime.

100. Herzen to Ogarev, Nov. 14, 1839, in *Sobranie sochinenii*, 22:54.

101. Herzen to Ogarev, Nov. 22, 1845, in *Sobranie sochinenii*, 22:245–46.

102. Herzen's words can only be gathered from Ogarev's response: "Stop repeating the old thought that it was unnecessary to attach a weak being, woman, to our lives. Drop that egoism. A woman does not fetter our will, only arbitrariness does" (Ogarev to Herzen, 1839, "Iz perepiski nedavnikh deiatelei," *Russkaia mysl'* 9, no. 11 [1888]: 7).

103. Ogarev to Herzen and Granovskii, June 12, 1844, in *Izbrannye sotsial'no-politicheskie i filosofskie proizvedeniia*, 2:335; Satin to Ogarev, Aug. 11, 1845, "Iz perepiski nedavnikh deiatelei," *Russkaia mysl'* 12, no. 8 (1891): 14–15.

104. Herzen, diary entry, Nov. 2, 1842, in *Sobranie sochinenii*, 2:239.

105. Herzen to Ketcher, n.d., papers of Nikolai Kh. Ketcher, RGB, f. 476, k. 5185, no. 8, l. 1. See also Granovskii to Ketcher, Jan. 1 or 2, 1845, in Granovskii, *T. N. Granovskii i ego perepiska*, 2:463: "What are you scolding me for, dog?" The most complete description of the deterioration of relations can be found in Herzen, *Byloe i dumy*, 9:228–33, 244–47.

106.   "We see each other often, but our conversations lack their former full-ness and liveliness" (Natal'ia Herzen to Ketcher, Nov. 9, 1843, in Herzen, *Sobranie sochinenii*, 22:156). "It used to be the case that when you were shouting, it seemed we would not mind if it were a bit quieter, but now everybody is acutely aware of the absence of that shout. Even now as I write to you, people are talking and making noise around me. Yet things are not as they used to be" (Evgenii Korsh to Ketcher, n.d., papers of Nikolai Kh. Ketcher, RGB, f. 476, k. 5185, d. 12, l. 1).

107.   Granovskaia to Ketcher, Dec. 13, 1843, papers of Nikolai Kh. Ketcher, RGB, f. 476, k. 5185, d. 9, l. 1–2, emphasis in original. See also Maria F. Korsh's attachment to the same letter (2 ob.): "Without you, it isn't good in our circle, somehow it's not complete." A similarly anguished denunciation of "every-one" from this period can be found in a letter Konstantin Kavelin wrote to his sister in September 1842. He belonged to the circle at this time (Kavelin, "Materialy dlia biografii iz semeinoi perepiski i vospominanii," 474–75).

108.   Annenkov, *The Extraordinary Decade*, 137–38.

109.   Ogarev to Herzen, 1840, "Iz perepiski nedavnikh deiatelei," *Russkaia mysl'* 10, no. 4 (1889): 3–4. See also Ogarev to Herzen, Feb. 20, 1840, in *Izbrannye sotsial'no-politicheskie i filosofskie proizvedeniia*, 2:305.

110.   Ogarev to Herzen, Feb. 2 [1845], in *Izbrannye sotsial'no-politicheskie i filosofskie proizvedeniia*, 2:367.

111.   Granovskii to Grigor'ev, Oct. 8, 1837, in "Pis'ma T. N. Granovskogo V. V. Grigor'evu," 10:85. Granovskii's letter was written in response to a letter from Grigor'ev in which he reported that he had been "seized by an unusual inclination for thought," leading to a crisis of faith. Yet he was determined to resolve those questions that "millions of people" never bothered to ask (Grigor'ev to Granovskii and Ianuarii M. Neverov, Sept. 24, 1837, papers of Timofei N. Granovskii, RGB, f. 84, kart. 3, no. 16. l. 1).

112.   Granovskii to Grigor'ev, Oct. 20, 1837, in "Pis'ma T. N. Granovskogo V. V. Grigor'evu," 86.

113.   See, for example, Granovskii to V. N. and A. N. Granovskii, Apr. 17, 1841, in *T. N. Granovskii i ego perepiska*, 2:123.

114.   Ogarev, "[T. N. Granovskomu]."

115.   Granovskii to Granovskaia, June 29, 1844, in *T. N. Granovskii i ego perepiska*, 2:261.

116.   Herzen to Granovskii, July 9, 1844, in *Sobranie sochinenii*, 22:190–91, emphasis in original.

117.   Granovskii to Ogarev, Jan. 1–10, 1845, in Herzen, *Sobranie sochinenii*, 22:221.

118.   Ogarev and Satin to Ketcher, Sept. 1–14, 1844, and Feb. 11–12, 1845, papers of Nikolai Kh. Ketcher, RGB, f. 476, k. 5185, no. 24, ll. 4 ob., 8 ob.

119.   Ogarev to Herzen and Granovskii, June 12, 1844, in *Izbrannye sotsial'no-politicheskie i filosofskie proizvedeniia*, 2:338.

120.   Natal'ia Herzen, Nov. 4, 1846, in "Dnevnik" [Diary], 1:235.

121.   Natal'ia Herzen, Nov. 4 and 5, 1846, in "Dnevnik," 1:236–37. Cf. Herzen, *Byloe i dumy*, 9:202, 209–10.

122.   Natal'ia Herzen, Oct. 20, 1846, in "Dnevnik," 1:233–34.

123.   Part 4 of *My Past and Thoughts*, which describes the period from 1840

to 1847 during which time the group confronted the Hegelians, first appeared in his London journal the *Polar Star* in 1855.

124. Herzen, "Kaprizy i razdum'e: Novye variatsii na starye temy," 2:89; Herzen, "Pis'ma ob izuchenii prirody," 3:126–28, 298–304. In *Letters on the Study of Nature*, he contrasts Locke and Hume, praising Hume for his intellectual "courage" and criticizing Locke for "stop[ing] half way."

125. Herzen to Tatiana A. and Sergei I. Astrakov, June 19, 1849, in *Sobranie sochinenii*, 23:155.

126. Qtd. in Roosevelt, *Apostle of Russian Liberalism*, 114.

127. See Schultze, *Wissarion Grigorjewitsch Belinskij*, 203.

128. Turgenev, *Stat'i i vospominaniia*, 163.

129. Satin to Ogarev, Mar. 3, 1845, "Iz perepiski nedavnikh deiatelei," *Russkaia mysl'* 12, no. 8 (1891): 6. The letter is dated 1844 in the journal, but this is probably a misprint.

130. Botkin to Ogarev, Feb. 17, 1845, in Botkin, *Literaturnaia kritika, publitsistika, pis'ma*, 251.

131. Ibid., 253–54.

132. Ogarev to Ketcher, Mar. 17–Apr. 4, 1845, in *Izbrannye sotsial'no-politicheskie i filosofskie proizvedeniia*, 2:377.

133. "Une chose m'occupe: réduire le problème de la vie à ses plus simples éléments et armé de ce matérialisme détroner entièrement tout idée mystique" (Ogarev to Tuchkova, Dec. 21, 1848, in *Russkie propilei*, 4:38).

134. Qtd. in Malia, *Alexander Herzen and the Birth of Russian Socialism*, 333.

135. Herzen, "S togo berega: Omnia mea mecum porto," 6:115–32.

136. Malia, *Alexander Herzen and the Birth of Russian Socialism*, 249.

137. Shpet comments on the identity of ideas, deeds, and "facts" in Herzen's thought (*Filosofskoe mirovozzrenie Gertsena*, 10).

138. He uses the French word *tué*, claiming that Venevitinov was "killed by society," that Lermontov and Pushkin were "killed in a duel," that Belinsky was "killed by misery and hunger," and that Ryleev, with whom the list begins, was "hanged by Nicholas" (Herzen, "Du développement des idées révolutionnaires en Russie," 77–78, 93).

Chapter 3. Atheists of 1849

1. Report by Nikolai Naumov, Apr. 11–12, 1849, Butashevich-Petrashevskii investigation and trial documents, RGVIA, f. 801, op. 84/28, d. 55, ch. 3, ll. 135–135 ob. All reports and interrogations are in f. 801, op. 84/28, d. 55.

2. In the 1840s the most widely prosecuted groups were sectarians, but there were two cases in 1849 and 1851 in which Nicholas I dispatched young men, a singer and a painter, to prison monasteries as punishment for alleged irreligious speech. The cases of Sergei Stepanov and Aleksei Orlovskii can be found in Chancellery of the Synod, RGIA, f. 796, op. 130, 1849 g., d. 845 and f. 796, op. 132, d. 1218, and Chancellery of the Overprocurator of the Synod, RGIA, f. 797, op. 19, 1849 g., d. 42858, and f. 797, op. 21, 1851 g., d. 46273. For a brief discussion of cases of this kind, see Grekulov, *Pravoslavnaia inkvizitsiia v Rossii*, 82–83.

3. Mironov, *Sotsial'naia istoriia Rossii*, 1:130.

4. Investigation summary, Apr. 21, 1849, Butashevich-Petrashevskii investigation and trial documents, RGVIA, ch. 2, l. 6 ob.; report by Petr Antonelli, Feb. 9, 1849, in *Delo petrashevtsev* (hereafter *DP*), 3:397. Tolstov's date of birth is unknown. Egorov surmises that he was born around 1826 (*Petrashevtsy*, 140).

5. Hildermeier, *Bürgertum und Stadt in Russland*, 574–79; Flynn, "Tuition and Social Class in the Russian Universities." Flynn quotes Uvarov, who remarked that "in institutions of higher and secondary education it is clear that there is a rising influx of young people, partly of those born in the lower social orders, for whom higher education is not useful, but only a luxury which takes them away from their original [life] situation, without benefit to them or to the state" (243).

6. Rieber, *Merchants and Entrepreneurs in Imperial Russia*, 25–26, 29n56; Owen, *Capitalism and Politics in Russia*, 23–25; Hildermeier, *Bürgertum und Stadt in Russland*, 562–63, 571, 579, 584.

7. Wirtschafter, *Structures of Society*, 102, 105. Wirtschafter remarks that the indeterminacy created by growing social mobility heightened feelings of "uncertainty and self-doubt" in all segments of the population (93).

8. The rise of the natural school is described in Tseitlin, *Stanovlenie realizma v russkoi literature*. According to Tseitlin, early examples of this genre were written in a conservative tone, emphasizing the humility and ultimate contentment of St. Petersburg's inhabitants (138). Only in the mid-1840s did the genre come to be seen as an investigation of the "degradation of humanity" in St. Petersburg (164–65, 238–39).

9. He also wrote dramas and poetry, which he discussed with Katenev (testimony of Gavrila Kurgannikov, [Aug. 17, 1849], Butashevich-Petrashevskii investigation and trial documents, RGVIA, ch. 1, l. 50; testimony of Andrei Glagolev, [Aug. 17, 1849], Butashevich-Petrashevskii investigation and trial documents, RGVIA, ch. 1, ll. 50–50 ob.

10. Katenev told his friend Grigorii Danilevskii (a student from the nobility) that he published two short stories in *Politseiskaia gazeta* (I have searched for these stories but have not been able to find them). He also claimed to be working on a novel and he said he wanted to use Shaposhnikov as a character in it (testimony of Grigorii Danilevskii, May 14, 1849, Butashevich-Petrashevskii investigation and trial documents, RGVIA, ch. 16, t. 2, ll. 41–42 ob.).

11. Shil'der, *Imperator Nikolai Pervyi: Ego zhizn' i tsarstvovanie*, 2:629.

12. Qtd. in Nifontov, *1848 god v Rossii*, 122–23.

13. Ignatii [Brianchaninov], "Po povodu politicheskikh sobytii v Evrope 1848 g.," 204–5, and "O neuklonnom," 224.

14. Filaret [Drozdov], "Slovo v den' vosshestviia na prestol Imperatora Nikolaia," 4:580, emphasis in original.

15. In the Russian Orthodox psalter, this is Psalm 143, and "great waters" is rendered as "vod mnogikh." Ignatii and Filaret used the term "potop"; the 1848 manifesto uses *potok*.

16. Platon [Levshin], "Slovo v den' rozhdeniia [. . .] Vel. Kniazia Pavla Petrovicha," 1:51–55, "Slovo v sviatyi i velikii piatok," 1:156, "Slovo o pol'ze uchenii v den' rozhdeniia ego Imp. Vysochestva," 1:359, "Slovo v nedeliu pravoslaviia," 3:319–24, "Slovo na kreshchenie Gospodne," 11:323–24, "Slovo na den' rozhdeniia Khristova," 14:586–87, and "Slovo na den' vozneseniia Gospodnia," 20:25–27;

Georgii [Konisskii], "Slovo v den' sv. Apostolov Petra i Pavla," 1:225, 229, 231–32, and "Slovo v sviatyi i velikii piatok," 1:124.

17. Georgii, "Slovo v den' sv. Apostolov Petra i Pavla," 1:230–31; Platon [Levshin], "Slovo v nedeliu pravoslaviia," 3:326–27.

18. Anastasii [Bratanovskii], "Slovo v nedeliu Fomy," 4:34, 37. Filaret (Gumilevskii) comments on this aspect of Anastasii's sermons; see *Obzor russkoi dukhovnoi literatury*, 395–96.

19. Georgii [Konisskii], "Slovo v den' novoletiia," 1:49; Anastasii, "Slovo v nedeliu Fomy," 4:34; Platon [Levshin], "Slovo v nedeliu vtoruiu velikogo posta," 4:287.

20. Tempters of this kind appear in Bulgarin's *Ivan Vyzhigin* (1829) and Zagoskin's *Iskusitel'* (1838). The phrase "demon of our time" is in the introduction to Zagoskin, *Iskusitel'*, 1:6.

21. Summary and assessment of investigation, [Aug. 17, 1849], Butashevich-Petrashevskii investigation and trial documents, RGVIA, ch. 1, l. 62. Liprandi also compared the "conspirators" he investigated to the French encyclopedists on the eve of the 1789 revolution (summary and assessment of investigation, [Aug. 17, 1849], Butashevich-Petrashevskii investigation and trial documents, RGVIA, ch. 1, l. 70 ob.). See also Liprandi, "Primechaniia," 19.

22. Eidel'man, *Iz potaennoi istorii Rossii XVIII–XIX vekov*, 453–55.

23. On the numbers of people arrested and questioned, see Desnitskii, preface, 1:xx, and Egorov, *Petrashevtsy*, 177. On the accuracy of the agents' reports, see Egorov, *Petrashevtsy*, 136n14. According to Egorov, Naumov and Vasilii Shaposhnikov were badly educated, but they faithfully related what they overheard. Where information in their reports is contradicted by the testimonies of Katenev, Shaposhnikov, and Tolstov, I refrain from using it or use it only with a clearly marked warning. By contrast, the reports of Petr Antonelli, who spied on Petrashevsky, were less reliable, a matter I return to.

24. Qtd. in Semevskii, "Petrashevtsy," pt. 2, 117; Alexander, *Der Petraševskij-Prozess*, 204; *DP*, 3:483.

25. Nifontov, *1848 god v Rossii*, 108–9; Berlin, *Russian Thinkers*, 4. As Berlin claims, Russia's anomalous status in Europe paradoxically inspired some observers, such as Alexander Herzen, to think that its future might also be anomalous: "uniquely happy and glorious." The merchants in this chapter did not share such nationalist, quasi-providentialist thoughts.

26. Monas, *The Third Section*, 239.

27. Report by Nikolai Naumov, Apr. 8 and 9, 1849, Butashevich-Petrashevskii investigation and trial documents, RGVIA, ch. 3, ll. 128 and 132 ob.

28. Reports by Vasilii Shaposhnikov, Apr. 18, 1849, Butashevich-Petrashevskii investigation and trial documents, RGVIA, ch. 3, l. 144. On April 16, Vasilii Shaposhnikov reported that Petr Shaposhnikov told him that the truth was "like the most beautiful, brazen woman," who would be dragged onto a public square. Further, Tolstov told Petr Shaposhnikov that he would put him to work as a public speaker after the revolution had broken out (case summary, Aug. 1849, in *DP*, 3:362).

29. Summary of reports, Apr. 11, 1849, Butashevich-Petrashevskii investigation and trial documents, RGVIA, ch. 2, l. 180. Under interrogation, Katenev

confirmed he had told Naumov that he had made such a speech but said he had been lying (summary of investigation, n.d., Butashevich-Petrashevskii investigation and trial documents, RGVIA, ch. 119, l. 368 ob.).

30. Under interrogation, Katenev denied having made the speech in the brothel (the police drew the information from two sources: Naumov heard it from Vasilii Pronin, who claimed to have accompanied Katenev on this occasion) (summary of investigation, n.d., RGVIA, ch. 119, l. 366 ob.). Petr Shaposhnikov also told Vasilii Shaposhnikov about it and claimed to have been there (report by Vasilii Shaposhnikov, Apr. 14, 1849, Butashevich-Petrashevskii investigation and trial documents, RGVIA, ch. 3, l. 138 ob.). The Trial Committee questioned the owner of the brothel, Gospozha Blium. She said she did not know Katenev and had heard no speech (testimony of Gospozha Blium, Aug. 1849, Butashevich-Petrashevskii investigation and trial documents, RGVIA, ch. 98, l. 13 ob.).

31. Reports by Nikolai Naumov, Apr. 9 and 11–12, 1849, Butashevich-Petrashevskii investigation and trial documents, RGVIA, ch. 3, l. 131 and 136 ob.

32. Wortman, *Scenarios of Power*, 1:280, 291, 299.

33. Report by Nikolai Naumov, Apr. 19, 1849, Butashevich-Petrashevskii investigation and trial documents, RGVIA, ch. 3, l. 145.

34. Report by Nikolai Naumov, Apr. 8, 1849, Butashevich-Petrashevskii investigation and trial documents, RGVIA, ch. 3, l. 128.

35. Report by Vasilii Shaposhnikov and Nikolai Naumov, Mar. 22, 1849, Butashevich-Petrashevskii investigation and trial documents, RGVIA, ch. 3, l. 98 ob. According to their testimony, Tolstov said he had been with the student Alexander Khanykov on that occasion. Khanykov denied this under questioning (interrogation of Aleksandr Khanykov, June 24, 1849, in *DP*, 3:38).

36. *Na meste etogo fonaria, zhelal by videt' poveshennogo nashego Tsaria*: "Instead of this lamp, I would like to see our hanged tsar." Katenev's acquaintance, Nikolai Kamenskii, claimed he had heard it from Katenev (interrogation of Nikolai Kamenskii, n.d., Butashevich-Petrashevskii investigation and trial documents, RGVIA, ch. 16, t. 2, l. 245). Katenev claimed to have heard it from Shaposhnikov. Shaposhnikov claimed to have read it in an antigovernment poem, of which he owned a collection (case summary, Aug. 1849, in *DP*, 3:356, 358). The cry "à la lanterne," associated with the French Revolution, was also heard during the 1848 revolutions. For example, in October 1848, the Austrian minister of war, Count Latour, was beaten to death by a crowd and hung naked from a lamppost. This event was widely used by conservatives in western Europe to discredit the revolutionaries.

37. Testimony of Aleksandr Tverskoi, ca. July 10, 1849, Butashevich-Petrashevskii investigation and trial documents, RGVIA, ch. 1, l. 36. Rumors of the impending arrests circulated in St. Petersburg a few weeks in advance (Voznyi, *Petrashevskii i tsarskaia tainaia politsiia*, 82).

38. The Russian version mistranslates the word "Christ" in the German title, "Mensch oder Christ? Sein oder Nichtsein? Die Religion der Zukunft." The German *Christ* means a person of Christian faith in this context. The Russian word *Khristos* means Christ. In most other regards, the Russian translation is accurate. *Mensch oder Christ?* was issued as the third volume of Friedrich Feuerbach's three-volume *Die Religion der Zukunft*.

39. See Friedrich Feuerbach, "Chelovek ili Khristos?" esp. 190.

40. Schuffenhauer, "Ludwig Feuerbach stellt des Bruders Schrift 'Gedanken und Thatsachen,' 1862 vor," 99.

41. Case summary, Aug. 1849, in *DP*, 3:361; testimony of Nikolai Naumov, n.d., Butashevich-Petrashevskii investigation and trial documents, RGVIA, ch. 3, ll. 160 ob.–61; interrogation of Nikolai Kamenskii, n.d., Butashevich-Petrashevskii investigation and trial documents, RGVIA, ch. 16, t. 3, l. 247. Utin claimed to have found his copy of "Religiia budushchnosti" inside a German copy of Ludwig Feuerbach's *Das Wesen des Christentums*, which he bought at the market (testimony of Boris Utin, July 15 and 26, 1849, in *DP*, 3:350). Most likely, Utin's copy was handwritten by Alexander Khanykov, a member of Petrashevsky's circle who knew Utin, Tolstov, and Shaposhnikov. Under questioning, Khanykov denied having given any document to the men in the tobacco store (testimony of Aleksandr Khanykov, June 24, 1849, in *DP*, 3:37). Because Khanykov's German was not very good (see Chernyshevsky's diaries), he could not have translated the pamphlet himself.

42. Voltaire, *Poema estestvennyi zakon*; report by Nikolai Naumov, Apr. 3, 1849, Butashevich-Petrashevskii investigation and trial documents, RGVIA, ch. 3, l. 122.

43. Voltaire, "Poème sur la loi naturelle," 273–74.

44. Febvre, *The Problem of Unbelief in the Sixteenth Century*, 354–55, 410–18. For critiques of Febvre's approach, see note 37 of the introduction to this book.

45. Katenev is accorded only a couple of sentences in two prominent Soviet histories of atheism; see Nikitina, "Ateizm petrashevtsev," 228, and Leikina-Svirskaia, "Ateizm petrashevtsev," 230. He, Tolstov, and Shaposhnikov are mentioned in passing in Seddon, *The Petrashevtsy*, 76, 78, 210–11, and in Alexander, *Der Petraševskij-Prozess*, 202–7. The fullest discussion is Egorov, *Petrashevtsy*, 135–55.

46. The group first entered the written historical record when Semevskii published his two-part article on the group in *Golos minuvshago*. Forty pages are devoted to them in *Delo Petrashevtsev*, the three-volume compendium of documentary evidence about the Petrashevsky trial: "Dokumenty sledstviia po delu P. G. Shaposhnikova, V. P. Kateneva, A. D. Tolstova, G. P. Danilevskogo, B. I. Utina i V. V. Vostrova," in *DP*, 3:333–73.

47. Vostrov testified that he, Pronin and Tverskoi boarded at Shaposhnikov's house (testimony of Vasilii Vostrov, July 21 and 26, 1849, in *DP*, 3:351).

48. Interrogation of Vasilii Pronin, n.d., Butashevich-Petrashevskii investigation and trial documents, RGVIA, ch. 16, t. 2, l. 297.

49. Interrogation of Aleksei Mazurin, n.d., Butashevich-Petrashevskii investigation and trial documents, RGVIA, ch. 16. t. 2, l. 374.

50. Testimony of Petr Shaposhnikov, n.d., in *DP*, 3:372.

51. Testimony of Aleksandr Tverskoi, ca. July 10, 1849, Butashevich-Petrashevskii investigation and trial documents, RGVIA, ch. 1, l. 35.

52. Testimony of Vasilii Pronin, [Aug. 17, 1849], Butashevich-Petrashevskii investigation and trial documents, RGVIA, ch. 1, l. 38 ob.

53. Testimony of Aleksei Mazurin, n.d., Butashevich-Petrashevskii investigation and trial documents, RGVIA, ch. 16, t. 2, l. 378.

54. Case summary, Aug. 1849, in *DP*, 3:358, 361. Shaposhnikov also wrote a

testimony for the police in which he denied, point by point, almost a dozen of the charges against him, though he did not deny having made antireligious remarks (testimony of Petr Shaposhnikov, n.d., in *DP*, 3:368–73).

55. Testimony of Andrei Glagolev, [Aug. 17, 1849], Butashevich-Petrashevskii investigation and trial documents, RGVIA, ch. 1, l. 50 ob.

56. Report by Nikolai Naumov, Apr. 11–12, 1849, Butashevich-Petrashevskii investigation and trial documents, RGVIA, ch. 3, ll. 135–135 ob. *Bog* ("god") in the second-to-last sentence is lowercase in the original. I follow this capitalization in my translation.

57. One eyewitness testimony came from Ivan Zhadovskii, who had been present at the tavern that night (testimony of Ivan Zhadovskii, [Aug. 17, 1849], Butashevich-Petrashevskii investigation and trial documents, RGVIA, ch. 1, l. 40 ob.). Another account was offered by Grigorii Danilevskii, who had heard about the speech thirdhand from an acquaintance (testimony of Grigorii Danilevskii, May 14, 1849, Butashevich-Petrashevskii investigation and trial documents, RGVIA, ch. 16, t. 2, l. 46). Danilevskii stated that he had not believed the rumor until Katenev told him it was true. Rumors about the event were also recounted in the testimony of Aleksandr Evropeus, June 23–24, 1849, in *DP*, 3: 183–84.

58. Testimony of Ivan Zhadovskii, [Aug. 17, 1849], Butashevich-Petrashevskii investigation and trial documents, RGVIA, ch. 1, l. 40 ob.

59. Alexander Evropeus heard the story from his brother Pavel, who had heard it from an acquaintance, who had heard it from an unnamed source. As Alexander Evropeus told it, Katenev "was talking about the miracles of Jesus Christ, explained them by Chaldean magic, and was smartly ridiculed by some unknown official, who, intervening, retorted, 'so, according to you, had you lived at the time, even you could have been Jesus Christ' but Katenev answered that well, yes, maybe" (testimony of Aleksandr Evropeus, June 23–24, 1849, in *DP*, 3:183–84).

60. Report by Nikolai Naumov, Apr. 11–12, 1849, Butashevich-Petrashevskii investigation and trial documents, RGVIA, ch. 3, ll. 135 ob.–136; testimony of Ivan Zhadovskii, [Aug. 17, 1849], RGVIA, ch. 1, l. 40 ob.

61. Case summary, Aug. 1849, in *DP*, 3:358–59; report by Vasilii Shaposhnikov, Apr. 13, 1849, Butashevich-Petrashevskii investigation and trial documents, RGVIA, ch. 3, l. 137 ob.

62. Testimony of Aleksandra L'vova (Petr Shaposhnikov's cousin), [Aug. 17, 1849], Butashevich-Petrashevskii investigation and trial documents, RGVIA ch. 1, l. 49 ob.; interrogation of Aleksandr Tverskoi, n.d., RGVIA, ch. 16, t. 2, l. 213 ob.; testimony of Vasilii Shaposhnikov, n.d., Butashevich-Petrashevskii investigation and trial documents, RGVIA, ch. 3, l. 153 ob.

63. Interrogation of Aleksei Mazurin, n.d., Butashevich-Petrashevskii investigation and trial documents, RGVIA, ch. 16, t. 2, l. 374. The same speech was retold slightly differently by Vasilii Pronin, who claimed under questioning that it was Mazurin who said that "We have no God, and the government means nothing for us, and those idiots the peasants respect them, without knowing whom" (interrogation of Vasilii Pronin, n.d., Butashevich-Petrashevskii investigation and trial documents, RGVIA, ch. 16, t. 2, l. 297).

64. Interrogation of Aleksei Mazurin, n.d., Butashevich-Petrashevskii investigation and trial documents, RGVIA, ch. 16, t. 2, l. 374.

65. Case summary, Aug. 1849, in *DP*, 3:368.

66. Testimony of Petr Shaposhnikov, n.d., in *DP*, 3:369; interrogation of Grigorii Danilevskii, May 14, 1849, Butashevich-Petrashevskii investigation and trial documents, RGVIA, ch. 16. t. 2, l. 42 ob.

67. Report by Vasilii Shaposhnikov, Apr. 9, 1849, Butashevich-Petrashevskii investigation and trial documents, RGVIA, ch. 3, l. 130.

68. Report by Vasilii Shaposhnikov, Apr. 8, 1849, Butashevich-Petrashevskii investigation and trial documents, RGVIA, ch. 3, l. 127 ob.

69. Report by Nikolai Naumov, Mar. 20, 1849, Butashevich-Petrashevskii investigation and trial documents, RGVIA, ch. 3, l. 93 ob.

70. Report by Nikolai Naumov, Mar. 30, 1849, Butashevich-Petrashevskii investigation and trial documents, RGVIA, ch. 3, l. 114. "Lamartinist" was presumably a reference to Alphonse de Lamartine, a key figure in the French provisional government in the spring and summer of 1848.

71. Katenev explained the "revolutionary" statements he made as "bragging" under interrogation. He said that he only wanted "to show his daring" in this way (case summary, Aug. 1849, in *DP*, 3:360).

72. Report by Vasilii Shaposhnikov, Apr. 13, 1849, Butashevich-Petrashevskii investigation and trial documents, RGVIA, ch. 3, l. 138.

73. Report by Nikolai Naumov, Apr. 13, 1849, Butashevich-Petrashevskii investigation and trial documents, RGVIA, ch. 3, l. 175 ob.

74. Testimony of Nikolai Naumov, n.d., Butashevich-Petrashevskii investigation and trial documents, RGVIA, ch. 3, l. 162.

75. Report by Nikolai Naumov, Apr. 8, 1849, Butashevich-Petrashevskii investigation and trial documents, RGVIA, ch. 3, l. 128. Egorov cites this statement and calls it "putting on the mask of the Romantic villain" (*Petrashevtsy*, 146).

76. Testimony of Vasilii Vostrov, May 12, 1849, in *DP*, 3:339–40.

77. On Katenev's drinking, see interrogation of Grigorii Danilevskii, May 14, 1849, Butashevich-Petrashevskii investigation and trial documents, RGVIA, ch. 16, t. 2, ll. 46, 46 ob.

78. Testimony of Vasilii Shaposhnikov, n.d., Butashevich-Petrashevskii investigation and trial documents, RGVIA, ch. 3, ll. 153 ob., 155; interrogation of Aleksei Mazurin, n.d., Butashevich-Petrashevskii investigation and trial documents, RGVIA, ch. 16, t. 2, l. 370; report by Nikolai Naumov, Apr. 8, 1849, Butashevich-Petrashevskii investigation and trial documents, RGVIA, ch. 3, l. 129.

79. Interrogation of Mikhail Semenov, n.d., Butashevich-Petrashevskii investigation and trial documents, RGVIA, ch. 16, t. 2, l. 267.

80. Report by Nikolai Naumov, Apr. 8, 1849, Butashevich-Petrashevskii investigation and trial documents, RGVIA, ch. 3, l. 128.

81. Interrogation of Grigorii Danilevskii, May 14, 1849, Butashevich-Petrashevskii investigation and trial documents, RGVIA, ch. 16, t. 2, ll. 40 ob.–41 ob.

82. The more cheerful description of the same type of behavior by Raphael Chernosvistov, one of the visitors at Petrashevsky's evening soirées, makes this

nuance stand out better: "Since I like educated society, I tried to spend and did in fact spend as much time as I could there, but I also spent time in taverns, eating houses, [...] bars and even went to more unworthy places. From there, I gathered more or less fresh observations about the life of our people and facts for science and practical existence" (testimony of Raphael A. Chernosvistov, n.d., in *DP*, 1: 475).

83. Report by Nikolai Naumov, Apr. 15, 1849, Butashevich-Petrashevskii investigation and trial documents, RGVIA, ch. 3, l. 139 ob.

84. Summary of Nikolai Naumov's reports, n.d., Butashevich-Petrashevskii investigation and trial documents, RGVIA, ch. 3, ll. 176–176 ob.

85. Report by Nikolai Naumov, Apr. 3, 1849, Butashevich-Petrashevskii investigation and trial documents, RGVIA, ch. 3, l. 122 ob.

86. Case summary, Aug. 1849, in *DP*, 3:361. See also 3:356, where this is phrased somewhat differently: "Katenev testifies that Shaposhnikov inculcated in him depraved ideas about religion and the state; indeed [Shaposhnikov] made rousing speeches about popular government and the speaker's platform. He turned him, Katenev, away from religion, denied Scripture [*zakony*], stating that all this was a pure invention of the human mind, using fear of punishment in the future life to bind us. [Shaposhnikov also] expressed free thoughts [*vol'nodumstvoval*] about marriage and morality and cursed all forms and rituals that inhibit pleasure."

87. For Tolstov's confession, see case summary, Aug. 1849, in *DP*, 3:363–67. Tolstov was pardoned by Nicholas I but not set free; his death sentence was commuted to military service in the Caucasus (ibid., 368). He survived and was allowed to return to St. Petersburg in 1857.

88. Lermontov, *Geroi nashego vremeni*, 4:405. The original reads "ne to otchaian'e, kotoroe lechat dulom pistoleta, no kholodnoe, bessil'noe, otchaian'e, prikrytoe liubeznost'iu."

89. Tolstov's words were "Snachala ia byl ozloblen, potom sdelalsia ugrium." The narrator in Pushkin's *Eugene Onegin* says "Ia byl ozloblen, on ugrium" (*Evgenii Onegin*, 6:23). Pechorin in Lermontov's *A Hero of Our Time* says, "Ia stal zlopamiaten; ia byl ugrium" (*Geroi nashego vremeni*, 4:405). No doubt Lermontov was gesturing at Pushkin here.

90. Tolstov testified that after first having lost faith and then finding it again, he had a second crisis of faith but that it too had passed (case summary, Aug. 1849, in *DP*, 3:365).

91. *Russkii invalid*, Dec. 22, 1849, reproduced in *Politicheskie protsessy niko-laevsoi epokhi*, 3.

92. This statement contradicts the standard Soviet narrative.

93. Alexander, *Der Petraševskij-Prozess*, 214–15.

94. Kolakowski, *Main Currents of Marxism*, 1:199; Riasanovsky, *The Teaching of Charles Fourier*, 103. For the influence of Fourier on Petrashevsky and his guests, see Riasanovsky, *A Parting of Ways*, 240.

95. See, for example, testimony of Aleksandr Evropeus, May 11, 1849, in *DP*, 3:176. Pavel Filippov wrote a commentary on the Ten Commandments, interpreting them in such a way as to justify socialist reform; see "Desiat' zapovedei."

96. Atheism was mentioned in a lecture by Nikolai Kashkin in the winter of 1848. It was, he said, a consequence of people's frustration over the seeming incompatibility between the existence of evil and God's providential role in the world. Yet Kashkin repudiated unbelief, calling for a faith reminiscent of Fourierism ("Rech' o zadachakh obshchestvennykh nauk," 660).

97. Report of the general auditor, Dec. 17, in Shchegolev, *Petrashevtsy*, 3:51; interrogation summary of Nikolai Danilevskii, n.d., in *DP*, 2:288.

98. Summary of the testimonies of Nikolai Mombelli, May 31–June 6, 1849, in *DP*, 1:335; testimony and interrogation of Nikolai Danilevskii, n.d. and July 15, 1849, in *DP*, 2:323, 333.

99. Speshnev, "Pis'ma k K. E. Khoetskomu." These letters are sometimes misinterpreted as evidence of Speshnev's "atheism." See, for example, Seddon, *The Petrashevtsy*, 79, and Leikina-Svirskaia, "Petrashevets N. A. Speshnev v svete novykh materialov," 136. A sounder analysis is presented in Saraskina, *Nikolai Speshnev*, 163.

100. Khanykov recalled Speshnev's promise to give the lecture (testimony of Aleksandr Khanykov, June 24, 1849, in *DP*, 3:29).

101. The manuscript was lost along with Speshnev's file in the Butashevich-Petrashevskii investigation and trial documents, RGVIA. A summary and extract from it are contained in the general auditor's report, Dec. 17, 1849, in Shchegolev, *Petrashevtsy*, 3:53.

102. Interrogation of Nikolai Mombelli, May 28, 1849, in *DP*, 1:326.

103. Report of the general auditor, Dec. 17, 1849, in Shchegolev, *Petrashevtsy*, 3:51.

104. Testimony of Feliks Tol', n.d., in *DP*, 2:165.

105. Tol said that the speech was only a summary of the views of Ludwig Feuerbach and Bruno Bauer and did not reflect his own opinion (n.d., in *DP*, 2:165–66). This statement sounds disingenuous. Tol repeated the claim (though without mentioning Bauer) in later testimony (June 21–23, 1849, in *DP*, 2:180).

106. Testimony of Feliks Tol', n.d., in *DP*, 2:166.

107. Tol argued that religion arose as a product of fear in "undeveloped" societies. People assigned supernatural powers to natural phenomena they could not understand. Popular religious beliefs became more abstract, tending toward monotheism, as people gained knowledge about the laws of nature. Meanwhile, the growing complexity of societies militated that human relationships be mediated by some higher authority. An imagined god-man was made to serve this function. Tol listed a range of examples, from Jehovah, Osiris, Buddha, and Zoroaster to Orpheus and Christ (Tol', "Nabrosok rechi o proiskhozhdenii religii").

108. Report by Petr Antonelli, Mar. 13, 1849, in *DP*, 3:414–15.

109. Interrogation of Aleksandr Maderskii, n.d., Butashevich-Petrashevskii investigation and trial documents, RGVIA, ch. 38, ll. 4, 17.

110. Eyewitness testimonies, n.d., in *DP*, 2:173–74.

111. Other guests—Balasoglo, Kaidanov, L'vov, Lamanskii, and Akhshamurov—all argued with him specifically about the fear theory.

112. Testimonies and interrogation of Aleksandr Balasoglo, May 14, June 22, and June 23, 1849, in *DP*, 2:94, 114. It should be noted that Balasoglo was not

an uncritical defender of Orthodoxy; he had been one of the most enthusiastic listeners to Dostoevsky's reading of Belinsky's letter.

113.   The unfavorable impression he made on his prosecutors had much to do with the report that the agent, Antonelli, wrote about his lecture and with subsequent comments Antonelli made about his character. After the lecture was over, he and Antonelli left Petrashevsky's house together, took a walk, and had some more drinks. Tol evidently took a liking to the young man, and if Antonelli's report can be believed, poured out his troubled heart to him. Antonelli, however, had little sympathy for his interlocutor. His report combined factual evidence about the conversation he had with Tol with sharp condemnation of Tol's character: "Tol is a person who has lived a lot, boozed a lot, gambled a lot. In a word, he did many foolish things which, of course, he did not get away with, and for this reason he says that he has suffered greatly, taken many blows of fate, that his strength has been exhausted, that he is sick of the world and of people, that he does not believe in anything, that he is prepared for anything, and that he impatiently waits for the thread which ties him to life—his father and mother—to break, and then a bullet in the forehead and it's all over. And he will do just right, because may God keep us away from such people" (report by Petr Antonelli, Mar. 13, 1849, in *DP*, 3:416).

114.   See, for example, Malia, *Alexander Herzen and the Birth of Russian Socialism*, 355.

115.   "Why did you have to get Christ mixed into it? What did he have in common, in your view, with some church, much less the Orthodox Church? He was the first to announce to people the teaching of freedom, equality, and brotherhood, and through martyrdom, he imprinted and confirmed the truth of his teaching." And "Whoever is capable of suffering at the sight of another's suffering, whoever is weighed down by the spectacle of the oppression of people he does not know, that person carries Christ in his heart [*v grudi svoei*]" (Belinskii, "Pis'mo k N. V. Gogoliu, 15 June n.s. 1847," 10:214, 218).

116.   Interrogation of Aleksandr Maderskii, n.d., Butashevich-Petrashevskii investigation and trial documents, RGVIA, ch. 38, ll. 8 ob.–9 ob. According to Maderskii, Balasoglo and Iastrzhembskii (who was known in the group for his anticlerical inclinations) had been especially enthusiastic. Tol further testified that Iastrzhembskii had attacked the institution of monasteries as well as icons, which, according to Tol, he called an "anachronism" (interrogation of Feliks Tol', June 21 and 23, 1849, in *DP*, 2:181).

117.   Frank, *Dostoevsky: Seeds of Revolt*, 282, 287.

118.   See Evans, *The Petraševskij Circle*, 16. The conflict between Petrashevsky and his school's director provides a parallel with Katenev. Katenev had apparently been unable to graduate from the gymnasium he attended owing to a conflict with its director. See testimony of Grigorii Danilevskii, May 14, 1849, Butashevich-Petrashevskii investigation and trial documents, RGVIA, ch. 16, t. 2, l. 41 ob. Unfortunately, Danilevskii did not indicate which gymnasium Katenev attended: some did not admit sons of merchants in this period.

119.   Report by Ivan Liprandi, Apr. 21, 1849, Butashevich-Petrashevskii investigation and trial documents, RGVIA, ch. 2, ll. 4–4 ob.; report to Aleksei Orlov by Lieutenant Chulkov, "O titululiarnom sovetnike Mikhaile

Butasheviche-Petrashevskom," documents of the Third Section, GARF, f. 109, 1849, op. 24, d. 214, ch. 4 (1), l. 3.

120.   "Unloved by his mother in childhood, and later, upon entering the Lyceum, persecuted by the Director and—as a result of that, by everyone else— he grew embittered. He began to seek sympathy in a circle of scoundrels—the natural enemies of his enemy, the Director—among his fellows" (report by Petr Antonelli, n.d., Butashevich-Petrashevskii investigation and trial documents, RGVIA, ch. 1, l. 10 ob.; see also report by Petr Antonelli, Mar. 1, 1849, in *DP*, 3: 410–11).

121.   Summary of agents' reports and assessment, n.d., Butashevich-Petrashevskii investigation and trial documents, RGVIA, ch. 2, l. 63 ob. See also secret report, Apr. 23, 1848, Chancellery of the Ministry of Internal Affairs, RGIA, f. 1282, op. 1, 1848 g., d. 1, l. 4. Beards (that is, full beards) were considered a sign of a liberal disposition in western Europe and Russia at this time. Russian men who wore full beards attracted the attention of the Third Section; the wearing of a beard was apparently considered legitimate evidence that a man was ill intentioned.

122.   It was said that he recommended Abbé Barruel's *Mémoires pour servir à l'histoire du Jacobinisme* with especial warmth. This was a history of the French Revolution, centering on the roles of Voltaire, Rousseau, and other philosophes in promoting immorality and lawlessness (Evans, *The Petraševskij Circle*, 18).

123.   Testimony of D. B. Bronevskii, director of the lyceum, May 18, 1849, in *DP*, 1:6; Evans, *The Petraševskij Circle*, 20–21.

124.   Interrogation of Aleksandr Maderskii, n.d., Butashevich-Petrashevskii investigation and trial documents, RGVIA, ch. 38, ll. 45 ob.; Butashevich-Petrashevskii, "Chernovik pis'ma K. I. Timkovskomu," 1:531; interrogation and testimony of Butashevich-Petrashevskii, June 24–29, and July 1–2, 1849, in *DP*, 1:151, 167.

125.   Testimony of Vasilii Serebriakov, [Aug. 17, 1849], Butashevich-Petrashevskii investigation and trial documents, RGVIA, ch. 1, l. 47; interrogation of Mikhail Butashevich-Petrashevskii, June 24–29, 1849, in *DP*, 1:151. Serebriakov did not make it clear who exactly said he did not "recognize God" (whether it was Petrashevsky, or someone else). Moreover, the four or more years that had elapsed may have clouded his memory.

126.   Interrogation of Nikolai Grigor'ev, June 14 and 15, 1849, in *DP*, 3: 248–49. In the same deposition, he repeated several times that the entire trial was Petrashevsky's fault, adding "Petrashevsky and Belinsky are to blame for everything." Belinsky's name was inserted later, apparently added as an afterthought (251).

127.   Petrashevsky's escapade in the cathedral must have taken place between 1843 and 1845, if it occurred at all. Serebriakov, who boarded at Petrashevsky's house between 1843 and 1845 claimed to have heard about the incident at that time (testimony of Vasilii Serebriakov, [Aug. 17, 1849], Butashevich-Petrashevskii investigation and trial documents, RGVIA, ch. 1, l. 47). Numerous different accounts of the incident exist. See, e.g., Evans, *The Petraševskij Circle*, 19, and Seddon, *The Petrashevtsy*, 78. While some accounts place the event at Kazan Cathedral on Nevskii Prospect, others place it at

Pokrovskaia Church, which was very close to Petrashevsky's house at the corner of Sadovaia Street (on which Petrashevsky lived) and Angliiskii Prospect.

128. Bel'chikov, *Dostoevskii v protsesse Petrashevtsev*, 75.

129. Butashevich-Petrashevskii, "Otryvochnye zametki: O znachenii cheloveka v otnoshenii k chelovechestvu," 1:550.

130. A person of this kind "triumphantly proclaims himself to be a radical social reformer but is nevertheless worried lest social reforms darken the shine of his patent-leather gloves, lest they place an indecent wrinkle in his clothing" (Butashevich-Petrashevskii to Timkovskii, n.d., in *DP*, 1:538).

131. Butashevich-Petrashevskii, "Zapas obshchepoleznogo," 1:553.

132. For example, Petrashevsky referred to Christ as "that famous demagogue who ended his career somewhat unsuccessfully" (Butashevich-Petrashevskii to Timkovskii, in *DP*, 1:525).

133. Testimony of Mikhail Butashevich-Petrashevskii, ca. June 20, 1849, in *DP*, 1:116–19. At the time he wrote this deposition, Petrashevsky apparently still believed that such a confession might display a willingness to cooperate and thereby sway investigators in his favor. On Petrashevsky's depositions, see Alexander, *Der Petraševskij-Prozess*, 54, 39, 47.

134. Testimony of Mikhail Butashevich-Petrashevskii, July 1–2, 1849, in *DP*, 1:167–73.

135. Desnitskii, preface, 1:xix.

136. Dostoevskii, *Zapiski iz mertvogo doma*, 4:88. Dostoevsky's treatment of this dynamic in *Notes from Underground* (1864) is also well known. Dostoevskii, *Zapiski iz podpol'ia*, 5:102, 104–5.

137. Testimony of Petr Shaposhnikov, n.d., Butashevich-Petrashevskii investigation and trial documents, RGVIA, ch. 3, l. 155.

138. Actors in the 1840s were commoners, forming their own small social category, and they were usually trained for the stage from early childhood on. For examples, see Varneke, *Istoriia russkogo teatra XVII–XIX vekov*, 207–34.

Chapter 4. Atheism as the Predicate for Salvation

1. Chernyshevskii, "Esteticheskie otnosheniia iskusstva k deistvitel'nosti," 2:26, 35–36.

2. Manchester, *Holy Fathers, Secular Sons*, 12, 18–19; Freeze, *The Parish Clergy in Nineteenth-Century Russia*, 144–64.

3. Florovskii, *Ways of Russian Theology*, 266–68; Freeze, *The Parish Clergy in Nineteenth-Century Russia*, 119–22.

4. Chernyshevskaia, *Letopis' zhizni i deiatel'nosti N. G. Chernyshevskogo*, 17; Reiser, *Letopis' zhizni i deiatel'nosti N. A. Dobroliubova*, 50.

5. Dobroliubov, Mar. 15, 1853, in "Dnevniki" [Diary], 8:451.

6. Ivan Davydov was the former tutor of the Wisdom Lovers. After having been dismissed from his chair as professor of philosophy at Moscow University in 1826 because of his Schellingian views, Davydov was successful in acquiring a professorship in rhetoric at the university in 1831. He was known for his skill at cultivating the right contacts. In the 1830s and 1840s he became an ardent promoter of Nicholaevan state ideology. In 1847 he was rewarded, becoming

director of the Main Pedagogical Institute in St. Petersburg. Dobroliubov and his friends detested Davydov for not only his authoritarian style of directorship but also his tearful displays of piety and patriotism. To express their contempt, they would refer to him only in the diminutive, as "Vanka." During the 1850s, Davydov was considered a reactionary.

7. These lectures were conducted by the institute's resident priest, archpriest Pavel Soliarskii, who held a master's degree from St. Petersburg Theological Academy (*Akt dvadtsatipiatiletnego iubileia Glavnogo pedagogicheskogo instituta*, 38, 41, 48, 49).

8. Grigor'ev, *Imperatorskii S. Peterburgskii universitet v techenie pervykh piatidesiati let ego sushchestvovaniia*, 132.

9. Chernyshevskii, "Polemicheskie krasoty," 7:725–26, 763, 769–73.

10. Ruge, *Zwei Jahre in Paris*, 2:59–60.

11. Chernyshevskii, Nov. 23, 1848, in "Dnevniki," 1:178–79.

12. Chernyshevskii, Sept. 25, 1848, in "Dnevniki," 1:132.

13. Chernyshevskaia, *Letopis' zhizni i deiatel'nosti N. G. Chernyshevskogo*, 16, 30.

14. Chernyshevskii, Oct. 8, 1848, Dec. 10, 1848, and July 11, 1849, in "Dnevniki," 1:143, 193, 298.

15. Chernyshevskii, Sept. 23 and Oct. 2, 1848, in "Dnevniki," 1:128, 139. Irina Paperno describes the young Chernyshevsky as "gripped at once by a deep sense of inadequacy and desire for glory" (*Chernyshevsky and the Age of Realism*, 40).

16. In his diary, Chernyshevsky recorded a conversation with Alexandra Klientova, an old friend of Natalia Herzen, in which he declared that he admired Alexander Herzen more than any other Russian, adding that "there is nothing I would not do for him" (June 19, 1850, in "Dnevniki," 1:381).

17. Herzen, "Kaprizy i razdum'e: Novye variatsii na starye temy," 2:89, emphasis in original, and "Realizm," in "Pis'ma ob izuchenii prirody," 3:298, 303. Chernyshevsky assigned special importance to *Letters on the Study of Nature*, which he wished Khanykov to read (Chernyshevskii, Mar. 18, 1849, in "Dnevniki," 265).

18. Chernyshevskii, Dec. 4, 1848, in "Dnevniki," 1:188.

19. Chernyshevskii, Dec. 10, 1848, in "Dnevniki," 1:193.

20. Chernyshevskii, [Mar. 4, 1849], in "Dnevniki," 1:248.

21. Feuerbach, *Das Wesen des Christenthums*, 6:160–62; Feuerbach, "Vorrede zur Zweiten Auflage vom 'Wesen des Christenthums,'" 7:287–89.

22. Chernyshevskii, [Mar. 4, 1849], in "Dnevniki," 1:248.

23. Chernyshevskii, July 11, 1849, in "Dnevniki," 1:297.

24. Chernyshevskii, Jan. 19, 1850, in "Dnevniki," 1:354. Chernyshevsky's circumlocutions in this context are remarkable: "And this is another characteristic of my cowardice concerning my religious . . . it's not exactly unbelief, but something of that sort; that is, I am not a Christian by conviction, that is, I would not be a Christian if I had the courage of spirit, the fearlessness in the face of that, in which I see no point in believing."

25. Chernyshevskii, Jan. 20, 1850, in "Dnevniki," 1:358.

26. "Skepticism in the matter of religion has developed inside me to the point, where I am almost completely devoted from the soul to the teachings of

Feuerbach, and yet, for example, I was ashamed before mommy not to go to church on the 13th" (Chernyshevskii, Sept. 15, 1850, in "Dnevniki," 1:391).

27. Chernyshevskii, [late Mar. 1851], in "Dnevniki," 1:402. Though many scholars have claimed that Feuerbach had a seminal influence on Chernyshevsky's thought, Gustav Shpet found scant traces of any such influence in Chernyshevsky's writings ("Antropologizm Lavrova v svete istorii filosofii," 91–94).

28. Here I depart from Paperno, *Chernyshevsky and the Age of Realism*, 206, who says that it was unclear whether or not Chernyshevsky had lost faith in God.

29. Chernyshevskii, "Esteticheskie otnosheniia iskusstva k deistvitel'nosti," 2:26, 35–36.

30. The fullest account can be found in Steklov, *N. G. Chernyshevskii*, 1: 135–43.

31. Chernyshevskii, Feb. 21, 185[3], in "Dnevniki," 1:419.

32. Qtd. in Ovsianiko-Kulikovskii, "K psikhologii Dobroliubova," 5:47–48.

33. See, e.g., Reiser, *Letopis' zhizni i deiatel'nosti N. A. Dobroliubova*, 51, 58.

34. See, e.g., Kogan, "K voprosu o formirovanii mirovozzreniia Dobroliubova," 291. Cf. the interpretation of Ovsianiko-Kulikovskii, "K psikhologii Dobroliubova," 5:47. He characterized Dobroliubov as a "deeply religious boy" whose declarations of guilt cohered with the "traditional morals" of his family milieu.

35. Manchester, *Holy Fathers, Secular Sons*, 72.

36. Both figure separately in John Climacus's *Ladder of Divine Ascent*, one of the most widely translated and read patristic texts in Russia. "Dejection" (*unynie*) is listed under step 13 together with laziness, while "numbness" (*nechuvstvie*) appears as a sin under step 18. See, e.g., Ignatii [Brianchaninov], *Prinoshenie sovremennomu monashestvu*, 5:334: "When the soul gives up on a spiritual feat, or—what amounts to the same thing—performs it negligently, superficially, and coldly. [. . .] Then the monk develops a false sense of security/calm [*spokoistvie*]. [. . .] Such security, or rather, lulling to sleep of the soul, is the opposite of compunction [*umilenie*]. [. . .] The church fathers call it numbness [*nechuvstvie*], the mortification of the soul, the death of the mind even as the body remains alive." A footnote refers to step 18 in John Climacus's *Ladder of Divine Ascent*.

37. Paperno, *Chernyshevsky and the Age of Realism*, 41, 47. Paperno comments on numbness without, however, mentioning acedia.

38. Dobroliubov, Mar. 15, 1853, in "Dnevniki," 8:450.

39. Dobroliubov, Mar. 7, 1853, "Psikhatorium," in "Dnevniki," 8:454–56.

40. Dobroliubov, Apr. 7, 1853, "Psikhatorium," in "Dnevniki," 8:458. Chernyshevsky, who destroyed a large part of the diary, claimed that there had originally been entries for thirty-four days, totaling thirty-two pages. See notes to *Sobranie*, 8:658.

41. Dobroliubov to A. I. and Z. V. Dobroliubov, Mar. 17, 1854, Dobroliubov to F. V. and M. I. Blagoobrazov, Apr. 1 and 15, 1854, and Dobroliubov to A. I. Dobroliubov, May 24, 1854, in *Sobranie*, 9:118, 128, 135, 146.

42. Dobroliubov to A. I. Dobroliubov, Apr. 20, 1854, in *Sobranie*, 9:138.

43. One gathers this from the shamefaced tone of some letters Dobroliubov wrote to a friend from the institute, Dmitrii F. Shcheglov, on July 25, 1854, during his first summer vacation. He guiltily confessed to having been to church and having prayed: "Finally, I set off with my sisters for mass, where I arrived toward

the end, but—I must admit—I prayed heartily [. . .] everything awoke feelings that were long gone, long forgotten, that had been mocked long ago" (*Sobranie*, 9:159–60). Dobroliubov is clearly posturing in front of his friend when he writes that these feelings were "long forgotten"; the letters he wrote to his father in preceding months were full of them.

44. Dobroliubov to Shcheglov, Aug. 9, 1854, in *Sobranie*, 9:161.

45. "*You* will be celebrating, when you receive my letter. . . . There will be no celebration for me, no resurrection of the dead. I salute you at the commencement of the feast, but do so coldly, without any feeling of the heart. I hope it will be a merry one for you. . . . Do not wish me the same" (Dobroliubov to V. V. and L. I. Kolosovskii, Mar. 24, 1855, in *Sobranie*, 9:184, emphasis in original).

46. Dobroliubov, Dec. 18, 1855, in "Dnevniki," 8:463–64.

47. Reiser, "Neizdannye teksty N. A. Dobroliubova," 244–45. There is some scholarly disagreement over when Dobroliubov first became familiar with Feuerbach's works—whether it happened in 1855, as Reiser suggests, through friends at the institute, or in the spring of 1856, when he first met Chernyshevsky. Dobroliubov's first references to Feuerbach in his correspondence date to 1857, in which he mentions the circulation of books by Feuerbach and Bruno Bauer among his friends. See Dobroliubov to A. P. Zlatovratskii, June 23, 1857, and Dobroliubov to B. I. Stsiborskii, July 6, 1857, in *Sobranie*, 9:276, 284, and A. P. Zlatovratskii to Dobroliubov, late June/early July 1857 and late summer 1857, in Chernyshevskii, *Materialy dlia biografii N. A. Dobroliubova*, 381, 394.

48. Chernyshevskii, "Esteticheskie otnosheniia iskusstva k deistvitel'nosti," 2:96–98.

49. Dobroliubov, "Blagodetel'," 76–77.

50. Dobroliubov, "Pamiati ottsa," 93–94.

Благословен тот час печальный, / Когда ошибок детских мгла
Вслед колесницы погребальной / С души озлобленной сошла. [. . .]
Не уловлял мечты туманной / И пред иконами святых
Мольбой смиренно-покаянной / Не опозорил чувств моих. [. . .]
На битву жизни вышел смело, / И жизнь свободно протекла . . .
И делал я благое дело / Среди царующего зла . . . (94)

[Blessed be the sad hour, when behind a funeral carriage, the mist of childish mistakes fell from an embittered soul. [. . .] I did not detect a hazy hope and did not demean my feelings with a prayer of submissive penitence before the holy icons. [. . .] Bravely, I went into the battle of life, and life passed in freedom . . . And I did a good deed amidst a reign of evil . . .]

51. Qtd. in Ovsianiko-Kulikovskii, "K psikhologii Dobroliubova," 47–48.

52. Dobroliubov to E. N. Peshchurova, July 8, 1858, in *Sobranie*, 9:307: "By my very nature, I cannot belong to the number of ordinary people and cannot pass through life unnoticed" (*Ia po nature svoei ne dolzhen prinadlezhat' k chislu liudei diuzhinnykh*); Dobroliubov, Dec. 18, 1855, in "Dnevniki," 8:463–64.

53. The timing of their meeting has been the subject of some debate. See Reiser, *Letopis' zhizni i deiatel'nosti N. A. Dobroliubova*, 124–25.

54. See *Turgenev i krug "Sovremennika,"* 39, 172, 181–82, 186; Steklov, N. G. *Chernyshevskii,* 2:19–20n4. Some of these writers, notably Ivan Turgenev, modified their attitudes toward Chernyshevsky when *Essays on the Gogol Period in Russian Literature* began to appear.

55. Chernyshevsky to Dobroliubov, Aug. 11, 1858, in *Polnoe sobranie sochinenii,* 14:359–60.

56. The sociologist Vladimir Nahirny once alleged that "neither [. . .] Chernyshevskii, nor Dobroliubov had a single personal friend" ("The Russian Intelligentsia," 423). Nahirny argued that in the 1830s and 1840s, men such as Herzen and Ogarev, who belonged to the nobility, had cultivated personal relationships as ends in themselves. Chernyshevsky and Dobroliubov, by contrast, came from a generation that concerned itself with ideas or "convictions" to the exclusion of personal, affective relationships. Nahirny's views evidently stand in need of modification, but they do contain a grain of truth.

57. Chernyshevskii, "Stikhotvoreniia N. Ogareva," 3:563–64.

58. See chapter 2.

59. Ivan Panaev, editor of the journal, offered this figure in a letter to Vasilii Botkin (June 28, 1857, in *Turgenev i krug "Sovremennika,"* 423).

60. Herzen, "Eshche raz Bazarov," 20.1.348–49.

61. The most explicit discussion of this can be found in Chernyshevskii, "Lessing, ego vremia, ego zhizn' i deiatel'nost'," 4:71, and "Sochineniia T. N. Granovskogo," 3:356–57. Chernyshevsky also hinted at the relative lack of influence by statesmen in the introduction to *Essays on the Gogol Period in Russian Literature,* where he noted that Byron was "hardly less important than Napoleon in the history of humankind" (*Ocherki gogolevskogo perioda russkoi literatury,* 3:11). The word "intelligentsia" does not appear in either passage.

62. Chernyshevskii, *Ocherki gogolevskogo perioda russkoi literatury,* 3:11, 302–3. The latter passage was cut by censors. See also Chernyshevskii, "Lessing, ego vremia, ego zhizn' i deiatel'nost'," 4:9.

63. Dobroliubov, "Sobesednik liubitelei rossiiskogo slova," 1:32.

64. Chernyshevskii, *Ocherki gogolevskogo perioda russkoi literatury,* 3:7, 177, 183, 299, 305–7.

65. Ibid., 3:20, 298–301, 216–17.

66. Ibid., 3:6–7, 309.

67. Chernyshevsky claimed that Russians had been dozing since the seventeenth century ("Sochineniia Granovskogo," 3:351).

68. Chernyshevskii, "Russkii chelovek na rendez-vous," 5:158–60.

69. Dobroliubov, "Chto takoe oblomovshchina?" 2:11–13; Chernyshevskii, "Russkii chelovek na rendez-vous," 5:168–71.

70. Chernyshevsky inserted these remarks into 1855 and 1857 reviews of collected works of Pushkin and Gogol, respectively; see Chernyshevskii, "Sochineniia Pushkina," 2:440, and "Sochineniia i pis'ma N. V. Gogolia," 4:662.

71. Chernyshevskii, "Russkii chelovek na rendez-vous," 5:171–74. The impending danger Chernyshevsky—and all other Russians—had in mind was peasant rebellion.

72. Chernyshevskii, "Stikhotvoreniia N. Ogareva," 3:567.

73. Annenkov, "Literaturnyi tip slabogo cheloveka," 2:160. See also the

anonymous "Starye bogi i novye bogi," 893, 898-99. There, similar accusations were leveled against Maksim Antonovich.

74. Herzen, "Very Dangerous!!!" 14:118-20.

75. Steklov, *N. G. Chernyshevskii,* 2:43-60; Woehrlin, *Chernyshevskii,* 251-57. Both authors represent Chernyshevsky and Dobroliubov's estrangement from Herzen as having resulted from a disagreement over political convictions, specifically whether Alexander II could be relied on to see through necessary reforms or whether revolution was inevitable. Although it is true that there were important differences in political outlook, these were not the only differences that created the rift.

76. Dobroliubov, "Kogda zhe pridet nastoiashchii den'?" 2:236-37, 231-32.

77. Dobroliubov, "Zabitye liudi," 2:396-97. This passage was cut by censors.

78. Ibid., 2:386-87.

79. See n. 75 above.

80. For a discussion that balances the myth of the late nineteenth-century battle between science and religion, see Chadwick, *The Secularization of the European Mind in the Nineteenth Century,* 161-65. Chadwick argues that anti-religious writers projected their priorities backward in time to mythologize an age-old conflict between science and religion.

81. Gregory, *Scientific Materialism in Nineteenth-Century Germany,* 1, 88.

82. Though Vogt and Moleschott also used it, the phrase "no force without matter" is now most widely associated with Ludwig Büchner; see his *Kraft und Stoff,* 2.

83. Dobroliubov, "Zhizn' Magometa," 3:338; Dobroliubov, "Organicheskoe razvitie cheloveka v sviazi s ego umstvennoi i nravstvennoi deiatel'nost'iu," 3: 93, 97; Chernyshevskii, "Etiudy," 10:482.

84. Dobroliubov, "Aleksandr Sergeevich Pushkin," 1:108-9; Chernyshevskii, "Sochineniia Pushkina," 2:440.

85. Dobroliubov, "Organicheskoe razvitie cheloveka v sviazi s ego umstvennoi i nravstvennoi deiatel'nost'iu," 3:93-94; Dobroliubov, "Buddizm, rassmatrivaemyi v otnoshenii k posledovateliam ego, obitaiushchim v Sibiri," 3:412-13; Dobroliubov, "Vzgliad na istoriiu i sovremennoe sostoianie Ost-Indii," 3:32, 34, 39.

86. Commenting on the biography of Pushkin, Dobroliubov claimed that by embracing religion in the 1830s, Pushkin cut off the possibility of further intellectual development ("Aleksandr Sergeevich Pushkin," 1:117).

87. Dobroliubov, "Svatovstvo Chenskogo ili materialism i idealism," 2:498-99. Ahriman and Ormuzd are Zoroastrian gods of good and evil.

88. Chadwick, *The Secularization of the European Mind in the Nineteenth Century,* 173; Büchner, *Last Words on Materialism,* 9-10.

89. Pereira, *The Thought and Teachings of N. G. Černyševskij,* 38. Steklov attributes Chernyshevsky's ethical views to the influence not only of Bentham and J. S. Mill but also Feuerbach, Diderot, Lamettrie, and Helvetius (*N. G. Chernyshevskii,* 1:276-87). His emphasis on the French philosophers reflects the early Soviet interest in French Enlightenment philosophy more than it does Chernyshevsky's reading habits.

90. Chernyshevskii, "Antropologicheskii printsip v filosofii," 7:265, 267, 285-87; Dobroliubov, "Organicheskoe razvitie cheloveka v sviazi s ego umstvennoi

i nravstvennoi deiatel'nost'iu," 3:111–12. Dobroliubov also speaks of the generation of new people as capable of acting on the basis of instinct, because they are
unburdened by prejudice. These are "whole people, carried away, from childhood
on, by an idea." They are characterized by the "harmony of heart and thought,"
which gives them energy ("Kogda zhe pridet nastoiashchii den'?" 2:239–40).

91. I discuss this more fully in Frede, "Materialism and the Radical Intelligentsia," 79–82.

92. Ostrovskii, "Groza," 248.

93. In a section that the censors cut out, Dobroliubov explains that "the rites
in church are not what interests her; nor does she hear anything they sing and
read. There is a different music in her soul, different visions, and the service
ends without her noticing, as if in a single second" ("Luch sveta v temnom
tsarstve," 2:351).

94. Dobroliubov, "Luch sveta v temnom tsarstve," 2:353. "In religious practice,
by attending church," "dreamed of angels, singing in a cloud of dust, lit by the
sun, she cannot," and "the saints' faces severe, and the liturgical readings are
threatening, and the tales of the pilgrims are monstrous. . . . In essence, they are
all as they were before, they have not changed at all; she is the one who has
changed" were cut by censors.

95. Ibid., 2:359.

96. Dobroliubov to Stepan T. Slavutinskii, Mar. 24, 1860, in *Sobranie*, 9:408.

97. Dobroliubov, "Zabitye liudi," 2:391.

98. Ibid., 2:399. The last sentence was excised by the censor.

99. Dobroliubov, "Kogda zhe pridet nastoiashchii den'?" 2:209–10.

100. Chernyshevskii, *Chto delat'?* 411.

101. Ibid., 68–71.

102. Paperno, *Chernyshevsky and the Age of Realism*, 207.

103. Ibid., 206, 204.

Chapter 5. Atheism and Apocalypse

1. Isaiah Berlin used the phrase "apocalyptic assumption" to characterize
the worldview of Russian Populists. "Its heart is the pattern of sin and fall and
resurrection—of the road to earthly paradise the gates of which will only open
if men find the one true way and follow it" (introduction, xiii–xiv).

2. Brower, *Training the Nihilists*, 87–88, 114.

3. Kupriianov, *Gorodskaia kul'tura russkoi provintsii*, 320–21.

4. The influence of Chernyshevsky and Dobroliubov on the student population of the 1860s is discussed in Steklov, *N. G. Chernyshevskii*, 2:211–22. Some of
the figures I discuss in this chapter knew Chernyshevsky and Dobroliubov
personally or had friends who knew them. See, e.g., Krasnoperov, *Zapiski
raznochintsa*, 62–63, and Pinaev, "M. K. Elpidin," 6.

5. Kavelin to Herzen and Ogarev, Aug. 1857, in *Pis'ma K. D. Kavelina i I. S.
Turgeneva k A. I. Gertsenu*, 5.

6. Richard Wortman, *Scenarios of Power*, 2:74–78. According to Wortman, the
commemoration in 1862 of the thousand-year anniversary of the foundation
of Rus' may have played a part in such expectations. Irina Paperno notes that

contemporaries celebrated the announcement of the Emancipation by drawing on the prayers, incantations, and rituals of Easter and the Feast of the Presentation of the Lord, with its prayer, "Rejoice thou also, pious elder, who took in thy arms the liberator of souls, who bestows on us resurrection" ("The Liberation of the Serfs as a Cultural Symbol," 424–27).

7. Zaionchkovskii, *Provedenie v zhizn' krest'ianskoi reformy 1861 g.*, 56.

8. For a discussion of Old-Believer Apocalypticism, see Cherniavsky, "Old Believers and the New Religion," 10–39.

9. Zhuk, *Russia's Lost Reformation*, 11, 106, 114.

10. On revolutionaries and sectarians more generally, see Engelstein, *Castration and the Heavenly Kingdom*, 72–77.

11. Wayne Meeks explains that apocalyptic language appeals largely to people whose position in society has been subject to sudden and drastic change (a crisis). They are hence inclined to feel that the world is out of joint, to be receptive the promise of imminent and radical transformation, and to see in the apocalyptic message a guideline for solidarity in a new community of believers (*The First Urban Christians*, 172–77).

12. Rowley, *The Relevance of Apocalyptic*, 9, 20, 36, 155; Schmithals, *The Apocalyptic Movement*, 24, 27, 37.

13. Derevenskii, *Uchenie ob Antikhriste v drevnosti i srednevekov'e*, 123–25. According to Derevenskii, these two explanations stood side by side rather than fusing.

14. Behm, "καινός," 3:449–50; Martyn, *Galatians*, 565. This interpretation is not so far fetched, if one considers 2 Corinthians 5:17: "Therefore, if any one is in Christ, he is a new creation; the old has passed away, behold, the new has come."

15. *Znameniia prishestviia Antikhrista po ucheniiu sviashchennago pisaniia*, 4–6. Despite the injunction against speculation, it proved irresistible. One clergyman saw the Antichrist in Chernyshevsky, precisely because Chernyshevsky seemed so innocent in person: "The devil [*bes*] takes on the lightest [*samyi svetlyi*] image of angels and even of Christ himself, and that is when the devil is most dangerous" (Kostomarov, "Avtobiografiia," 1:158).

16. See, e.g., Ignatii [Brianchaninov], "Pouchenie v nedeliu miasopustnuiu," 4:50–52. Even the just knew that it was God's mercy, and God's mercy alone, that would save them. This was not to deny the importance of the will in salvation; the person to be saved did also have to want to be saved but the mere fact that one wanted to be saved should not lead to a confident expectation of God's mercy.

17. The only such reference I have found is in an epistle by Feofan (Govorov) in which he summarized what the New Testament (primarily II Peter 3, not Revelation) had to say on the Second Coming of Christ and Judgment Day. He did not, however, comment on the "new people" and "new world." Instead, he reprimanded the addressee for having speculated about life after death (*Pis'ma k raznym litsam*, 38).

18. See Makarii [Bulgakov], *Pravoslavno-dogmaticheskoe bogoslovie*, 2:294; Platon [Fiveiskii], *Sokrashchennoe izlozhenie dogmatov very*, 138, 189. Neither discusses the new people in the context of the Apocalypse. Nor are they discussed

in corresponding sections of Filaret [Gumilevskii], *Pravoslavno-dogmaticheskoe bogoslovie*. The only reference to the "new man" I could find here was in the context of his discussion of God's creation of Adam (1:195–96).

19. Ignatii [Brianchaninov],"K nekotoromu nastoiateliu o liubvi k bratii," 111. See also Ignatii [Brianchaninov], "Pouchenie vtoroe v dvadtsat' piatuiu nedeliu," 1:133. Here, he contrasts the "newness" of the Gospels to the "old, worn-out" nature of the human heart. The path to renewal is through the Gospels and through love in Christ.

20. Filaret [Drozdov], "Beseda o novom rozhdenii svyshe," 4:347–51.

21. Dobroliubov, "Kogda zhe pridet nastoiashchii den'?" 2:209–10: "New people have grown up, for whom love of the truth and honesty of endeavor are no longer a rarity. Slowly but surely, from childhood on, they have been soaking up those concepts and goals that the best people of earlier days had to fight, doubt, and suffer for in their mature years. [. . .] You will hear from the high school student, the average cadet, and even sometimes from a decent seminarian the expression of such convictions, for which someone like Belinsky had to argue and rave in previous times." The article is described at length in Müller, *Der Topos des neuen Menschen in der russischen und sowjetrussichen Geistesgeschichte*, 35–39.

22. Pomialovskii, "Meshchanskoe schast'e," 1:61–62. On 75, Pomialovskii plays on the Latin, *homo novus*, a historical term that refers to the first male in a family to attain the rank of senator.

23. Chernyshevskii, *Chto delat'?* 231–33. He claims in this passage that the character Rakhmetov, who does seem to possess superhuman traits, is introduced merely to show how ordinary the other characters are.

24. Chernyshvevskii, *Chto delat'?* 149.

25. There is some disagreement as to who wrote this manifesto. Iastrebov makes a convincing case for Nikolai Raevskii and Mitrofan Muravskii (*Revoliutsionnye demokraty na Ukraine*, 136–37). Koz'min claims that Raevskii had no role to play in the writing the manifesto (*Khar'kovskie zagovorshchiki*, 57).

26. The envelope made its way into the hands of the governor of Kharkov province, who initially took the whole incident for a schoolboy's prank (Koz'min, *Khar'kovskie zagovorshchiki*, 14–15). The writing on the envelope, however, had the look of a threat. Alexander II was made aware of the group's activities and was furious that they could not be identified.

27. "We thank you for not attempting to achieve true enlightenment but for sleeping in the darkness of ignorance, having entrusted yourselves to our servants, your robbers—the bishops and priests—who trade in your conscience and in the truths of the teaching of the Gospel" (Koz'min, *Khar'kovskie zagovorshchiki*, 14).

28. Iastrebov, *Revoliutsionnye demokraty na Ukraine*, 156.

29. Reproduced in Koz'min, "M. D. Muravskii v khar'kovskom tainom obshchestve," 136. These lines again recall the New Testament, specifically the reference to darkness and light in Colossians 1:12–13: "Giving thanks unto the Father, which hath made us meet to be partakers of the inheritance of the saints in light / Who hath delivered us from the power of darkness and hath translated us into the kingdom of his dear Son."

30. See, for example, the letter by Nikandr Rashevskii to A. A. Tyshinskii

(who had been a close friend of Zavadskii and Efimenko since 1856), Feb. 23, 1858. Having remarked that the "head" of the state had been "possessed" by a "demon of evil," he went on to say that "worldly idols and policemen have confused everyone so thoroughly, that they are more of afraid of breaking the fundamental laws than [of breaking] the laws of nature, the Divine laws. [. . .] How can the majority possibly believe that all [earthly] power comes from God? That is only just on the basis of the saying: the voice of the people is the voice of God, and by no means on the basis of the fundamental laws and the writings of Church Fathers" (documents of the Third Section, GARF, f. 109, 1 eksp., 1860, op. 35, d. 26, ch. 1, lit. B, ch. 2, ll. 493 ob.–94).

31. Testimony of Petr Efimenko, documents of the Third Section, GARF, f. 109, 1 eksp, 1860 g., op. 35, d. 26, ch. 1, lit. D, l. 94 ob.

32. According to the brief history Zavadskii wrote of the group, they decided to form a literary club and to devote themselves to "self-preparation [*prigotovlenie samikh sebia*]" (Iastrebov, *Revoliutsionnye demokraty na Ukraine*, 171). Soon, even this seemed too much. Several began to feel that "our activities consist only of empty words" (Koz'min, *Khar'kovskie zagovorshchiki*, 70).

33. Zavadskii said this when asked to summarize an article he had written on the Sunday school movement (documents of the Third Section, GARF, f. 109, 1 eksp., 1860, op. 35, d. 26, ch. 2, lit B, l. 204).

34. Pokrovskii, "Pravila dlia voskresnykh shkol moskovskogo uchebnogo okruga," 164.

35. Muravskii to Viachaslav A. Manasein, Feb. 19, 1861, in Lemke, "Molodost' 'Ottsa Mitrofana'," 316.

36. This emerged largely in testimonies by Mitrofan Levchenko, a close friend of Muravskii, and in documents seized by the police (documents of the Third Section, GARF, f. 109, 1 eksp., 1860 g., op. 35, d. 26, ch. 1, ll. 31, 69, 74 ob., 87 ob.). Ukrainian nationalism was very important to some members of the group.

37. Muravskii to Manasein, Jan. 20, 1861, in Lemke, "Molodost' 'Ottsa Mitrofana'," 313–14. It should be noted, however, that Veniamin Portugalov, a Jew, joined the group at some point in 1856, and his friend, Leon Zelenskii, also associated with some of them.

38. After his arrest and exile in 1860, for example, he found fault with one new acquaintance because he did not observe Orthodox fasts (Muravskii to Manasein, Jan. 20, 1861, in Lemke, "Molodost' 'Ottsa Mitrofana'," 313).

39. Muravskii to Zavadskii, Jan. 29–Mar. 19, 1861, in Lemke, "Molodost' 'Ottsa Mitrofana'," 296.

40. Breshko-Breshkovskaia, *Iz moikh vospominanii*, 31.

41. Muravskii was not the only one who gave investigators information, but he may have been the first to provide a full confession, and his admission was much more detailed than those offered by most of his friends. The group was caught only by coincidence. In 1860 an enraged nobleman, Mikhail Garshin, denounced Zavadskii to the authorities for having "seduced the soul" of Garshin's wife (he ran off with her, taking Garshin's son with them). Zavadskii might consider himself a "learned man, a genius, a naturalist," Garshin said, but he was in fact nothing but a "shabby seminarian" (Koz'min, *Khar'kovskie*

zagovorshchiki, 26). Authorities searched Zavadskii's apartment for Garshina and the child. Although they did not find them, they did find compromising documents, allowing them to arrest Zavadskii and to begin arresting his friends.

42. Documents of the Third Section, GARF, f. 109, 1 eksp., 1860, op. 35, d. 26, ch. 7, l. 82.

43. On the reasons for political repression, see Venturi, *Roots*, 175–76. The number of arrests further increased following the Polish uprising of 1863–64. According to one source, thirty-six thousand people were arrested and exiled in connection with that event (Izmozik, "Politicheskie ssyl'nye i kontrol' za ikh perepiskoi v 60–70-kh gg. XIX v.," 471).

44. On the role of priests in dealing with radical detainees, see Verhoeven, *The Odd Man Karakozov*, 159.

45. Zhuk, *Russia's Lost Reformation*, 109–112. They consisted largely of "Shalaputs" and German Mennonites.

46. Koz'min, *Khar'kovskie zagovorshchiki*, 58.

47. Documents of the Third Section, GARF, f. 109, 1 eksp., 1860 g., op. 35, d. 26, ch. 1, lit. B, ch. 2, l. 414.

48. Feuerbach, *Vorlesungen über das Wesen der Religion*, 8:31, 39, 200–207, 296–303, 312–13, 358–60.

49. The original letter was lost. The contents are paraphrased and quoted in Muravskii to Manasein, Feb. 19, 1861, in Lemke, "Molodost' 'Ottsa Mitrofana'," 318.

50. [Morigerovskii and Efimenko], "Poslanie startsa Kondratiia," 11:427–29.

51. Under interrogation, Morigerovskii claimed to have found the epistle in St. Petersburg when he visited there in 1857–58, but this claim has been dismissed, partly because the epistle refers to events that took place in 1861. Morigerovskii was the principal author. See Gorovoi, *Revoliutsionno-demokraticheskoe dvizhenie v permskoi gubernii v 60-kh godakh XIX veka*, 45–46. One of Morigerovskii's associates testified that Morigerovskii had written it with the help of one other person. Efimenko is generally supposed to have been that other person.

52. Gorovoi, *Revoliutsionno-demokraticheskoe dvizhenie v permskoi gubernii v 60-kh godakh XIX veka*, 47. Before the group was arrested, four copies were taken out of Perm: two were taken to Shadrinsk district by a seminary student and two more were taken to Krasnoufimsk district by Efimenko. One further copy may have turned up in Kazan; one of the arrestees, Ivan Orlov, referred to it in garbled terms under interrogation (testimony of Ivan Orlov, Aug. 14, 1863, in *Russko-pol'skie revoliutsionnye sviazi* [hereafter *RPRS*], 3.2.377–78).

53. Herzen's works were widely read in Perm in 1860; they were smuggled there by a local merchant who frequently traveled abroad and by a student at Kazan University who regularly sent parcels to a Perm bookstore that doubled as a library and distribution center for underground literature. In 1860, Perm seminarians had even set up their own journal, the *Seminar Bell* (*Seminarskii zvonok*), in which they printed extracts from Herzen's journal, the *Bell* (*Kolokol*) (Khotiakov, "Nelegal'naia rabota biblioteki A. I. Ikonnikova," 55–56; Gorovoi, *Revoliutsionno-demokraticheskoe dvizhenie v permskoi gubernii v 60-kh godakh XIX veka*, 55).

54. In the early 1850s, Herzen and Ogarev had begun to look to peasant rebellion, specifically one involving Old Believers, as the only possible source for a successful revolution in Russia. Five hundred copies of *Visions* were shipped to Istanbul in order to be distributed in Moldavia (Linkov, *Revoliutsionnaia bor'ba A. I. Gertsena i N. P. Ogareva i tainoe obshchestvo "Zemlia i volia" 1860-kh godov*, 44–48).

55. [Engelson], "Videniia sv. Ottsa Kondratiia," 56–59.

56. The first commandment is rather abstract and the second is slightly bizarre. It orders people to become conscious of their actions ("Vedai, chto tvorishi!") ([Engelson], "Videniia sv. Ottsa Kondratiia," 62–64). The text specifies that this means demanding accountability from the state, avoiding drunkenness, and acting in a measured and reasonable way, without requiring unconditional obedience from one another. People should not interpret the Bible in a literal manner either. The second was to act immediately ("Ne khoroni!") ([Engelson], "Videniia," 64–66). This meant making full use of one's talents, not saving one's money, and preferring cremation to burial.

57. [Morigerovskii and Efimenko], "Poslanie startsa Kondratiia," 428, 425.

58. Ibid., 413–14n1.

59. Ibid., 425–26, 428. The second commandment is to enrich one's reason through study and conversation. The third and fourth commandments are to unite and form a representative government (426–28).

60. Ibid., 413, 417. This may be contrasted to [Engelson], "Videniia sv. Ottsa Kondratiia," where Jesus is mentioned numerous times (on 56, 57, 62, and 66–67). True, his resurrection is not noted there either, but he is mentioned as a judge in the afterlife: "My soul, my soul, rise up! Why do you sleep? The end is drawing near, you must arouse yourself, therefore rejoice. May Christ the God protect you, [for he] is everywhere and in all things" (66–67).

61. [Morigerovskii and Efimenko], "Poslanie startsa Kondratiia," 427, 428.

62. Ibid., 425, 418, 429.

63. Here I am contradicting the view, standard among western historians of Russia, that the emancipation of the serfs caused radicalization. Disillusionment was already pervasive by the time emancipation was proclaimed.

64. According to one estimate, 107 peasants were killed immediately and many more died after having fled the scene. Officially, the state acknowledged only 55 dead, while the Third Section placed the number around 70 (Field, *Rebels in the Name of the Tsar*, 67). Students estimated about 200 dead. See the proclamation "B'iu chelom narodu pravoslavnomu," 3.2.285.

65. Irina Paperno points out that peasants seem to have viewed themselves this way, too ("The Liberation of the Serfs as a Cultural Symbol," 429, 431).

66. Herzen, "12 aprelia 1861," 849. Translation modified from Field, *Rebels*, 94.

67. In an article on the Kazan Requiem, Gregory Freeze represents the requiem as principally planned and carried out by students at the Kazan Theological Academy. The requiem, he claims, was the manifestation of a new movement among elements of the Orthodox Church to reflect on social developments ("A Social Mission for Russian Orthodoxy," 115–35). In this deeply researched article, Freeze may overdraw the boundaries that separated students at the

university from those at the academy. Similarly, his assertion that "secular philosophy [. . .] possessed only marginal significance at the time" is too strong (128).

68. The Christian meaning of these days was firmly imprinted on the minds
of participants. Years later, Arkadii Biriukov, one of the participants in the
requiem, remembered that the Saturday had been "Lazarus Saturday," the day
that commemorated Christ's resurrection of Lazarus from the dead ("Universitet
i studenty v nachale 6o-kh godov," 877).

69. Students themselves sometimes referred to the "Kruzhok" with a capital
"K" and seem to have thought of it as a group with distinct aims. It is probably
unwise, however, to treat this circle as a coherent organization with a fixed
membership, as Soviet scholars did. They provided contradictory lists of
members and also overstated the case in claiming that the circle was a branch of
the revolutionary organization Zemlia i volia in St. Petersburg.

70. Biriukov, "Universitet i studenty v nachale 6o-kh godov," 874.

71. Vul'fson and Bushkanets, *Obshchestvenno-politicheskaia bor'ba v Kazanskom
universitete v 1859–1861 godakh,* 77, 80. A poem found in the possession of a
Perm seminarian celebrated Shchapov as an "apostle" who called on the people
to arise from their "dead sleep" (Chernyshev, "Materialy po istorii klassovoi
bor'by v Rossii v 6o-kh godakh XIX veka," 97).

72. Shchapov, "Rech' posle panikhidy po ubitym v s. Bezdne krest'ianam,"
410.

73. Biriukov, "Universitet i studenty v nachale 6o-kh godov," 878. Specifically,
Biriukov remembered Shchapov as having said that "justice has always been
persecuted by force; from the beginning of the world to the present time, not
one prophet in the world has died a natural death; and even the God-man, the
greatest of all prophets, who brought peace and love with him, was crucified on
a level with robbers" (878). Here, Christ's status as God has been restored.

74. As the manuscript shows, Shchapov was apparently not sure how to
express himself. He originally wrote "Mythical Democrat," but then struck out
the word "mythical" and wrote "until now mythical [*dosele mificheskii*]" ("Rech'
posle panikhidy po ubitym v s. Bezdne krest'ianam," 409).

75. Here, he refers to those peasant rebels and pretenders who appeared in
the seventeenth century claiming to be Jesus Christ. Shchapov described them
in his 1862 pamphlet "Zemstvo i raskol," 264–65.

76. An outline of the speech Shchapov apparently produced in advance
contained no references to Christ at all. The only Christian word in the outline is "martyr," and it does not appear in the text of the speech itself.
Vul'fson proposes that Shchapov thought he would be delivering the speech at
a different type of function when he wrote the outline (*Iz istorii raznochinno-
demokraticheskogo dvizheniia v Povolzh'e i na Urale,* 54). The outline is reproduced
in Vul'fson and Bushkanets, *Obshchestvenno-politicheskaia bor'ba v Kazanskom
universitete v 1859–1861 godakh,* 74–75n4.

77. Shchapov, "Rech' posle panikhidy po ubitym v s. Bezdne krest'ianam,"
409, emphasis mine.

78. Freeze, "A Social Mission for Russian Orthodoxy," 121.

79. According to the memoirs of Arkadii Biriukov, they also hoped to lend
medical assistance to wounded peasants ("Universitet i studenty v nachale 6o-kh
godov," 877).

80. Here and below, most biographical information about the Kazan students is taken from volume 1 of *Kazanskii universitet: Biobibliograficheskii slovar'*.

81. Testimony of Mikhail Elpidin, n.d., in Iampol'skaia and Gutman, *Bezdnenskoe vosstanie 1861 goda*, 35; Vul'fson and Bushkanets, *Obshchestvenno-politicheskaia bor'ba v Kazanskom universitete v 1859–1861 godakh*, 72.

82. Vul'fson, *Iz istorii raznochinno-demokraticheskogo dvizheniia v Povolzh'e i na Urale*, 64.

83. "B'iu chelom narodu pravoslavnomu," in *RPRS*; "Dolgo davili vas, brattsy," in *RPRS*. Both texts draw heavily on a July 1861 proclamation by Nikolai Ogarev, "Chto nuzhno narodu?"

84. "B'iu chelom narodu pravoslavnomu," 285. God's name is invoked positively only twice in this text—once, where it is said that God will help the sacred cause and once where it is asserted that the terms of the emancipation are contrary to "divine and human truth" (284). There is no mention of Christ.

85. "Dolgo davili vas, brattsy," 298. In the Orthodox bible, this is 1 Kings 8. The Kazan authors may have borrowed the quote from Ogarev's "What do the People Need?" though it comes across differently in their version. In Ogarev's version ("Chto nuzhno narodu?" 856), the reference to Samuel's prophecy is used as a likeness. After soldiers shot into the crowd in Bezdna, Ogarev claimed, peasants could see in the new tsar what the prophet Samuel had said about the rule of a future king to the people of Israel, when he warned them not to take a new king (the king would exploit the people and their daughters). In the Kazan proclamation, by contrast, the quote is inserted without a proper introduction, so that it sounds much more prophetic.

86. "Dolgo davili vas, brattsy," 298–99. The reference to a life without sorrow is drawn from the Book of Revelation 7:16 and 21:4: God "shall wipe away all tears from their eyes; and there shall be no more death, neither sorrow, nor crying; neither shall there be any more pain, for the former things are passed away."

87. Pinaev, "M. K. Elpidin," 9. "Iisus navin" is the Russian name for Joshua, the author of the Old Testament Book of Joshua.

88. Chancellery of the Ministry of Internal Affairs, RGIA, f. 1282, op. 1, d. 141, ll. 253 ob.–54. He told investigators that he intended to refute these ideas, a claim that seems improbable given the manner in which the manuscript was laid out.

89. "B'iu chelom narodu pravoslavnomu," 284.

90. "Dolgo davili vas, brattsy," 298. This was a point that had not been made in Ogarev's tract, "Chto nuzhno narodu."

91. Qtd. in a report by the police in Viatka to Ministry of Internal Affairs, May 23, 1863, in *RPRS*, 3.2.327.

92. Krasnoperov, *Zapiski raznochintsa*, 70. He specified that this was a manuscript copy, most like a Russian lithograph.

93. Krasnoperov, *Zapiski raznochintsa*, 101.

94. Lavrskii to Zolotov, Mar. 6, 1863, in *RPRS*, 3.2.306, 307.

95. Ershov, "Kazanskii zagovor 1863 g.," pt. 1, 207–9.

96. "Volzhskii manifest," 16:333–34.

97. Ershov, "Kazanskii zagovor 1863 g.," pt. 1, 209–11; Leikina-Svirskaia, "'Kazanskii zagovor' 1863 g.," 434–35.

98. Koz'min, *Kazanskii zagovor 1863 goda*, 17–18; Leikina-Svirskaia, "'Kazanskii zagovor' 1863 g.," 445.

99. Bazanov, *Russkie revoliutsionnye demokraty i narodoznanie*, 244–46. The proclamations the students took included the two that were produced in Kazan, "B'iu chelom narodu pravoslavnomu" and "Dolgo davili vas, brattsy," as well as proclamations produced in St. Petersburg and elsewhere, such as "Zemlia i volia: Svoboda veroispovedaniia, brattsy!" "L'etsia pol'skaia krov'," and "Svoboda." Later, in mid-April, Polish students arrived in Kazan from St. Petersburg to distribute the Polish manifesto themselves.

100. Biriukov's roommate, Lavrskii, noted that "there are some good passages in those texts: 'I have not come to bring peace, but a sword' [Matthew 10:34], all of them are underlined in it" (Lavrskii to Zolotov, Mar. 6, 1863, in *RPRS*, 3.2.306).

101. Ershov, "Kazanskii zagovor 1863 g.," pt. 1, 218–19n1.

102. Biriukov, "Sdelannye vypiski," in *RPRS*, 3.2.308. The extracts come from *Zerkalo dlia dukhvnogo vnutrennego cheloveka* in Kel'siev, *Sbornik pravitel'stvennykh svedenii o raskol'nikakh*, 1:211.

103. [Elpidin], "Kazanskii zagovor (1863–1865)," 136–37.

104. Ershov, "Kazanskii zagovor 1863 g.," pt. 1, 218.

105. Ibid., 215; Chancellery of the Ministry of Internal Affairs, RGIA, f. 1282, op. 1, 1863, d. 160, ll. 26–27 ob.

106. Orlov to Skliarovskii, Mar. 15, 1863, in *RPRS*, 3.2.324. Indeed, he said that he cared little about possible peasant responses to the proclamations: "I was in no in mood for it, and may God quickly give me legs" (qtd. in a report by Adamovich to Dolgorukii, Minister of Internal Affairs, May 23, 1863, in *RPRS*, 3.2.324). Cheremis, Votiaks, and Besseriakhs are nineteenth-century designations for people who came to be known as Mari, Udmurt, and Besermiane (relatives of Udmurts).

107. The seminarian Il'ya Ponomarev had been bedridden for three days as a result (Bazanov, *Russkie revoliutsionnye demokraty i narodoznanie*, 245n1).

108. Ershov, "Kazanskii zagovor 1863 g.," pt. 1, 217.

109. "Volzhskii Manifest," 16:360.

110. There was certainly some bravado involved in these missions. Under interrogation, Biriukov testified that part of the appeal in taking proclamations into the countryside was that one got to show them off to the fellow priests' sons (who, in most cases, were priests themselves): "He wanted to show it and read it to his acquaintances among the clergy, he wanted to show off with this proclamation as a *wild rarity* in the *dark kingdom*" ("Volzhskii Manifest," 16:363). These words are italicized as in the original and presumably refer to Dobroliubov's works.

111. Lavrskii to Zolotov, Mar. 6, 1863, in *RPRS*, 3.2.306.

112. Bazanov claims that the Kazan students borrowed this term from Ogarev. Ogarev had used it in a piece he wrote on revolutionary conspiracy in 1859 titled "Ideals." These "apostles" would be leaders of revolutionary centers throughout Russia, popularizing revolutionary ideas (*Revoliutsionnye demokraty i narodoznanie*, 227). See also Nechkina, "N. G. Chernyshevskii i A. I. Gertsen v gody revoliutsionnoi situatsii," 58. "Ideals" was never published, however, and there is no evidence that it circulated in Russia.

113. Literally, the word *apostolos* derives from the Greek verb "to send," so that an apostle is "one who is sent." They gain their authority from the fact that

they are "sent" by God on a commission or by Jesus Christ on God's initiative. It is not a function that the individual can arrogate to himself. See Rengstorf, "ἀποστέλλω—ἀποστολή," 1:399, 405, 424, 426.

114. Rengstorf, "ἀποστέλλω— ἀποστολή," 431; Schmithals, *The Office of Apostle in the Early Church*, 22–57, esp. 24.

115. The Russian reads:

В виду имеюших совершиться для обшаго блага событий, сей человек взял на себя роль апостола-проповедника, роль, в высшей степени прекрасная и полезная. Прошу принять зтого апостола радушно и исполнять те поручения, которые он на Вас возложит . . . Время близко; старому свету приближается конец, и Россия воспрянет от сна. Верю, что Вы принимаете в зтом деле непосредственное участие.

Да здравствует демократическая конституция!

(Krasnoperov to A. A. Krasovskii, Feb. 7, 1863, Chancellery of the Ministry of Internal Affairs, RGIA, f. 1282, op. 1, d. 160, 1863, ll. 5–5 ob.). It has been reproduced in various forms by historians. A slightly different version is found in Sergeev, *Revniteli revoliutsionnogo neterpeniia*, 10.

116. Torrey, *The Apocalypse of John*, 160.

117. *Imeiushchie sovershit'sia sobytiia* appears to be a standard Russian Orthodox synonym for apocalyptic events. See, e.g., *O poslednikh sobytiiakh, imeiushchikh sovershit'sia v kontse mira*. The first edition was published in 1884.

118. "He [Krasnoperov] understands the phrases 'the time is drawing near [. . .] sleep' as follows: the time for the emancipation of the peasants from serfdom is drawing near, that Russia was as if mentally asleep during the age of serfdom but that she will live with new life [*zhit' novoiu zhizn'iu*] when the peasants become free" (Ershov, "Kazanskii zagovor 1863 g.," pt. 1, 216).

119. See Müller, *Der Topos des neuen Menschen in der russischen und sowjet-russichen Geistesgeschichte*.

Chapter 6. Doubt after Atheism

1. For the fullest discussion of Pisarev's contribution to Russian intellectual life in the second half of the nineteenth century, see Pozefsky, *The Nihilist Imagination*, 167–203, quotes on 192–95.

2. Pozefsky, *The Nihilist Imagination*, 169–70, 175–77.

3. Qtd. in Plotkin, *Pisarev i literaturno-obshchestvennoe dvizhenie shestidesiatykh godov*, 6–7. In particular, one may point to Ivan Ivanov and Akim Volynsky, both influential as historians of the Russian intelligentsia and Russian literary criticism in the late nineteenth and early twentieth centuries.

4. Pisarev, "Nasha universitetskaia nauka," 5:60–62.

5. Ginzburg, *O psikhologicheskoi proze*, 246, 256–57.

6. Joravsky, *Russian Psychology*, 56.

7. Pozefsky, *The Nihilist Imagination*, 27.

8. Some of these scandals are described in Danilov, "Neskol'ko otryvochnykh vospominanii o D. I. Pisareve."

9. Pisarev, letter to his parents, Dec. 15, 1851, in "Pis'ma D. I. Pisareva k roditeliam," 110.

10. Shcherbakov, "Universitetskii dnevnik Pisareva," 198.

11. Gleason, *Young Russia*, 133, 137–59.

12. Korotkov, *Pisarev*, 53–59.

13. Solov'ev, *D. I. Pisarev*, 43.

14. Skabichevskii, "Dmitrii Ivanovich Pisarev," 49, 51. See also Skabichevskii, *Literaturnye vospominaniia*, 107–8. Petr Polevoi offered a different account in 1868, highlighting disagreements over the status of women and Pisarev's review of the character Olga in Goncharov's *Oblomov* ("Vospominaniia o Dmitrie Ivanoviche Pisareve," *Sanktpeterburgskie vedomosti*, no. 194).

15. Pisarev, "Nasha universitetskaia nauka," 5:57.

16. See Elizavetina, "Pisarev i zhurnal 'Rassvet'," 1:365.

17. Pisarev's student diary of 1857 is full of references to the Orthodox devotional practices of his St. Petersburg family, which included regular church attendance and fasting. See Shcherbakov, "Universitetskii dnevnik Pisareva," 190, 192, 195.

18. The author, Heinrich Zschokke, was Swiss and began to publish his meditations in 1809 in German under the title *Stunden der Andacht zur Beförderung wahren Christentums und häuslicher Gottesverehrung*. This work became extremely popular, translated into eight languages, including Russian (where it appeared in four editions between 1834 and 1845). At the time it first appeared, it was highly controversial owing to its mixture of pietism, Catholicism, and deism. On its publication history and the controversy it sparked, see Hartmann, *Heinrich Zschokkes Stunden der Andacht*, 18–23, 26–27, 119, 137–81. Pisarev commented on it several times, including in a December 11, 1851, letter to his mother ("Pis'ma D. I. Pisareva k roditeliam," 110).

19. Pisarev to Koreneva, Oct. 15, [1858], "Iz neopublikovannoi perepiski D. I. Pisareva," 652. Skabichevskii describes his spiritual crisis in *Literaturnye vospominaniia*, 108–11. Here, he claims that his crisis in 1858 started when, intending to preach the Gospel to others, he began to study the Bible (in French translation). He began with the Old Testament and found the contents incredible. Though his description of this crisis, which he says lasted for two months, was clearly inspired by Russian romantic models of the 1830s and 1840s, it is the only account I have come across in which reading the Bible itself is represented as the source of the crisis.

20. Pisarev to Pisareva, [1859], in Elizavetina, *Pisarev—kritik: Nachalo puti*, 99. See also Skabichevskii, *Literaturnye vospominaniia*, 125–26.

21. Pisarev to Pisareva, [1859], in Solov'ev, *Pisarev*, 60.

22. Describing the views of Epictetus in "Apollonius of Tyana" (1861), he would note that "man renounces the joys of life not in the name of a higher, embodied idea of the good, nor in the name of love for one's neighbor, but only because these joys can betray [him] over time" (3:108). This theme of betrayal remained dominant in his writings of the 1860s.

23. "He started speaking to me and to all of us much less often about himself, and much more rarely did he share his dreams and thoughts with us" (Polevoi, "Vospominaniia").

24. Pisarev to Treskin, [summer 1859], in Solov'ev, *Pisarev*, 57. Pisarev would level the same accusation at his mother and other family members in subsequent years. See, for example, Pisarev to Pisareva, [1863], in Solov'ev, *Pisarev*, 20.

25. Elizavetina, *Pisarev—kritik: Nachalo puti*, 95.

26. Pisarev, "Minuty uedinennykh razmyshlenii Khristianina," 1:86. In this review, he mentions Zschokke's *Religious Meditations*, comparing the work under review to it. See also Pisarev, "O podrazhanii Khristu," 1:158.

27. Pisarev, "Byt' i kazat'sia" and "O vospitanii devochek," 1:240, 1:258.

28. Pisarev, "Dvorianskoe gnezdo," 1:314.

29. Pisarev, "O vospitanii devochek," 1:258.

30. Pisarev, "Dvorianskoe gnezdo," 1:313–16.

31. In early 1861, when he was still fishing around for a permanent position at a journal, he applied to the liberal journal *Russian Speech* (*Russkaia rech'*) and to the Orthodox-Christian *Wanderer* (*Strannik*). See Elizavetina, *Pisarev—kritik: Ispytanie estetikoi*, 14–17.

32. Some historians have argued that Pisarev became a radical under Blagosvetlov's influence. See, e.g., Plotkin, *Pisarev i literaturno-obshchestvennoe dvizhenie shestidesiatykh godov*, 172–86. On journalists' reflections on the changing place of *raznochintsy* in the literary sphere, see Wirtschafter, *Structures of Society*, 106–7.

33. He could not say so explicitly, but his meaning is clear: "Thus, a life force, as something independent, indivisible, does not exist" (Pisarev, "Protsess zhizni," 3:180).

34. Pisarev, "Fiziologicheskie kartiny," 4:71–72. This 1862 article is a review of Ludwig Büchner's *Physiologische Bilder*. Pisarev's comments on primitive religion (specifically, on sun worship) take their point of departure from Büchner, *Physiologische Bilder*, 1:127. The remarks on primitive religion here are Pisarev's; they are not in Büchner's book.

35. Pisarev, "Apollonii Tianskii," 3:53–54.

36. "The broader and deeper our knowledge becomes, the more fully and utterly it will disperse those awkward phantoms of Ormuzd and Ahriman, which once frightened the trusting childhoods of individuals and entire nations" (Pisarev, "'Fiziologicheskie eskizy' Moleshotta," 3:174). Dobroliubov had made a very similar statement in 1859 in the *Contemporary* ("Svatovstvo Chenskogo," 2:498–99).

37. Pisarev, "Idealizm Platona," 2:242; "Apollonii Tianskii," 3:104.

38. Pisarev, "Apollonii Tianskii," 3:104–5.

39. Pisarev, "Idealizm Platona," 2:241–42.

40. Pisarev, "Skholastika XIX veka," 2:270.

41. "Healthy faith in reality is replaced by faith in the existence and unattainable perfection of an invisible, spectral world beyond the clouds, [a world] of fantasy, which develops to the point of hallucination" ("Idealizm Platona," 2:242).

42. Pisarev, "Zhenskie tipy v romanakh i povestiakh Pisemskogo, Turgeneva i Goncharova," 3:380.

43. Pisarev, "Idealizm Platona," 2:234; "Skholastika XIX veka," 2:270.

44. Pisarev, "Zhenskie tipy v romanakh i povestiakh Pisemskogo, Turgeneva i Goncharova," 3:380.

45. Pisarev, "Skholastika XIX veka," 2:270.

46. Pisarev, "Idealizm Platona," 2:235.

47. Although the word "religion" does not appear in this sentence, it does in the preceding passage (Pisarev, "Skholastika," 2:270).

48. Pisarev is speculating about the inner world of Ivan Kireevsky here ("Russkii Don Kikhot," 4:96).

49. "Believers tossed from side to side, strained themselves to a breaking point and never found satisfaction anywhere" (Pisarev, "Apollonii Tianskii," 3: 52); "The majority did not believe, and doubted, and was afraid to doubt [. . .] and yet [these people] could not resolve to discard a single, foolish ritual as superstition" (ibid., 78).

50. Pisarev, "Idealizm Platona," 2:248.

51. Pisarev, "Skholastika XIX veka," 2:269, 282, 284. On 273, he makes it clear that he rejects philosophical skepticism with respect to the reliability of processes of perception and cognition in furnishing accurate information about the surrounding world. Instead, he claims that "skepticism" means accepting as true only those observations that accord with one's sensory impressions. See also "Apollonii Tianskii," 3:52, where he associates skepticism with rejection of everything that cannot be "tangibly proven," including faith in the afterlife.

52. Pisarev, "Bazarov," 4:175.

53. Pisarev, "Bednaia russkaia mysl'," 4:227.

54. Pisarev, "Russkii Don Kikhot," 4:98. See also "Apollonii Tianskii," 3:78, where he notes that many people are "too cowardly" for this way of life.

55. Pisarev, "Idealizm Platona," 2:237.

56. Ibid., 238–39.

57. Pisarev, "Skholastika XIX veka," 2:270.

58. Ibid., 255.

59. Pisarev, "Bazarov," 4:166–68.

60. Ibid., 167, 175. Pisarev would repeat that it is a grave mistake to base one's self-worth on worldly success. In an 1864 piece, he wrote that a person who "evaluates himself only according to the outward success of his under-takings [. . .] changes in his own eyes, just as the rate of exchange of a stock of dubious value will fluctuate on the market" (Pisarev, "Motivy russkoi dramy," 5:372–73).

61. According to Polevoi, Pisarev had annoyed his friends in 1860 by arguing that "everything that is natural is moral" (*Chto vse, chto estestvenno, to i nravstvenno*) ("Vospominaniia").

62. Pisarev, "Skholastika XIX veka," 2:271. See also Pisarev, "Posmertnye stikhotvoreniia Geine," 3:281.

63. Pisarev, "Skholastika XIX veka," 2:269.

64. Pozefsky, *The Nihilist Imagination*, 15. Pozefsky also refers here to the assessment of Ivanov-Razumnik and Armand Coquart.

65. Ginzburg, *O psikhologicheskoi proze*, 246.

66. As he explains in "Realists" (1864), one of his most important articles of the prison period, people are suggestible. Feelings that seem spontaneous are often only internalized cultural norms. For example, many young women claimed to adore men in uniform: "They hotly substantiated their position by referring to the voice of unmediated feeling, and they were prepared to swear that this was just how nature made them, that they could neither feel nor think any other way." Pisarev was certain that the preference for men in uniform was

unnatural ("Realisty," 6:275). Pisarev also addresses society's deformation of personal preference through contemporary child-rearing practices, in "Motivy russkoi dramy," 5:371.

67. Pisarev, "Skholastika XIX veka," 2:270.

68. Pisarev, "Oblomov," 1:295. See also Pisarev, "'Bratets,'" 1:49. In "'Bratets'" ("'Brother Dearest'" [1859]), he praises the heroine of Nadezhda D. Khvoshchin-skaia's novel, because she "unwillingly harbored all of her strengths inside herself, withdrew inside herself, concentrated, and ceased to speak her mind. Happy are those, whose characters are capable of concentrating in this way, who have something to withdraw into." See also Pisarev, "Apollonii Tianskii," 3:133: "Apollonius felt not the slightest need to share his thoughts and hopes with anyone at all."

69. Pisarev, "Bazarov," 4:168–69. He qualifies this statement slightly by explaining that this was because no one he knew was worth taking seriously (184). See also Pisarev, "Realisty," 6:263.

70. Pisarev, "Posmotrim!" 8:55.

71. Pisarev, "Genrikh Geine," 9:407.

72. Elizavetina, *Pisarev—kritik: Posle "Russkogo slova,"* 177.

73. Koreneva to Pisareva, Feb. 17, 1862, in "Pis'ma D. I. Pisareva i o Pisareve," 40–41. Pisarev's love of cards had indeed gotten out of control at this point. By the summer of 1862, his gambling debts had mounted to three thousand rubles (Shcherbakov, "Universitetskii dnevnik Pisareva," 193).

74. Koreneva's situation at this point was precarious. In 1861 Pisarev's uncle, Andrei Danilov published a roman à clef, *Svezhye sily*, about the Pisarevs' family life at Grunets, which appeared in the journal *Razvlechenie* in 1861. In it, Danilov not only heavily criticized Pisarev's mother, but described his erotic feelings for Koreneva. In two poems, published in *Razvlechenie* that year, he graphically described their relationship as sexual. These assertions were certainly slanderous. It is unclear whether they were true, and it is not known how Pisarev, who wished to marry his cousin, responded to them.

75. Korotkov, *Pisarev*, 160–61.

76. Titled "Shedo-Ferroti's Stupid Little Book" (1862), the tract was more of an expression of exasperation than a call to arms. Alexander Herzen had complained about receiving an anonymous death threat, which he thought was written by an agent of the imperial government. Shedo-Ferroti, a conservative, had responded with an indictment of Herzen, claiming that he was a traitor and deserved little better. Pisarev attacked Shedo-Ferroti, arguing that the imperial state's administrators had forfeited any right to loyalty because of their ineptitude, stupidity, and utter lack of moral standards. To any "honest person," support for revolution was a foregone conclusion (Pisarev, "Glupaia knizhonka Shedo-Ferroti," 4:270–75).

77. This was only possible with prisoners whose cells were directly adjacent, and Pisarev did not always have neighbors (Korotkov, *Pisarev*, 247).

78. Pisarev to Pisareva, Jan. 17, 1865, in Solov'ev, *Pisarev*, 99.

79. Pisarev, "Motivy russkoi dramy," 5:374.

80. Ibid., 5:373; Pisarev, "Novyi tip," 8:221–22, 218.

81. Pisarev, "Motivy russkoi dramy," 5:385.

82. Pisarev, "Promakhi nezreloi mysli" and "Tsvety nevinnogo iumora," 6: 440–41, 5:355.

83. Pisarev, "Promakhi nezreloi mysli," 6:449, 462.

84. Ibid., 441; "Tsvety nevinnogo iumora," 5:356.

85. Pisarev, "Istoricheskoe razvitie evropeiskoi mysli," 6:386. Pisarev couched this remark amid reflection on the suppression of science by the medieval Catholic church.

86. Pisarev, "Istoricheskie idei Ogiusta Konta," 8:142–43.

87. Pisarev, "Posmotrim!" 8:21, 40–41, 61–65; Pisarev, "Pushkin i Belinskii: Evgenii Onegin," 7:216.

88. Pisarev, "Obrazovannaia tolpa," 9:38. One should note that Pisarev urges readers to be selective about their actions. The yearning to "wear a crown of thorns," that is, to sacrifice oneself only for the sake of becoming a martyr, he says, is rather childish ("Obrazovannaia tolpa," 9:60).

89. Pisarev, "Genrikh Geine," 9:432. Pisarev makes these comments in connection with pointing out Heinrich Heine's dislike of German "radicals" of the 1830s.

90. Pisarev, "Novyi tip," 8:222, 239, 241; Pisarev, "Roman kiseinoi devushki," 7:11–12. In "The New Type," 8:241, he remarks that "the future will become the present precisely at that moment when ordinary people will truly begin to feel like human beings and will truly begin to respect their human dignity."

91. "It would appear that the disjuncture between dream and reality is in no way harmful, if, that is, the dreaming person seriously believes in his dream, looks attentively at life, compares his observations with his castles in the sand, and is generally conscientious about working to make his fantasy come true. When there is some kind of a contact between the dream and life, then everything is geared for success" (Pisarev, "Promakhi nezreloi mysli," 6:438).

92. Pisarev, "Istoricheskie idei Ogiusta Konta," 8:82–83.

93. Ibid., 8:73–74, 204.

94. See Volodin, "Raskol'nikov i Karakozov." The review was interpreted as signaling a turn away from violence by Kirpotin, *Radikal'nyi raznochinets D. I. Pisarev*, 375–81. Here, Kirpotin enters into a polemic against the Soviet historian, Boris P. Koz'min, asserting that Pisarev went so far as to reject the radical cause as such. Other Soviet historians insisted that Pisarev's late works did not represent a rightward shift. See, for example, Kazanovich, "D. I. Pisarev posle kreposti," 626–27.

95. In February 1866 the *Contemporary* published a review by Grigorii Z. Eliseev of the first installment, attacking the novel as a caricature of the radical movement. Eliseev appears to have viewed Raskolnikov as a latter-day Bazarov. See Elizavetina, *Pisarev—kritik: Posle "Russkogo slova,"* 57.

96. Verhoeven, *The Odd Man Karakozov*, 86.

97. Pisarev, "Bor'ba za zhizn'," 9:148.

98. Ibid., 9:145–46.

99. Pisarev, "Geinrikh Geine," 9:419, 430, 432.

100. Pisarev to Turgenev, May 18, 1867, in Turgenev, "Perepiska s D. I. Pisarevym," 215–17.

101. Coquart, *Dmitri Pisarev et l'idéologie du nihilisme Russe*, 377–78.

102. Pisarev, "Staroe barstvo," 10:87, 89.
103. Ibid., 10:97.
104. Ibid., 10:96.
105. Pisarev, "Romany Andre Leo," 10:22.
106. Pisarev, "Bor'ba za zhizn'," 9:156–57.
107. Pisarev to Markovich, Nov. 30, [1867], Dec. 3, [1867], Dec. 4, [1867], in "Pis'ma D. I. Pisareva k M. A. Markovich," 155, 158, 159.
108. The most complete description of Pisarev's death comes from Coquart, who also fully discusses the rumors of suicide that circulated among Pisarev's friends. Coquart is inclined to think that Pisarev took his life (*Dmitri Pisarev*, 380–83). Other biographers, including Kazanovich and Korotkov, insist that his death was an accident.
109. See the poem by Nekrasov, "Ne rydai tak bezumno nad nim."
110. Herzen, "Eshche raz Bazarov," 20.1.346, 348, 350.
111. Pisarev, "Genrikh Geine," 9:391.

Conclusion

1. Panteleev, *Vospominaniia*, 164.
2. Herzen, *Byloe i dumy*, 9:27.
3. Herzen, *Byloe i dumy*, 9:32.
4. In this conversation, Bezukhov convinces Bolkonsky that there is a God and that the soul is immortal, not through "proofs" (which Bolkonsky rejects) but by helping Bolkonsky recognize that he already believes in both and that he believes in them on the basis of personal experience (Tolstoi, *Voina i mir*, 5:119).
5. Dostoevskii, *Brat'ia Karamazovy*, 14:224.
6. Chadwick, *The Secularization of the European Mind in the Nineteenth Century*, 244.
7. Ibid., 248.
8. Dostoevskii, *Zapiski iz podpol'ia*, 5:103–4.
9. Qtd. in Perrie, *The Agrarian Policy of the Russian Socialist-Revolutionary Party*, 19.
10. Van den Bercken, *Ideology and Atheism in the Soviet Union*, 74.
11. Thrower, *Marxist-Leninist "Scientific Atheism" and the Study of Religion and Atheism in the USSR*, 89–124, 305–6; Bociurkiw, "Lenin and Religion," 110–11; McLellan, *Marxism and Religion*, 91.
12. Here, I contradict William Husband's assertion that atheism occupied a relatively unimportant place in the priorities of the intelligentsia and among the early Bolsheviks. "Antireligiosity and anti-clericalism became common among the radical intelligentsia as the twentieth century approached, but no significant broad and sustained effort to promote atheism as an independent goal took shape. In this environment, the Bolshevik position on atheism developed only gradually and without special urgency" (*"Godless Communists,"* 34).
13. Berdiaev, *The Origin of Russian Communism*, 145, 158, 168–69, 187.

Bibliography

Archives

Gosudarstvennyi arkhiv Rossiiskoi Federatsii, Moscow (GARF)
    Documents of the Third Section: f. 109, 1 esksp.
    Documents of the Investigative Committee on the Spread of Revolutionary
        Propaganda: f. 95.
Rossiiskaia gosudarstvennaia biblioteka, Otdel rukopisei, Moscow (RGB)
    Papers of Mikhail P. Pogodin: f. 231.
    Papers of Nikolai Kh. Ketcher: f. 476.
    Papers of Timofei N. Granovskii: f. 84.
Rossiiskii gosudarstvennyi istoricheskii arkhiv, St. Petersburg (RGIA)
    Chancellery of the Synod: f. 796.
    Chancellery of the Overprocurator of the Synod: f. 797.
    Chancellery of the Ministry of Internal Affairs: f. 1282.
    Chancellery of the Ministry of Justice: f. 1405.
Rossiiskii gosudarstvennyi voenno-istoricheskii arkhiv, Moscow (RGVIA)
    Butashevich-Petrashevskii investigation and trial documents: f. 801, opis'
        84/28, delo 55.
Rossiiskaia natsional'naia biblioteka, Otdel rukopisei, St. Petersburg (RNB)
    Papers of Vladimir F. Odoevskii: f. 539.

Primary Sources

Akt dvadtsatipiatiletnego iubileia Glavnogo pedagogicheskogo instituta. St. Petersburg:
    Akademiia nauk, 1853.
Anastasii [Bratanovskii]. "Slovo v nedeliu Fomy." In *Pouchitel'nye slova pri
    vysochaishem dvore i v drugikh mestakh s 1792 goda po 1796 god skazyvannyia*, 4:
    31–38. 4 vols. Moscow: Sinodal'naia tipografiia, 1814.
Annenkov, Pavel V. *The Extraordinary Decade*. Translated by Irwin R. Titunik.
    Ann Arbor: University of Michigan Press, 1968.

———. "Literaturnyi tip slabogo cheloveka." In *Vospominaniia i kriticheskie ocherki: Sobranie statei i zametok*, 2:149–72. 3 vols. St. Petersburg: Stasiulevich, 1877–79.

Barruel, Augustin. *Volteriantsy, ili istoriia o Iakobintsakh, otkryvaiushchaia vse protivu Khristianskie zloumyshleniia i tainstva masonskikh lozh, imeiushchikh vliianie na vse Evropeiskie derzhavy*. 12 vols. Translated by Petr Domogatskii. Moscow: Reshetnikov, 1805–9.

Belinskii, Vissarion G. "Mentsel', kritik Gete." In *Polnoe sobranie sochinenii*, 3: 385–419. 13 vols. Moscow: Akademiia nauk, 1953–59.

———. "Pis'mo k N. V. Gogoliu, 15 iiulia n.s. 1847." In *Polnoe sobranie sochinenii*, 10:212–20. 13 vols. Moscow: Akademiia nauk, 1953–59.

———. *Polnoe sobranie sochinenii*. 13 vols. Moscow: Akademiia nauk, 1953–59.

———. "Russkaia literatura v 1840 godu." In *Polnoe sobranie sochinenii*, 4:408–47. 13 vols. Moscow: Akademiia nauk, 1953–59.

———. "Russkaia literatura v 1841 godu." In *Polnoe sobranie sochinenii*, 5:521–88. 13 vols. Moscow: Akademiia nauk, 1953–59.

"B'iu chelom narodu pravoslavnomu." In *Russko-pol'skie revoliutsionnye sviazi*, 3.2.284–87. 3 vols. Moscow: Akademiia nauk, 1961–63.

Biriukov, Arkadii. "Universitet i studenty v nachale 60-kh godov." *Uchenye zapiski Kazanskogo gosudarstvennogo universiteta* 90, no. 5 (1930): 861–78.

———. "Sdelannye vypiski." In *Russko-pol'skie revoliutsionnye sviazi*, 3.2.308. 3 vols. Moscow: Akademiia nauk, 1961–63.

Botkin, Vasilii P. *Literaturnaia kritika, publitsistika, pis'ma*. Moscow: Sovetskaia Rossiia, 1984.

———. "Pis'ma k M. A. Bakuninu." In *Ezhegodnik rukopisnogo otdela pushkinskogo doma na 1978 god*, 88–128. Leningrad: Nauka, 1980.

Breshko-Breshkovskaia, Ekaterina. *Iz moikh vospominanii*. St. Petersburg: Raspopov, 1906.

Büchner, Ludwig. *Kraft und Stoff: Empirisch-naturphilosophische Studien*. Frankfurt am Main: Meidinger, 1855.

———. *Last Words on Materialism*. Translated by Joseph McCabe. London: Rationalist Press Association, 1901.

———. *Physiologische Bilder*. 2 vols. Leipzig: Thomas, 1861–75.

Bulgarin, Faddei V. *Ivan Vyzhigin*. Vol. 1 of *Polnoe sobranie sochinenii*. 5 vols. St. Petersburg: Grech, 1839–44.

Butashevich-Petrashevskii, Mikhail V. "Chernovik pis'ma K. I. Timkovskomu." In *Delo petrashevtsev*, edited by Vasilii A. Desnitskii, 1:523–40. 3 vols. Moscow: Akademiia nauk, 1937–51.

———. "Zapas obshchepoleznogo." In *Delo petrashevtsev*, edited by Vasilii A. Desnitskii, 1:552–58. 3 vols. Moscow: Akademiia nauk, 1937–51.

———. "O znachenii cheloveka v otnoshenii k chelovechestvu." In *Delo petrashevtsev*, edited by Vasilii A. Desnitskii, 1:550–51. 3 vols. Moscow: Akademiia nauk, 1937–51.

Chaadaev, Petr Ia. "Lettres philosophiques adressées à une dame: Lettre première." In *Polnoe sobranie sochinenii i izbrannye pis'ma*, 1:86–106. 2 vols. Moscow: Nauka, 1991.

Chernyshevskii, Nikolai. G. "Antropologicheskii printsip v filosofii." In *Polnoe sobranie sochinenii*, edited by Valerii Ia. Kirpotin et al., 7:222–95. 16 vols. Moscow: Gosudarstvennoe izdatel'stvo khudozhestvennoi literatury, 1939–53.

———. *Chto delat'? Iz rasskazov o novykh liudiakh.* Edited by Tamara I. Ornatskaia and Solomon A. Reiser. Leningrad: Nauka, 1975.

———. "Dnevniki" [Diary]. In *Polnoe sobranie sochinenii*, edited by Valerii Ia. Kirpotin et al., 1:29–563. 16 vols. Moscow: Gosudarstvennoe izdatel'stvo khudozhestvennoi literatury, 1939–53.

———. "Esteticheskie otnosheniia iskusstva k deistvitel'nosti." In *Polnoe sobranie sochinenii*, edited by Valerii Ia. Kirpotin et al., 2:5–92. 16 vols. Moscow: Gosudarstvennoe izdatel'stvo khudozhestvennoi literatury, 1939–53.

———. "Etiudy: Populiarnye chteniia Shleidena." In *Polnoe sobranie sochinenii*, edited by Valerii Ia. Kirpotin et al., 10:480–85. 16 vols. Moscow: Gosudarstvennoe izdatel'stvo khudozhestvennoi literatury, 1939–53.

———. "Lessing, ego vremia, ego zhizn' i deiatel'nost'." In *Polnoe sobranie sochinenii*, edited by Valerii Ia. Kirpotin et al., 4:5–221. 16 vols. Moscow: Gosudarstvennoe izdatel'stvo khudozhestvennoi literatury, 1939–53.

———, ed. *Materialy dlia biografii N. A. Dobroliubova.* Moscow: Soldatenkov, 1890.

———. *Ocherki gogolevskogo perioda russkoi literatury.* In *Polnoe sobranie sochinenii*, edited by Valerii Ia. Kirpotin et al., 3:5–309. 16 vols. Moscow: Gosudarstvennoe izdatel'stvo khudozhestvennoi literatury, 1939–53.

———. "Polemicheskie krasoty." In *Polnoe sobranie sochinenii*, edited by Valerii Ia. Kirpotin et al., 7:707–74. 16 vols. Moscow: Gosudarstvennoe izdatel'stvo khudozhestvennoi literatury, 1939–53.

———. *Polnoe sobranie sochinenii.* 16 vols. Edited by Valerii Ia. Kirpotin et al. Moscow: Gosudarstvennoe izdatel'stvo khudozhestvennoi literatury, 1939–53.

———. "Russkii chelovek na rendez-vous." In *Polnoe sobranie sochinenii*, edited by Valerii Ia. Kirpotin et al., 5:156–74. 16 vols. Moscow: Gosudarstvennoe izdatel'stvo khudozhestvennoi literatury, 1939–53.

———. "Stikhotvoreniia N. Ogareva." In *Polnoe sobranie sochinenii*, edited by Valerii Ia. Kirpotin et al., 3:561–68. 16 vols. Moscow: Gosudarstvennoe izdatel'stvo khudozhestvennoi literatury, 1939–53.

———. "Sochineniia i pis'ma N. V. Gogolia." In *Polnoe sobranie sochinenii*, edited by Valerii Ia. Kirpotin et al., 4:626–65. 16 vols. Moscow: Gosudarstvennoe izdatel'stvo khudozhestvennoi literatury, 1939–53.

———. "Sochineniia Pushkina." In *Polnoe sobranie sochinenii*, edited by Valerii Ia. Kirpotin et al., 2:424–516. 16 vols. Moscow: Gosudarstvennoe izdatel'stvo khudozhestvennoi literatury, 1939–53.

———. "Sochineniia T. N. Granovskogo." In *Polnoe sobranie sochinenii*, edited by Valerii Ia. Kirpotin et al., 3:346–68. 16 vols. Moscow: Gosudarstvennoe izdatel'stvo khudozhestvennoi literatury, 1939–53.

Davydov, Ivan I. "Aforizmy iz nravstvennogo liubomudriia." *Vestnik Evropy*, nos. 11–12 (1822): 201–32.

Delo petrashevtsev [*DP*]. 3 vols. Edited by Vasilii A. Desnitskii. Moscow: Akademiia nauk, 1937–51.

Danilov, Andrei D. "Neskol'ko otryvochnykh vospominanii o D. I. Pisareve." *Literaturnyi arkhiv: Materialy po istorii literatury i obshchestvennogo dvizheniia* 3 (1951): 48–67.

Dobroliubov, Nikolai A. "Aleksandr Sergeevich Pushkin." In *Polnoe sobranie sochinenii*, edited by Pavel I. Lebedev-Polianskii, 1:107–18. 6 vols. Moscow: Gosudarstvennoe izdatel'stvo khudozhestvennoi literatury, 1934–41.

———. "Blagodetel'." In *Polnoe sobranie stikhotvorenii*, edited by Boris Ia. Bukhshtab, 76–77. Leningrad: Sovetskii pisatel', 1969.

———. "Buddizm, rassmatrivaemyi v otnoshenii k posledovateliam ego, obitaiushchim v Sibiri." In *Polnoe sobranie sochinenii*, edited by Pavel I. Lebedev-Polianskii, 3:412–23. 6 vols. Moscow: Gosudarstvennoe izdatel'stvo khudozhestvennoi literatury, 1934–41.

———. "Chto takoe oblomovshchina?" In *Polnoe sobranie sochinenii*, edited by Pavel I. Lebedev-Polianskii, 2:5–35. 6 vols. Moscow: Gosudarstvennoe izdatel'stvo khudozhestvennoi literatury, 1934–41.

———. "Dnevniki" [Diary]. In *Sobranie sochinenii*, 8:413–570. 9 vols. Leningrad: Gosudarstvennoe izdatel'stvo khudozhestvennoi literatury, 1961–64.

———. "Dobroliubov—perevodchik Feierbakha." Edited by Solomon Reiser. *Literaturnoe nasledstvo* 25–26 (1936): 243–45.

———. "Kogda zhe pridet nastoiashchii den'?" In *Polnoe sobranie sochinenii*, edited by Pavel I. Lebedev-Polianskii, 2:206–40. 6 vols. Moscow: Gosudarstvennoe izdatel'stvo khudozhestvennoi literatury, 1934–41.

———. "Luch sveta v temnom tsarstve." In *Polnoe sobranie sochinenii*, edited by Pavel I. Lebedev-Polianskii, 2:310–66. 6 vols. Moscow: Gosudarstvennoe izdatel'stvo khudozhestvennoi literatury, 1934–41.

———. "Organicheskoe razvitie cheloveka v sviazi s ego umstvennoi i nravstvennoi deiatel'nost'iu." In *Polnoe sobranie sochinenii*, edited by Pavel I. Lebedev-Polianskii, 3:90–113. 6 vols. Moscow: Gosudarstvennoe izdatel'stvo khudozhestvennoi literatury, 1934–41.

———. "Pamiati ottsa." In *Polnoe sobranie stikhotvorenii*, edited by Boris Ia. Bukhshtab, 93–94. Leningrad: Sovetskii pisatel', 1969.

———. *Polnoe sobranie sochinenii*. 6 vols. Edited by Pavel I. Lebedev-Polianskii. Moscow: Gosudarstvennoe izdatel'stvo khudozhestvennoi literatury, 1934–41.

———. *Polnoe sobranie stikhotvorenii*. Edited by Boris Ia. Bukhshtab. Leningrad: Sovetskii pisatel', 1969.

———. "Sobesednik liubitelei rossiiskogo slova." In *Polnoe sobranie sochinenii*, edited by Pavel I. Lebedev-Polianskii, 1:29–100. 6 vols. Moscow: Gosudarstvennoe izdatel'stvo khudozhestvennoi literatury, 1934–41.

———. *Sobranie sochinenii*. 9 vols. Leningrad: Gosudarstvennoe izdatel'stvo khudozhestvennoi literatury, 1961–64.

———. "Svatovstvo Chenskogo ili materialism i idealism; O neizbezhnosti idealizma v materializme Iu. Savicha." In *Polnoe sobranie sochenenii*, edited by Pavel I. Lebedev-Polianskii, 2:498–507. 6 vols. Moscow: Gosudarstvennoe izdatel'stvo khudozhestvennoi literatury, 1934–41.

———. "Vzgliad na istoriiu i sovremennoe sostoianie Ost-Indii." In *Polnoe sobranie sochinenii*, edited by Pavel I. Lebedev-Polianskii, 3:30–61. 6 vols. Moscow: Gosudarstvennoe izdatel'stvo khudozhestvennoi literatury, 1934–41.

———. "Zabitye liudi." In *Polnoe sobranie sochinenii*, edited by Pavel I. Lebedev-Polianskii, 2:367–405. 6 vols. Moscow: Gosudarstvennoe izdatel'stvo khudozhestvennoi literatury, 1934–41.

———. "Zhizn' Magometa," in *Polnoe sobranie sochenenii*, edited by Pavel I. Lebedev-Polianskii, 3:334–39. 6 vols. Moscow: Gosudarstvennoe izdatel'stvo khudozhestvennoi literatury, 1934–41.

"Dolgo davili vas, brattsy." In *Russko-pol'skie revoliutsionnye sviazi*, 3.2.297–99. 3 vols. Moscow: Akademiia nauk, 1961–63.

Dostoevskii, Fedor. M. *Besy*. Vol. 10 of *Polnoe sobranie sochinenii*. 30 vols. Edited by Viktor G. Bazanov. Leningrad: Nauka, 1972–90.

———. *Brat'ia Karamazovy*. Vols. 14–15 of *Polnoe sobranie sochinenii*. 30 vols. Edited by Viktor G. Bazanov. Leningrad: Nauka, 1972–90.

———. *Polnoe sobranie sochinenii*. 30 vols. Edited by Viktor G. Bazanov. Leningrad: Nauka, 1972–90.

———. *Zapiski iz mertvogo doma*. Vol. 4 of *Polnoe sobranie sochinenii*. 30 vols. Edited by Viktor G. Bazanov. Leningrad: Nauka, 1972–90.

———. "Zapiski iz podpol'ia." In *Polnoe sobranie sochinenii*, edited by Viktor G. Bazanov, 5:99–179. 30 vols. Leningrad: Nauka, 1972–90.

[Elpidin, Mikhail K.]. "Kazanskii zagovor. (1863–1865)." In *Materialy dlia istorii revoliutsionnogo dvizheniia v Rossii v 60-kh gg: Pervoe prilozhenie k sbornikam*, edited by B. Bazilevskii [Vasilii Bogucharskii], 134–47. St. Petersburg: Russkaia skoropechatnia, [1905].

[Engelson, Vladimir A.]. "Videniia sv. Ottsa Kondratiia." In *Desiatiletie vol'noi russkoi tipografii v Londone*, edited by Liudvig Chernetskii, 53–68. Leningrad: Akademiia nauk, 1935.

Evgenii [Bolkhovitinov]. "Slovo 7. v nedeliu sv. Apostola Fomy." In *Sobranie pouchitel'nykh slov, v raznyia vremena i v raznykh eparkhiiakh propovedannykh*, 1: 46–56. 4 vols. Kiev: Kievopecherskaia lavra, 1834.

———. "Slovo 8. v tuiuzhde nedeliu sv. Apostola Fomy." In *Sobranie pouchitel'nykh slov, v raznyia vremena i v raznykh eparkhiiakh propovedannykh*, 1:57–65. 4 vols. Kiev: Kievopecherskaia lavra, 1834.

———. "Slovo 23. v nedeliu 7. po piatdesiatnitse." In *Sobranie pouchitel'nykh slov, v raznyia vremena i v raznykh eparkhiiakh propovedannykh*, 1:203–13. 4 vols. Kiev: Kievopecherskaia lavra, 1834.

———. *Sobranie pouchitel'nykh slov, v raznyia vremena i v raznykh eparkhiiakh propovedannykh*. 4 vols. Kiev: Kievopecherskaia lavra, 1834.

Feofan [Govorov]. *Pis'ma k raznym litsam*. Moscow: Blagovest, 2001.

Feuerbach, Friedrich. "Chelovek ili Khristos? Byt' ili ne byt'? Religiia budushchnosti." In *Petrashevtsy ob ateizme, religii i tserkvi*, edited by Vera R. Leikina-Svirskaia and Faina G. Nikitina, 188–98. Moscow: Mysl', 1986.

———. *Die Religion der Zukunft*. 3 vols. Zürich: Verlag des literarischen Comptoirs, 1843–45.

Feuerbach, Ludwig. *Das Wesen des Christenthhums*. Vol. 6 of *Sämtliche Werke*. 2nd ed. 13 vols. Edited by Wilhelm Bolin and Friedrich Jodl. Stuttgart: Frommann, 1959–64.

———. *Sämtliche Werke*. 2nd ed. 13 vols. Edited by Wilhelm Bolin and Friedrich Jodl. Stuttgart: Frommann, 1959–64.

————. *Vorlesungen über das Wesen der Religion.* Vol. 8 of *Sämtliche Werke.* 2nd ed. 13 vols. Edited by Wilhelm Bolin and Friedrich Jodl. Stuttgart: Frommann, 1959-64.

————."Vorrede zur zweiten Auflage vom 'Wesen des Christenthums.'" In *Sämtliche Werke*, edited by Wilhelm Bolin and Friedrich Jodl, 7:275-94. 2nd ed. 13 vols. Stuttgart: Frommann, 1959-64.

————. *Sushchnost' khristianstva.* Translated by Iakov Khanykov. London: Trübner, 1861.

Filaret [Drozdov]. "Beseda iz pritchi o plevelakh." In *Sochineniia*, 2:234-40. 5 vols. Moscow: Mamontov, 1873-85.

————. "Beseda o novom rozhdenii svyshe." In *Sochineniia*, 4:345-51. 5 vols. Moscow: Mamontov, 1873-85.

————. "Rech' Blagochestiveishemu Gosudariu Imperatoru Nikolaiu Pavlovichu, pred vstupleniem Ego Velichestva v Uspenskii sobor." In *Sochineniia*, 3:49-50. 5 vols. Moscow: Mamontov, 1873-85.

————. "Slovo v den' Blagoveshcheniia Presviatyia Bogoroditsy." In *Sochineniia*, 2:64-70. 5 vols. Moscow: Mamontov, 1873-85.

————. "Slovo v den' sobora sviatago arkhistratiga Mikhaila." In *Sochineniia*, 2: 24-30. 5 vols. Moscow: Mamontov, 1873-85.

————. "Slovo v den' vosshestviia na Vserossiiskii Prestol Blagochestiveishogo Gosudaria Imperatora Nikolaia Pavlovicha." In *Sochineniia*, 4:576-81. 5 vols. Moscow: Mamontov, 1873-85.

————. *Sochineniia.* 5 vols. Moscow: Mamontov, 1873-85.

Filaret [Gumilevskii]. *Obzor russkoi dukhovnoi literatury: Knigi pervaya i vtoraia, 1862-1863.* 3rd ed. St. Petersburg: Tuzov, 1884.

————. *Pravoslavno-dogmaticheskoe bogoslovie.* 3rd ed. 2 vols. St. Petersburg: Tuzov, 1882.

Filippov, Pavel. "Desiat' zapovedei." In *Filosofskie i obshchestvenno-politicheskie proizvedeniia petrashevtsev*, edited by Vasilii E. Evgrafov, 637-42. Moscow: Gosudarstvennoe izdatel'stvo politicheskoi literatury, 1953.

Georgii [Konisskii]. "Slovo v den' novoletiia." In *Sobranie sochinenii*, 1:45-53. 2 vols. St. Petersburg: Imperatorskaia akademiia nauk, 1835.

————. "Slovo v den' sv. Apostolov Petra i Pavla." In *Sobranie sochinenii*, 1:224-37. 2 vols. St. Petersburg: Imperatorskaia akademiia nauk, 1835.

————. "Slovo v sviatyi i velikii piatok." In *Sobranie sochinenii*, 1:119-29. 2 vols. St. Petersburg: Imperatorskaia akademiia nauk, 1835.

————. *Sobranie sochinenii.* 2 vols. St. Petersburg: Imperatorskaia akademiia nauk, 1835.

Granovskii, Timofei N. "Pis'ma T. N. Granovskogo V. V. Grigor'evu." In *Shchukinskii sbornik*, 10:81-108. 10 vols. Moscow: Sinodal'naia tipografiia, 1902-12.

————. *T. N. Granovskii i ego perepiska.* 2 vols. Moscow: Mamontov, 1897.

Herzen, Aleksandr I. "12 aprelia 1861." *Kolokol* 4, no. 101 (1861): 847-49.

————. *Byloe i dumy.* Vols. 8-11 of *Sobranie sochinenii.* 30 vols. Edited by Viacheslav P. Volgin et al. Moscow: Akademiia nauk, 1954-65.

————. "Den' byl dushnyi." In *Sobranie sochinenii*, edited by Viacheslav P. Volgin et al., 1:52-55. 30 vols. Moscow: Akademiia nauk, 1954-65.

————. "Du développement des idées révolutionnaires en Russie." In *Sobranie sochinenii*, edited by Viacheslav P. Volgin et al., 7:5–132. 30 vols. Moscow: Akademiia nauk, 1954–65.

———. "Eshche raz Bazarov." In *Sobranie sochinenii*, edited by Viacheslav P. Volgin et al., 20.1:335–50. 30 vols. Moscow: Akademiia nauk, 1954–65.

———. "O meste cheloveka v prirode." In *Sobranie sochinenii*, edited by Viacheslav P. Volgin et al., 1:13–25. 30 vols. Moscow: Akademiia nauk, 1954–65.

———. "Kaprizy i razdum'e: Novye variatsii na starye temy." In *Sobranie sochinenii*, edited by Viacheslav P. Volgin et al., 2:86–102. 30 vols. Moscow: Akademiia nauk, 1954–65.

———. "Pis'ma ob izuchenii prirody." In *Sobranie sochinenii*, edited by Viacheslav P. Volgin et al., 3:89–315. 30 vols. Moscow: Akademiia nauk, 1954–65.

———. *Polnoe sobranie sochinenii*. 22 vols. Edited by Mikhail K. Lemke. Petrograd: Literaturno-izdatel'skii otdel Narkomprosa, 1919–25.

———. "Programma i plan izdaniia zhurnala." In *Sobranie sochinenii*, edited by Viacheslav P. Volgin et al., 1:59–61. 30 vols. Moscow: Akademiia nauk, 1954–65.

———. *Sobranie sochinenii*. 30 vols. Edited by Viacheslav P. Volgin et al. Moscow: Akademiia nauk, 1954–65.

———. *Sochineniia A. I. Gertsena i perepiska s N. A. Zakhar'inoi*. 7 vols. St. Petersburg: Pavlenkov, 1905.

———. "S togo berega." In *Sobranie sochinenii*, edited by Viacheslav P. Volgin et al., 6:7–142. 30 vols. Moscow: Akademiia nauk, 1954–65.

———. "Very Dangerous!!!" In *Sobranie sochinenii*, edited by Viacheslav P. Volgin et al., 14:116–21. 30 vols. Moscow: Akademiia nauk, 1954–65.

Herzen, Natal'ia A. "Dnevnik" [Diary]. In *Russkie propilei: Materialy po istorii russkoi mysli i literatury*, edited by Mikhail O. Gershenzon, 1:233–38. 6 vols. Moscow: Shabashnikovy, 1915–30.

———. "Kopiia predsmertnoi zapiski, napisannoi karandashom." *Russkie zapiski* 3, no. 14 (1939): 118–19.

———. "Pis'ma T. A. Astrakovoi." Edited by I. M. Rudaia and Iu. P. Blagovolina. *Literaturnoe nasledstvo* 99, no. 1 (1997): 577–659.

Ignatii [Brianchaninov]. "K nekotoromu nastoiateliu o liubvi k bratii, umnoi molitve i pokaianii." In *Pis'ma o podvizhnicheskoi zhizni*, 111–17. Paris: Bibliothèque slave de Paris, 1996.

———. "O neuklonnom." In *Pis'ma o podvizhnicheskoi zhizni*, 222–25. Paris: Bibliothèque slave de Paris, 1996.

———. *Pis'ma o podvizhnicheskoi zhizni*. Paris: Bibliothèque slave de Paris, 1996.

———. "Po povodu politicheskikh sobytii v Evrope 1848 g." In *Pis'ma o podvizhnicheskoi zhizni*, 204–5. Paris: Bibliothèque slave de Paris, 1996.

———. "Pouchenie v nedeliu miasopustnuiu: O vtorom prishestvii Khristovom." In *Sobranie sochinenii*, 4:47–53. 8 vols. Moscow: Blagovest, 2001.

———. "Pouchenie vtoroe v dvadtsat' piatuiu nedeliu: O liubvi k blizhnemu." In *Sobranie sochinenii*, 4:320–24. 8 vols. Moscow: Blagovest, 2001.

———. *Prinoshenie sovremennomu monashestvu*. Vol. 5 of *Sobranie sochinenii*. 8 vols. Moscow: Blagovest, 2001.

———. *Sobranie sochinenii*. 8 vols. Moscow: Blagovest, 2001.

"Iz perepiski nedavnikh deiatelei." *Russkaia mysl'* 9, no. 7 (1888): 1–10; 9, no. 9 (1888): 1–16; 9, no. 10 (1888): 1–15; 9, no. 11 (1888): 1–15; 10, no. 1 (1889): 1–16;

10, no. 4 (1889): 1–16; 11, no. 3 (1890): 1–10; 11, no. 8 (1890): 1–18; 11, no. 9 (1890): 1–13; 11, no. 10 (1890): 1–13; 12, no. 8 (1891): 1–25; 13, no. 9 (1892): 1–11.

Kavelin, Konstantin D. "Materialy dlia biografii iz semeinoi perepiski i vospominanii." Edited by Dmitri A. Korsakov. *Vestnik Evropy*, no. 6 (1886): 445–91.

———. *Pis'ma K. D. Kavelina i I. S. Turgeneva k A. I. Gertsenu.* Geneva: Ukrainskaia tipografiia, 1892.

Kashkin, Nikolai. "Rech' o zadachakh obshchestvennykh nauk." In *Filosofskie i obshchestvenno-politicheskie proizvedeniia petrashevtsev*, edited by Vasilii E. Evgrafov, 653–60. Moscow: Gosudarstvennoe izdatel'stvo politicheskoi literatury, 1953.

Kel'siev, Vasilii. *Zerkalo dlia dukhvnogo vnutrennego cheloveka.* In *Sbornik pravitel'stvennykh svedenii o raskol'nikakh*, 1:209–15. 4 vols. London: Trübner, 1860–62.

Khomiakov, Aleksei S. "Molodost'." In *Stikhotvoreniia i dramy*, edited by Boris F. Egorov, 70–71. Leningrad: Sovetskii pisatel', 1969.

———. "Poet." In *Stikhotvoreniia i dramy*, edited by Boris F. Egorov, 73. Leningrad: Sovetskii pisatel', 1969.

———. *Stikhotvoreniia i dramy.* Edited by Boris F. Egorov. Leningrad: Sovetskii pisatel', 1969.

Khomiakova, M. A. "Vospominaniia ob A. S." In Aleksei S. Khomiakov, *A. S. Khomiakov v vospominaniiakh sovremennikov*, 2:52–66. 2 vols. Tula: Peresvet, 2004.

Koshelev, Aleksandr I. "Moi vospominaniia ob A. S. Khomiakove." In *Zapiski Aleksandra Ivanovicha Kosheleva, 1812–1883 gody: S sem'iu prilozheniiami*, edited by Tatiana F. Pirozhkova, 345–54. Moscow: Nauka, 2002.

———. *Zapiski Aleksandra Ivanovicha Kosheleva, 1812–1883 gody: S sem'iu prilozheniiami.* Edited by Tatiana F. Pirozhkova. Moscow: Nauka, 2002.

Kostomarov, Nikolai I. "Avtobiografiia." In *N. G. Chernyshevskii v vospominaniiakh sovremennikov*, edited by Iulian G. Oksman, 1:156–60. 2 vols. Saratov: Saratovskoe knizhnoe izdatel'stvo, 1958.

Krasnoperov, Ivan M. *Zapiski raznochintsa.* Leningrad: Molodaia gvardiia, 1929.

Lakhtin, Aleksei K. "Pis'mo k Ogarevu." *Literaturnoe nasledstvo* 63 (1956): 294–96.

Lermontov, Mikhail Iu. *Geroi nashego vremeni.* In *Sobranie sochinenii*, 4:275–474. 4 vols. Leningrad: Akademiia nauk, 1958–59.

Liprandi, Ivan. "Primechaniia." In *Politicheskie protsessy nikolaevskoi epokhi: Petrashevtsy*, edited by V. M. Sablin, 17–25. Moscow: Sablin, 1907.

Makarii [Mikhail Bulgakov]. *Pravoslavno-dogmaticheskoe bogoslovie.* 5th ed. 2 vols. St. Petersburg: Golike, 1895.

"Manifest 13 iiulia 1826 g." In *Vosstanie dekabristov*: Dokumenty, 17:252–53. 21 vols. Moscow: Gosudarstvennoe izdatel'stvo, 1925–.

[Morigerovskii, Aleksei, and Petr Efimenko]. "Poslanie startsa Kondratiia." In Aleksandr I. Herzen, *Polnoe sobranie sochinenii*, edited by Mikhail K. Lemke, 11:407–29. 22 vols. Petrograd: Literaturno-izdatel'skii otdel Narkomprosa, 1919–25.

Nekrasov, Nikolai. A. "Ne rydai tak bezumno nad nim." In *Polnoe sobranie stikhotvorenii*, 2:273–74. 3 vols. Leningrad: Sovetskii pisatel', 1967.

Obolenskii, V. I. "Pervaia subbota tvoreniia." In *Severnaia lira na 1827 god*, 76–78. Reprint, Moscow: Nauka, 1984.

Odoevskii, Vladimir F. "Eshche dva apologa: 'Novyi demon,' 'Moia upravitel'nitsa.'" *Mnemozina* 4 (1825): 35–48.

———. "Opyt teorii iziashchnykh iskusstv." In *Russkie esteticheskie traktaty pervoi treti XIX veka*, edited by Zakhar A. Kamenskii, 2:156–68. 2 vols. Moscow: Iskusstvo, 1974.

———. "Aforizmy iz razlichnykh pisatelei, po chasti sovremennogo germanskogo liubomudriia." *Mnemozina* 2 (1824): 73–84.

———. "Sekta idealistiko-eleaticheskaia (otryvok iz Slovaria istorii filosofii)." *Mnemozina* 4 (1825): 160–92.

Ogarev, Nikolai P. "Chto nuzhno narodu?" *Kolokol* 4, no. 102 (1861): 853–60.

———. "Crescendo aus der Symphonie meines Ichs im Verhältnisse zu seinen Freunden." In *Izbrannye proizvedeniia*, 1:40–44. 2 vols. Moscow: Gosudarstvennoe izdatel'stvo khudozhestvennoi literatury, 1956.

———. *Izbrannye proizvedeniia*. 2 vols. Moscow: Gosudarstvennoe izdatel'stvo khudozhestvennoi literatury, 1956.

———. *Izbrannye sotsial'no-politicheskie i filosofskie proizvedeniia*. 2 vols. Edited by Mikhail T. Iovchuk and Nikolai G. Tarakanov. Moscow: Gosudarstvennoe izdatel'stvo politicheskoi literatury, 1952–56.

———. *O literature i iskusstve*. Edited by Georgii Krasnov et al. Moscow: Sovremennik, 1988.

———. "Profession de foi." In *Russkie propilei: Materialy po istorii russkoi mysli i literatury*, edited by Mikhail O. Gershenzon, 2:111–42. 6 vols. Moscow: Shabashnikovy, 1915–30.

———. "Razlad." In *Izbrannye proizvedeniia*, 1:97. 2 vols. Moscow: Gosudarstvennoe izdatel'stvo khudozhestvennoi literatury, 1956.

———. "Razorvannost'." In *Izbrannye proizvedeniia*, 1:146. 2 vols. Moscow: Gosudarstvennoe izdatel'stvo khudozhestvennoi literatury, 1956.

———. "[T. N. Granovskomu]." In *Izbrannye proizvedeniia*, 1:177–83. 2 vols. Moscow: Gosudarstvennoe izdatel'stvo khudozhestvennoi literatury, 1956.

———. "Tuman upal na sneg polei." In *Izbrannye proizvedeniia*, 1:143. 2 vols. Moscow: Gosudarstvennoe izdatel'stvo khudozhestvennoi literatury, 1956.

O poslednikh sobytiiakh, imeiushchikh sovershit'sia v kontse mira. 3rd ed. Moscow: Svetliachok, 1994.

"O religii kak osnove istinnogo prosveshcheniia." In *Izbrannye sochineniia i perevody v proze i stikhakh: Trudy blagorodnykh vospitannikov universitetskogo pansiona*, 1:3–15. 3 vols. Moscow: Universitetskaia tipografiia, 1824–25.

Ostrovskii, Aleksandr N. "Groza." In *P'esy*, edited by Aleksandr A. Reviakin, 235–94. Moscow: Sovremennik, 1973.

Panteleev, Longin F. *Vospominaniia*. Moscow: Gosudarstvennoe izdatel'stvo khudozhestvennoi literatury, 1958.

Passek, Tatiana P. *Iz dal'nikh let*. 2 vols. Moscow: Gosudarstvennoe izdatel'stvo khudozhestvennoi literatury, 1963.

Pisarev, Dmitrii. I. "Apollonii Tianskii." In *Polnoe sobranie sochinenii*, 3:7–152. 12 vols. Moscow: Nauka, 2000–.

———. "Bazarov." In *Polnoe sobranie sochinenii*, 4:164–201. 12 vols. Moscow: Nauka, 2000–.

———. "Bednaia russkaia mysl'." In *Polnoe sobranie sochinenii*, 4:202–42. 12 vols. Moscow: Nauka, 2000–.

———."Bor'ba za zhizn'." In *Polnoe sobranie sochinenii*, 9:118–71. 12 vols. Moscow: Nauka, 2000–.

———. "'Bratets'." In *Polnoe sobranie sochinenii*, 1:47–51. 12 vols. Moscow: Nauka, 2000–.

———. "'Byt' i kazat'sia.'" In *Polnoe sobranie sochinenii*, 1:237–42. 12 vols. Moscow: Nauka, 2000–.

———. "'Dvorianskoe gnezdo.'" In *Polnoe sobranie sochinenii*, 1:304–18. 12 vols. Moscow: Nauka, 2000–.

———. "'Fiziologicheskie eskizy' Moleshotta." In *Polnoe sobranie sochinenii*, 3:153–75. 12 vols. Moscow: Nauka, 2000–.

———. "'Fiziologicheskie kartiny' po Biukhneru." In *Polnoe sobranie sochinenii*, 4:51–86. 12 vols. Moscow: Nauka, 2000–.

———. "Genrikh Geine." In *Polnoe sobranie sochinenii*, 9:391–440. 12 vols. Moscow: Nauka, 2000–.

———. "Glupaia knizhonka Shedo-Ferroti." In *Polnoe sobranie sochinenii*, 4:270–75. 12 vols. Moscow: Nauka, 2000–.

———. "Idealizm Platona." In *Polnoe sobranie sochinenii*, 2:230–49. 12 vols. Moscow: Nauka, 2000–.

———. "Istoricheskie idei Ogiusta Konta." In *Polnoe sobranie sochinenii*, 8:71–204. 12 vols. Moscow: Nauka, 2000–.

———. "Istoricheskoe razvitie evropeiskoi mysli." In *Polnoe sobranie sochinenii*, 6:356–427. 12 vols. Moscow: Nauka, 2000–.

———. "Minuty uedinennykh razmyshlenii khristianina." In *Polnoe sobranie sochinenii*, 1:85–89. 12 vols. Moscow: Nauka, 2000–.

———. "Motivy russkoi dramy." In *Polnoe sobranie sochinenii*, 5:359–88. 12 vols. Moscow: Nauka, 2000–.

———. "Iz neopublikovannoi perepiski D. I. Pisareva." Edited by Boris. P. Koz'min. *Literaturnoe nasledstvo* 25–26 (1936): 645–54.

———."Nasha universitetskaia nauka." In *Polnoe sobranie sochinenii*, 5:7–106. 12 vols. Moscow: Nauka, 2000–.

———. "Novyi tip." In *Polnoe sobranie sochinenii*, 8:205–47. 12 vols. Moscow: Nauka, 2000–.

———. "Oblomov." In *Polnoe sobranie sochinenii*, 1:289–301. 12 vols. Moscow: Nauka, 2000–.

———. "Obrazovannaia tolpa." In *Polnoe sobranie sochinenii*, 9:15–70. 12 vols. Moscow: Nauka, 2000–.

———. "O podrazhanii Khristu." In *Polnoe sobranie sochinenii*, 1:156–58. 12 vols. Moscow: Nauka, 2000–.

———. "Pis'ma D. I. Pisareva i o Pisareve." Edited by Boris P. Koz'min. *Zapiski otdela rukopisei: Gosudarstvennaia biblioteka SSSR imeni V. I. Lenina* 9 (1940): 19–50.

———. "Pis'ma D. I. Pisareva k M. A. Markovich." Edited by Evlaliia P. Kazanovich. In *Shestidesiatye gody: Materialy po istorii literatury i obshchestvennomu dvizheniiu*, edited by Nikolai K. Piksanov and Orest V. Tsekhnovitser, 154–72. Leningrad: Akademiia nauk, 1940.

"Pis'ma D. I. Pisareva k roditeliam." Edited by Evlaliia P. Kazanovich. In *Shestidesiatye gody: Materialy po istorii literatury i obshchestvennomu dvizheniiu*, edited by Nikolai K. Piksanov and Orest V. Tsekhnovitser, 108–42. Leningrad: Akademiia nauk, 1940.

———. *Polnoe sobranie sochinenii.* 12 vols. Moscow: Nauka, 2000–.

———. "Posmertnye stikhotvoreniia Geine." In *Polnoe sobranie sochinenii*, 3:269–84. 12 vols. Moscow: Nauka, 2000–.

———. "Posmotrim!" In *Polnoe sobranie sochinenii*, 8:7–67. 12 vols. Moscow: Nauka, 2000–.

———. "Promakhi nezreloi mysli." In *Polnoe sobranie sochinenii*, 6:428–73. 12 vols. Moscow: Nauka, 2000–.

———. "Protsess zhizni: 'Fiziologicheskie pis'ma' Karla Fokhta." In *Polnoe sobranie sochinenii*, 3:176–95. 12 vols. Moscow: Nauka, 2000–.

———. "Pushkin i Belinskii: 'Evgenii Onegin.'" In *Polnoe sobranie sochinenii*, 7: 206–316. 12 vols. Moscow: Nauka, 2000–.

———. "Realisty." In *Polnoe sobranie sochinenii*, 6:222–353. 12 vols. Moscow: Nauka, 2000–.

———. "Roman kiseinoi devushki." In *Polnoe sobranie sochinenii*, 7:7–39. 12 vols. Moscow: Nauka, 2000–.

———. "Romany Andre Leo." In *Polnoe sobranie sochinenii*, 10:7–72. 12 vols. Moscow: Nauka, 2000–.

———. "Russkii Don-Kikhot." In *Polnoe sobranie sochinenii*, 4:87–103. 12 vols. Moscow: Nauka, 2000–.

———. "Skholastika XIX veka." In *Polnoe sobranie sochinenii*, 2:250–306. 12 vols. Moscow: Nauka, 2000–.

———. "Staroe barstvo." In *Polnoe sobranie sochinenii*, 10:73–100. 12 vols. Moscow: Nauka, 2000–.

———. "Tsvety nevinnogo iumora." In *Polnoe sobranie sochinenii*, 5:325–58. 12 vols. Moscow: Nauka, 2000–.

———. "O vospitanii devochek." In *Polnoe sobranie sochinenii*, 1:254–61. 12 vols. Moscow: Nauka, 2000–.

———. "Zhenskie tipy v romanakh i povestiakh Pisemskogo, Turgeneva i Goncharova." In *Polnoe sobranie sochinenii*, 3:347–85. 12 vols. Moscow: Nauka, 2000–.

Platon [Fiveiskii]. *Sokrashchennoe izlozhenie dogmatov very.* 1869. Reprint, Moscow: Lestvitsa, 1999.

Platon [Levshin]. *Pouchitel'nye slova pri Vysochaishem Dvore eia Imperatorskogo Velichestva skazyvannye.* 20 vols. Moscow: Senatskaia tipografiia, 1779–1806.

———. "Slovo na den' rozhdeniia Khristova." In *Pouchitel'nye slova pri Vysochaishem Dvore eia Imperatorskogo Velichestva skazyvannye*, 14:581–89. 20 vols. Moscow: Senatskaia tipografiia, 1779–1806.

———. "Slovo na den' vozneseniia Gospodnia." In *Pouchitel'nye slova pri Vysochaishem Dvore eia Imperatorskogo Velichestva skazyvannye*, 20:19–27. 20 vols. Moscow: Senatskaia tipografiia, 1779–1806.

———. "Slovo na kreshchenie Gospodne." In *Pouchitel'nye slova pri Vysochaishem Dvore eia Imperatorskogo Velichestva skazyvannye*, 11:319–26. 20 vols. Moscow: Senatskaia tipografiia, 1779–1806.

————. "Slovo o pol'ze uchenii v den' rozhdeniia ego Imp. Vysochestva." In *Pouchitel'nye slova pri Vysochaishem Dvore eia Imperatorskogo Velichestva skazyvannye*, 1:351–63. 20 vols. Moscow: Senatskaia tipografiia, 1779–1806.

————. "Slovo v den' rozhdeniia [. . .] Vel. Kniazia Pavla Petrovicha." In *Pouchitel'nye slova pri Vysochaishem Dvore eia Imperatorskogo Velichestva skazyvannye*, 1:48–60. 20 vols. Moscow: Senatskaia tipografiia, 1779–1806.

————. "Slovo v nedeliu pravoslaviia." In *Pouchitel'nye slova pri Vysochaishem Dvore eia Imperatorskogo Velichestva skazyvannye*, 3:316–27. 20 vols. Moscow: Senatskaia tipografiia, 1779–1806.

————. "Slovo v nedeliu vtoruiu velikogo posta." In *Pouchitel'nye slova pri Vysochaishem Dvore eia Imperatorskogo Velichestva skazyvannye*, 4:281–88. 20 vols. Moscow: Senatskaia tipografiia, 1779–1806.

————. "Slovo v sviatyi i velikii piatok." In *Pouchitel'nye slova pri Vysochaishem Dvore eia Imperatorskogo Velichestva skazyvannye*, 1:150–61. 20 vols. Moscow: Senatskaia tipografiia, 1779–1806.

Poety 1820–1830-kh godov. Edited by Vera S. Kiseleva-Sergenina and Lidiia Ia. Ginzburg. 2 vols. Leningrad: Sovetskii pisatel', 1972.

Pogodin, Mikhail P. "Vospominanie o kniaze Vladimire Fedoroviche Odoevskom." In *V pamiat' o Kniaze Vladimire Fedoroviche Odoevskom*, 43–68. Moscow: Tipografiia Russkogo, 1869.

Polevoi, Petr N. "Vospominaniia o Dmitrie Ivanoviche Pisareve." *Sanktpeterburgskie vedomosti*, nos. 193–94, Jul. 17–18, 1868.

Pokrovskii, A. P. "Pravila dlia voskresnykh shkol moskovskogo uchebnogo okruga." In *Politicheskie protsessy 60-kh gg.*, edited by Vasilii P. Alekseev and Boris P. Koz'min, 156–69. Moscow: Gosudarstvennoe izdatel'stvo, 1923.

Pomialovskii, Nikolai G. "Meshchanskoe schast'e." In *Polnoe sobranie sochinenii*, 1:55–136. 2 vols. Moscow: Academia, 1935.

"Prostota very." *Khristianskoe chtenie* 15 (1824): 215–25.

Pushkin, Aleksandr S. "Demon." In *Polnoe sobranie sochinenii*, 2.1.299. 17 vols. Leningrad: Akademiia nauk, 1937–59.

————. *Evgenii Onegin*. Vol. 6 of *Polnoe sobranie sochinenii*. 17 vols. Leningrad: Akademiia nauk, 1937–59.

————. "Moi demon." *Mnemozina* 3 (1824): 11–12.

————. "[O stikhotvorenii 'demon']." In *Polnoe sobranie sochinenii*, 11:30. 17 vols. Leningrad: Akademiia nauk, 1937–59.

————. *Polnoe sobranie sochinenii*. 17 vols. Leningrad: Akademiia nauk, 1937–59.

Rozhalin, Nikolai. "Nechto o spore po povodu Onegina (pis'mo k redaktoru Vestnika Evropy)." *Vestnik Evropy* 17 (September 1825): 23–34.

Ruge, Arnold. *Zwei Jahre in Paris: Studien und Erinnerungen*. 2 vols. Leipzig: Jurany, 1846.

Russkie propilei: Materialy po istorii russkoi mysli i literatury. 6 vols. Edited by Mikhail O. Gershenzon. Moscow: Shabashnikovy, 1915–30.

Russko-pol'skie revoliutsionnye sviazi. 3 vols. Moscow: Akademiia nauk, 1961–63.

Satin, Nikolai M. "Nozhka." In *Russkie propilei: Materialy po istorii russkoi mysli i literatury*, edited by Mikhail O. Gershenzon, 1:165–94. 6 vols. Moscow: Shabashnikovy, 1915–30.

————. "Raskaianie poeta: Fantaziia." In *Poety 1820–1830-kh godov*, edited by

Vera S. Kiseleva-Sergenina and Lidiia Ia. Ginzburg, 2:430–45. 2 vols. Leningrad: Sovetskii pisatel', 1972.

———. "Umiraiushchii khudozhnik." In *Poety 1820–1830-kh godov*, edited by Vera S. Kiseleva-Sergenina and Lidiia Ia. Ginzburg, 2:421–25. 2 vols. Leningrad: Sovetskii pisatel', 1972.

Schelling, Friedrich Wilhem Joseph. "Philosophische Untersuchungen über das Wesen der menschlichen Freiheit." In *Werke*, 4:223–308. 6 vols. Munich: Beck, 1958–59.

Schiller, Friedrich. "Das eigne Ideal." In *Gesammelte Werke*, 1:239. 8 vols. Berlin: Aufbau, 1959.

———. *Gesammelte Werke*. 8 vols. Berlin: Aufbau, 1959.

———. "Tabulae Votivae: Mein Glaube." In *Gesammelte Werke*, 1:237. 8 vols. Berlin: Aufbau, 1959.

———. "Rousseau." In *Gesammelte Werke*, 1:71. 8 vols. Berlin: Aufbau, 1959.

———. "Vorrede zur ersten Ausgabe der 'Räuber.'" In *Gesammelte Werke*, 2:7–11. 8 vols. Berlin: Aufbau, 1959.

———. "Zuversicht der Unsterblichkeit." In *Gesammelte Werke*, 1:90. 8 vols. Berlin: Aufbau, 1959.

Shchapov, Afanasii P. "Zemstvo i raskol." In *Izbrannoe*, 245–326. Irkutsk: Ottisk, 2001.

———. "Rech' posle panikhidy po ubitym v s. Bezdne krest'ianam." *Krasnyi arkhiv* 4 (1923): 407–10.

Shchegolev, Pavel E., ed. *Petrashevtsy v vospominaniiakh sovremennikov*. 3 vols. Moscow: Gosudarstvennoe izdatel'stvo, 1926.

Shevyrev, Stepan P. "Ia esm'." In Dmitrii Venevitinov, Stepan P. Shevyrev, Aleksei Khomiakov, *Stikhotvoreniia*, 111–13. Leningrad: Sovetskii pisatel', 1937.

———. "Obozrenie russkikh zhurnalov v 1827 godu: Moskovskii telegraf." *Moskovskii vestnik* 8, no. 5 (1828): 61–105.

———. "Razgovor o vozmozhnosti naidti edinyi zakon dlia iziashchnogo." In *Russkie esteticheskie traktaty pervoi treti XIX veka*, edited by Zakhar A. Kamenskii, 2:508–17. 2 vols. Moscow: Iskusstvo, 1974.

———. *Stikhotvoreniia*. Edited by Mark Aronson. Leningrad: Sovetskii pisatel', 1939.

Shelgunov, Nikolai V. "Beskharakternost' nashei intelligentsii." Pt. 1. *Delo*, no. 11 (1873): 1–32

———. "Beskharakternost' nashei intelligentsii." Pt. 2. *Delo*, no. 12 (1873): 1–36.

Skabichevskii, Aleksandr M. "Dmitrii Ivanovich Pisarev." *Otechestvennye zapiski* 182, no. 1 (1869): 41–94.

———. *Literaturnye vospominaniia*. Edited by Boris Koz'min. Moscow: Zemlia i fabrika, 1928.

Snegirev, Ivan M. "Dnevnik" [Diary]. Edited by Andrei Titov. *Russkii arkhiv* 2, no. 6 (1902): 177–212; 2, no. 7, 369–435; 2, no. 8, 529–76.

Sokolovskii, Vladmir I. *Odna i dve ili liubov' poeta: Roman iz chastnoi zhizni*. 4 vols. Moscow: Stepanov, 1834.

———. "Russkii imperator." In *Poety 1820–1830-kh godov*, edited by Vera S. Kiseleva-Sergenina and Lidiia Ia. Ginzburg, 2:368. 2 vols. Leningrad: Sovetskii pisatel', 1972.

"Starye bogi i novye bogi." *Russkii vestnik* 31, nos. 1–2 (1861): 891–904.

Speshnev, Nikolai. "Pis'ma k K. E. Khoetskomu." In *Filosofskie i obshchestvenno-politicheskie proizvedeniia petrashevtsev*, edited by Vasilii E. Evgrafov, 477–502. Moscow: Gosudarstvennoe izdatel'stvo politicheskoi literatury, 1953.

Titov, Vladimir P. "O dostoinstve poeta (teoriia iziashchnykh iskusstv)." *Moskovskii vestnik* 2, no. 7 (1827): 230–36.

Tol', Feliks. "Nabrosok rechi o proiskhozhdenii religii." In *Filosofskie i obshchestvenno-politicheskie proizvedeniia petrashevtsev*, edited by Vasilii E. Evgrafov, 699–702. Moscow: Gosudarstvennoe izdatel'stvo politicheskoi literatury, 1953.

Tolstoi, Leo N. *Voina i mir*. Vols. 4–7 of *Sobranie sochinenii*. 14 vols. Moscow: Gosudarstvennoe izdatel'stvo khudozhestvennoi literatury, 1951–53.

Turgenev, Ivan S. "Perepiska s D. I. Pisarevym." Edited by Evlaliia P. Kazanovich. In *Raduga: Al'manakh Pushkinskogo doma*, 207–25. Petrograd: Kooperativnoe izdatel'stvo literatorov i uchenykh, 1922.

———. *Polnoe sobranie sochinenii i pisem*. 30 vols. Moscow: Nauka, 1978–.

———. *Stat'i i vospominaniia*. Edited by S. E. Shatalova. Moscow: Sovremennik, 1981.

Venevitinov, Dmitrii V. "Elegiia." In *Stikhotvoreniia, Proza*, edited by Evgenii A. Maimin and M. A. Chernyshev, 68. Moscow: Nauka, 1980.

———. "K moemu perstniu." In *Stikhotvoreniia, Proza*, edited by Evgenii A. Maimin and M. A. Chernyshev, 48–49. Moscow: Nauka, 1980.

———. "O matematicheskoi filosofii." In *Stikhotvoreniia, Proza*, edited by Evgenii A. Maimin and M. A. Chernyshev, 235–40. Moscow: Nauka, 1980.

———. "Neskol'ko myslei v plan zhurnala." In *Stikhotvoreniia, Proza*, edited by Evgenii A. Maimin and M. A. Chernyshev, 128–33. Moscow: Nauka, 1980.

———. *Polnoe sobranie sochinenii*. Moscow: Academia, 1934.

———. "Poslanie k R[ozhali]nu." In *Stikhotvoreniia, Proza*, edited by Evgenii A. Maimin and M. A. Chernyshev, 43–45. Moscow: Nauka, 1980.

———. *Stikhotvoreniia, Proza*. Edited by Evgenii A. Maimin and M. A. Chernyshev. Moscow: Nauka, 1980.

———. "XXXV." In *Stikhotvoreniia, Proza*, edited by Evgenii A. Maimin and M. A. Chernyshev, 72–73. Moscow: Nauka, 1980.

Venevitinov, Dmitrii, Stepan P. Shevyrev, and Aleksei Khomiakov. *Stikhotvoreniia*. Edited by Mark Aronson and Ivan Sergievskii. Leningrad: Sovetskii pisatel', 1937.

Venevitinov, Mikhail. "K biografii poeta D. V. Venevitinova." *Russkii arkhiv*, no. 1 (1885): 113–31.

Voltaire. *Poema estestvennyi zakon*. St. Petersburg: Imperatorskaia tipografiia, 1802.

———. "Poème sur la loi naturelle." In *Mélanges*, edited by Jacques van de Heuvel, 271–87. Paris: Gallimard, 1961.

"Volzhskii manifest." In Aleksandr I. Herzen, *Polnoe sobranie sochinenii*, edited by Mikhail K. Lemke, 16:194–96. 22 vols. Petrograd: Literaturno-izdatel'skii otdel Narkomprosa, 1919–25.

Zagoskin, Mikhail N. *Iskusitel'*. 3 vols. Moscow: Stepanov, 1838.

Znameniia prishestviia Antikhrista po ucheniiu sviashchennago pisaniia. 5th ed. Moscow: Svetliachok, 1994.

Secondary Sources

Abrams, M. H. *Natural Supernaturalism: Tradition and Revolution in Romantic Literature*. New York: Norton, 1971.

Aizlewood, Robin. "Revisiting Russian Identity in Russian Thought: From Chaadaev to the Early Twentieth Century." *Slavonic and East European Review* 78, no. 1 (2000): 20–43.

Alexander, Manfred. *Der Petraševskij-Prozess: Eine "Verschwörung der Ideen" und ihre Verfolgung im Russland von Nicholas I*. Wiesbaden: Steiner, 1979.

Barsukov, Nikolai. *Zhizn' i trudy M. P. Pogodina*. 22 vols. St. Petersburg: Stasiulevich, 1888–1911.

Bazanov, Vasilii. *Russkie revoliutsionnye demokraty i narodoznanie*. Leningrad: Sovetskii pisatel', 1974.

Behm, Johannes. "καινός." In *Theological Dictionary of the New Testament*, edited by Gerhard Kittel and translated by Geoffrey Bromiley, 3:447–54. 10 vols. Grand Rapids, Mich.: Eerdmans, 1964–76.

Beiser, Frederick C. *The Fate of Reason: German Philosophy from Kant to Fichte*. Cambridge, Mass.: Harvard University Press, 1987.

———. *The Romantic Imperative: The Concept of Early German Romanticism*. Cambridge, Mass.: Harvard University Press, 2003.

Bel'chikov, Nikolai F. *Dostoevskii v protsesse Petrashevtsev*. Moscow: Akademiia nauk, 1936.

Berdiaev, Nikolai. *The Origin of Russian Communism*. Translated by R. M. French. London: Bles, 1937.

———. "Philosophical Verity and Intelligentsia Truth." In *Signposts*, translated by Marshall S. Shatz and Judith E. Zimmerman, 1–16. Irvine, Calif.: Schlacks, 1986.

———. *The Russian Idea*. Translated by R. M. French. Hudson, N.Y.: Lindesfarne, 1992.

Berelowitch, Wladimir. "La vie mondaine sous Catherine II." In *Catherine II et l'Europe*, edited by Anita Davidenkoff, 99–106. Paris: Institut d'études slaves, 1997.

Berlin, Isaiah. Introduction to Franco Venturi, *Roots of Revolution: A History of the Populist and Socialist Movements in Nineteenth Century Russia*, vii–xxx. Translated by Francis Haskell. London: Phoenix, 2001.

———. *Russian Thinkers*. Edited by Henry Hardy and Aileen Kelly. London: Penguin, 1994.

Bielfeldt, Siegrun. *Selbst oder Natur: Schellings Anfang in Rußland*. Munich: Sagner, 2008.

Bociurkiw, Bohdan R. "Lenin and Religion." In *Lenin: The Man, the Theorist, the Leader*, edited by Leonard Shapiro and Peter Reddaway, 107–35. London: Praeger, 1967.

Bréhier, Émile. *Schelling*. Paris: Alcan, 1912.

Brodskii, Nikolai. L. "Moskovskii universitetskii blagorodnyi pansion epokhi Lermontova (iz neizdannykh vospominanii grafa D. A. Miliutina)." In *M. Iu. Lermontov: Stat'i i materialy*, 3–15. Moscow: Sotsial'no-ekonomicheskoe izdatel'stvo, 1939.

Brower, Daniel. "The Problem of the Russian Intelligentsia." *Slavic Review* 26, no. 4 (1967): 638–47.

———. *Training the Nihilists: Education and Radicalism in Tsarist Russia*. Ithaca, N.Y.: Cornell University Press, 1975.

Brown, Edward J. *Stankevich and His Moscow Circle, 1830–1840*. Stanford, Calif.: Stanford University Press, 1966.

Bulgakov, Sergei. "Heroism and Asceticism (Reflections on the Religious Nature of the Russian Intelligentsia)." In *Signposts*, translated by Marshall S. Shatz and Judith E. Zimmerman, 17–49. Irvine, Calif.: Schlacks, 1986.

Cabantous, Alain. *Blasphemy: Impious Speech in the West from the Seventeenth to the Nineteenth Century*. Translated by Eric Rauth. New York: Columbia University Press, 2002.

Cassedy, Steven. *Dostoevsky's Religion*. Stanford, Calif.: Stanford University Press, 2005.

Chadwick, Owen. *The Secularization of the European Mind in the Nineteenth Century*. Cambridge: Cambridge University Press, 1975.

Cherniavsky, Michael. "The Old Believers and the New Religion." *Slavic Review* 25, no. 1 (1966): 1–39.

Chernyshev, E. "Materialy po istorii klassovoi bor'by v Rossii v 60-kh godakh XIX veka." *Izvestiia obshchestva arkheologii, istorii i etnografii pri Kazanskom gosudarstvennom universitete* 33, no. 4 (1927): 75–97.

Chernyshevskaia, Nina M. *Letopis' zhizni i deiatel'nosti N. G. Chernyshevskogo*. Moscow: Gosudarstvennoe izdatel'stvo khudozhestvennoi literatury, 1953.

Chizhevskii, Dmitrii I. *Gegel' v Rossii*. Paris: Dom knigi, 1939.

Confino, Michael. "On Intellectuals and Intellectual Traditions in Eighteenth- and Nineteenth-Century Russia." *Daedalus* 101, no. 2 (1972): 117–49.

Coquart, Armand. *Dmitri Pisarev et l'idéologie du nihilisme russe*. Paris: Institut d'études slaves, 1946.

Corbin, Alain. "Backstage." In *From the Fires of Revolution to the Great War*. Vol. 4 of *A History of Private Life*, edited by Michelle Perrot, 453–667. Translated by Arthur Goldhammer. Cambridge, Mass.: Belknap Press of Harvard University Press, 1990.

Cracraft, James. *The Church Reform of Peter the Great*. London: Macmillan, 1971.

Derevenskii, Boris. G. *Uchenie ob Antikhriste v drevnosti i srednevekov'e*. St. Petersburg: Aleteiia, 2000.

Desnitskii, Vasilii A. Predislovie. In *Delo petrashevtsev*, edited by Vasilii A. Desnitskii, 1:v–xxiii. 3 vols. Moscow: Akademiia nauk, 1937–51.

Edwards, John. "Religious Faith and Doubt in Late Medieval Spain: Soria ca. 1450–1500." *Past and Present* 120 (1988): 3–25.

Egorov, Boris F. *Petrashevtsy*. Leningrad: Nauka, 1988.

Eidel'man, Natan. *Iz potaennoi istorii Rossii XVIII–XIX vekov*. Moscow: Vysshaia shkola, 1993.

Elizavetina, Galina G. *Pisarev—kritik: Nachalo puti*. Moscow: Nasledie, 1992.

———. *Pisarev—kritik: Ispytanie estetikoi*. Moscow: Nasledie, 1999.

———. *Pisarev—kritik: Posle "Russkogo slova."* Moscow: Institut mirovoi literatury RAN, 2003.

———. "Pisarev i zhurnal 'Rassvet'." In Pisarev, *Polnoe sobranie sochinenii*, 1: 359–92. 12 vols. Moscow: Nauka, 2000–.

Engelstein, Laura. *Castration and the Heavenly Kingdom*. Ithaca, N.Y.: Cornell University Press, 1999.

———. *Slavophile Empire: Imperial Russia's Illiberal Path*. Ithaca, N.Y.: Cornell University Press, 2009.

Ershov, A. "Kazanskii zagovor 1863 g. Epizod iz pol'skogo vosstaniia." Pt. 1. *Golos minuvshago*, no. 6 (1913): 199–232.

———. "Kazanskii zagovor 1863 g. Epizod iz pol'skogo vosstaniia." Pt. 2. *Golos minuvshago*, no. 7 (1913): 199–228.

Eßbach, Wolfgang. *Die Junghegelianer: Soziologie einer Intellektuellengruppe*. Munich: Fink, 1998.

Evans, John L. *The Petraševskij Circle*. The Hague: Mouton, 1974.

Febvre, Lucien. *The Problem of Unbelief in the Sixteenth Century: The Religion of Rabelais*. Translated by Beatrice Gottlieb. Cambridge, Mass.: Harvard University Press, 1982.

Feoktistov, Evgenii. *Materialy dlia istorii prosveshcheniia v Rossii: I. Magnitskii*. St. Petersburg: Tipografiia Kesnevilia, 1865.

Field, Daniel. *Rebels in the Name of the Tsar*. Boston: Unwyn Hyman, 1989.

Florovskii, Georgii V. "Iskaniia molodogo Gertsena." In *Iz proshlogo russkoi mysli*, 358–411. Moscow: Agraf, 1998.

———. "Michael Gerschensohn." Translated by D. S. Mirsky. *Slavonic Review* 5, no. 14 (1926): 315–31.

———. *Ways of Russian Theology*. 2 vols. Translated by Robert L. Nichols. Belmont, Mass.: Nordland, 1979–87.

Flynn, James T. "Tuition and Social Class in the Russian Universities: S. S. Uvarov and 'Reaction' in the Russia of Nicholas I." *Slavic Review* 35, no. 2 (1976): 232–48.

Frank, Joseph. *Dostoevsky: The Miraculous Years, 1865–1871*. Princeton, N.J.: Princeton University Press, 1995.

———. *Dostoevsky: The Seeds of Revolt, 1821–1849*. Princeton, N.J.: Princeton University Press, 1976.

Frank, Semen. "The Ethic of Nihilism (A Characterization of the Russian Intelligentsia's Moral Outlook)." In *Signposts*, translated by Marshall S. Shatz and Judith E. Zimmerman, 131–55. Irvine, Calif.: Schlacks, 1986.

Frede, Victoria S. "Materialism and the Radical Intelligentsia, the 1860s." In *A History of Russian Philosophy, 1830–1930: Faith, Reason, and the Defense of Human Dignity*, edited by Gary M. Hamburg and Randall Poole, 69–89. Cambridge: Cambridge University Press, 2010.

———. "The Rise of Unbelief among Educated Russians in the Late Imperial Period." PhD diss., University of California, Berkeley, 2002.

Freeze, Gregory L. "Handmaiden of the State? The Church in Imperial Russia Reconsidered." *Journal of Ecclesiastical History* 36, no. 1 (1985): 82–102.

———. *The Parish Clergy in Nineteenth-Century Russia*. Princeton, N.J.: Princeton University Press, 1983.

———. *The Russian Levites: Parish Clergy in the Eighteenth Century*. Cambridge, Mass.: Harvard University Press, 1977.

————. "A Social Mission for Russian Orthodoxy: The Kazan Requiem of 1861 for the Peasants in Bezdna." In *Imperial Russia, 1700–1917: State, Society, Opposition,* edited by Ezra Mendelsohn and Marhsall S. Shatz, 115–35. DeKalb: Northern Illinois University Press, 1988.

Fricke, Gerhard. *Der religiöse Sinn der Klassik Schillers: Zum Verhältnis von Idealismus und Christentum.* Darmstadt: Wissenschaftiche Buchgesellschaft, 1968.

Gernet, Mikhail N. *Istoriia tsarskoi tiur'my.* 3rd ed. 5 vols. Moscow: Gosudarstvennoe izdatel'stvo iuridicheskoi literatury, 1960–63.

Gershenzon, Mikhail O., ed. "Creative Self-Consciousness." In *Signposts,* translated by Marshall S. Shatz and Judith E. Zimmerman, 51–69. Irvine, Calif.: Schlacks, 1986.

————. *Istoriia molodoi Rossii.* In *Izbrannoe,* 2:7–176. 4 vols. Moscow: Universitetskaia kniga, 2000.

————. *Izbrannoe,* 4 vols. Moscow: Universitetskaia kniga, 2000.

————. "Liubov' N. P. Ogareva." In *Izbrannoe,* 3:250–424. 4 vols. Moscow: Universitetskaia kniga, 2000.

————. *P. Ia. Chaadaev.* St. Petersburg: Stasiulevich, 1908.

————. "Tvorcheskoe samosoznanie." In *Vekhi; Intelligentsiia v Rossii,* edited by Mikhail O. Gersehnzon, 85–108. Moscow: Molodaia gvardiia, 1991.

Ginzburg, Lidiia Ia. *Literatura v poiskakh real'nosti.* Leningrad: Sovetskii pisatel', 1987.

————. "Opyt filosofskoi liriki." In *O starom i o novom,* 194–228. Leningrad: Sovetskii pisatel', 1982.

————. *O psikhologicheskoi proze.* Moscow: Intrada, 1999.

————. "Poeziia mysli." In *O lirike,* edited by Aleksandr S. Kushner, 50–119. Moscow: Intrada, 1997.

————. *Tvorcheskii put' Lermontova.* Leningrad: Khudozhestvennaia literatura, 1940.

Gleason, Abbott. *Young Russia: The Genesis of Russian Radicalism in the 1860s.* New York: Viking, 1980.

Gorovoi, Fedor S. *Revoliutsionno-demokraticheskoe dvizhenie v permskoi gubernii v 60-kh godakh XIX veka.* Molotov: Molotovskoe oblastnoe gosudarstvennoe izdatel'stvo, 1952.

Gotovtseva, Anastasiia G., and A. I. Kiianskaia. "Dvizhenie dekabristov v gosudarstvennoi propagande, 1825–1826 gg." In *Dekabristy: Aktual'nye problemy i novye podkhody,* edited by Oksana I. Kiianskaia, 477–93. Moscow: Rossiiskii gosudarstvennyi gumanitarnyi universitet, 2008.

Greenleaf, Monika. *Pushkin and Romantic Fashion: Fragment, Elegy, Orient, Irony.* Stanford, Calif.: Stanford University Press, 1994.

Grekulov, Efim F. *Pravoslavnaia inkvizitsiia v Rossii.* Moscow: Nauka, 1964.

Gregory, Frederick. *Scientific Materialism in Nineteenth Century Germany.* Dordrecht: Reidel, 1977.

Grigor'ev, Vasilii V. *Imperatorskii S. Peterburgskii universitet v techenie pervykh piatidesiati let ego sushchestvovaniia.* St. Petersburg: Bezobrazov, 1870.

Hartmann, Wilhelm. *Heinrich Zschokkes Stunden der Andacht.* Gütersloh: Bertelsmann, 1932.

Hayner, Paul Collins. *Reason and Existence: Schelling's Philosophy of History.* Leiden: Brill, 1967.

Hecht, Jennifer Michael. *The End of the Soul: Scientific Modernity, Atheism, and Anthropology in France.* New York: Columbia University Press, 2003.

Hildermeier, Manfred. *Bürgertum und Stadt in Russland, 1760–1870.* Cologne: Böhlau, 1986.

Huch, Ricarda. *Die Romantik: Ausbreitung Blütezeit und Verfall.* Tübingen: Wunderlich, 1951.

Hunter, Michael, and David Wootton, eds. *Atheism from the Reformation to the Enlightenment.* Oxford: Clarendon Press, 1992.

Husband, William. *"Godless Communists": Atheism and Society in Soviet Russia, 1917–1932.* DeKalb: Northern Illinois University Press, 2000.

Iampol'skaia, A. I., and David S. Gutman. *Bezdnenskoe vosstanie 1861 goda.* Kazan: Tatgosizdat, 1948.

Iastrebov, Fedir O. *Revoliutsionnye demokraty na Ukraine: Vtoraia polovina 50-kh-nachalo 60-kh godov XIX st.* Kiev: Akademiia nauk Ukrainskoi SSR, 1960.

Immerwahr, Raymond. "The Subjectivity or Objectivity of Friedrich Schlegel's Poetic Irony." *Germanic Review* 26, no. 3 (1951): 173–91.

Istoriia Moskovskogo universiteta. 2 vols. Moscow: Moskovskii universitet, 1955.

Ivanov-Razumnik, Razumnik V. *Chto takoe intelligentsiia?* Berlin: Skify, 1920.

———. "Obshchestvennye i umstvennye techeniia 30-kh godov." In *Istoriia russkoi literatury XIX v.*, edited by Dmitrii N. Ovsianiko-Kulikovskii, 1:247–76. 5 vols. Moscow: Mir, 1908–11.

Izmozik, Vladlen S. "Politicheskie ssyl'nye i kontrol' za ikh perepiskoi v 60–70-kh gg. XIX v." In *Iz istorii russkoi intelligentsii*, 469–83. St. Petersburg: Bulanin, 2003.

Jakovenko, Boris. *Geschichte des Hegelianismus in Russland.* Prague: Bartl, 1940.

Joravsky, David. *Russian Psychology: A Critical History.* Oxford: Blackwell, 1989.

Kamenskii, Zakhar A. *Moskovskii kruzhok liubomudrov.* Moscow: Nauka, 1980.

Kanunova, Faina Z., and Irina A. Aizikova. *Nravstvenno-esteticheskie iskaniia russkogo romantizma i religiia.* Novosibirsk: Sibirskii khronograf, 2001.

Kazanovich, Evlaliia P. "D. I. Pisarev posle kreposti." *Zven'ia* 6 (1936): 625–49.

Khotiakov, Iakov I. "Nelegal'naia rabota biblioteki A. I. Ikonnikova, 1859–1862 gg." *Sovetskaia bibliografiia: Sbornik statei* 33, no. 2 (1952): 49–59.

Kirichenko, Oleg. *Dvorianskoe blagochestie: XVIII vek.* Moscow: Palomnik, 2002.

Kirpotin, Valerii Ia. *Radikal'nyi raznochinets D. I. Pisarev.* Moscow: Sovetskaia literatura, 1933.

Kiseleva-Serginina, Vera S. "N. M. Satin." In *Poety 1820–1830-kh godov*, edited by Vera S. Kiseleva-Sergenina and Lidiia Ia. Ginzburg, 2:415–20. 2 vols. Leningrad: Sovetskii pisatel', 1972.

Kline, George L. *Religious and Anti-Religious Thought in Russia.* Chicago: University of Chicago Press, 1968.

Knight, Nathaniel. "Was the Intelligentsia Part of the Nation? Visions of Society in Post-Emancipation Russia." *Kritika* 7, no. 4 (2006): 733–58.

Kogan, Lev. "K voprosu o formirovanii mirovozzreniia Dobroliubova." *Literaturnyi kritik*, nos. 9–10 (1938): 273–92.

Kogan, Iurii Ia. *Ocherki po istorii russkoi ateisticheskoi mysli XVIII v.* Moscow: Akademiia nauk, 1962.

Kolakowski, Leszek. *Main Currents of Marxism.* 3 vols. Translated by Paul S. Falla. Oxford: Oxford University Press, 1978.

Koliupanov, Nil P. *Biografiia Aleksandra Ivanovicha Kosheleva*. 2 vols. Moscow: Kosheleva, 1889–92.

Kornilov, Aleksandr A. *Molodye gody Mikhaila Bakunina: Iz istorii russkogo romantizma*. Moscow: Sabashnikovy, 1915.

Korotkov, Iurii. *Pisarev*. Moscow: Molodaia gvardiia, 1976.

Kors, Alan Charles. "The Atheism of D'Holbach and Naigeon." In *Atheism from the Reformation to the Enlightenment*, edited by Michael Hunter and David Wootton, 273–300. Oxford: Clarendon Press, 1992.

———. *D'Holbach's Coterie: An Enlightenment in Paris*. Princeton, N.J.: Princeton University Press, 1976.

———. *The Orthodox Sources of Disbelief*. Vol. 1 of *Atheism in France, 1650–1729*. Princeton, N.J.: Princeton University Press, 1990.

Kotovich, Aleksei. *Dukhovnaia tsenzura v Rossii, 1799–1855 gg*. St. Petersburg: Rodnik, 1909.

Koyré, Alexandre. *La philosophie et le problème national en Russie au début du XIXe siècle*. Paris: Champion, 1929.

Koz'min, Boris P. *Kazanskii zogovor 1863 goda*. Moscow: Obshchestvo politkatorzhan, 1929.

———. *Khar'kovskie zagovorshchiki, 1856–1858*. Kharkov: Proletarii, 1930.

———. "M. D. Muravskii v khar'kovskom tainom obshchestve, 1856–1858 gg." *Katorga i ssylka* 41, no. 4 (1928): 125–39.

Kupriianov, Aleksandr. *Gorodskaia kul'tura russkoi provintsii*. Moscow: Novyi khronograf, 2007.

Labry, Raoul. *Alexandre Ivanovič Herzen: Essai sur la formation et le développement de ses idées*. Paris: Bossard, 1928.

Lankheit, Klaus. *Das Freundschaftsbild der Romantik*. Heidelberg: Winter, 1952.

Laughland, John. *Schelling versus Hegel: From German Idealism to Christian Metaphysics*. Aldershot, U.K.: Ashgate, 2007.

Leikina-Svirskaia, Vera R. "Ateizm Petrashevtsev." *Voprosy istorii religii i ateizma* 3 (1955): 214–36.

———. "Formirovanie raznochinskoi intelligentsii v Rossii v 40-kh godakh XIX v." *Istoriia SSSR*, no. 1 (1958): 83–103.

———. "'Kazanskii zagovor' 1863 g." *Revoliutsionnaia situatsiia v Rossii v 1859–1861 gg*. 1 (1960): 423–49.

———. "Petrashevets N. A. Speshnev v svete novykh materialov." *Istoriia SSSR*, no. 4 (1978): 128–40.

Lemke, Mikhail K. *Nikolaevskie zhandarmy i literatura, 1826–1855 gg*. The Hague: Europe Printing, 1966.

———. "Molodost' 'Ottsa Mitrofana'. In *Ocherki osvoboditel'nogo dvizheniia "shestidesiatykh godov,"* 279–331. St. Petersburg: Popova, 1908.

Levin, Iurii D. "N. Kh. Ketcher." In *Russkie pisateli, 1800–1917*, 2:529–30. 5 vols. Moscow: Sovetskaia entsiklopediia, 1989–2007.

Liaskovskii, Valerii. *Brat'ia Kireevskie: Zhizn' i trudy ikh*. St. Petersburg: Balashev, 1899.

Linkov, Iakov I. *Revoliutsionnaia bor'ba A. I. Gertsena i N. P. Ogareva i tainoe obshchestvo "Zemlia i volia" 1860-kh godov*. Moscow: Nauka, 1964.

Lotman, Iurii M. *Pushkin*. St. Petersburg: Iskusstvo-SPB, 1995.

———. "The Decembrist in Daily Life." Translated by Andrea Bessing. In *The Semiotics of Russian Cultural History: Essays,* edited by Alexander D. Nakhimovsky and Alice Stone Nakhimovsky, 95-149. Ithaca, N.Y.: Cornell University Press, 1985.

Lovell, Stephen. "Biography, History, and Finitude: Understanding the Life Span in Early-Nineteenth-Century Russia." *Slavonic and East European Review* 82, no. 2 (2004): 246-67.

Maimin, Evgenii A. *Pushkin: Zhizn' i tvorchestvo.* Moscow: Nauka, 1981.

———. *Russkaia filosofskaia poeziia: Poety-liubomudry, A. S. Pushkin, F. I. Tiutchev.* Moscow: Nauka, 1976.

Malia, Martin. *Alexander Herzen and the Birth of Russian Socialism.* 2nd ed. New York: Grosset and Dunlap, 1965.

———. "What is the Intelligentsia?" In *The Russian Intelligentsia,* edited by Richard Pipes, 1-18. New York: Columbia University Press, 1961.

Manchester, Laurie. *Holy Fathers, Secular Sons: Clergy, Intelligentsia, and the Modern Self in Revolutionary Russia.* DeKalb: Northern Illinois University Press, 2008.

Marasinova, Elena N. *Psikhologiia elity rossiiskogo dvorianstva poslednei treti XVIII veka: Po materialam perepiski.* Moscow: Rossiiskaia politicheskaia entsiklopediia, 1999.

Marker, Gary. *Publishing, Printing, and the Origins of Intellectual Life in Russia, 1700-1800.* Princeton, N.J.: Princeton University Press, 1985.

Martin, Alexander M. *Romantics, Reformers, Reactionaries: Russian Conservative Thought and Politics in the Reign of Alexander I.* DeKalb: Northern Illinois University Press, 1997.

Martyn, J. Louis. *Galatians: A New Translation with Introduction and Commentary.* New York: Doubleday, 1997.

Masanov, Ivan F. *Slovar' psevdonimov russkikh pisatelei, uchenykh i obshchestvennykh deiatelei.* 4 vols. Moscow: Izdatel'stvo Vsesoiuznoi knizhnoi palaty, 1956-60.

Mason, Eudo C. *Goethe's Faust: Its Genesis and Purport.* Berkeley: University of California Press, 1967.

McLellan, David. *Marxism and Religion: A Description and Assessment of the Marxist Critique of Christianity.* London: Macmillan, 1987.

McNally, Raymond T. *Chaadayev and His Friends: An Intellectual History.* Tallahassee, Fla.: Diplomatic Press, 1971.

Meeks, Wayne A. *The First Urban Christians: The Social World of the Apostle Paul.* New Haven, Conn.: Yale University Press, 1983.

Mersereau, John. "Romanticism or Rubbish?" *Romantic Russia* 1 (1997): 5-16.

Mervaud, Michel. *Socialisme et liberté: La pensée et l'action de Nicolas Ogarev.* Mont Saint-Aignan and Paris: Université de Haute Normandie et Institut d'études slaves, 1984.

Meyendorff, John. *The Orthodox Church: Its Past and Its Role in the World Today.* Translated by John Chapin. New York: Pantheon, 1968.

Miliukov, Pavel N. "Liubov' u 'idealistov tridtsatykh godov'." In *Iz istorii russkoi intelligentsii,* 73-168. St. Petersburg: Kolpinskii, 1902.

Mironov, Boris N. *Sotsial'naia istoriia Rossii perioda imperii.* 2 vols. St. Petersburg: Bulanin, 1999.

Monas, Sidney. *The Third Section: Police and Society in Russia under Nicholas I.* Cambridge, Mass.: Harvard University Press, 1961.

Monod, Albert. *De Pascal à Chateaubriand: Les défenseurs français du Christianisme de 1670 à 1802.* Paris: Alcan, 1916.

Müller, Derek. *Der Topos des neuen Menschen in der russischen und sowjetrussichen Geistesgeschichte.* Bern: Peter Lang, 1998.

Müller, Eberhard. *Russischer Intellekt in europäischer Krise: Ivan V. Kireevskij.* Cologne: Böhlau, 1966.

Müller, Otto Wilhelm. *Intelligencija: Untersuchungen zur Geschichte eines politischen Schlagwortes.* Frankfurt: Athenäum, 1971.

Nahirny, Vladimir. "The Russian Intelligentsia: From Men of Convictions to Men of Ideas." *Comparative Studies in Society and History* 4, no. 4 (1962): 403–35.

Nasonkina, Lidiia I. *Moskovskii universitet posle vosstaniia dekabristov.* Moscow: Moskovskii universitet, 1972.

Nechkina, Militsa V. "N. G. Chernyshevskii i A. I. Gertsen v gody revoliutsionnoi situatsii, 1859–1861 gg." *Izvestiia Akademii nauk SSSR: Otdelenie literatury i iazyka* 13, no. 1 (1954): 48–65.

Nifontov, Aleksandr S. *1848 god v Rossii: Ocherki po istorii 40-kh godov.* Moscow: Gos. sotsial'no-ekonomicheskoe izdatel'stvo, 1931.

Nikitina, Faina G. "Ateizm petrashevtsev." In *Materializm i religiia,* edited by Il'ia D. Pantskhav, 221–33. Moscow: Krasnyi proletarii, 1958.

Ovsianiko-Kulikovskii, Dmitrii N. "K psikhologii Dobroliubova." In *Sobranie sochinenii,* 5:44–59. 9 vols. St. Petersburg: Stasiulevich, 1912–14.

Owen, Thomas C. *Capitalism and Politics in Russia: A Social History of the Moscow Merchants, 1855–1905.* Cambridge: Cambridge University Press, 1981.

Paperno, Irina. *Chernyshevsky and the Age of Realism: A Study in the Semiotics of Behavior.* Stanford, Calif.: Stanford University Press, 1988.

———. "Intimacy and History: The Gercen Family Drama Reconsidered." *Russian Literature* 61, nos. 1–2 (2007): 1–65.

———. "The Liberation of the Serfs as a Cultural Symbol." *Russian Review* 50, no. 4 (1991): 417–36.

———. *Suicide as a Cultural Institution in Dostoevsky's Russia.* Ithaca, N.Y.: Cornell University Press, 1997.

Papmehl, Kazimir A. *Freedom of Expression in Eighteenth Century Russia.* The Hague: Nijhoff, 1971.

Pattison, George, and Diane Oenning Thompson, eds. *Dostoevsky and the Christian Tradition.* Cambridge: Cambridge University Press, 2001.

Pereira, Norman G. O. *The Thought and Teachings of N. G. Černyševskij.* The Hague: Mouton, 1975.

Perrie, Maureen. *The Agrarian Policy of the Russian Socialist-Revolutionary Party: From Its Origins through the Revolution of 1905–1907.* Cambridge: Cambridge University Press, 1976.

Persits, Mark M. *Ateizm russkogo rabochego.* Moscow: Nauka, 1965.

———. "Russkii ateisticheskii rukopisnyi sbornik kontsa XVIII–nachala XIX v." *Voprosy istorii religii ateizma* 7 (1959): 361–93.

Peterson, A. "Rasskazy i anekdoty." *Russkii arkhiv,* no. 2 (1877): 361–68.

Piatkovskii, Aleksandr P. *Kniaz' V. F. Odoevskii i D. V. Venevitinov.* St. Petersburg: Tipografiia Glavnogo upravleniia udelov, 1901.

Pinaev, Mikhail T. "M. K. Elpidin—revoliutsioner, izdatel' i propagandist nasle-diia N. G. Chernyshevskogo." *Uchenye zapiski volgogradskogo gosudarstvennogo pedagogicheskogo instituta: Nekotorye voprosy russkoi literatury* 21 (1967): 3–79.

Plotkin, Lev A. *Pisarev i literaturno-obshchestvennoe dvizhenie shestidesiatykh godov.* Moscow: Akademiia nauk, 1945.

Pollard, Alan P. "The Russian Intelligentsia: The Mind of Russia." *California Slavic Studies* 3 (1964): 1–32.

Pomeau, René. *La religion de Voltaire.* Paris: Nizet, 1969.

Pozefsky, Peter. *The Nihilist Imagination: Dmitrii Pisarev and the Cultural Origins of Russian Radicalism, 1860–1868.* New York: Peter Lang, 2003.

Pustarnakov, Vladimir F., ed. *Filosofiia Shellinga v Rossii.* St. Petersburg: Russkii Khristianskii gumanitarnyi institut, 1998.

Pypin, Aleksandr N. *Religioznye dvizheniia pri Aleksandre I.* St. Petersburg: Akademicheskii proekt, 2000.

Raeff, Marc. *Origins of the Russian Intelligentsia: The Eighteenth-Century Nobility.* New York: Harcourt Brace Jovanovich, 1966.

Randolph, John. *The House in the Garden: The Bakunin Family and the Romance of Russian Idealism.* Ithaca, N.Y.: Cornell University Press, 2007.

Reid, Robert. "Lermontov's Demon: A Question of Identity." *Slavonic and East European Review* 60, no. 2 (1982): 189–210.

Reiser, Solomon A. *Letopis' zhizni i deiatel'nosti N. A. Dobroliubova.* Moscow: Goskul'tprosvetizdat, 1953.

———. "Neizdannye teksty N. A. Dobroliubova. I. Dobroliubov—perevodchik Feierbakha." *Literaturnoe nasledstvo* 25–26 (1936): 243–45.

Rengstorf, Karl Heinrich. "ἀποστέλλω—ἀποστολή." In *Theological Dictionary of the New Testament,* edited by Gerhard Kittel and translated by Geoffrey Bromiley, 1:398–447. 10 vols. Grand Rapids, Mich.: Eerdmans, 1964–76.

Riasanovsky, Nicholas V. *Nicholas I and Official Nationality in Russia, 1825–1855.* Berkeley: University of California Press, 1959.

———. *A Parting of Ways: Government and the Educated Public in Russia, 1801–1855.* Oxford: Clarendon Press, 1976.

———. *Russia and the West in the Teaching of the Slavophiles: A Study of Romantic Ideology.* Cambridge, Mass.: Harvard University Press, 1952.

———. *The Teaching of Charles Fourier.* Berkeley: University of California Press, 1969.

Rieber, Alfred J. *Merchants and Entrepreneurs in Imperial Russia.* Chapel Hill: University of North Carolina Press, 1982.

Roosevelt, Priscilla Reynolds. *Apostle of Russian Liberalism: Timofei Granovsky.* Newtonville, Mass.: Oriental Research Partners, 1986.

Rothe, Hans. *Religion und Kultur in den Regionen des russischen Reiches im 18. Jahrhundert.* Opladen: Westdeutscher Verlag, 1984.

Rowley, Harold H. *The Relevance of Apocalyptic: A Study of Jewish and Christian Apocalypses from Daniel to the Revelation.* 2nd ed. London: Lutterworth, 1961.

Russkie pisateli, 1800–1917. 5 vols. Moscow: Sovetskaia entsiklopediia, 1989–2007.

Sakulin, Pavel N. *Iz istorii russkago idealizma: Kniaz' V. F. Odoevskii: Myslitel', pisatel'.* 1 vol. in 2 pts. Moscow: Sabashnikovy, 1913.

Saraskina, Liudmila. *Nikolai Speshnev: Nesbyvshaiasia sud'ba.* Moscow: Nash dom-L'âge d'homme, 2000.

Scanlan, James P. *Dostoevsky the Thinker*. Ithaca, N.Y.: Cornell University Press, 2002.

Schmemann, Alexander. *The Historical Road of Eastern Orthodoxy*. Translated by Lydia W. Kesich. New York: Holt, Rinehart and Winston, 1963.

Schmithals, Walter. *The Apocalyptic Movement: Introduction and Interpretation*. Translated by John E. Steely. Nashville, Tenn.: Abingdon, 1975.

———. *The Office of Apostle in the Early Church*. Translated by John E. Steely. Nashville, Tenn.: Abingdon, 1969.

Schröder, Winfried. *Ursprünge des Atheismus: Untersuchungen zur Metaphysik- und Religionskritik des 17. und 18. Jahrhunderts*. Stuttgart: Frommann-Holzboog, 1998.

Schuffenhauer, Werner. "Ludwig Feuerbach stellt des Bruders Schrift, 'Gedanken und Thatsachen,' 1862 vor." *Aufklärung und Kritik* 3 (1999): 99–109.

Schultze, Bernhard. *Wissarion Grigorjewitsch Belinskij: Wegbereiter des revolutionären Atheismus in Rußland*. Munich: Pustet, 1958.

Seddon, J. H. *The Petrashevtsy: A Study of the Russian Revolutionaries of 1848*. Manchester, U.K.: Manchester University Press, 1985.

Semevskii, Vasilii I. *M. V. Butashevich-Petrashevskii i petrashevtsy*. Moscow: Zadruga, 1922.

———. "Petrashevtsy: studenty Tostov i G. P. Danilevskii, meshchanin P. G. Shaposhnikov, literator Katenev i B. I. Utin. (s portretom Shaposhnikova)." Pt. 1. *Golos minuvshago*, no. 11 (1916): 5–28.

———. "Petrashevtsy: studenty Tostov i G. P. Danilevskii, meshchanin P. G. Shaposhnikov, literator Katenev i B. I. Utin. (s portretom Shaposhnikova)." Pt. 2. *Golos minuvshago*, no. 12 (1916): 97–118.

Sergeev, V. D. *Revniteli revoliutsionnogo neterpeniia: Iz istorii Viatki*. Viatka: Kirovskaia oblastnaia nauchnaia biblioteka, 2000.

Setschkareff, Wsewolod. *Schellings Einfluß in der russischen Literatur der 20er und 30er Jahre des XIX. Jahrhunderts*. Nedeln: Kraus, 1968.

Shakhnovich, Mikhail. "Novyi pamiatnik russkogo svobodomysliia XVIII veka." *Zven'ia* 8 (1950): 735–51.

Shcherbakov, V. I. "Universitetskii dnevnik Pisareva." *D. I. Pisarev: Issledovaniia i materialy* 1 (1995): 186–214.

Shil'der, Nikolai. *Imperator Nikolai Pervyi: Ego zhizn' i tsarstvovanie*. 2 vols. St. Petersburg: Suvorin, 1903.

Shlapentokh, Dmitry. *The French Revolution in Russian Intellectual Life*. Westport, Conn.: Praeger, 1996.

Shpet, Gustav G. "Antropologizm Lavrova v svete istorii filosofii." In *P. L. Lavrov: Stat'i, vospominaniia, materialy*, 73–138. Petrograd: Kolos, 1922.

———. *Filosofskoe mirovozzrenie Gertsena*. Petrograd: Kolos, 1921.

Skabichevskii, Aleksandr M. *Ocherki istorii russkoi tsenzury, 1700–1863 g.* St. Petersburg: Pavlenkov, 1892.

Smilianskaia, Elena B. *Volshebniki, bogokhul'niki, eretiki: Narodnaia religioznost' i "dukhovnye prestupleniia" v Rossii v XVIII v.* Moscow: Indrik, 2003.

Smith, Douglas. *Working the Rough Stone: Freemasonry and Society in Eighteenth-Century Russia*. DeKalb: Northern Illinois University Press, 1999.

Smolitsch, Igor. "Die Stellung des russischen Kaisers zur orthodoxen Kirche in Russland vom 18. bis 20. Jahrhundert." *Forschungen zur osteuropäischen Geschichte* 2 (1955): 139–64.

Solov'ev, Evgenii. *D. I. Pisarev: Ego zhizn' i literaturnaia deiatel'nost'*. St. Petersburg: Evdokimov, 1894.

Steklov, Iurii. *N. G. Chernyshevskii: Ego zhizn' i deiatel'nost'*. 2 vols. Moscow: Gosudarstvennoe izdatel'stvo, 1928.

Struve, Petr. "The Intelligentsia and Revolution." In *Signposts*, translated by Marshall S. Shatz and Judith E. Zimmerman, 115–29. Irvine, Calif.: Schlacks, 1986.

Sukhomlinov, Mikhail I. *Issledovaniia i stat'i po russkoi literature i prosveshcheniiu*. 2 vols. St. Petersburg: Suvorin, 1889.

Thomson, Francis J. "The Corpus of Slavonic Translations Available in Muscovy: The Cause of Old Russia's Intellectual Silence and a Contributory Factor to Muscovite Cultural Autarky." *California Slavic Studies* 16 (1993): 179–214.

Thrower, James. *Marxist-Leninist "Scientific Atheism" and the Study of Religion and Atheism in the USSR*. Berlin: Mouton, 1983.

Torrey, Charles C. *The Apocalypse of John*. New Haven, Conn.: Yale University Press, 1958.

Tseitlin, Aleksandr G. *Stanovlenie realizma v russkoi literature: Russkii fiziologicheskii ocherk*. Moscow: Nauka, 1965.

Turgenev i krug "Sovremennika." Leningrad: Academia, 1930.

Tur'ian, Marietta A. *Strannaia moia sud'ba: O zhizni Vladimira Fedorovicha Odoevskogo*. Moscow: Kniga, 1991.

Turner, James. *Without God, Without Creed: The Origins of Unbelief in America*. Baltimore, Md.: Johns Hopkins University Press, 1985.

Udodov, Boris T. *M. Iu. Lermontov*. Voronezh: Voronezhskii universitet, 1973.

Usok, I. E. "Filosofskaia poeziia liubomudrov." In *K istorii russkogo romantizma*, edited by Iurii V. Mann et al., 107–28. Moscow: Nauka, 1973.

van den Bercken, William. *Ideology and Atheism in the Soviet Union*. Berlin: Mouton de Gruyter, 1988.

Varneke, Boris. *Istoriia russkogo teatra XVII–XIX vekov*. 3rd ed. Moscow: Iskusstvo, 1939.

Vatsuro, Vadim E. "K genezisu pushkinskogo 'Demona'." In *Pushkinskaia pora*, 128–34. St. Petersburg: Akademicheskii proekt, 2000.

Venturi, Franco. *Roots of Revolution: A History of the Populist and Socialist Movements in Nineteenth Century Russia*. Translated by Francis Haskell. London: Phoenix, 2001.

Verhoeven, Claudia. *The Odd Man Karakozov: Imperial Russia, Modernity, and the Birth of Terrorism*. Ithaca, N.Y.: Cornell University Press, 2009.

Virginskii, Viktor S. *Vladimir Fedorovich Odoevskii: Estestvenno-nauchnye vzgliady*. Moscow: Nauka, 1975.

Volodin, Aleksandr. "Raskol'nikov i Karakozov: K tvorcheskoi istorii D. I. Pisareva 'Bor'ba za zhizn'." *Novyi mir*, no. 11 (1969): 212–31.

Voronitsyn, Ivan P. *Istoriia ateizma*. 3rd ed. 5 vols. Moscow: Ateist, 1927–30.

Voznyi, Anatolii F. *Petrashevskii i tsarskaia tainaia politsiia*. Kiev: Naukova dumka, 1985.

Vucinich, Alexander. *Science in Russian Culture*. 2 vols. Stanford, Calif.: Stanford University Press, 1963–70.

Vul'fson, Grigorii N. *Iz istorii raznochinno-demokraticheskogo dvizheniia v Povolzh'e i na Urale*. Kazan: Kazanskii universitet, 1963.

——, ed. *Kazanskii universitet, 1804–2004: Biobibliograficheskii slovar'*. 3 vols. Kazan: Kazanskii universitet, 2002–2004.

Vul'fson, Grigorii N., and Efim G. Bushkanets. *Obshchestvenno-politicheskaia bor'ba v Kazanskom universitete v 1859–1861 godakh*. Kazan: Tatknigoizdat, 1955.

Wade, Ira O. *The "Philosophe" in the French Drama of the Eighteenth Century*. Princeton, N.J.: Princeton University Press, 1926.

Walicki, Andrzej. *The Slavophile Controversy: History of a Conservative Utopia in Nineteenth-Century Russian Thought*. Translated by Hilda Andrews-Rusiecka. Oxford: Clarendon Press, 1975.

Walker, Barbara. "On Reading Soviet Memoirs: A History of the 'Contemporaries' Genre as an Institution of Russian Intelligentsia Culture from the 1790s to 1970s." *Russian Review* 59, no. 3 (2000): 327–52.

Wirtschafter, Elise Kimerling. *Structures of Society: Imperial Russia's "People of Various Ranks."* DeKalb: Northern Illinois University Press, 1994.

Woehrlin, William F. *Chernyshevskii: The Man and the Journalist*. Cambridge, Mass.: Harvard University Press, 1971.

Wootton, David. "Lucien Febvre and the Problem of Unbelief in the Early Modern Period." *Journal of Modern History* 60, no. 4 (1988): 695–730.

Wortman, Richard S. *Development of a Russian Legal Consciousness*. Chicago: University of Chicago Press, 1976.

——. *Scenarios of Power: Myth and Ceremony in Russian Monarchy*. 2 vols. Princeton, N.J.: Princeton University Press, 1995–2000.

Wytrzens, Günther. *Dmitrij Vladimirovič Venevitinov als Dichter der russischen Romantik*. Graz-Cologne: Böhlau, 1962.

Zacek, Judith Cohen. "The Russian Bible Society and the Russian Orthodox Church." *Church History* 35, no. 4 (1966): 411–37.

Zaionchkovskii, Petr A. *Provedenie v zhizn' krest'ianskoi reformy 1861 g*. Moscow: Izdatel'stvo sotsial'no-ekonomicheskoi literatury, 1958.

Zelnik, Reginald E. "'To the Unaccustomed Eye:' Religion and Irreligion in the Experience of St. Petersburg Workers in the 1870s." *California Slavic Studies* 17 (1994): 49–82.

Zhivov, Viktor. *Iz tserkovnoi istorii vremen Petra Velikogo: Issledovaniia i materialy*. Moscow: Novoe literaturnoe obozrenie, 2004.

——. "Marginal'naia kul'tura v Rossii i rozhdenie intelligentsii." *Novoe literaturnoe obozrenie* 37, no. 3 (1999): 37–51.

Zhuk, Sergei I. *Russia's Lost Reformation: Peasants, Millennialism, and Radical Sects in Southern Russia and Ukraine, 1830–1917*. Washington, D.C.: Woodrow Wilson Center Press, 2004.

Zimmerman, Judith E. "Natalie Herzen and the Early Intelligentsia." *Russian Review* 41, no. 3 (1982): 249–72.

Zorin, Andrei. *Kormia dvuglavogo orla . . . : Literatura i gosudarstvennaia ideologiia v Rossii v poslednei treti XVIII—pervoi treti XIX veka*. Moscow: Novoe literaturnoe obozrenie, 2001.

Index

acedia, 130, 137–38, 139, 141, 170, 188; in Orthodox theology, 130, 246n36; as spiritual aridity, 41, 46, 47

afterlife. *See* immortality

agnosticism, 3, 211

Alexander I, 8, 23, 28, 32, 205

Alexander II, 140, 155, 170, 202, 252n26; as Antichrist, 167; associated with Orthodox Church, 161, 162; false manifestos attributed to, 160, 174; and the Great Reforms, 13, 136, 140, 156, 249n75

Anastasii (Bratanovskii), 93, 106

Annenkov, Pavel V., 79, 138–39

antiauthoritarianism, 98; directed against God, 98, 100; directed against teachers and school directors, 113, 123, 184, 242n118, 243n120, 244n6; directed against the state, 56, 98, 103, 136. *See also* authority

Antichrist, 93, 115, 156, 251n15; in Bible, 157; Old Believer views of, 156, 175–76; Prince of darkness, 28; in revolutionary propaganda, 166, 167, 175–76

Antonelli, Petr D., 95, 111, 112, 116, 235n23, 242n113

Apocalypse, 155, 156–58; and atheism, 154, 167–68, 178; in Bible, 156–58; expectation of, among revolutionaries, 17, 148, 153, 159–60, 164, 173–74, 250n1; millenarianism among Old Believers and sectarians, 165; millenarianism and intelligentsia, 15, 213; Orthodox Christian views of, 158; in revolutionary

manifestos, 161–63, 166–68, 169; sociological explanations of, 157, 251n11

apostle, 147; appellation for revolutionary propagandists, 125, 170, 178, 256n71; in the Christian tradition, 177, 178, 258–59n113

atheism, 4, 11–12, 89–208; as an assertion of human independence, 98–99, 101, 103, 128, 132, 144, 165–68, 173; deemed unspeakable by the nobility, 84–85, 92, 109–12, 140; definition of, 3; in the eighteenth century, 4, 10–12; history of the term, 4, 215n3; image of the atheist as anarchic, 4, 12, 28, 93–94, 109, 116; image of the atheist as depraved, 4, 84, 93–94, 96, 106–9; image of the atheist as fool, 93; image of the atheist as tempter, 93–94, 107, 108, 113, 240n86; as a political statement, 104, 109, 140, 172–73; as a religion, 14–15, 20; in the Soviet Union, 15, 18, 154, 180, 212–13, 249n89. *See also* God; Left Hegelianism; materialism; science; suicide

authority, 100; of the Bible, 167, 173; of political rulers, 15, 29, 55, 94, 205; of the Russian Orthodox Church, 9–10, 164. *See also* antiauthoritarianism

autocracy, 8; opposition to, 64, 73, 121, 136, 170, 198, 263n76; and the Russian Orthodox Church, 8–9, 55, 58, 64

Bakunin, Mikhail A., 52, 67, 70, 72, 219n56

Bauer, Bruno, 124, 247n47

293